MILLER'S
CollectableS
PRICE ◆ GUIDE
1989-90

(Volume I)

Compiled and Edited by
Judith and Martin Miller

General Editor: Robert Murfin.

D0410684

MILLERS PUBLICATIONS

The Lion and 2 Monkeys
money bank in cast iron,
9in (23cm).
£150-200 *P*

MILLER'S COLLECTABLES PRICE GUIDE 1989/90

Compiled, edited and designed by
M.J.M. Publishing Projects for
Millers Publications Limited
The Mitchell Beazley Group
Sissinghurst Court, Sissinghurst
Cranbrook, Kent TN17 2JA
Telephone: (0580) 713890

British Library Cataloguing in Publication Data
Miller's collectables price guide — Vol. 1 (1989-1990)
1. Collecting — Serials
790.1'32'05

ISBN 0-905879-52-X

Typeset by Ardek Photosetters, St Leonards-on-Sea
Printed and bound in England by William Clowes Ltd
Beccles and London

Introduction

Since Martin and I produced the first *Miller's Antiques Price Guide* in 1979 antiques in general have become more popular, and consequently more and more expensive. I started collecting porcelain (mostly damaged pieces, I must admit) for a few pennies as a student at Edinburgh University. Some of these same pieces are now worth several hundred pounds. So what can a would-be collector do?

There is no doubt collecting does become a passion. Martin and I have filled our hotel, Chilston Park, with many different collections – we are still the victims of the same affliction – the love of buying a find! This is as strong when you collect postcards or rock memorabilia as it is when you collect Ming porcelain or Chippendale furniture. The wonderful thing about 'collectables' is that anyone with just a few extra pounds can become a collector. This is *not* the province of the extremely wealthy – anyone who is prepared to do a little research can begin. And research *is* essential. Find out about your subject. Read up as much as you can. Search out a friendly dealer and go to some specialist auctions. This book should help you get a feel for what is around and the sort of price you should pay. Pricing is always difficult and our price guides are what they say. This is a price *guide* – NOT a price *list*.

The wonderful thing about collecting is that it is such fun. The research on your chosen subject shouldn't be boring – it can open up so many areas of interest. Through my own collections I have learnt much about social history, I've puzzled over Victorian gadgets and games and been amazed at how much my pair of Beatles stockings would have been worth now if I hadn't laddered them!

Collections and collectors are fascinating – why not write to tell us about your collection? Maybe we should have a prize for 'Bizarre' collection of the year or the 'Most Unusual' collecting area? We will change every photograph in this book every year, so if your particular area isn't covered, write to us. We love getting your suggestions.

This first edition of *Miller's Collectables Price Guide* is filled with many fascinating pieces. I do hope it will provide you with solid information, interesting facts, photographs and prices, and help to make collecting even more fun. Good hunting!

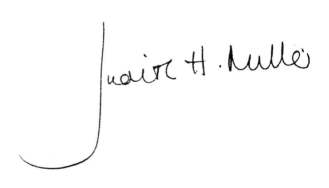

Acknowledgements

The publishers would like to acknowledge the great assistance given by our consultants.

AERONAUTICA, AUTOMOBILIA, RAILWAYS & SHIPPING:	**Patrick Bogue, John Jenkins,** *Onslow's, Metro Store, Townmead Road, London, SW6.*
CAMERAS:	**David Lawrence,** *Jessops, 67 Great Russell Street, London, WC1.*
ART DECO:	**Beverley,** *30 Church Street, London, NW8.*
ROYAL DOULTON:	**Eric Knowles,** *Bonhams, Knightsbridge, London, SW7.* **Tom Power,** *The Collector, Alfies Antique Market, 13-25 Church Street, London, NW8.*
STAFFORDSHIRE FIGURES:	**Ron Beech,** *150 Portland Road, Hove, Sussex.*
GOSS & CRESTED WARE:	**Nicholas Pine,** *Goss & Crested China Ltd., 62 Murray Road, Horndean, Hants.*
EPHEMERA:	**Trevor Vennett-Smith and his Staff** *at Neales of Nottingham, 192 Mansfield Road, Nottingham.*
FISHING:	**Jamie Maxtone Graham,** *Lyne Haugh, Lyne Station, Peebles, Scotland.*
MONART GLASS:	**Frank Andrews,** *Stall 21, Portobello Road, 290 Westbourne Grove, London, W11.*
MILITARIA:	**Roy Butler,** *Wallis & Wallis, West Street Auction Galleries, Lewes, East Sussex.*
MEDALS, BUTTONS & BADGES:	**Jim Bullock,** *Romsey Medal Centre, 101 The Hundred, Romsey, Hants.*
PLAYING CARDS:	**Yasha,** *Intercol, 1A Camden Walk, Islington Green, London, N1.*
POLICE ITEMS:	**Mervyn Mitton,** *161 The Albany, Manor Road, Bournemouth, Dorset.*
SEWING ITEMS:	**Deborah Felts,** *Phillips West Two, 10 Salem Road, London, W2.*
TOYS, SPORTING ITEMS:	**Duncan Chilcott,** *Bonhams, 65-69 Lots Road, London, SW10.*

Key to Illustrations

Each illustration and descriptive caption is accompanied by a letter-code. By reference to the following list of Auctioneers (denoted by *) and Dealers (•), the source of any item may be immediately determined. In no way does this constitute or imply a contract or binding offer on the part of any of our contributors to supply or sell the goods illustrated, or similar articles, at the prices stated. Advertisers in this year's directory are denoted by †.

AC • Angela Charlesworth, 99 Dodsworth Road, Barnsley, S. Yorks. Tel: (0226) 282097

AD • Alan Douglas, Bartlett Street, Antique Market, Bath, Avon.

AG * Anderson & Garland, Marlborough House, Marlborough Crescent, Newcastle-upon-Tyne. Tel: 091-232 6278

AL †• Ann Lingard, Ropewalk Antiques, Ropewalk, Rye, Sussex. Tel: (0797) 223486

AP • Angela Page, Tunbridge Wells, Kent. Tel: (0892) 22217

AW • A. Waine, Tweedale, Rye Mill Lane, Feering, Colchester, Essex. Tel: (0376) 71078.

BAL †• Sharon Ball, Stratford-on-Avon Antique Centre, Ely Street, Stratford-on-Avon, Warks. Tel: (0789) 204180

BC • British Collectables, 1st Floor, Georgian Village, Camden Passage, Islington, London N1. Tel: 01-359 4560

Bea * Bearnes, Rainbow, Avenue Road, Torquay, Devon. Tel: (0803) 26277

BEV †• Beverley, 30 Church Street, London NW8. Tel: 01-262 1576

BIG * Bigwoods (Colliers, Bigwood, Bewlay), The Old School, Tiddington, Stratford-upon-Avon, Warks. Tel: (0789) 69415

Bon †* Bonhams, Montpelier Galleries, Montpelier Street, Knightsbridge, London SW7. Tel: 01-584 9161 and 65-69 Lots Road, SW10. Tel: 01-351 7111

BUR • David Burns, 116 Chestnut Grove, New Malden, Surrey. Tel: 01-949 7356 (See DBu)

C * Christie, Manson & Woods Ltd, 8 King Street,

St James's, London SW1. Tel: 01-839 9060

CAC ● Cranbrook Antique Centre, Stone Street, Cranbrook, Kent. Tel: (0580) 712173

Cas ● Simon Castle, 38B Kensington Church Street, London W8. Tel: 01-892 2840

CB ● Christine Bridge Antiques, 78 Castelnau, London SW13. Tel: 01-741 5501

CBA ● Chateaubriand Antiques Centre, High Street, Burwash, East Sussex. Tel: (0435) 882535

CCC †● The Crested China Co, The Station House, Driffield, East Yorks. Tel: (0377) 47042

CDC * Capes Dunn & Co, Auction Galleries, 38 Charles Street, off Princess Street, Manchester. Tel: 061-273 1911

CEd * Christie's & Edmiston's Ltd, 164-166 Bath Street, Glasgow. Tel: 041-332 8134

CHA †● Charles Antiques, 101 The Hundred, Romsey, Hants. Tel: (0794) 512885

CL ● Carr Linford, 10-11 Walcot Buildings, London Road, Bath, Avon. Tel: (0225) 317516

CNY * Christie, Manson & Woods International Inc, 502 Park Avenue, New York, NY 10022, USA. Tel: (212) 546 1000 (including Christie's East)

COB †● Cobwebs, 78 Northam Road, Southampton. Tel: (0703) 227458

CSK * Christie's (South Kensington) Ltd, 85 Old Brompton Road, London SW7. Tel: 01-581 7611

D ● Dudley, Alfie's Antique Market, 13-25 Church Street, London NW8. Tel: (Home) 01-633 0507

DBu ● David Burns, 116 Chestnut Grove, New Malden, Surrey. Tel: 01-949 7356 (see BUR)

DEC †● Decodence, 59 Brighton Road, Surbiton, Surrey. Tel: 01-390 1778

DL ● Dunsdale Lodge Antiques, Westerham, Kent. Tel: (0959) 62160

DN * Drewett Neate, Donnington Priory, Donnington, Newbury, Berks. Tel: (0635) 31234

DSH * Dacre, Son & Hartley, 1-5 The Grove, Ilkley, West Yorks. Tel: (0943) 600655

EUR ● Eureka Antiques, 18 Northenden Road, Sale, Cheshire. Tel: 061-962 5629 and 105 Portobello Road, W11 (Saturdays)

FA ● Frank Andrews, Unit 21, 290 Westbourne Grove, London W11. Tel: 01-881 0658

FAL ● Falstaff Antiques, 63-67 High Street, Rolvenden (Motor Museum). Tel: (0580) 241234

GA * GA Property Services, Clevedon, Avon (Hoddell Pritchard) (see HOD).

G&CC †● Goss & Crested China Ltd, Nicholas J. Pine, 62 Murray Road, Horndean, Hants. Tel: (0705) 597440

GD * Garth Denham, Horsham Auction Galleries, Warnham, Nr Horsham, West Sussex. Tel: (0403) 55699 & 53837

GEN ● Lionel Geneen Ltd, 781 Christchurch Road, Boscombe, Bournemouth. Tel: (0202) 422961

GHE * Graham H. Evans, FRICS, FRVA, The Market Place, Kilgetty, Pembrokeshire, Dyfed. Tel: (0834) 811151

GKR †● GKR Bonds Ltd, PO Box 1, Kelvedon, Essex. Tel: (0376) 71711

GW ● George Weiner, 2 Market Street, The Lanes, Brighton, East Sussex. Tel: (0273) 729948

HCH * Hobbs & Chambers, Market Place, Cirencester, Glos. Tel: (0285) 4736

HE ● Heroes, 21 Canonbury Lane, Islington, London N1. Tel: 01-359 8329

HOD * Hoddell, GA Property Services, Six Ways, Clevedon, Avon. Tel: (0272) 876699

HP * Hobbs Parker, Romney House, Ashford Market, Elwick Road, Ashford, Kent. Tel: (0233) 22222

HSS * Henry Spencer & Sons, 20 The Square, Retford, Notts. Tel: (0777) 708633

IMA ● Images (Peter Stockham), 16 Cecil Court, Charing Cross Road, London WC2. Tel: 01-836 8661

IC †● InterCol London, Yasha Beresiner, 1A Camden Walk, Islington Green, London N1. Tel: 01-354 2599

J †● Jessops, 67 Great Russell Street, London WC1. Tel: 01-831 3640

JAS ● Jasmin Cameron, 259 Kings Road, SW3. Tel: 01-352 0837

JBB †● Jessie's Button Box, Great Western Antique Centre, Stand 17, Bartlett Street, Bath, Avon. Tel: (0272) 299065

JBO ● Jane and Bjarne Olsen, Alfie's Antique Market, T.103/104, 13-15 Church Street, London NW8. Tel: 01-706 2969

JMG †● Jamie Maxtone Graham, Lyne Haugh, Lyne Station, Peebles, Scotland. Tel: (072 14) 304

JO †● Jacqueline Oosthuizen, Shop 12 (1st Floor) Georgian Village, Camden Passage, London N1. Tel: 01-226 5393/01-352 5581 and Chelsea Antique Market, 253 Kings Road, SW3. Tel: 01-352 6071/5581

JW * John H. Walter & Sons, No. 1 Mint Lane, Lincoln. Tel: (0522) 25454

K †● Keith, Old Advertising, Unit 14, 155A Northcote Road Antiques Market, Battersea, London SW11. Tel: 01-228 0741/01-228 6850

KOL ● Kollectomania, 4 Catherine Street, Rochester, Kent. Tel: (0634) 45099

L * Lawrence Fine Art of Crewkerne, South Street, Crewkerne, Somerset . Tel: (0460) 73041

LAM ● Penny Lampard, 28 High Street, Headcorn, Kent. Tel: (0622) 890682

LAY * David Lay ASVA, Penzance Auction House, Alverton, Penzance, Cornwall. Tel: (0736) 61414

LB †● The Lace Basket, 1a East Cross, Tenterden, Kent. Tel: (05806) 3923

LG ● Lynn Greenwold, Digbeth, Digbeth Street, Stow-on-the-Wold, Glos. Tel: (0451) 30398

LR ● Leonard Russell, 21 Kings Avenue, Denton, Newhaven, East Sussex . Tel: (0273) 515153

LRG * Lots Road Chelsea Auction Galleries, 71 Lots Road, London SW10. Tel: 01-352 2349

MAN †● F. C. Manser & Son Ltd, 53-54 Wyle Cop, Shrewsbury. Tel: (0743) 51120

MB †● Mostly Boxes, 92 & 52b High Street, Eton. Tel: Windsor 858470

McC * McCartneys, 25 Corve Street, Ludlow, Shropshire. Tel: (0584) 2636

MG • Michael G. German, 38B Kensington Church Street, London W8. Tel: 01-937 2771

MGM * Michael G. Matthews, Devon Fine Art Auction House, Dowell Street, Honiton, Devon. Tel: (0404) 41872/3137

MIN • Mint & Boxed, 110 High Street, Edgware, Middx. Tel: 01-952 2002

MIT • Mervyn A. Mitton, 161 The Albany, Manor Road, Bournemouth.

MOR * Wm. Morey & Sons, Salerooms, St Michaels Lane, Bridport. Tel: (0308) 22078

MS †• Mike Sturge, 39 Union Street, Maidstone, Kent. Tel: (0622) 54702

N †* Neales of Nottingham, The Nottingham Salerooms, 192 Mansfield Road, Nottingham. Tel: (0602) 624141

NM • Nick Marchant, Bartlett Street Antique Market, Bath, Avon. Tel: Bath 310457

OBJ • Objects, Stand T.101, Alfie's Antique Market, 13-25 Church Street, London NW8. Tel: 01-706 2969/01-801 6626

OMH • The Old Mint House, Pevensey, East Sussex. Tel: (0323) 762337/761251

ONS * Onslow's, Metro Store, Townmead Road, London, SW6. Tel: 01-793 0240

OR • The Originals, Alfie's Antique Market, Stand 37, 13-25 Church Street, NW8. Tel: 01-724 3439/7

OSc • Old School Antiques (P. Rumble), Chittering, Cambridge. Tel: (0223) 861831

OT * Osmond Tricks, Regent Street Auction Rooms, Clifton, Bristol. Tel: (0272) 737201

P * Phillips, Blenstock House, 7 Blenheim Street, New Bond Street, London W1. Tel: 01-629 6602/01-229 9090

PAC • Polegate Antique Centre, Station Road, Polegate, East Sussex. Tel: (032 12) 5277

PAT • Patrician, 1st Floor, Georgian Village, Camden Passage, Islington, London N1. Tel: 01-359 4560/01-435 3159

PC Private Collection

PCh * Peter Cheney, Western Road Auction Rooms, Western Road, Littlehampton, West Sussex. Tel: (0903) 722264 and 713418

PGA †• Paul Gibbs Antiques, 25 Castle Street, Conwy, N. Wales. Tel: (0492) 593429

P[Re] Prudential Fine Art (Reeds Rains), Trinity House, 114 Northenden Road, Sale, Manchester. Tel: 061-962 9237

PVH • Peter & Valerie Howkins, 39, 40 & 135 King Street, Gt Yarmouth, Norfolk. Tel: (0493) 844639

PWA • Pat Walker, Georgian Village, Camden Passage, Islington, London N1. Tel: 01-226 1571/01-731 0999

RBB * Russell Baldwin & Bright Property, 38 South Street, Leominster, Hereford. Tel: (0568) 4123

RBE • Ron Beech, 150 Portland Road, Hove, West Sussex. Tel: (0273) 724477

RS • Roger Summers, 92 Nursery Road, Edgbaston, Birmingham.

SAD • Old Saddlers Antiques, Church Road, Goudhurst, Kent. Tel: (0580) 211458

SAR • Sarah Baddiel, The Book Gallery, B12 Grays Mews, Davies Mews, London W1. Tel: 01-408 1239/01-452 7243

SC • The Scottish Connection, Alfie's Antique Market, 13-25 Church Street, Marylebone NW8. Tel: 01-723 6066

Som • Somervale Antiques, 6 Radstock Road, Midsomer Norton, Bath. Tel: (0761) 412686

ST • Simon Tracy, 18 Church Street, London NW8. Tel: 01-724 5890

SWa †• Stephen Watson, Alfie's Antique Market, 13-25 Church Street, Marylebone NW8. Tel: 01-723 0678

SWO * Sworders, G. E. Sworder & Sons, 15 Northgate End, Bishops Stortford. Tel: (0279) 51388

TAV * Taviner's Auction Rooms, Prewett Street, Redcliffe, Bristol. Tel: (0272) 265996

TM * Thos. Mawer & Son, The Lincoln Saleroom, 63 Monks Road, Lincoln. Tel: (0522) 24984

TP †• Tom Power, Alfie's Antique Market, 13-25 Church Street, London NW8. Tel: 01-883 0024

Tri • Trio, Stand L24, Grays Mews, 1-7 Davies Mews, London W1. Tel: 01-629 1184

VB †• Variety Box, 16 Chapel Place, Tunbridge Wells, Kent. Tel: (0892) 31868/21589

VDB • Van Den Bosch, 1st Floor, Georgian Village, Camden Passage, Islington N1. Tel: 01-359 4560/01-398 5410

VF • Victorian Fireplaces, Simon Priestley, Ground Floor, Cardiff Antique Centre, 69/71 St Mary Street, Cardiff. Tel: (0222) 230970/226049

WAL †* Wallis & Wallis, West Street Auction Galleries, Lewes, East Sussex BN7 2NJ. Tel: (0273) 480208

WD * Weller & Dufty, 141 Bromsgrove Street, Birmingham. Tel: 021-692 1414/5

WHA †• Wych House Antiques, Wych Hill, Woking, Surrey. Tel: (04862) 64636

WIL * Peter Wilson, Victoria Gallery, Market Street, Nantwich, Cheshire. Tel: (0270) 623878

WIN • Winstone Stamp Co, Gt Western Antique Market, Bartlett Street, Bath, Avon. Tel: (0225) 310388

WRe • Walcot Reclamations, 108 Walcot Street, Bath, Avon. Tel: (0225) 66291/63245

WW * Woolley & Wallis, The Castle Auction Mart, Castle Street, Salisbury. Tel: (0722) 21711

ZIG • Ziggurat, Stand J22, Grays Mews, 1-7 Davies Mews, London W1. Tel: 01-629 3788

CONTENTS

Contents

A Royal Doulton jug
entitled The Collector.
£100-130 *TP*

CALENDAR OF FAIRS from May 1989

This calendar is in no way complete. If you wish your event to be included in next year's edition or if you have a change of address or telephone number, please could you inform us by December 31st 1989. Finally we would advise readers to make contact by telephone before a visit, therefore avoiding a wasted journey, which nowadays is both time consuming and expensive.

London

Sat May 6th
The London Decorative Arts Fair, Kensington Town Hall, W8. 11-4.30pm
Bagatelle Antiques Fairs. Tel: 01-391 2339

Sun May 7th
Antiques Fair, London Marriott Hotel, Grosvenor Square, W1
Harvey (Management Services) Ltd. Tel: 01-624 5173

Picketts Lock Leisure Centre, Picketts Lock Lane, N9. 11-5pm
Jax Fairs. Tel: (0444) 400570

The Park Lane Hotel, Piccadilly, W1. 11-6pm
Monway Ltd. Tel: 01-603 0380

Sun May 14th
The Café Royal, W1
Harvey (Management Services) Ltd. Tel: 01-624 5173

The Gloucester, 4 Harrington Gardens, SW7. 11-6pm
Monway Ltd. Tel: 01-603 0380

Great Hall, Alexandra Palace, N22. 11.30-5pm
Pig & Whistle Promotions. Tel: 01-883 7061

Sun May 21st
London Hilton, W1
Harvey (Management Services) Ltd. Tel: 01-624 5173

The Park Lane Hotel, W1. 11-6pm
Monway Ltd. Tel: 01-603 0380

Tues May 23rd
Sandown Park Race Course
Wonder Whistle Enterprises. Tel: 01-249 4050

Sun May 28th
The Rembrandt Hotel, SW7. 11-6pm
Monway Ltd. Tel: 01-603 0380

Tues May 23rd
Sandown Park Race Course
Wonder Whistle Enterprises. Tel: 01-249 4050

Sun May 28th
The Rembrandt Hotel, SW7. 11-6pm
Monway Ltd. Tel: 01-603 0380

Sun June 4th
Kensington Hilton, W11
Harvey (Management Services) Ltd. Tel: 01-624 5173

Picketts Lock Leisure Centre, N9. 11-5pm
Jax Fairs. Tel: (0444) 400570

The Gloucester Hotel, SW7. 11-6pm
Monway Ltd. Tel: 01-603 0380

Thurs June 8th-18th (closed Mon)
Grand Hall, Olympia. 2-8pm
Philbeach Events Ltd. Tel: 01-370 8188/8205

Fri June 9th, Sat 10th, Sun 11th
Wakefield Ceramic Fair, The Cumberland Hotel, Marble Arch, W1. Tel: (0634) 723461

Sat June 10th
The Kensington Brocante Antiques Fair, Kensington Town Hall, W8
Bagatelle Antiques Fairs. Tel: 01-391 2339

Sun June 11th
Le Meridien, Piccadilly, W1
Harvey (Management Services) Ltd. Tel: 01-624 5173

Sheraton Park Hotel, W1. 11-6pm
Monway Ltd. Tel: 01-603 0380

Sun June 18th
London Hilton, W1
Harvey (Management Services) Ltd. Tel: 01-624 5173

Sun June 25th
Kensington Palace Hotel, W8
Harvey (Management Services) Ltd. Tel: 01-624 5173

Rembrandt Hotel, SW7. 11-6pm
Monway Ltd. Tel: 01-603-0380

Wed July 5th-9th
London International Antiques & Fine Art Fair, Connaught Rooms, Gt Queen Street, WC2
Raymond Gubbay Exhibition Ltd. Tel: 01-441 8940

Fri July 14th-16th
Annual Fine Art & Antiques Fair, Alexandra Palace
Alan & Ludi Kipping. Tel: 01-249 4050

Thurs August 17th-20th
West London Antiques Fair, Kensington Town Hall, Hornton Street, W8
Penman Antiques Fairs. Tel: (04447) 4531/2514

Sun Sept 3rd
Picketts Lock Leisure Centre. 11-5pm
Picketts Lock Lane, N9
Jax Fairs. Tel: (0444) 400570

Sat Sept 9th
The London Decorative Arts Fair, Kensington Town Hall, W8
Bagatelle Antiques Fairs. Tel: 01-391 2339

Tues 12th Sept-23rd
Chelsea Old Town Hall, Kings Road, SW3

Penman Antiques Fairs. Tel: (04447) 4531/2514

Sun Sept 17th
Alexandra Palace, Wood Green, N22. 11.30-5pm
Pig & Whistle Promotions. Tel: 01-883 7061

Sat Sept 23rd
The Kensington Brocante Antiques Fair, Kensington Town Hall
Bagatelle Antiques Fairs. Tel: 01-391 2339

Sun Oct 1st
Picketts Lock Leisure Centre. 11-5pm
Picketts Lock Lane, N9
Jax Fairs. Tel: (0444) 400570

Mon Oct 23rd & Tues 24th
Little Chelsea Antiques Fair, Chelsea Town Hall, Kings Road, SW3
Ravenscott Fairs. Tel: 01-727 5045

Fri Nov 3rd-11th
The Burlington House Fair, The Royal College of Art, Kensington Gore, SW7

Sun Nov 12th
Picketts Lock Leisure Centre. 11-5pm
Picketts Lock Lane, N9
Jax Fairs. Tel: (0444) 400570

Tues Nov 21st-26th
City of London Antiques & Art Fair, Barbican Exhibition Halls, Golden Lane, EC2
Penman Antiques Fairs. Tel: (04447) 4531/2514

Sat Nov 25th
The London Decorative Arts Fair, Kensington Town Hall, W8
Bagatelle Antiques Fairs. Tel: 01-391 2339

Sun Dec 3rd
Picketts Lock Leisure Centre. 11-5pm
Picketts Lock Lane, N9
Jax Fairs. Tel: (0444) 400570

Mon Dec 4th-5th
Little Chelsea Antiques Fair, Chelsea Town Hall, Kings Road, SW3
Ravenscott Fairs. Tel: 01-727 5045

Fri Jan 5th-7th 1990
Winter London Ceramics Fair, The Cumberland Hotel, Marble Arch, W1
Wakefield Ceramic Fairs. Tel: (0634) 723461

Avon

Tues May 9th-10th
Bristol Spring Antiques Collectors & Book Fair, City Docks Exhibition Centre, Bristol
West Country Antiques & Collectors Fairs. Tel: (0364) 52182

Tues Aug 8th-10th
Bath Guildhall Antiques Fair, The Guildhall, High Street, Bath
Antiques in Britain Fairs. Tel: (05474) 356/464

Bedfordshire

Sun May 7th
Slip End Village Hall, Nr Luton. 10-5pm
Frank & Shirley Fairs. Tel: (0582) 405281

Sun May 14th
Dagnell Village Hall, Nr Whipsnade. 10-5pm
Frank & Shirley Fairs. Tel: (0582) 405281

Sun May 21st
The Weatherley Centre, Eagle Farm Road, Biggleswade. 10-5pm
Biggleswade Antiques Fairs. Tel: (0767) 40190

Wing Village Hall, Nr Leighton Buzzard. 10-5pm
Frank & Shirley Fairs. Tel: (0582) 405281

Sun June 4th
Slip End Village Hall, Nr Luton. 10-5pm
Frank & Shirley Fairs. Tel: (0582) 405281

Sun June 11th
Dagnell Village Hall, Nr Whipsnade
Frank & Shirley Fairs. Tel: (0582) 405281

Sun June 18th
The Weatherley Centre, Eagle Farm Road, Biggleswade
Biggleswade Antiques Fairs. Tel: (0767) 40190

Wing Village Hall, Nr Leighton Buzzard. 10-5pm
Frank & Shirley Fairs. Tel: (0582) 405281/38624

Berkshire

Sun May 7th
Village Hall, Hurley. 11-5pm
Harris & May Antiques Fairs. Tel: (0628) 30766/(0494) 715927

Crest Hotel, Maidenhead. 10-5pm
Reg Cooper Fairs. Tel: (0860) 537153

FAIRS

Sat May 13th-14th
Spring American Bazaar,
Crafts, Antiques & Gifts, RAF
Greenham Common, Newbury.
11-5pm
Four Seasons Antiques &
Collectors Fairs.
Tel: (0787) 281855

Sun May 14th
Antiques & Collectors Fair, The
Racecourse, Maidenhead Road,
Windsor. 10.30-5pm
Chiltern Fairs. Tel: (09278) 2144

Sun May 28th
The Racecourse, Maidenhead
Road, Windsor. 10.30-5pm
Chiltern Fairs. Tel: (09278) 2144

Sun June 11th
The Racecourse, Maidenhead
Road, Windsor. 10.30-5pm
Chiltern Fairs. Tel: (09278) 2144

Sun June 25th
The Racecourse, Maidenhead
Road, Windsor. 10.30-5pm
Chiltern Fairs. Tel: (09278) 2144

Sun Oct 1st
Village Hall, Hurley
Harris & May Fairs.
Tel: (0628) 30766/(0494) 715927

Sun Nov 5th
Village Hall, Hurley
Harris & May Fairs.
Tel: (0628) 30766/(0494) 715927

Sun Dec 3rd
Village Hall, Hurley
Harris & May Fairs.
Tel: (0628) 30766/(0494) 715927

Buckinghamshire
Mon May 1st
Olney Church Hall, Olney.
10-5pm
Magpie Antiques & Collectors
Fairs. Tel: (0604) 890107

Sun May 7th
Centre for Epilepsy, Chalfont St
Peter. 10-5pm
Chiltern Fairs. Tel: (09278) 2144

Sat May 13th
Memorial Hall, Great
Missenden. 10-4pm
Harris & May Antiques Fairs.
Tel: (0628) 30766

Sun May 21st
Woughton Centre, Milton
Keynes. 10-5pm
Sovereign Fairs.
Tel: (0234) 50600

Sun May 29th
Olney Church Hall, Olney.
10-5pm
Magpie Antiques & Collectors
Fairs. Tel: (0604) 890107

Sun June 4th
Centre for Epilepsy, Chalfont St
Peter. 10.30-5pm
Chiltern Fairs. Tel: (09278) 2144

Sat Sept 9th
Memorial Hall, Great
Missenden
Harris & May Fairs.
Tel: (0628) 30766

Sat Oct 14th
Memorial Hall, Great
Missenden
Harris & May Fairs.
Tel: (0628) 30766

Sat Nov 11th
Memorial Hall, Great
Missenden
Harris & May Fairs.
Tel: (0628) 30766

Thur Nov 16th-18th
Town Hall, High Wycombe
Norton Antiques.
Tel: (0494) 673674

Sat Dec 9th
Memorial Hall, Great
Missenden
Harris & May Fairs.
Tel: (0628) 30766

Cambridgeshire
Sat May 6th
Cambridge Corn Exchange.
9-4pm
T H C Fairs. Tel: (0220 23) 2802

Sun May 7th
Bushfield Sports Centre,
Peterborough. 10.30-5pm
Four-in-One Promotions.
Tel: (0533) 712589

Sat May 13th
Peterborough Wirrina Stadium.
9-4pm
T H C Fairs. Tel: (0220 23) 2802

Sun June 4th
Sawston Hall, Cambridge.
10-5pm
Swift Antiques Fairs. Tel: (0733)
242033/(035478) 277

Sat June 10th
Peterborough Wirrina Stadium.
9-4pm
T H C Fairs. Tel: (0220 23) 2802

Sun June 25th
Mammoth Antiques &
Collectors Fair, East of England
Showground, Peterborough.
8am
Four-in-One Promotions.
Tel: (0533) 712589

Sun Sept 3rd
Sawston Hall, Cambridge.
10-5pm
Swift Antique Fairs.
Tel: (0733) 242033/(035478) 277

Tues Oct 3rd
East of England Showground,
Peterborough
Four-in-One Promotions.
Tel: (0533) 712589

Sun Oct 13th
Sawston Hall, Cambridge.
10-5pm
Swift Antique Fairs.
Tel: (0733) 242033/(035478) 277

Sun Dec 10th
Sawston Hall, Cambridge.
10-5pm
Swift Antique Fairs.
Tel: (0733) 242033/(035478) 277

Cheshire
Mon May 1st
Northgate Arena, Victoria
Road, Chester. 10-5pm
Pamela Robertson Antiques &
Collectors Fairs.
Tel: (0244) 678106

Mon May 29th
Northgate Arena, Victoria
Road, Chester. 10-5pm
Pamela Robertson Antiques &
Collectors Fairs.
Tel: (0244) 678106

Sat June 24th
Northgate Arena, Victoria
Road, Chester. 10-5pm
Pamela Robertson Antique &
Collectors Fairs.
Tel: (0244) 678106

Cornwall
Sun May 14th
Headland Hotel, Newquay.
10-5pm
Fairs Promotions West.
Tel: (0637) 830566
Lord Eliot Hotel, Liskeard.
10-4pm
Kernow Fairs.
Tel: (0726) 842957

Mon May 15th
Wadebridge Town Hall,
Wadebridge. 10-4pm
Fairs Promotions West.
Tel: (0637) 830566

Sun May 21st
Penventon Hotel, Redruth.
Fairs Promotions West.
Tel: (0637) 830566

Mon May 22nd
Wadebridge Town Hall. 10-4pm
Fairs Promotions West.
Tel: (0637) 830566

Sun May 28th
Treganna Castle Hotel, St Ives.
10-5pm
Fairs Promotions West.
Tel: (0637) 830566

Mon May 29th
Treganna Castle Hotel, St Ives.
10-5pm
Fairs Promotions West.
Tel: (0637) 830566

Sun June 11th
Headland Hotel, Newquay.
10-5pm
Fairs Promotions West.
Tel: (0637) 830566
The Lord Eliot Hotel, Liskeard.
10-4pm
Kernow Fairs.
Tel: (0726) 842957

Sun June 18th
Peventon Hotel, Redruth.
10-4pm
Fairs Promotions West.
Tel: (0637) 830566

Mon June 19th
Wadebridge Town Hall. 10-4pm
Fairs Promotions West.
Tel: (0637) 830566

Sun June 25th
Treganna Castle Hotel, St Ives.
10-5pm
Fairs Promotions West.
Tel: (0637) 830566

Cumbria
Mon May 1st
The Wordsworth Hotel,
Grasmere. 10-5pm
Lake District Fairs.
Tel: (096 64) 41389

Sat May 27th-29th
The Wordsworth Hotel,
Grasmere. 11-5pm
Lake District Fairs.
Tel: (096 64) 41389

Derbyshire
Sun May 14th
Courtaulds Acetate, Spondon.
10-5pm
Temple Fairs.
Tel: (0332) 663197

Sat June 3rd-4th
Buxton Pavilion Gardens.
10-5pm
Unicorn Fairs.
Tel: 061-773 7001

Sun June 18th
Community College, Castle
Donnington. 10-5pm
Temple Fairs.
Tel: (0332) 663197

Sat July 15th-16th
Buxton Pavilion Gardens
Unicorn Fairs.
Tel: 061-773 7001

Sat Sept 9th & Sun Sept 19th
Wakefield Ceramic Fair, The
Royal Crown Derby Museum,
Derby
Tel: (0634) 723461

Sat Sept 30th & Sun Oct 1st
Buxton Pavilion Gardens
Unicorn Fairs.
Tel: 061-773 7001

Sat Nov 11th-12th
Buxton Pavilion Gardens
Unicorn Fairs.
Tel: 061-773 7001

Sun Jan 1st, 1990
Buxton Pavilion Gardens
Unicorn Fairs.
Tel: 061-773 7001

Devon
Mon May 1st
Exmouth Spring Bank Holiday
Antiques and Collectors Fair,
The Pavilion, Exmouth.
10.30-5pm
West Country Antiques &
Collectors Fairs.
Tel: (0364) 52182

Fri May 26th-27th
Budleigh Salterton Spring
Antiques and Collectors Fair,
The Masonic Hall, Budleigh
Salterton. 2-8pm, 10-5pm
West Country Antiques &
Collectors Fairs.
Tel: (0364) 52182

Mon May 29th
Exmouth Whitsun Antiques
and Collectors Fair, The
Pavilion, Exmouth. 10.30-5pm
West Country Antiques &
Collectors Fairs.
Tel: (0364) 52182

Thur June 1st-2nd
North Devon Antiques Dealers
Fair, The Queens Hall,
Barnstaple. 10-5pm, 10-3pm
West Country Antiques &
Collectors Fairs.
Tel: (0364) 52182

Fri June 9th-10th
Devon County Showground,
Exeter
Devon County Antiques &
Collectors Fairs.
Tel: (03633) 571

Wed June 14th-15th
Newton Abbott Giant Antiques
and Collectors Fair at The
Racecourse. 2-8pm, 10-5pm
West Country Antiques &
Collectors Fairs.
Tel: (0364) 52182

Wed July 26th
Newton Abbot giant summer
drive-in fair, The Racecourse.
8-5pm
West Country Antiques &
Collectors Fairs.
Tel: (0364) 52182

Fri July 28th-29th
Budleigh Salterton Summer
Antique and Collectors Fair,
The Racecourse. 2-8pm, 10-5pm
West Country Antiques &
Collectors Fairs.
Tel: (0364) 52182

Thur Aug 24th-25th
Barnstaple Antique and
Collectors Fairs, Queens Hall,
Barnstaple. 10-5pm, 10-3pm
West Country Antiques &
Collectors Fairs.
Tel: (0364) 52182

Dorset
Sat Oct 7th-8th
The Coach House Inn, Trickett's
Cross, Ferndown. 11-5pm
Ron Beech Antique Fairs.
Tel: (0273) 724477

Durham
Sun May 14th
Meadowfield Sports Centre,
Durham. 10-5pm
Memories Antiques Fairs.
Tel: (09693) 463

Essex
Mon May 1st
Antiques Drive-in and Country
Fair, Orsett Hall, Orsett. 10-5pm
Etonia Promotions.
Tel: (0268) 774977/(0702) 74833
Sun May 14th
Furze Hill Banqueting Centre,
Margaretting, Nr Chelmsford.
10.30-5pm
Emporium Fairs.
Tel: (0440) 704632

Orsett Hall, Orsett. 10-5pm
Etonia Promotions. Tel: (0268)
774977/(0702) 74833
Sun May 21st
Marconi Club, Beehive Lane,
Chelmsford. 10-5pm
Etonia Promotions. Tel: (0268)
774977/(0702) 74833
Sun June 18th
Orsett Hall, Orsett. 10-5pm
Etonia Promotions. Tel: (0268)
774977/(0702) 74833
Sun June 25th
The Barn, Cranes Farm Road,
Basildon. 10-5pm
Etonia Promotions. Tel: (0268)
774977/(0702) 74833
Sun July 2nd
Airport Moathouse Hotel,
Aviation Way, Southend.
10-5pm
Etonia Promotions. Tel: (0268)
774977/(0702) 74833

Gloucestershire
Sun May 14th
Bingham Hall, Cirencester.
10.30-4.30pm
Keith Smith Fairs.
Tel: (0684) 575126
Sun May 28th
The Prestbury Suite,
Cheltenham Racecourse.
10-4.30pm
Steve & Valda Mitchell.
Tel: (0934) 624854
Mon May 29th
Giant Fleamarket, Bingham
Hall, Cirencester. 10.30-4.30pm
Keith Smith Fairs.
Tel: (0684) 575126
Sun June 11th
Bingham Hall, Cirencester.
10.30-4.30pm
Keith Smith Fairs.
Tel: (0684) 575126
Sun June 25th
The Prestbury Suite,
Cheltenham Racecourse.
10-4.30pm
Steve & Valda Mitchell.
Tel: (0934) 624854

Hampshire
Mon May 1st
River Park Leisure Centre,
Gordon Road, Winchester.
10-4.30pm
Magnum Antiques Fairs.
Tel: (0491) 681009
Sun May 7th
Balmer Lawn Hotel,
Brockenhurst. 10.30-5pm
Kingston Promotions.
Tel: (0329) 661780

Old Basingstoke Village Hall.
10-4.30pm
Magnum Antiques Fairs.
Tel: (0491) 681009
Mon May 8th
Bellvue Hotel, Lee on Solent.
10.30-5pm
Kingston Promotions.
Tel: (0329) 661780

Sun May 14th
The Pyramids, Southsea.
10-5pm
Kingston Promotions.
Tel: (0329) 661780
Sun May 28th
The Guildhall, Portsmouth.
10.30-5pm
Kingston Promotions.
Tel: (0329) 661780
Mon May 29th
Bellvue Hotel, Lee on Solent.
10.30-5pm
Kingston Promotions.
Tel: (0329) 661780

River Park Leisure Centre,
Gordon Road, Winchester.
10-4.30pm
Magnum Antiques Fairs.
Tel: (0491) 681009
Thur June 1st-3rd
The Town Hall, Petersfield.
11-8pm, 11-8pm, 11-5pm
Gamlin Exhibition Services.
Tel: (0452) 862557
Sun June 4th
Balmer Lawn Hotel,
Brockenhurst. 10.30-5pm
Kingston Promotions.
Tel: (0329) 661780
Sun June 11th
The Pyramids, Southsea.
10-5pm
Kingston Promotions.
Tel: (0329) 661780
Sun June 18th
Lyndhurst Park Hotel,
Lyndhurst. 10.30-5pm
Kingston Promotions.
Tel: (0329) 661780
Sun June 25th
Botleigh Grange Hotel, Hedge
End, Nr Southampton.
10.30-5pm
Kingston Promotions.
Tel: (0329) 661780
Wed Sept 6th-9th
The Town Hall, Petersfield
Gamlin Exhibition Services.
Tel: (0452) 862557

Hereford & Worcs
Sun May 14th
The Winter Gardens, Malvern.
10-5pm
Triangle Fairs. Tel: (0531) 4878
Tues Oct 10th-12th
19th Annual Hereford Antiques
Fair, Hereford Moat House,
Belmont Road
Antiques in Britain, Fairs.
Tel: (05474) 356/464
Sat Oct 28th-29th
Wakefield Ceramic Fair, The
Dyson Perrins Museum,
Worcester
Tel: (0634) 723461
Fri Dec 1st-2nd
Midland Antiques Ceramics
Fair, Royal Oak Hotel, South
Street, Leominster
Antiques in Britain, Fairs.
Tel: (05474) 356/464

Hertfordshire
Sat May 6th
Memorial Hall, Common Road,
Chorleywood. 10-4pm
Chiltern Fairs. (09278) 2144
Sun May 14th
Knebworth Village Hall, Nr
Stevenage. 10.30-4.30pm
G & Y Services.
Tel: (0438) 355049
Sat May 20th
Castle Hall, Hertford.
10.30-5pm
Camfairs. Tel: (0440) 704632
Sun May 21st
Hatfield Polytechnic, College
Lane, Hatfield. 10.30-5pm
Chiltern Fairs. Tel: (09278) 2144
Tues May 23rd
Public Hall, Harpenden. 10-4pm
Chiltern Fairs. Tel: (09278) 2144
Sun May 28th
Moathouse Hotel, Ware.
10.30-6pm
Rochefort-Bulman Fairs.
Tel: 01-886 4779/01-363 0910
Sat June 3rd
Memorial Hall, Common Road,
Chorleywood. 10-4pm
Chiltern Fairs. Tel: (09278) 2144
Sun June 4th
Blakemore Hotel, Little
Wymondly, Hitchin. 10-5pm
Biggleswade Antiques Fairs.
Tel: (0767) 40190
Sun June 11th
Knebworth Village Hall, Nr
Stevenage. 10.30-4.30pm
G & Y Services.
Tel: (0438) 355049
Sat June 17th
Castle Hall, Hertford.
10.30-5pm
Camfairs. Tel: (0440) 704632
Tues June 27th
The Public Hall, Harpenden.
10-4pm
Chiltern Fairs. Tel: (09278) 2144
Sun July 23rd
Ware Moat House Hotel, Ware.
10.30-6pm
Rochefort-Bulman Fairs.
Tel: 01-886 4779/01-363 0910

N. Humberside
Sun May 21st
Willerby Manor, Hull. 10-5pm
Abbey Antique Fairs.
Tel: (0482) 445785

Kent
Mon May 1st
Sandwich Antique Fair
Tel: (0843) 588731
Sat May 6th
Hoodeners Antiques Fair, Red
Cross Centre, Lower Chantry
Lane, Canterbury
Tel: (0227) 70437
Sun May 7th
Chilham Antiques Fair
Tel: (0227) 710304

13

FAIRS

Sun May 14th
Barham Antiques Fair, Village Hall. 10-4.30pm
Tel: (0843) 62069

Sun May 21st
Sandwich Antique Fair
Tel: (0843) 588731

Sun May 28th-29th
Cobham Hall, Cobham
Wakefield Antiques Fairs
Tel: (0634) 723461

Mon May 29th
Barham Antiques Fair, Village Hall. 10-4.30pm
Tel: (0843) 62069

Sandwich Antiques Fair
Tel: (0843) 588731

Sat June 3rd
Hoodeners Antiques Fair, Red Cross Centre, Lower Chantry Lane, Canterbury
Tel: (0227) 70437

Sun June 4th
Chilham Antiques Fair
Tel: (0227) 710304

Sun June 18th
Sandwich Antiques Fair
Tel: (0843) 588731

Sat July 1st
Hoodeners Antiques Fair, Red Cross Centre, Lower Chantry Lane, Canterbury
Tel: (0227) 70437

Sun July 9th
Barham Antiques Fair, Village Hall. 10-4.30pm
Tel: (0843) 62069

Sat Aug 5th
Hoodeners Antiques Fair, Red Cross Centre, Lower Chantry Lane, Canterbury
Tel: (0227) 70437

Sun August 27th-28th
Sutton Valence School
Sutton Valence
Nr. Maidstone
Wakefield Antiques Fairs
Tel: (0634) 723461

Mon Aug 28th
Barham Antiques Fair, Village Hall. 10-4.30pm
Tel: (0843) 62069

Sat Sept 2nd
Hoodeners Antiques Fair, Red Cross Centre, Lower Chantry Lane, Canterbury
Tel: (0227) 70437

Sun Sept 10th
Barham Antiques Fair, Village Hall. 10-4.30pm
Tel: (0843) 62069

Sat Oct 7th
Hoodeners Antiques Fair, Red Cross Centre, Lower Chantry Lane, Canterbury
Tel: (0227) 70437

Sat Nov 4th
Hoodeners Antiques Fair, Red Cross Centre, Lower Chantry Lane, Canterbury
Tel: (0227) 70437

Sun Nov 12th
Barham Antiques Fair, Village Hall. 10-4.30pm
Tel: (0843) 62069

Sat Dec 2nd
Hoodeners Antiques Fair, Red Cross Centre, Lower Chantry Lane, Canterbury
Tel: (0227) 70437

Sun Dec 10th
Barham Antiques Fair, Village Hall. 10-4.30pm
Tel: (0843) 62069

Lancashire

Mon May 1st
Haslingden Sports Centre, Rossendale. 10-5pm
Dualco Promotions.
Tel: 061-766 2012

Stretford Sports Centre, Stretford, Manchester
Dualco Promotions.
Tel: 061-766 2012

Sun May 7th
Park Hall, Charnock Richard. 8.30-4pm
Unicorn Fairs.
Tel: 061-773 7001

Sun May 14th
Whitworth Civic Hall, Nr Rochdale. 10-5pm
Dualco Promotions.
Tel: 061-766 2012

Park Hall, Charnock Richard. 8.30-4pm
Unicorn Fairs.
Tel: 061-773 7001

Sun May 21st
Bower Hotel, Chadderton, Oldham. 10-5pm
Dualco Promotions.
Tel: 061-766 2021

Park Hall, Charnock Richard. 8.30-4pm
Unicorn Fairs.
Tel: 061-773 7001

Sun May 28th
Park Hall, Charnock Richard. 8.30-4pm
Unicorn Fairs.
Tel: 061-773 7001

Mon May 29th
Stretford Sports Centre, Stretford, Manchester. 10-5pm
Dualco Promotions.
Tel: 061-766 2012

Sun June 4th
Clayton Arms Sports Centre, Oldham
Dualco Promotions.
Tel: 061-766 2012

Park Hall, Charnock Richard. 8.30-4pm
Unicorn Fairs.
Tel: 061-773 7001

Sun June 11th
Whitworth Civic Centre, Nr Rochdale. 10-5pm
Dualco Promotions.
Tel: 061-766 2012

Park Hall, Charnock Richard. 8.30-4pm
Unicorn Fairs.
Tel: 061-773 7001

Sun June 18th
Park Hall, Charnock Richard. 8.30-4pm
Unicorn Fairs.
Tel: 061-773 7001

Sun June 25th
Park Hall, Charnock Richard. 8.30-4pm
Unicorn Fairs.
Tel: 061-773 7001

Leicestershire

Mon May 1st
Hood Park Leisure Centre, Ashby-de-la-Zouch. 10-5pm
Temple Fairs.
Tel: (0332) 663197

Sun May 14th
Leys Leisure Centre, Leicester. 10.30-5pm
Four-in-One Promotions.
Tel: (0533) 712589

Hinckley Island Hotel, Leicester. 10.30-5pm
Prestige Promotions.
Tel: (0533) 516045

Sun May 28th
School Sports Centre, Oakham. 10.30-5pm
Four-in-One Promotions.
Tel: (0533) 712589

Community College, Heath Lane, Earl Shilton. 10-5pm
Temple Fairs.
Tel: (0332) 663197

Mon May 29th
Hood Park Leisure Centre, Ashby-de-la-Zouch. 10-5pm
Temple Fairs.
Tel: (0332) 663197

Sun June 4th
Welland Park College, Market Harborough. 10.30-5pm
Four-in-One Promotions.
Tel: (0533) 712589

Sun June 24th
Hinckley Island Hotel, Leicester. 10.30-5pm
Prestige Promotions.
Tel: (0533) 516045

Sat Oct 28th-29th
Leicester Antiques Ceramics Fair, Moat House Hotel, Wigston Road, Oadby
Antiques in Britain Fairs.
Tel: (05474) 356/464

Lincolnshire

Fri May 26th-29th
The Harlaxton Manor Antiques Fair, Grantham
Robert Bailey Antique Fairs.
Tel: 01-550 5435

East Midlands

Sun May 21st
Donnington Park Exhibition Centre, Donnington. 8am
Four-in-One Promotions.
Tel: (0533) 712589

Park Hall, Charnock Richard. 8.30-4pm
Unicorn Fairs.
Tel: 061-773 7001

Sun June 18th
Park Hall, Charnock Richard. 8.30-4pm
Unicorn Fairs.
Tel: 061-773 7001

Sun June 25th
Park Hall, Charnock Richard. 8.30-4pm
Unicorn Fairs.
Tel: 061-773 7001

Sun July 23rd
Donnington Park Exhibition Centre, Donnington. 8am
Four-in-One Promotions.
Tel: (0533) 712589

Sun Oct 22nd
Donnington Park Exhibition Centre, Donnington. 8am
Four-in-One Promotions.
Tel: (0533) 712589

Middlesex

Tues May 2nd
Harrow Leisure Centre, Christchurch Avenue, Harrow. 11-5pm
Jax Fairs. Tel: (0444) 400570

Mon May 29th
Harrow Leisure Centre, Christchurch Avenue, Harrow. 11-5pm
Jax Fairs. Tel: (0444) 400570

Mon Aug 28th
Harrow Leisure Centre, Christchurch Avenue, Harrow
Jax Fairs. Tel: (0444) 400570

Tues Oct 3rd
Harrow Leisure Centre, Christchurch Avenue, Harrow
Jax Fairs. Tel: (0444) 400570

Tues Nov 14th
Harrow Leisure Centre, Christchurch Avenue, Harrow
Jax Fairs. Tel: (0444) 400570

Tues Dec 26th
Harrow Leisure Centre, Christchurch Avenue, Harrow. 11-5pm
Jax Fairs. Tel: (0444) 400570

Northamptonshire

Mon May 1st
St Georges Hall, Northampton. 10-5pm
Sovereign Fairs.
Tel: (0234) 50600

Mon May 29th
Moathouse Hotel, Northampton. 10-4pm
Sovereign Fairs.
Tel: (0234) 50600

Sun June 18th
Village Hall, Cogenhoe, Nr Northampton. 10.30-5pm
Magpie Antiques Fairs.
Tel: (0604) 890107

Nottingham

Tues June 6th
Newark and Notts Showground, Winthorpe, Nr Newark. 7-4pm
International Antique & Collectors Fairs.
Tel: (0636) 702326

Fri June 23rd-25th
The Thoresby Hall Antiques and Fine Art Fair, Thoresby Park Exhibition Centre, Ollerton, Nr Newark
Whittington Exhibitions.
Tel: 01-644 9327

Fri July 7th-9th
The Welbeck Abbey Antiques
Fair, Worksop
Robert Bailey. Tel: 01-550 5435

Fri Sept 1st-3rd
Thoresby Hall Antiques and
Fine Art Fair, Thoresby Park
Exhibition Centre, Ollerton, Nr
Newark
Whittington Exhibitions.
Tel: 01-644 9327

Oxfordshire
Sun May 21st
Shiplake Memorial Hall,
Shiplake, Nr Henley. 11-5pm
Harris & May Antique Fairs.
Tel: (0628) 30766/(0494) 715927

Henley on Thames Rugby Club.
10-4.30pm
Magnum Antiques Fairs.
Tel: (0491) 681009

Sun June 25th
Henley on Thames Rugby Club,
Henley on Thames. 10-4.30pm
Magnum Antiques Fairs.
Tel: (0491) 681009

Spread Eagle Hotel, Thame.
10-5pm
Tel: (084421) 3661

Sun August 20th
Shiplake Memorial Hall, Nr
Henley
Harris & May Fairs.
Tel: (0628) 30766/(0296) 625335

Fri Sept 15th-16th
Oxford City Antiques Fair,
Clarendon Press Centre,
Walton Street, Oxford
Antiques in Britain Fairs.
Tel: (05474) 356/464

Sun Sept 17th
Shiplake Memorial Hall, Nr
Henley
Harris & May Fairs.
Tel: (0628) 30766/(0296) 625335

Sun Oct 15th
Shiplake Memorial Hall, Nr
Henley
Harris & May Fairs.
Tel: (0628) 30766/(0296) 625335

Sun Oct 22nd
Spread Eagle Hotel, Thame
Mrs S. Barrington.
Tel: (0844 21) 3661

Sun Nov 19th
Shiplake Memorial Hall, Nr
Henley
Harris & May Fairs.
Tel: (0628) 30766/(0296) 625335

Sun Dec 17th
Shiplake Memorial Hall, Nr
Henley
Harris & May Fairs.
Tel: (0628) 625335

Shropshire
Mon May 1st
Mount Vernon Hospital,
Northwood. 10.30-5pm
Chiltern Fairs. Tel: (09278) 2144

Mon May 29th
Mount Vernon Hospital,
Northwood. 10.30-5pm
Chiltern Fairs. Tel: (09278) 2144

Tues July 11th-13th
Shropshire Summer Antiques
Fair, The Lion Hotel, Wyle Cop,
Shrewsbury
Antiques in Britain Fairs.
Tel: (05474) 356/464

Bridgenorth Leisure Centre,
By-monthly Antique Fairs
(Sundays)
Waverley Antiques Fairs.
Tel: (0905) 620697/
021-550 0309

Somerset
Sat Nov 18th-19th
Royal Bath and West
Showground, Shepton Mallet.
10-5pm
Merlin Fairs. Tel: (0278) 691616

Staffordshire
Mon, May 1st
Leisure Centre, Swadlincote.
10.30-5pm
Four-in-One Promotions.
Tel: (0533) 712589

Tues May 30th
Leisure Centre, Swadlincote.
10.30-5pm
Four-in-One Promotions.
Tel: (0533) 712589

Sun June 11th
Kings Hall, Stoke on Trent.
10.30-5pm
Four-in-One Promotions.
Tel: (0533) 712589

Fri June 16th-18th
Bingley Hall County
Showground, Stafford. 10-5pm
Bowman Antique Fairs.
Tel: (0532) 843333

Kinver Community Centre,
Antique Fairs, 1st Sat in month,
10-5pm
Waverley Fairs. Tel: (0905)
620697/021-550 0309

Wombourne Community
Centre, Monthly Antique Fairs
(Sundays)
Waverley Fairs. Tel: (0905)
620697/021-550 0309

Suffolk
Thur May 4th
Horringer Community Hall, Nr
Bury St Edmunds. 10-4pm
Trash & Treasures.
Tel: (0284) 4507/810398

Thur June 1st
Horringer Community Hall, Nr
Bury St Edmunds. 10-4pm
Trash & Treasures.
Tel: (0284) 810398

Sun June 11th
RAF Lakenheath, Nr Brandon.
11-5pm
Four Seasons Antique &
Collectors Fairs.
Tel: (0787) 281855

15

FAIRS

Thur July 27th-29th
Wakefield Ceramic Fair, The
Athenaeum, Bury St Edmunds
Tel: (0634) 723461

Thur Sept 7th-9th
23rd Annual East Anglian
Antique Fair, Athenaeum,
Angel Hill, Bury St Edmunds
Antiques in Britain Fairs.
Tel: (05474) 356/464

Surrey
Sun May 7th
Preston Cross Hotel and
Country Club, Rectory Lane,
Bookham. 10-5pm
Falcon Antique & Collectors
Fairs. Tel: 01-681 3312/
(0737 81) 2989

Sun May 14th
Woodlands Park Hotel, Stoke
D'Abernon, Cobham. 10-5pm
Falcon Antique & Collectors
Fairs. Tel: 01-681 3312/
(0737 81) 2989

Sat May 20th
St Mary's Parish Hall, Church
Street, Leatherhead. 9-4pm
Antique Dealers Co-operative.
Tel: (0372) 379795

Sun May 28th
Oatlands Park Hotel, Oatlands
Drive, Weybridge. 10-5pm
Falcon Antiques.
Tel: 01-681 3312

Sat June 3rd
Preston Cross Hotel and
Country Club, Rectory Lane,
Bookham. 10-5pm
Falcon Antique & Collectors
Fairs. Tel: 01-681 3312/
(0737 81) 2989

Sat June 17th
St Mary's Parish Hall, Church
Street, Leatherhead. 9-4pm
Antique Dealers Co-operative.
Tel: (0372) 379795

Sun June 25th
Oatlands Park Hotel, Oatlands
Drive, Weybridge. 10-5pm
Falcon Antique Collectors
Fairs. Tel: 01-681 3312/
(0737 81) 2989

Thur Oct 26th-28th
The Church House, Farnham
Gamlin Exhibition Services.
Tel: (0452) 862557

East Sussex
Thur July 6th-9th
Brighton Antiques Fair, The
Corn Exchange, Royal Pavilion
Grounds
Penman Antique Fairs.
Tel: (04447) 4531/2514

Sun July 30th
Winter Garden, Eastbourne
Brenda Lay. Tel: (07983) 3822

Sun Oct 29th
Winter Garden, Eastbourne
Brenda Lay. Tel: (07983) 3822

West Sussex
Mon May 1st
Goodwood Racecourse, Nr
Chichester. 10-5pm
Falcon Antique & Collectors
Fairs.
Tel: 01-681 3312/(0737 81) 2989

Sat May 6th-7th
The Village Hall, Wivelsfield
Green, Nr Haywards Heath.
11-5pm
Ron Beech Antique Fairs.
Tel: (0273) 724477

Mon May 29th
Goodwood Racecourse, Nr
Chichester. 10-5pm
Falcon Antique & Collectors
Fairs.
Tel: 01-681 3312/(0737 81) 2989

Sun June 4th
The Grange Centre, Repton
Road, Midhurst. 10-4.30pm
Magnum Antique Fairs.
Tel: (0491) 681009

Sat Sept 30th, Sun Oct 1st
Wakefield Ceramic Fair, The
Felbridge Hotel, East Grinstead
Tel: (0634) 723461

Sat Nov 4th-5th
The Village Hall, Wivelsfield
Green, Nr Haywards Heath
Ron Beech Antiques Fairs.
Tel: (0273) 724477

Tyne & Wear
Wed May 3rd-7th
Newcastle upon Tyne Antiques
Fair
Robert Bailey. Tel: 01-550 5435

Warwickshire
Sat May 6th
Royal Sports Centre,
Leamington Spa. 10.30-5pm
Four-in-One Promotions.
Tel: (0533) 712589

Sun May 7th
College of Technology and Art,
Nuneaton. 10-5pm
Temple Fairs.
Tel: (0332) 663197

Sun June 11th
Welcome Hotel, Stratford upon
Avon. 10-5pm
Reg Cooper Fairs.
Tel: (0860) 537153

Sun June 18th
Bell Hall, Rugby. 10.30-5pm
Four-in-One Promotions.
Tel: (0533) 712589

West Midlands
Mon May 1st
Warwickshire County Cricket
Ground, Edgbaston,
Birmingham. 11-6pm
Warwickshire County Antique
Fairs.
Tel: 021-743 2259/021-443 4606

Sun May 21st
The Manor Hotel, Meriden.
10.30-5pm
Prestige Promotions.
Tel: (0533) 516045

Sun June 11th
The Belfry National Golf
Centre, Sutton Coldfield.
10.30-5pm
Prestige Promotions.
Tel: (0533) 516045

Thur Sept 21st-23rd
Warwickshire County Cricket
Ground
Tel: 021-743 2259/021-443 4606

Thur Nov 9th-11th
Warwickshire County Cricket
Ground
Tel: 021-743 2259/021 443 4606

Wiltshire
Thur Nov 24th-26th
Wakefield Ceramic Fair, The
Michael Herbert Hall, Wilton
Tel: (0634) 723461

N. Yorkshire
Tues May 2nd
Conservative Club, Hawes.
10-5pm
Memories Antique Fairs.
Tel: (09693) 463

Fri May 5th
Leyburn Market Place
Memories Antique Fairs.
Tel: (09693) 463

Tues May 9th
Conservative Club, Hawes.
10-5pm
Memories Antique Fairs.
Tel: (09693) 463

Fri May 12th
Leyburn Market Place
Memories Antique Fairs.
Tel: (09693) 463

Sun May 14th
Old Swan Hotel, Harrogate.
10-5pm
Abbey Antique Fairs.
Tel: (0482) 445785

Tues May 16th
Conservative Club, Hawes.
10-5pm
Memories Antique Fairs.
Tel: (09693) 463

Wed May 17th
Skipton Town Hall
Memories Antique Fairs.
Tel: (09693) 463

Fri May 19th
Leyburn Market Place
Memories Antique Fairs.
Tel: (09693) 463

Sat May 20th
Kings Head, Richmond. 10-5pm
Memories Antique Fairs.
Tel: (09693) 463

Ripley Town Hall. 10-5pm
Memories Antique Fairs.
Tel: (09693) 463

Tues May 23rd
Conservative Club, Hawes
Memories Antique Fairs.
Tel: (09693) 463

Wed May 24th
Skipton Town Hall
Memories Antique Fairs.
Tel: (09693) 463

Fri May 26th
Leyburn Market Place
Memories Antique Fairs.
Tel: (09693) 463

Sat May 27th-29th
Hawes Market Hall, Skipton.
10-5pm
Memories Antique Fairs.
Tel: (09693) 463

Tues May 30th
Conservative Club, Hawes
Memories Antique Fairs.
Tel: (09693) 463

Mon May 31st
Skipton Town Hall
Memories Antique Fairs.
Tel: (09693) 463

Fri June 2nd
Leyburn Market Place
Memories Antique Fairs.
Tel: (09693) 463

Sun June 4th
Old Swan Hotel, Harrogate.
10-5pm
Abbey Antique Fairs.
Tel: (0482) 445785

Tues June 6th
Conservative Club, Hawes
Memories Antique Fairs.
Tel: (09693) 463

Wed June 7th
Skipton Town Hall
Memories Antique Fairs.
Tel: (09693) 463

Fri June 9th
Leyburn Market Place
Memories Antique Fairs.
Tel: (09693) 463

Sun June 11th
Devonshire Arms Hotel, Bolton
Abbey, Nr Skipton
Memories Antique Fairs.
Tel: (09693) 463

Tues June 13th
Conservative Club, Hawes
Memories Antique Fairs.
Tel: (09693) 463

Wed June 14th
Skipton Town Hall
Memories Antique Fairs.
Tel: (09693) 463

Fri June 16th
Leyburn Market Place
Memories Antique Fairs.
Tel: (09693) 463

Tues June 20th
Conservative Club, Hawes
Memories Antique Fairs.
Tel: (09693) 463

Wed June 21st
Skipton Town Hall
Memories Antique Fairs.
Tel: (09693) 463

Thur June 22nd-24th
York Summer Antique Fair, De Grey Rooms, Exhibition Sq, York
Antiques in Britain Fairs.
Tel: (05474) 464

Fri June 23rd
Leyburn Market Place
Memories Antique Fairs.
Tel: (09693) 463

Tues, June 27th
Conservative Club, Hawes
Memories Antique Fairs.
Tel: (09693) 463

Wed June 28th
Skipton Town Hall
Memories Antique Fairs.
Tel: (09693) 463

Fri June 30th
Leyburn Market Place
Memories Antique Fairs.
Tel: (09693) 463

Thur Oct 19th-21st
22nd Annual York Antiques Fair, De Grey Rooms, Exhibition Sq, York
Antiques in Britain Fairs.
Tel: (05474) 356/464

Fri Nov 10th-12th
Wakefield Ceramic Fair, The Crown Hotel, Harrogate
Tel: (0634) 723461

S. Yorkshire

Sun May 14th
Keresforth Hall, Barnsley.
10-5pm
Abbey Antique Fairs.
Tel: (0482) 445785

Sun June 11th
Keresforth Hall, Barnsley.
10-5pm
Abbey Antique Fairs.
Tel: (0482) 445785

Sun June 18th
Moathouse, Doncaster
Memories Antique Fairs.
Tel: (09693) 463

W. Yorkshire

Mon May 1st
Antiques Fair, Hilton National Hotel, Garforth, Leeds. 10-5pm
Abbey Antique Fairs.
Tel: (0482) 445785

Sun May 7th
Antiques Fair, Bankfield Hotel, Bingley. 10-5pm
Abbey Antique Fairs.
Tel: (0482) 445785

Northbridge Sports Centre, Halifax. 10-5pm
Dualco Promotions.
Tel: 061-766 2012

Mansion House, Roundhay Park, Leeds. 10-5pm
Memories Antique Fairs.
Tel: (09693) 463

Sun May 21st
Morley Sports Centre, Morley, Leeds. 10-5pm
Dualco Promotions.
Tel: 061-766 2012

Sun May 28th
Hilton National Hotel, Garforth, Leeds. 10-5pm
Abbey Antique Fairs.
Tel: (0482) 445785

Mon May 29th
Bankfield Hotel, Bingley.
10-5pm
Abbey Antique Fairs.
Tel: (0482) 445785

Sun June 18th
Bankfield Hotel, Bingley.
10-5pm
Abbey Antique Fairs.
Tel: (0482) 445785

Pudsey Civic Hall, Leeds.
10-5pm
Dualco Promotions.
Tel: 061-766 2012

Scotland

Sat May 6th
Albert Hall, Stirling
Scotfairs. Tel: (0764) 3592

Fri May 5th-7th
13th Annual Perthshire Antiques Fair, Station Hotel, Leonard Street, Perth
Antiques in Britain Fairs.
Tel: (05474) 356/464

Sun May 7th
Skean Dhu Hotel, Dyce, Aberdeen
Scotfairs. Tel: (0764) 3592

Sun May 21st
Marry at Hall, City Square, Dundee
Scotfairs. Tel: (0764) 3592

Mitchell Theatre, Granville Street, Glasgow
Scotfairs. Tel: (0764) 3592

Sun June 18th
Marry at Hall, City Square, Dundee

City Halls, Candleriggs, Glasgow
Scotfairs. Tel: (0764) 3592

Sat June 24th
Albert Hall, Stirling
Scotfairs. Tel: (0764) 3592

Sun 25th June
Mitchell Theatre, Granville Street, Glasgow
Scotfairs. Tel: (0764) 3592

Tues July 25th-27th
18th Annual Edinburgh Antiques Fair, Roxburghe Hotel, Charlotte Square, Edinburgh
Antiques in Britain Fairs.
Tel: (05474) 356/464

Fri Sept 29th-Oct 1st
Perthshire Autumn Antiques Fair, Station Hotel, Leonard Street, Perth

Antiques in Britain Fairs.
Tel: (05474) 356/464

Fri Nov 17th-19th
13th Annual Edinburgh Winter Antiques Fair, Roxburghe Hotel, Charlotte Square, Edinburgh
Antiques in Britain Fairs.
Tel: (05474) 356/464

Wales

Sun May 14th
St Mellons Hotel and Country Club, St Mellons, Cardiff.
10-5pm
David Robinson Fairs.
Tel: (0222) 620520

Tues May 16th
Royal Welsh Showground, Builth Wells, Powys. 7-4pm
International Antique & Collectors Fairs.
Tel: (0636) 702326

Sun May 21st
Glyn Clydach Hotel, Longford Road, Neath Abbey, Neath.
10-5pm
David Robinson Fairs.
Tel: (0222) 620520

Sun May 28th
Leisure Centre, Chepstow, Gwent
Puzzle House Fairs.
Tel: (0594) 60653

Sun June 11th
St Mellons Hotel and Country Club, St Mellons, Cardiff.
10-5pm
David Robinson Fairs.
Tel: (0222) 260520

Sun June 18th
Glyn Clydach Hotel, Longford Road, Neath Abbey
David Robinson Fairs.
Tel: (0222) 620520

Sun June 25th
The Leisure Centre, Chepstow, Gwent
Puzzle House Fairs.
Tel: (0594) 60653

Aeronautica

The Aeronautica collectables market continues to increase at a constant pace; although a smaller market than Automobilia, collectables have been commanding high prices. Ballooning is a growth area, as is Pioneer Aviation, including early programmes, manufacturers' brochures and catalogues, from the First World War through to the Post War period.

Ballooning

A French chocolate box, with painted scene from 'The Capture', a French drama published in 1798, 3in (7.5cm) diam.
£400-500 *CSK*

A walnut box from the French school, painted with the ascent of the sheep, the cock and the duck in the Montgolfier balloon from Versailles, 19th September 1783, 3in (8cm) diam.
£450-550 *CSK*

Schmidt — A crowd watching the ascent of the French balloonist Etienne Robertson, a verre églomisé inked engraving, signed by the artist, inscribed Robertson's Lüftreyse bëy Dresden au 8 May 1816.
£800-850 *CSK*

A letterpress poster, 1845.
£30-50 *N*

A pair of French ivory miniatures, painted with ballooning scenes, both inscribed on reverse, 18thC, 3in (7cm).
£400-500 *CSK*

A Staffordshire jug, printed with balloon scenes below a border of vines, c1830, 9in (23cm) wide.
£500-600 *CSK*

A postcard, 'Balloon Post', 1903.
£550-650 *N*

A collection of 13 mounted prints and engravings, including The Great Nassau Balloon and Parachute, some coloured, various sizes.
£300-350 *CSK*

A chromium plated balloonist's altimeter, inscribed Barometre altimétrique du Colonel Goulier Compensé, 4½in (11cm) diam.
£350-450 *CSK*

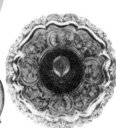

A silver salver with grapevine borders, the commemorative inscription dated October 16th 1839, 16in (40cm) diam.
£800-1,000 *CSK*

Books & Programmes

'With the Airmen',
published in 1913.
£25-30 *COB*

A set of books about
armed services,
Coronation 1937.
£6-8 *COB*

Schneider Trophy,
Official Souvenir
programme, 1931,
Circuit of Britain, 1,010
Miles Air Race 1911,
Blackpool Pageant Air
Display, 1928, Official
Souvenir Programme,
and Spitfire
Achievements, 1939-
1945.
£110-150 *CSK*

An Amy Johnson Daily
Mail souvenir, 1930.
£10-12 *COB*

A collection of
aeronautical ephemera
including 1960s publicity
pamphlets, a 1929
Schneider Trophy
programme and other
items.
£70-120 *CSK*

A souvenir programme
for Blackpool Aviation
Week, 1909.
£60-80 *N*

A monthly gazette
printed by Qantas, 1941.
£6-10 each *COB*

An official programme
with decorative cover,
Bournemouth, July
6th-16th, 1910.
£70-100 *CSK*

A journal for members of
the Royal Naval Air
Service, December 1917.
£6-10 *COB*

A collection of fully
illustrated catalogues of
engines and the aircraft
fitted with them, c1920.
£180-200 *CSK*

Magazines for the
Services, published in
1937.
£4-6 *COB*

General

An R.A.F. officer's car mascot, c1940.
£25-35 *COB*

A bell made for R.A.F.A. from the metal of German aircraft shot down during the war.
£20-40 *COB*

A piston from a Messerschmitt aircraft.
£20-30 *COB*

A piece of a Zeppelin mounted for presentation, 1916.
£40-50 *COB*

A photograph of a First World War pilot.
£5-10 *COB*

A silver cup with presentation inscription, for the Blackpool Aviation Meeting, 1910, 8½in (21cm) diam.
£600-800 *CSK*

A silver cigarette case depicting a Miles Magister, Birmingham 1938, 4in (11cm) high.
£70-100 *CSK*

A green painted and gilt bronze figure of the aviator Amy Johnson, 33½in (85cm) high, on marble and alabaster base, with bronze plaque showing Europe and Africa, signed and dated, Otakar Steinberger, 1932.
£450-550 *CSK*

A white metal tin of Crosse & Blackwell tomato soup, with presentation inscription, commemorating the MacRobertson England to Australia Air Race, 1934, 4½in (11.5cm) high.
£800-1,000 *CSK*

A flying boat cigarette lighter, 1930.
£65-85 *COB*

A Spitfire car mascot, 1940.
£45-50 *COB*

A fruitwood Luftwaffe eagle, clutching a swastika, 40in (101cm) wingspan.
£1,000-1,400 *CSK*

Reputed to have been removed from a Luftwaffe Mess in 1945.

A contemporary tobacco jar modelled as a Royal Flying Corps pilot's head, 6½in (16cm) high.
£110-150 *CSK*

MAKE THE MOST OF MILLER'S
Condition is absolutely vital when assessing the value of any item. Damaged pieces appreciate much less than perfect examples. However, a rare, desirable piece may command a high price even when damaged.

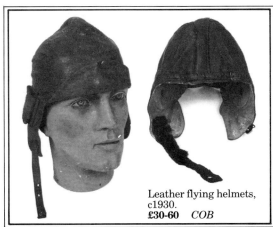

Leather flying helmets,
c1930.
£30-60 *COB*

A collection of 3 wings
from a World War I scout
aircraft, 156 by 62in (396
by 157cm).
£50-150 *CSK*

A Harrods Flying Kit
advertisement, 2nd
December, 1919.
£7-10 *COB*

A BOAC lighter, c1960.
£17-20 *COB*

A presentation turbo
blade from the first-ever
Harrier, c1970.
£45-50 *COB*

Laminated wood two-
blade propellers, c1915.
£250-500 each *CSK*

A set of Aeroplane
Recognition Tests, c1940.
£3-8 *COB*

A BOAC water jug,
c1960.
£15-20 *COB*

A BEA cap, c1950.
£12-15 *COB*

A BOAC route map and
flight information
booklet, c1960.
£4-6 *COB*

Models & Toys

A wooden model of a Harrier, c1970, 12in (30.5cm) long.
£35-45 *COB*

An Aeromodels Hawker Typhoon kit, in original box, price 6s 3d, c1940.
£20-25 *COB*

A manufacturer's model of Skybolt missile, c1960, 14in (35.5cm) long.
£40-60 *COB*

A plated model of a Westland Whirlwind helicopter, c1956, 10½in (26.5cm) long.
£50-70 *CSK*

A contemporary wooden recognition model of a Focke-Wulf 190, finished in camouflage green paint, flaking, 41½in (105cm) wingspan.
£80-120 *CSK*

A Skybirds Hawker Hurricane model kit, c1940.
£20-24 *COB*

A printed and painted tinplate four-engine airliner, 'Strato Clipper', by Gama, slightly chipped, c1956, wingspan 20in (51cm).
£100-120 *CSK*

A collection of Dinky pre-war aeroplanes.
£250-350 each set
CSK

Dinky pre-war No. 60 aeroplane set, 1st issue, including Imperial Airways liner, D. H. Leopard Moth, Percival Gull, Low wing monoplane, General Monospar and a Cierva Autogyro, in original paintwork, helicopter damaged, with box.
£2,200-2,500 *CSK*

Cross Reference
Toys
Diecast Aircraft

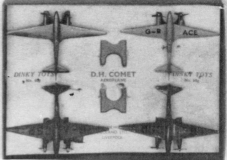

Dinky pre-war 60g D. H. Comet aeroplanes, including 2 red aircraft 'G-ACSR', a gold finished aeroplane and a yellow painted post-war 'Light Racer' 'G-RACE', in original box.
£600-650 *CSK*

Posters & Prints

A poster from Illustrated London News, c1926.
£8-10 *COB*

A colour lithograph poster, after Geo. Dorival, c1910, 30 by 22in (76 by 56cm).
£200-220 *CSK*

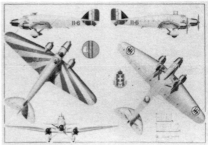

A James Goulding Savoia Marchetti S.M.81, signed, 16½ by 24in (42 by 61.5cm).
£100-150 *CSK*

A colour lithograph poster, after A. Solon, 35 by 25in (89 by 63.5cm).
£70-100 *CSK*

An original watercolour of a cartoon, 1944.
£45-50 *COB*

BACK THEM UP!

A collection of colour lithograph posters, in folio.
£150-200 *CSK*

A watercolour of a reconnaissance Spitfire, c1945.
£60-70 *COB*

A Howard Leigh signed etching, Fokker D VII, c1919.
£40-50 *COB*

A Cecil Bernard watercolour, signed and dated 1918, 9½ by 15in (24 by 38cm).
£70-100 *CSK*

Cross Reference
Ephemera
Postcards
Posters
Toys

FURTHER READING

Dallas, Brett, R. *History of British Aviation*, 2 vols. 1908-14 and 1913-14.
Duval, G. R. *British Flying Boats and Amphibians*, 1909-52. London 1953.
Funderburk, Thomas R. *The Fighters: The Men and Machines of the First Air War*. London 1966.
Hodgson, J. E. *The History of Aeronautics in Britain*, 1924.
Janes All the World's Aircraft — published annually.
Mackay, James A. *Airmails 1870-1970*. London 1971.
Swanborough, F. C. *Combat Aircraft of the World*. London 1962.
Warring, R. H. *Aeromodelling*. London 1965.

Automobilia

Just about anything to do with transport is collectable, particularly vehicles. The field is enormous, from car badges, accessories, spare parts, original promotional artwork, brochures, posters, magazines, books, oil and petrol, up to and including motor cars themselves. The market is currently very active with good prices being obtained for most items.

Accessories

l. A pair of nickel plated C.A.V. sidelights, 4in (10cm) long, and a Heath's parking light.
£30-40
r. A pair of nickel plated C.A.V. sidelights, 5½in (14cm) diam.
£55-70   *ONS*

A pair of Lucas P100 headlamps, original lenses and mirrors, 12in (30.5cm) diam.
£600-800   *C*

A brass boa constrictor horn with trumpet head attachment, 66in (168cm) long.
£40-60   *ONS*

A Lucas 'Calcia King' headlamp, in original box, price 17s 6d.
£30-40   *FAL*

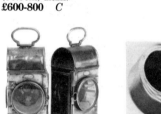

A pair of copper and brass fire engine sidelights, with oil burners, 12in (30.5cm) high.
£110-150   *ONS*

A Lucas 'Owl Eye' tail lamp.
£400-450   *C*

A nickel plated Heath's bulb horn, with nickel plated flexible extension and mounting bracket.
£125-150   *ONS*

l. A black painted aluminium-cased Lucas 'Owls Eye' rear light, 6in (15cm) wide.
£200-250
r. A brass electric Klaxon horn, suitable for Rolls Royce, 9in (23cm) high.
£80-100   *ONS*

A 1937 coronation commemorative car pennant.
£20-30   *FAL*

'Tut-Tut' or 'A Run In A Motor Car' game.
£70-100   *ONS*

A selection of dashboard instruments.
£70-130 each   *ONS*

Cross Reference
Tools

Badges

An R.A.C. windscreen clip-on badge.
£5-10 *FAL*

A chromium plated and enamelled B.R.D.C. badge, stamped 767 Boshier-Jones, 4½in (11cm) high.
£200-300 *ONS*

An R.A.C. Life Members Badge, by Elkington & Co. Ltd., No. B2346, on plinth, 7in (18cm) high.
£550-600 *C*

Car badges
£30-50   **£450-500**
£120-140   *ONS*

Car badges
£100-150
£400-450
£500-550   *ONS*

A Ladies B.A.R.C. marcasite brooch.
£30-50 *FAL*

Mascots

A radiator cap with Austin winged steering wheel.
£200-250 *FAL*

An early pixie car mascot.
£600-800 *FAL*

Mascots were often painted before plated mascots were made.

A brass figure of Charlie Chaplin, on beechwood plinth, 5in (12cm) high.
£200-250 *CSK*

A Jaguar radiator cap with Rolls Royce mascot.
£40-60 *FAL*

A chromed metal figure, stamped Riley Ski Lady R.D. 759377, on metal stand, c1930, 7in (18cm) high.
£300-350 *CSK*

AUTOMOBILIA

The original Morgan stork mascot.
£400-500   FAL

This is possibly the only remaining example.

A winged mascot.
£10-20   FAL

A chromium plated speed nymph, mounted on a radiator cap, 5½in (14cm).
£70-100   ONS

A Daily Express commemorative plaque, 1,000 miles car rally, 1950.
£10-15   FAL

Trophies

A pair of silver trophies, inscribed Essex Motor Club, Brooklands, August 13th, 1921, H. Merton, 2nd Prize, 4in (10cm) high.
£200-300   ONS

An R.A.C. rally trophy, on marble base, inscribed R.A.C. Rally, Eastbourne 1935, 12in (30.5cm).
£650-750   C

A chromium plated trophy, modelled as a Bugatti radiator grill and badge, on wood stand, inscribed F.C.K. Wharton, Prescott Hill Climb Champion, 1951-52, 9in (23cm) high.
£550-600   ONS

A plated desk companion, modelled as an Edwardian Grand Prix racing car at speed, signed on base W. Zurick, 16in (40.5cm) long.
£1,500-2,000   CSK

Prints

Frederick Gordon Crosby, an impression of how road-type racing might look on a proposed artificial circuit at Brooklands Motor Course, signed, pencil and watercolour, 14 by 13½in (35.5 by 34cm).
£3,500-4,000   CSK

Dion Pears — Stirling Moss driving a Maserati 250M at Monaco, signed watercolour 23 by 31in (58.5 by 78cm).
£150-200   CSK

Avus 1937 Auto Unions, signed, watercolour, 8½ by 10½in (21.5 by 26.5cm).
£60-80   ONS

Frederick Gordon Crosby, the artist in his MG 16/80, signed and dated 1929, watercolour, 24 by 19in (61 by 48cm).
£1,500-2,000   ONS

Bryan de Grineau, Sir Malcolm Campbell's 'Bluebird', signed and dated 1928, watercolour, 19½ by 30in (49 by 76cm).
£1,500-2,000   CSK

DID YOU KNOW?
Miller's Collectables Price Guide is designed to build up, year by year, into the most comprehensive reference system available.

26

Books & Motoring Ephemera

Le Sport & Le Tourisme Automobile, June 1925, French text, mounted plates.
£80-100 *ONS*

The Ministry of Transport Highway Code, 1931, price 1d.
£2-5 *FAL*

A programme for a luncheon in honour of Major H. O. D. Segrave after he achieved the land speed record and the Motor Boat Championship of the World Trophy, 1929.
£70-100 *CSK*

A Price's car manual, 1929.
£10-18 *FAL*

A sales brochure for the Bentley 3 litre, No. 7, issued October 1924.
£250-300 *ONS*

A silk handkerchief, XVIII Mille Miglia 1951, framed and glazed, 31in (79cm) square.
£200-300 *ONS*

A selection of race programmes.
£50-100 each *ONS*

Pre-War race programmes.
£30-50 each *ONS*

THIS IS A PRICE GUIDE NOT A PRICE LIST

The price ranges quoted indicate the *average* price a purchaser should pay for similar items. However, there are many other factors which should be taken into account when assessing the value of a piece. These include:

Condition
Rarity of design or pattern
Size
Colour
Provenance
Restoration
If sought after

When buying or selling, remember that prices can be greatly affected by condition. Unless otherwise stated all goods illustrated are of good saleable quality, and the price ranges reflect this. Pieces offered for sale in exceptionally fine or in poor condition may reasonably be expected to be priced considerably higher or lower than the estimates quoted here.

Signs

A collection of enamel double-sided advertising signs.
Humber.
£80-100
Castrol.
£80-100
Shell.
£100-120
Vacuum Motor Car Oils.
£60-80
Bedford Trucks.
£70-80
Pratts.
£70-100
National Benzole.
£70-100
B.P.
£350-400
Shell.
£100-120   *ONS*

Glass petrol pump globes.
National Benzole.
£80-100   *FAL*
B.P.
£40-50   *ONS*
Shell.
£80-100   *ONS*
Regent.
£40-45   *FAL*
Esso.
£80-100   *ONS*

Redex advertising items.
top:
£30-35
bottom:
£5-10 each   *FAL*

Duckham's advertising board, with thermometer, 43in (109cm) high.
£140-160   *CSK*

Enamel advertising badges.
£10-15 each   *FAL*

Branded Products

Two gallon petrol cans.
£25-30 each *ONS*

Morris Motors Ltd., The
Clear-All Adapter, 'will
clear all obstructions in
your petrol pipes, jets and
oil pipes in a few seconds',
original box.
£1-3 *FAL*

Ferodo brake linings for
Austin 7 h.p., in original
box.
£5-10 *FAL*

Cross Reference
Ephemera
Posters
Postcards
Ceramics
Toys

Petrol and oil cans.
Speedwell.
£10-20
Bluecol.
£2-5
Maxima.
£2-5
Ford.
£2-5
Price's.
£5-10
De Dion-Bouton.
£60-70
B.P.
£1-3
Shell.
£10-15 *FAL*

Lodge sparking
plug tin.
£5-10
Plug, c1914.
£3-4 *FAL*

Duckhams, Wear-Cure
tablets, 'of special value
for running-in new
engines'.
£1-3 *FAL*

Osram Automobile lamp
bulb, in original box.
£1-2 *FAL*

Barometers

Stick

A mahogany and
boxwood strung stick
barometer, signed
Negretti & Co., fecit,
London, 38in (99cm).
£450-500 *CSK*

A mahogany stick
barometer, the silvered
scale signed Cary,
London, late 18thC.
£600-700 *P*

A Scottish pattern
mahogany stick
barometer, with ivory
scale, signed Swaddell,
Glasgow, the cistern
signed in ink, Josh
Somalvico, 18 Charles
St., Hatton Garden,
London, early 19thC.
£600-650 *P*

A rosewood stick
barometer, with twin
glazed ivory scales
signed Warranted
Correct, Improved
Barometer,
Wolverhampton, mid-
19thC, 37in (94cm).
£420-500 *P*

A mahogany stick
barometer, the scale
signed Leoni Fecit, late
18thC.
£450-500 *P*

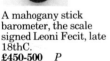

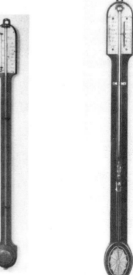

A mahogany bowfront
stick barometer, the
silvered scale signed
F. Pastorelli, Cross
Street, Hatton Garden,
London, c1815.
£2,000-2,500 *P*

A mahogany stick
barometer, signed Frans
Pelegrino fecit, early
19thC, 38in (96cm).
£850-950 *CSK*

A mahogany stick
barometer, signed
Domco. Manticha Fecit,
restored, early 19thC.
£700-750 *P*

An oak stick barometer,
vernier and thermometer
inscribed S. Margoschis,
Leamington, 36in
(91.5cm).
£250-300 *CSK*

A mahogany stick
barometer, signed Will.
Barclay, damaged, late
18thC, 35in (89cm).
£550-650 *P*

Wheel (Banjo)

A mahogany, ebony and boxwood strung wheel barometer, the silvered dial signed Marzorati & Rivolta, warranted, 38½in (97cm).
£400-450   *CSK*

A mahogany and boxwood strung barometer, the silvered dial signed F. Potti, Pontefract, 38in (96.5cm).
£350-400   *CSK*

A mahogany wheel barometer, the silver dial inscribed J. Polty, fecit, 39in (99cm).
£400-450   *CSK*

A Victorian rosewood barometer, the silvered dial signed John Hansford, Ilminster, 37in (94cm).
£200-250   *CSK*

A mahogany and boxwood strung wheel barometer, the spirit level signed Tagliabue & Casella, 23 Hatton Garden, London, 38in (96.5cm).
£400-450   *CSK*

A rosewood wheel barometer, the silvered dial signed Tagliabue & Casella, 25 Hatton Garden, London, 39in (99cm).
£400-450   *CSK*

A mahogany and boxwood wheel barometer, the spirit level signed A. Cattanio, Worcester, 38½in (96.5cm).
£250-300   *CSK*

A mahogany wheel barometer, the dial with well engraved centre signed Robert Carr Woods, Meteorological Instrument Maker, 47 Hatton Garden, Holborn, London, with spirit level, 19thC, 43½in (110cm).
£500-550   *CSK*

Other Types

A rosewood marine barometer, with twin glazed ivory scales, signed Wallace, Ardrossan, mounted with Improved Sympiesometer, mid-19thC.
£1,300-1,500   *P*

A mahogany and chequered strung pillar barometer, signed I. Pozzy, Glasgow, 38in (96.5cm).
£550-650   *CSK*

DID YOU KNOW?
Barometers usually carry a maker's mark and/or name, often with a registration number. The earliest types were stick, diagonal and pediment barometers; these can date back to the late 17th century. The wheel (or banjo) barometer came into general use from the late 18th century and was being mass-produced by the middle of the 19th.

31

Bicycling

An Ordinary bicycle, finished in green paintwork, c1890, driving wheel 51½in (130cm).
£1,300-1,500 *CSK*

An Ordinary Hillman-Herbert and Cooper bicycle, etched on the saddle spring 'Popular Premier', with some original spokes to front wheel, crescent rims, Cooper patented front and rear bearings, nickel plated brake parts, recovered and correct saddle, turned hand grips, c1885, 54in (137cm).
£500-1,000 *P*

A 'boneshaker' bicycle, with iron frame, wooden wheels and spokes, and iron tyres, the handlebar with wooden hand grips, twisting to operate the rear wheel brake, c1869.
£1,000-1,500 *CDC*

A Triumph Moller autogale.
£450-500 *TM*

A Victorian three-wheeled wicker bath chair.
£50-100 *TM*

A tricycle, convertible to ladies or gentlemen, with moving crossbar.
£250-350 *TM*

A cantilever-powered 2-gear invalid tricycle.
£80-120 *TM*

A Kendricity tricycle.
£200-300 *TM*

A Golden Sunbeam bicycle, black enamelling retouched, some damage to pedal, with front and rear lamps, c1907.
£200-250 *CSK*

A James tricycle.
£80-120 *TM*

A butcher's trade cycle.
£210-250 *TM*

Johnson's Nu-Cycle bicycle polish.
£5-10 *FAL*

Burning cycle oil.
£10-20 *FAL*

A nickel plated bell, c1912.
£7-10 *CAC*

Patchquick puncture kit.
£5-10 *FAL*

The Halford Cycle Co., Ltd., 'Rutico' oil injector for motor cyclists.
£5-10 *FAL*

A carbide bicycle lamp.
£20-25 *FAL*

A Continentale bicycle saddle.
£20-30 *FAL*

An Imperial Rover and Meteor Cycles enamel plaque, 24½in (62cm) high.
£200-250 *ONS*

A Motor Cycling Club triple award trophy.
£30-35 *FAL*

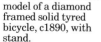

A silver scratch-built model of a diamond framed solid tyred bicycle, c1890, with stand.
£30-40 *P*

Raleigh advertising posters, unmounted.
£40-60 each *P*

A Stuart bicycle plaque.
£10-15 *FAL*

Bottles

Bottle collecting is not as popular as it was a few years ago, although a collecting area to watch for a revival. Condition is all important; check carefully for cracks and chips, especially inside the rim and on the base of the bottle.

Stoneware

Small brown stoneware bottles for everyday commodities.
£2-8   *FAL*

A plain brown bottle with pourer spout.
£10-15   *FAL*

l. Boots Ginger Beer, c1920.
£8-10
r. James Rowland Derby Stoneware bottle, c1902.
£30-35   *COB*

Ginger beer.
£8-12   *FAL*

Royal Doulton 2 gallon bottle, c1920, 19½in (49cm) high.
£35-40   *COB*

A brown stoneware bottle, impressed 'Maidstone'.
£15-20   *FAL*

A stone cider keg, 11in (28cm).
£10-15   *WHA*

'Southampton' stone bottles, c1900.
£10-12 each   *COB*

Glass

A selection of glass bottles for a variety of household uses.
£5-12 each   *FAL*

In 1875 Hiram Codd patented his glass bottle. These had a marble inside the neck which was forced onto a rubber ring in the neck of the bottle by the gas generated by carbonised drink.

Dark blue glass Codd bottles are very scarce.

Beware of bottles with black or blue marbles as they may be modern Indian examples.

Bovril bottles, c1890-1920.
£3-4 each   *FAL*

A Codd mineral water bottle, c1900.
£4-6   *FAL*

A green glass bottle, W. J. Cremer & Son, Sittingbourne.
£4-6   *FAL*

Medicine

A blue sealed bottle, 7in (18cm) high.
£30-40   *CAC*

Chemists' bottles, 7 to 9in (18 to 23cm) high.
£10-12   *AL*

Three German Schnapps bottles.
£16-18 each   *WHA*

Ten blue glass labelled chemists' bottles.
£230-250   *TM*

The late 18thC saw the arrival of pointed bottles used to hold medicinal soda water. These had to be laid down thereby keeping the cork wet and retaining the gas. These were first used by chemist Jacob Schweppe.

Eight green poison bottles.
£80-100   *TM*

Boxes

General

A Victorian satinwood and birch coin collector's cabinet, 15in (38cm) wide.
£125-175 *MB*

A George III mahogany cutlery urn, inlaid with boxwood lines, with fitted interior, 25½in (64.5cm) high.
£800-1,000 *C*

A Victorian mahogany artist's box, 9in (23cm) wide.
£45-65 *MB*

A Victorian artist's box, J. Reeves & Woodyer, complete with original embossed paints, brushes and mixing accessories.
£300-400 *PC*

A George III mahogany apothecary box, with original interior, 7in (18cm) high.
£350-400 *MB*

A missionary's medicine chest, containing a complete selection of drugs and first aid accessories, late 19thC.
£600-700 *PC*

A Victorian ebonised decanter box, inlaid with brass and tortoiseshell, containing 15 glasses and 4 decanters, one glass missing.
£500-600 *MB*

A George III mahogany decanter box, with original decanters, 10in (25.5cm) high.
£400-450 *MB*

A George III mahogany knife box, outlined with corded banding, the crossbanded sloping front inlaid with a fan medallion and enclosing a fitted interior, the front with a Sheffield plate escutcheon, 14½in (37cm) high.
£400-450 *Bea*

A pair of George III mahogany sloping fronted knife boxes, with serpentine fronts, 14½in (37cm).
£900-1,200 *CSK*

An Edwardian metal hat box, clasp missing.
£10-12 *LB*

Two cardboard hat boxes, c1930.
£10-15 each *LB*

A Victorian fruitwood collector's cabinet, complete with butterflies and insects, 17in (43cm) high.
£200-250 *MB*

An early walnut inlaid chest, 10in (25.5cm) high.
£140-160 *MB*

A Regency table cabinet, with leather inlay, 9½in (24cm) high.
£360-400 *MB*

A Regency gilt metal mounted leather sarcophagus shaped casket, the lid engraved with a 'C', the interior of the cover set with 2 coloured engraved portraits of Queen Caroline and Princess Charlotte in gilt slips, 15½in (39cm) wide.
£450-500 *C*

A carved casket, late 18thC, 15in (38cm) wide.
£300-350 *MB*

MAKE THE MOST OF _____
MILLER'S
Price ranges in this book reflect what one should expect to *pay* for a similar example. When selling, however, one should expect to receive a lower figure. This will fluctuate according to a dealer's stock, saleability at a particular time, etc. It is always advisable, when selling, to approach a reputable specialist dealer or an auction house which has specialist sales.

BOXES

A counter box, in ivory painted beechwood with gilding, c1775, 7½in (19cm) wide.
£300-350 *CL*

A spa counter box, with individual lacquered counter boxes in a tray, containing bone counters, c1860, 11½ by 9½in (29 by 24cm).
£250-300 *CL*

An early quill box.
£17-25 *MB*

Tunbridge & Souvenir woodware, by Pinto

A painted box with lock and fittings, c1820, 5in (12.5cm) wide.
£80-100 *CL*

A pencil box, with hand coloured engraving, c1830, 7 by 2in (18 by 5cm).
£50-60 *CL*

An inlaid box, with hand coloured engraving, c1840.
£30-40 *CL*

A box with simple motif, c1840.
£40-60 *CL*

A mid-Victorian gilt metal-mounted green painted stationery box, 8in (20.5cm) wide.
£350-400 *C*

A Victorian oak stationery box, with original leather.
£180-200 *MB*

A walnut and brass coal box.
£60-100 *MB*

A George III Sheraton dome top box, in lime, boxwood and partridge wood, 12in (30.5cm) wide.
£180-200 *MB*

A Victorian burr walnut box, c1840.
£350-400 *MB*

A rosewood box, 8½in (22cm) high.
£35-55 *MB*

An early Victorian oak and holly letter box, the top with a slot, the fall front with glazed flap, 9in (23cm) wide.
£350-400 *C*

A Sheraton style inlaid mahogany letter box, with mirror front, 12in (30.5cm) high.
£170-200 *MB*

A crossbanded collar/
jewel box, 19thC.
£100-120 *MB*

A Georgian Sheraton
inlaid mahogany
gentleman's bedside box,
15in (38cm) high.
£400-450 *MB*

A Georgian coromandel
gentleman's vanity box,
c1815, 12½in (30.5cm)
wide.
£400-450 *MB*

A Victorian vanity box,
with silver accessories.
£1,000-1,200 *MB*

A Victorian coromandel
brass bound vanity box,
c1852, 12in (30.5cm)
wide.
£500-600 *MB*

An oak bible box, the
hinged cover bearing the
date 1718, 29in (74cm)
wide.
£175-200 *CSK*

A French box, with
reeded and dot decoration
and engraved with floret,
marks probably for
Dijon, c1758, and marks
for Seurre, 4in (10cm).
£200-250 *DN*

A French kingwood and
rosewood glove box, 11in
(28cm) wide.
£300-350 *MB*

A Japanese barrel-
shaped gold lacquered
box and cover, decorated
in relief with a dragon
within a border of clouds,
4½in (11.5cm) diam.
£200-250 *CSK*

A Georgian Napoleonic
prisoner-of-war straw-
work box, 10in (25.5cm)
wide.
£230-260 *MB*

An ivory silk
embroidered box, the fall
front flap revealing one
long and 2 short drawers,
lined in pink silk,
mid-17thC, 8½in (21cm)
wide.
£1,200-1,500 *P*

A late Ming blue and
white oval box and cover,
painted with a scholar
seated in a landscape
within panels of flowers
divided by swastika
pattern, Wanli, 5in
(12.5cm) wide.
£350-400 *CSK*

A Japanese ivory box
and cover, carved in
relief with a monkey and
young catching bats,
signed, 7½in (19cm).
£500-550 *CSK*

A Russian box, with
peasant scene, c1835.
£260-280 *CL*

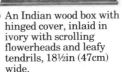

An Indian wood box with
hinged cover, inlaid in
ivory with scrolling
flowerheads and leafy
tendrils, 18½in (47cm)
wide.
£700-750 *CSK*

BOXES

Jewel

An early Victorian rosewood jewel box.
£85-100   *MB*

A Victorian walnut jewel box, with brass banding, c1860.
£175-200   *MB*

A Victorian walnut jewel box, with tulipwood edging, c1850.
£115-130   *MB*

A Victorian jewel box.
£60-65   *CAC*

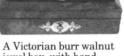

A Victorian mahogany trinket box, 10in (25.5cm) wide.
£45-65   *MB*

A jewel box.
£12-15   *VB*

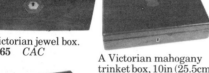

A Victorian burr walnut jewel box, with hand painted plaque, c1860.
£180-200   *MB*

A late Georgian coromandel brass bound jewel box, 12in (30.5cm) wide.
£225-250   *MB*

A Victorian rosewood inlaid jewel box, c1850, 8in (20.5cm) square.
£170-200   *MB*

Sewing

A coromandel sewing box, 12in (30.5cm) wide.
£200-250   *MB*

A William IV inlaid rosewood and mother-of-pearl fitted sewing box, c1835, 13in (33cm).
£400-450   *MB*

A Victorian coromandel fitted sewing box, inlaid with mother-of-pearl, c1850, 12in (30.5cm) wide.
£225-250   *MB*

A Regency lacquered work box, with original contents, c1820, 14½in (35.5cm) wide.
£260-300   *MB*

A William IV ebony fitted sewing box, inlaid with mother-of-pearl, c1830, 12½in (31.5cm) wide.
£400-450   *MB*

A William IV mahogany fitted sewing box, banded with pewter, with rosewood inlay, c1830, 12in (30.5cm) wide.
£350-400   *MB*

A Victorian walnut sewing box, 1870, 11½in (29cm) wide.
£70-100   *MB*

Writing Slopes

A coromandel brass bound box, c1850, 13in (33cm) wide.
£275-300 *MB*

A mahogany brass bound writing slope, with secret drawer, c1840, 20in (51cm) wide.
£300-350 *MB*

A Victorian walnut brass bound writing slope, with secret drawer, c1880, 20in (51cm) wide.
£260-300 *MB*

A Regency writing slope in burr oak, cedar, rosewood and birch, with secret drawers, c1825.
£400-450 *MB*

A Georgian mahogany writing slope.
£100-150 *MB*

A teak brass bound inlaid writing slope, with secret drawers.
£200-250 *MB*

A walnut writing box.
£70-80 *CAC*

A Victorian coromandel brass inlaid writing slope, with original contents, c1850, 16in (40.5cm) wide.
£450-500 *MB*

A Persian rosewood travelling writing box, crossbanded and inlaid in ivory with stylised foliage, 19thC, 23½in (60cm) wide.
£750-800 *CSK*

A rosewood writing slope, inlaid with mother-of-pearl, 16in (40.5cm) wide.
£75-100 *PAC*

A bird's-eye maple writing slope, inlaid with rosewood, 14in (35.5cm) wide.
£75-100 *PAC*

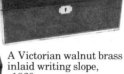

A Victorian walnut brass inlaid writing slope, c1860.
£175-200 *MB*

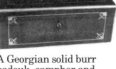

A Georgian solid burr padouk, camphor and ebony writing slope, with secret drawers, c1810.
£500-550 *MB*

A William IV rosewood mother-of-pearl inlaid writing slope, c1835.
£165-185 *MB*

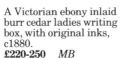

A Victorian ebony inlaid burr cedar ladies writing box, with original inks, c1880.
£220-250 *MB*

FURTHER READING
Bedford, John. *All Kinds of Small Boxes*. London 1964.
Delieb, Eric. *Silver Boxes*. London 1968.

Buckles

A Georgian shoe buckle.
£10-15 *JBB*

A Georgian silver and
steel buckle.
£45-55 *JBB*

A Georgian silver buckle.
£20-30 *JBB*

A cloisonné clasp, c1890.
£85-100 *JBB*

A silver and silver plate
buckle, dated 1865.
£60-80 *JBB*

A silver buckle, marked
London 1901.
£25-30 *JBB*

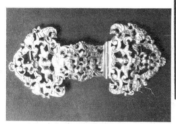

A silver clasp, marked
London 1889.
£120-150 *JBB*

A three-piece glass, paste
and brass plated clasp,
c1890.
£80-100 *JBB*

A pair of French pressed
steel shoe buckles, c1890.
£12-15 *JBB*

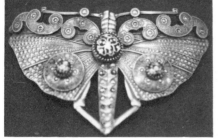

An Art Nouveau
Austrian Studios
pewter clasp.
£130-150 *JBB*

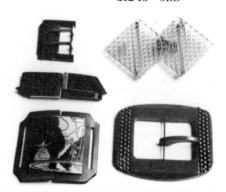

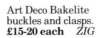

Art Deco Bakelite
buckles and clasps.
£15-20 each *ZIG*

Art Deco Bakelite
buckles and clasps.
£45-65 each   *ZIG*

An enamelled one-piece
clasp, 20thC.
£60-80   *JBB*

A porcelain and metal
clasp, c1920.
£40-60   *JBB*

A selection of Art Deco
buckles and clasps.
£10-20 each   *JBB*

A pair of shoe buckles,
c1930.
£12-15   *JBB*

**MAKE THE MOST OF
MILLER'S**
Condition is absolutely
vital when assessing the
value of any item.
Damaged pieces
appreciate much less
than perfect examples.
However, a rare,
desirable piece may
command a high price
even when damaged.

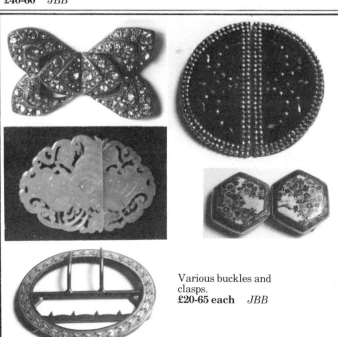

Various buckles and
clasps.
£20-65 each   *JBB*

Buttons

Porcelain buttons of the 18th and 19th centuries are particularly sought after. Most porcelain manufacturers produced buttons, the most notable from Sèvres, Tournai and Copenhagen. Other continental factories include Meissen, Limoges and Delft and in England buttons were produced by such factories as Wedgwood, Ruskin, Pilkington and Minton. Oriental buttons, especially Satsuma ware, are also in demand. 20th century designer buttons by Lalique and Salvador Dali are highly prized; buttons by Fabergé can sell for thousands of pounds.

A set of 6 mid-Victorian cut steel buttons, 1860.
£30-40   *JBB*

A French enamelled button, marked E. M. Paris, c1880.
£14-18   *JBB*

An enamel and silver button, with crimson background, c1890.
£15-20   *JBB*

A set of Art Nouveau silver buttons.
£65-75   *JBB*

Six blue enamel and paste buttons, in original box, early 19thC.
£125-150   *JBB*

A cut steel button, with blue stone, 18thC.
£12-15   *JBB*

A Guild of Craftsmen pewter button, with green ceramic centre.
£5-10   *JBB*

A set of 6 late Victorian painted enamel buttons.
£45-55   *JBB*

An Art Nouveau button.
£10-12   *VB*

A set of Arts and Crafts Movement buttons, in silver, enamel and pearls.
£85-95   *JBB*

A set of Victorian
enamelled glass buttons.
£25-30 *JBB*

A set of glass and paste
buttons, c1930.
£12-15 *JBB*

An enamel and silver
button and buckle set,
marked Birmingham,
c1910, in original box.
£175-200 *JBB*

An ivory button, c1900.
£5-10 *JBB*

A pressed steel button.
£5-10 *JBB*

A single paste button,
c1915.
£4-8 *JBB*

A late Victorian painted
enamel button.
£5-10 *JBB*

DID YOU KNOW?
Many porcelain factories produced buttons, mostly to
show their particular factory's patterns in miniature.

A set of cut steel with
enamel paste buttons.
£55-65 *JBB*

A silver button,
Birmingham 1901.
£12-15 *JBB*

A cut steel and enamel
button.
£6-10 *JBB*

BUTTONS

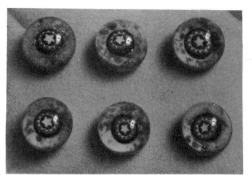

A set of 6 Canadian paperweight buttons, 20thC.
£45-55   *JBB*

An ivory button, 20thC.
£5-10   *JBB*

An ivory dog button, 20thC.
£5-10   *JBB*

A set of 15ct gold and enamel buttons with diamonds.
£550-600   *JBB*

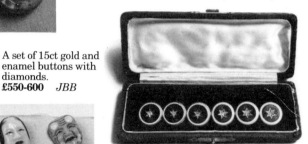

A set of Imari present day mask buttons.
£45-55   *JBB*

A Satsuma button, with silver mount.
£14-18   *JBB*

A set of Japanese Satsuma buttons, produced for the European market.
£60-80   *JBB*

A sporting button.
£5-10   *JBB*

A set of 6 Mikado 'Yum Yum' picture buttons.
£50-60   *JBB*

Satsuma buttons.
£10-15 each   *JBB*

DID YOU KNOW?____
Casein buttons are made from milk!

46

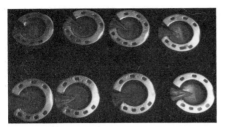

A set of horn horseshoe buttons.
£20-25 *JBB*

A glass button, with a yacht painting under glass, with brass backing.
£16-18 *JBB*

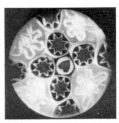

A single paperweight glass button.
£12-15 *JBB*

An enamelled button.
£2-5 *VB*

An imitation cut steel button.
£10-15 *JBB*

A silver cat button, marked.
£20-25 *JBB*

A set of Imari buttons, 'Seven Gods of Wisdom'
£45-55 *JBB*

A set of picture buttons, Incroyable Merveilleuse.
£45-55 *JBB*

An enamel button with cut steel decoration.
£14-18 *JBB*

A set of 4 silver and enamel buttons, Birmingham 1900.
£55-65 *JBB*

A set of paste buttons, set in silver.
£45-55 *JBB*

An Italian mosaic button, with silver mount.
£22-25 *JBB*

FURTHER READING
Albert, Lilian Smith and Kent, Cathryn. *The Complete Button Book*. London 1952.
Luscomb, Sally C. *The Collector's Encyclopedia of Buttons*. New York 1967.
Peacock, Primrose. *Buttons for the Collector*. Newton Abbot 1972.
Squire, Gwen. *Buttons: A Guide for Collectors*. London 1972.

Button Hooks

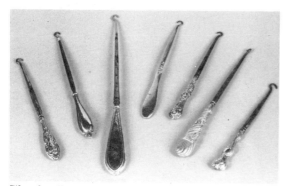

Silver handled button hooks.
£10-15 each *VB*

Button hooks and a collar buttoner.
£1-12 each *VB*

A folding ivory button hook.
£6-7
A folding mother-of-pearl knife and button hook.
£13-15 *VB*

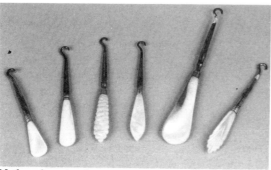

Mother-of-pearl and ivory button hooks.
£5-7 each *VB*

A pair of ivory handled boot hooks.
£14-16 *VB*

Two button hooks.
£18-20 each *VB*

DID YOU KNOW?

Tiny button hooks, little more than an inch or two long, were used to fasten the buttons on ladies' elbow length gloves.

A Victorian silver and ivory button hook/shoe horn, 9½in (24cm) long.
£25-35 *MB*

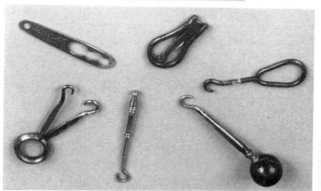

A selection of button hooks.
£4-9 *VB*

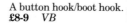

A button hook/boot hook.
£8-9 *VB*

A folding mother-of-pearl
button hook.
£13-15 *VB*

Button hooks and heel
pads.
£3-10 each *VB*

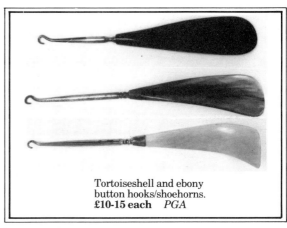

Tortoiseshell and ebony
button hooks/shoehorns.
£10-15 each *PGA*

An ivory-handle button
hook and shoe horn.
£7-9 *VB*

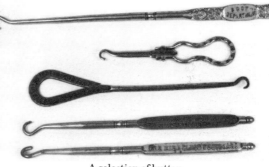

A selection of button
hooks, advertising
footware.
£10-20 each *PGA*

DID YOU KNOW?
Button hooks are a boon
when pulling up long zips
on the backs of dresses.

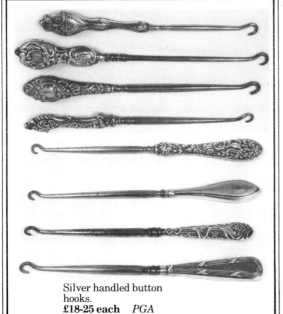

Silver handled button
hooks.
£18-25 each *PGA*

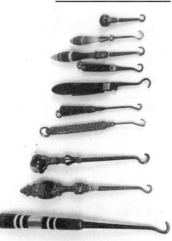

A selection of glove
hooks, with agate,
cornelian and jade
handles.
£15-20 each *PGA*

49

Cameras

A Gandolfi whole plate camera.
£375-400 *J*

A quarter plate Special B camera, by Newman and Guardia Ltd., London, No. SB1451, with a Ross Zeiss Patent 9in lens and 3 integral d.d.s.
£180-200 *CSK*

An Anthony PDQ detective box camera, c1890, 6in (15cm) high.
£950-1,000 *J*

A Nodark camera, from The Popular Photograph Company.
£950-1,000 *J*

A Kodak Panoram No. 4 camera.
£225-250 *J*

A Kodak Rainbow Hawkeye No. 2 camera, c1931.
£25-35 *J*

A Rex magazine camera.
£200-250 *J*

A Buisson detective plate camera.
£800-900 *J*

A Beck Frena D/Lux detective camera.
£150-200 *J*

An Amourette camera No. 010359, with a Double Miniscope 35mm f6.3 lens.
£250-300 *CSK*

A Kodak Bulls-Eye Special camera.
£75-100 *J*

A McKellen double pinion treble Patent mahogany folding field camera with black bellows, Thornton-Pickard roller blind shutter, Cooke f8 lens No. 4170, Ross No. s Symmetrical lens, a tripod and leather case.
£100-150 *Bon*

A Cine-Kodak, 'model A', 16mm movie camera, No. 02483.
£65-75 *Bon*

A Compass camera, Le Coultre et Cie, Switzerland, No. 2522 with a CCC3N anastigmat f3.5 35mm lens with a Compass roll film back, plate developing tank, film spool holders, Compass Pocket Tripod in maker's box.
£700-750 *CSK*

A 10 by 15cm tropical Nettel camera with polished teak body, and a Carl Zeiss Jena Tessar f3.5 16.5cm lens No. 917920, in a leather fitted case.
£700-800 *CSK*

A Brownie box camera and instruction book, Eastman Kodak Co.
£40-50 *FAL*

A 35mm 18 x 24mm Sept camera, No. VO8778, with an H Roussel, Paris Stylor f3.5 50mm lens No. 42581 camera front engraved 'Societe Francaise Sept Paris', and 'Construit Par les Etablissements Andre Debrie Paris', and 3 Sept film cassettes.
£175-200 *CSK*

The Sept camera was introduced in 1922. It was primarily intended as a movie camera, but also offered the option of single and time exposures.

A Houghton 'Ticka' pocket watch style camera, with film and original sales box, for A. W. Gamage Ltd., Holborn, London E.C.
£140-150 *Bon*

A Leica IIIg camera No. 880421 with Leitz Elmar 5cm f2.8 lens No. 1538326.
£300-400 *Bon*

A black Leica M5 camera No. 1353918 with Leitz Summicron 50mm f2 lens No. 2534590, with lens hood and cap.
£650-750 *Bon*

A Physiographe monocular detective camera No. 1856, by Watson/Bloch, with Cooke lens, 12 dark slides and fitted leather binocular-style case.
£500-600 *Bon*

A Zeiss Super Nettel 35mm folding camera with black door, and Tessar f3.5 5cm lens No. 1402696, and leather case.
£100-150 *Bon*

CAMERAS

A Sanderson Tropical camera.
£600-650 *J*

A Thornton-Pickard half plate Royal Ruby field camera.
£550-600 *J*

A quarter plate Sibyl de luxe camera, Newman and Guardia Ltd., London, No. D109, with a Zeiss Protarlinse 224mm lens No. 110135 and 4 s.m.s., all in maker's leather fitted case.
£260-300 *CSK*

A Contessa Nettel Adoro camera, c1921.
£40-50 *J*

A Kodak No. 4 cartridge camera.
£75-85 *J*

An APeM reflex camera.
£100-120 *J*

A Kodak folding Brownie No. 2 camera.
£50-60 *J*

A Voigtlander Bessa camera.
£30-40 *J*

A Leica IIIg camera No. 971764, Leitz, in maker's leather case.
£300-400 *Bon*

A Reid & Sigrist Leica III copy No. P 3084, with Taylor Hobson f2 2in lens No. 329175, and leather case.
£250-350 *Bon*

A Rolleiflex Automat Tessar 3.5 camera.
£125-150 *J*

A Leica style Canon IV series camera No. 160035, with Canon f1.5 50mm lens No. 18728, and leather case.
£150-250 *Bon*

A concealed vest camera, No. 1, for 6 exposures.
£500-600 *Bon*

A Franke & Heidecke Rolleidoscop camera.
£950-1,000 *J*

A Hasselblad 1000F complete camera.
£450-550 *J*

l. A Voigtlander
Prominent Inc. 50mm f2
camera.
£200-250
r. A Voigtlander
Bessamatic Inc. 50mm
f2.8 lens camera.
£100-120 *J*

A Leica Model 1 and 50
f3.5 Elmar and R1 finder.
£450-550 *J*

A Coronet 3-D stereo
camera.
£40-60 *J*

l. An Agfa Flexilette TLR
camera.
£90-100
r. A Werra Green camera.
£40-60 *J*

A Kodak stereo camera.
£200-250 *J*

A London Stereoscopic
Co. London camera
No. 305, and a Goerz
Dagor Serie 111 125mm
f6.8 lens No. 240747.
£800-900 *CSK*

A Braun Paxette Reflex
camera.
£60-80 *J*

A Magnacam
Wristamatic camera.
£50-75 *J*

A Minnigraph camera,
No. 1592, Levy-Roth,
Berlin, with 2 films, one
in maker's box.
£650-750 *CSK*

A Voigtlander Vito CSR
camera.
£25-35 *J*

A Rolleiflex Rollei 1.4
55mm wide angle
camera.
£1,400-1,500 *J*

CAMERAS

A Leica 250 model GG Reporter camera, No. 135624, with a Leitz Summar 5cm f2 lens No. 205334 and 2 250 cassettes, c1934.
£2,700-3,000   *CSK*

A rare chrome Night Exakta camera, Ihagee, Dresden, with Schneider Xenon f2.8cm lens No. 299723, in maker's leather e.r.c.
£200-300   *CSK*

A Leica Ig camera No. 925427 with a Leitz Elmar 5cm f3.5 lens No. 1344882 and a 50mm direct vision finder, all in maker's e.r.c.
£700-800   *CSK*

A Shanghai 58-11 camera No. 5855946, with a Shanghai f3.5 50mm lens, in leather e.r.c.
£350-450   *CSK*

A gold Leica presentation camera in 24ct gold, original wrapping, R.4 Summilux 50mm f1.4.
£3,000-4,000   *J*

A 35mm 3F camera No. 157298, Nicca Camera Co. Ltd. Japan, with a Leitz Elmar 5cm f3.5 lens, in maker's leather e.r.c.
£150-250   *CSK*

A Cub Scout flash camera with original box.
£25-45   *J*

A black dial Leica IIIf camera No. 586917 with a Leitz Elmar 9cm f4 lens No. 295241 and a VIOOH universal viewfinder.
£300-350   *CSK*

A Minox III black dummy miniature camera, 3½in (9cm) long.
£90-100   *J*

This was made for display and advertising purposes and rarity makes them valuable today.

An Erac Camera Co. Mercury 1 pistol camera, with built-in Merlin type camera, in maker's box.
£180-200   *CSK*

A rare 35mm Esco camera, Seischab, Germany, with a Steinheil anastigmat Cassar f3.5 3.5cm lens No. 167248.
£1,600-1,800   *CSK*

A Coronet Midget camera, 2½in (6cm) high.
£60-80   *J*

A Minicord miniature TLR camera No. 15201, by Goerz, with brown leather covering and Helgor f2 2.5cm lens, and leather case.
£200-250   *Bon*

A Newman & Sinclair 35mm movie camera, with polished and patterned aluminium body, Cooke F2 1in lens, and eye-level viewfinder.
£120-140   *Bon*

A Secret Sam spy weapon camera case, c1968, 15½ by 11½in (39 by 29cm).
£140-160   *J*

A Photoret camera with original instruction booklet, Magic Introduction Co. New York, in original box.
£400-450   *CSK*

A Houghton Ticka pocket watch camera.
£150-160   *J*

Lenses

Two Schneider Robot-fit Tele-Xenar f3.8 75mm lenses Nos. 4089302/3, each in individual leather cases and 2 Robot lens hoods.
£75-100   *CSK*

l. A rare Mountain Elmar 10.5cm f6.3 lens No. 128939, by Leitz, with reversible lens hood, c1932.
£450-550
r. A Mountain Elmar 10.5cm f6.3 lens No. 136721 by Leitz, with original lens hood and a Nebro lens cap, lens side engraved Zool Dept. Queens Coll. Dundee.
£400-450   *CSK*

Twenty-four Taylor Hobson 2in f2 anastigmat lenses, most with a Leitz Wetzlar bayonet to screw adaptor, in fitted box with engraved plaque Reid & Sigrist Ltd. Braunstone Works, Braunstone, Leicester.
£2,000-2,500   *CSK*

Miscellaneous

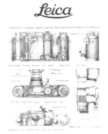

A very old projector, 6in (15cm) high.
£10-15   *AL*

A selection of Leica pamphlets, late 1930s.
£40-60   *CSK*

An original Leica advertising poster, c1930, 27 by 34in (68 by 85cm).
£130-150   *CSK*

A very old projector, 11in (29cm) high.
£10-15   *AL*

FURTHER READING
Holmes, Edward, *An Age of Cameras*, 1974.

Candlesticks

A pair of 'Heemskerk' type brass candlesticks, the bases engraved with crests, early 18thC, 9in (23cm) high.
£300-400 *Bon*

A pair of Victorian candlesticks, supported on 3 frog feet, 7in (18cm) high.
£180-200 *MB*

A coil steel spiral adjustable candle holder, with wood base, 18thC.
£200-300 *PC*

A George IV candlestick, 8½in (21cm).
£40-50 *SAD*

A Georgian candlestick.
£40-50 *SAD*

A pair of early Victorian candlesticks, 6in (15.5cm).
£60-80 *SAD*

A George III blackamoor taper holder, 7½in (19cm) high.
£150-180 *SAD*

DID YOU KNOW?

The Eddystone Lighthouse keepers eked out their meagre rations by eating the tallow lighthouse candles until the introduction of non-edible paraffin-wax candles in the mid 19th century.

A pair of candlesticks, c1835, 12in (30cm).
£110-140 *SAD*

A candlestick with knopped column and petal base, slight wear, 18thC, 8in (20cm) high.
£100-150 *WIL*

An early Victorian chamberstick, 3in (7.5cm) diam.
£40-60 *SAD*

A pair of Georgian candlesticks, 9½in (24cm).
£110-130 *SAD*

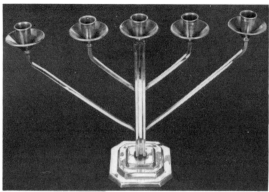

A pair of silver plated
candlesticks, John
Dixon, c1930.
£350-400   *BEV*

A pair of silver plated
candlesticks.
£45-55   *BEV*

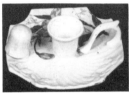

A silver rolled on brass
candlestick, c1890, 7in
(18cm) high.
£25-35   *PC*

A Victorian candle
holder, 6in (15cm) wide.
£20-25   *PAT*

A Danish cast metal
multi-candlestick, Jenz
Quistgaard, c1955, 18in
(46cm) high.
£85-100   *BEV*

A bronze Hagenat candle
holder, 4in (10cm) high.
£75-100   *VDB*

DID YOU KNOW?
The candle is said to have
been invented by the
Romans soon after the
birth of Christ.

A pair of chrome
candlesticks, with
stylised dogs, c1930.
£55-65   *BEV*

A Limoges candle holder.
£12-15   *VB*

An Art Deco green
opaque glass candle
holder.
£45-50   *PAT*

Devon and Torquay
Pottery — Candlesticks.
£35-40   *JO*

Devon and Torquay
Pottery — Candleholder.
£15-20   *JO*

A Clarice Cliff centre set,
comprising posy holders
and 4 candle holders.
£700-800   *VDB*

FURTHER READING
Grove, John R. *Antique Brass Candlesticks,
1450-1750*. London 1968.
Michaelis, R. F. *Old Domestic Base Metal
Candlesticks*. Antique Collectors' Club, Woodbridge,
Suffolk, 1978.
Wills, G. *Candlesticks*. Newton Abbot 1974.

Card Cases

Visiting cards came into general use at the beginning of the 19th Century. Originating in France, they quickly became fashionable and quite complicated rules governing their use evolved as an essential part of the etiquette of 'polite' society. At first the cards were carried in reticules and pocket books, but by the 1820s specially designed card cases had become universally popular.

Made in a wide variety of materials from silver to papier mâché and often finely worked and with elaborate decoration, card cases reflected Victorian taste and social aspirations. Gentlemen's cases are normally smaller than those made for ladies, but both often carry a small panel or cartouche intended for a name or initial. Tortoiseshell, ivory and mother-of-pearl cases are all very collectable, while cases made of wood and leather can still be found at relatively inexpensive prices. Especially sought after are unusual opening mechanisms, rare designs and pieces in good condition, with hinges, fastenings and edges showing little or no damage or wear.

A tortoiseshell card case, inlaid with mother-of-pearl, 4 by 3in (10 by 7.5cm).
£100-120 *CHA*

Three Victorian mother-of-pearl card cases, 4 by 3in (10 by 7.5cm).
£55-65 each *MAN*

A Victorian tortoiseshell card case, inlaid with mother-of-pearl and engraved.
£125-150 *MAN*

A ladies cigarette or card case, gilded on silver with onyx and marcasite trim, c1920, 3in (7.5cm) wide.
£300-400 *PAT*

A Victorian silver card case, with bracketed scroll outline and chased floral and scroll decoration, Birmingham 1852.
£100-150 *GD*

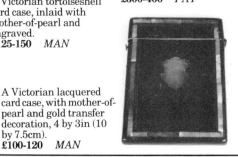

A Victorian lacquered card case, with mother-of-pearl and gold transfer decoration, 4 by 3in (10 by 7.5cm).
£100-120 *MAN*

A tortoiseshell card case.
£65-75 *CHA*

A Victorian tortoiseshell and mother-of-pearl card case.
£50-75 *MAN*

CERAMICS

Whilst all ceramics remain very collectable and are currently proving to be good investment material, we have in this book identified some of the more collectable fields. Amongst the most popular areas are the Art Deco and Art Nouveau periods. Art Nouveau, Moorcroft and Doulton notably, are becoming very expensive. However, many of the Art Deco, 20s and 30s potters, for example Shelley and Susie Cooper, can still be found at very reasonable prices; but not for long! Searching junk shops and early attendance at car boot fairs can still pay dividends. A word though regarding expensive pottery and porcelain of the more 'established' antique types, don't be deterred by damage; firstly, pieces will be much more affordable and secondly, it is without doubt the best way to learn new subjects.

On the following pages we have selected the more collectable factories and potters and then we have taken collectable areas. Don't forget to use the cross reference boxes and above all, good hunting!

Beswick

A set of ducks.
£70-85 *PGA*

A set of ducks, similar to Beswick, unmarked, made in England.
£28-35 *D*

A seagull.
£25-30 *COB*

A set of 5 ducks, c1930.
£130-150 *JBO*

A set of kingfishers, c1930.
£110-120 *JBO*

MAKE THE MOST OF _____
MILLER'S
Price ranges in this book reflect what one should expect to *pay* for a similar example. When selling, however, one should expect to receive a lower figure. This will fluctuate according to a dealer's stock, saleability at a particular time, etc. It is always advisable, when selling, to approach a reputable specialist dealer or an auction house which has specialist sales.

Clarice Cliff

A rare Dream Cottage pattern coffee set, with 5 cups and saucers.
£1,200-1,400 *VDB*

A selection of Crocus design items.
Bowl.
£90-100
Sugar sifter.
£95-110
Grapefruit bowl.
£55-65
Pepper pot.
£20-30 *BEV*

An Autumn Pastel plate, 10in (25.5cm) diam.
£350-400 *BEV*

A Clarice Cliff style pottery jug, with white and black design, 6½in (17cm) high.
£45-55 *PAT*

An egg cup set, with duck.
£350-450 *VDB*

Orange Alpine egg cups.
£25-30 each *BEV*

An Orange Alpine cup and saucer.
£135-150 *BEV*

A jug, 7in (18cm) high.
£300-330 *PAT*

Crocus design, c1929 onwards.
Cup and saucer.
£45-55
Candle holder.
£65-75
Sandwich dish.
£55-65 *BEV*

This design was widely produced, therefore the prices are lower than for other designs.

A milk jug and sugar basin.
£70-80 *VDB*

A Crocus pattern chamber pot.
£80-100 *PCh*

Sugar sifters.
£80-100 each *VDB*

A sugar sifter, 5in (12.5cm) high.
£140-150 *PAT*

A dinner service, comprising 25 pieces.
£700-750 *PAT*

A Secrets pattern vase, 5in (12.5cm) high.
£300-400 *VDB*

A Poppy Delicia vase, 6½in (16.5cm) high.
£225-250 *BEV*

A vase, 8in (20.5cm) high.
£400-500 *VDB*

A centre set, comprising posy holders and 4 candle holders.
£700-800 *VDB*

A Solomon Seal pattern teapot, Stamford shape.
£400-450 *PGA*

Clarice Cliff

A Harvest pattern teapot, c1935.
£150-200 *PGA*

A rare teapot, Le Bon Dieu pattern.
£450-550 *PGA*

A Shark's teeth pattern teapot, direct copy by Clarice Cliff from Edouard Benedictus original design.
£350-400 *PGA*

Susie Cooper

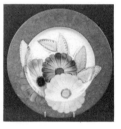

A plate, design for Grays, 10½in (26.5cm) diam.
£60-80 *BEV*

An animal design vase, c1930, 8½in (22cm) high.
£100-150 *BEV*

A Moon and Mountain design vase, 9½in (24cm) high.
£400-450 *BEV*

A lamp base.
£600-700 *VDB*

A sugar basin and milk jug.
£15-20 each *BEV*

Kestrel shape teapots, designed by Susie Cooper and made by Crown Ducal, c1939.
£65-85 each *PGA*

A Kestrel shape coffee pot.
£65-85 *PGA*

Coffee cups and saucers.
£15-20 each *BEV*

Susie Cooper

Six cups, sugar basin and milk jug.
£35-45   *PGA*

A half dinner service.
£100-150   *PGA*

Charlotte Rhead

A vase, c1930, 6in (15cm) high.
£95-120   *BEV*

A plate, 10in (25.5cm) diam.
£135-155   *BEV*

A Manchu pattern bowl, in shades of green, 10in (25.5cm) diam.
£85-100   *BEV*

A jug, c1930, 7in (18cm) high.
£125-150   *BEV*

63

Carlton Ware

A Buttercup design trefoil dish, in pink.
£35-50 *BEV*

These were made in pink, yellow and green, with pink being the rarest and most desirable.

A Daisy butter set and raspberry jam set, in original boxes.
£30-35 each *BEV*

A pair of candlesticks.
£25-30 each *BEV*

A jam pot, 5in (12.5cm) high.
£35-50 *BEV*

A small dish with Poppy and Daisy pattern.
£40-50 *BEV*

Feet egg cup, c1960.
£2-5 *PC*

Pictures on lids are an important indicator to assist in the dating of pieces.
£20-30 *BEV*

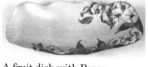

A fruit dish with Poppy and Daisy pattern, c1935, 12½in (31.5cm) wide.
£65-85 *BEV*

An Orange Transfer pattern powder bowl and puff, c1930, 6½in (16.5cm) high.
£100-150 *PAT*

A grey coffee set, with gold leaf trim, jug 9in (23cm) high.
£800-1,000 *PAT*

Marigold pattern cup and saucer, sugar basin, milk jug, and coffee pot.
£370-400
Biscuit barrel, c1932, 5½in (14cm) high.
£135-150 *BEV*

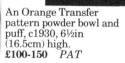

Expressions

ART DECO ORIGINALS

ceramics · furniture · mirrors
lighting · jewellery

17 PRINCESS STREET SHREWSBURY
Tel: 0743 51731

Jean.
Jane.
Old Nell.
Verona.
£200+ each
PC

Carlton Ware Figures
Carlton ware figures were copies of Royal Doulton figures with slight alterations. Royal Doulton took them to court to stop production and won their case. No one is sure how many were released — possibly only 12; they are very rare

A Poppy and Daisy pattern lamp base, 9in (23cm) high.
£120-150 *BEV*

A Flash Jazz pattern lustre ginger jar, c1930, 9in (23cm) high.
£450-500 *BEV*

Very collectable.

A Hydrangea pattern fruit dish, 14in (35.5cm) wide.
£75-100 *BEV*

Cross Reference
Egg cups
Teapots

DECODENCE
ART DECO

Sheena Taylor, 59 Brighton Road
Surbiton, Surrey K6 5NF
Hours of Business:
Mon., Fri. & Sat. 10am-5pm
Sun. (Trade Only) 11am-1pm
Tel: 01-390 1778

Shelley

A Rising Sun design
coffee set, with 6 cups
and saucers, c1928.
£225-250 *BEV*

A 21-piece tea set.
£250-300 *BEV*

A tea set, c1925.
£250-300 *BEV*

A plate, cup and saucer,
Vogue shape in green,
black and silver, c1930.
£85-100 *BEV*

A figure, c1937, 6½in
(16.5cm) high.
£500+ *BEV*

'The Golfer', by Mabel
Lucie Attwell, c1937,
6½in (16.5cm) high.
£500+ *BEV*

An Intarsia design vase,
by Walter Slater, c1915,
9in (23cm) high.
£200-250 *BEV*

A Shakespeare design
vase by Frederick Rhead,
Malvolio and Sir Toby
Belch, 9½in (24cm) high.
£200-250 *BEV*

A two-handled Intarsia
design vase, 10½in
(26.5cm) high.
£275-300 *BEV*

An Animal set teapot,
7in (18cm) high, milk jug
and sugar basin, c1928.
£450-500 *BEV*

A bedside light, c1937,
9in (23cm) high.
£500+ *BEV*

A cream jug with
stencilled flowers, and
butterfly handle.
£40-50 *BEV*

A figural table lamp,
designed by Mabel Lucie
Attwell, painted artist's
marks, on wooden base,
12½in (31.5cm) high.
£1,000-1,500 *P*

A Shelley porcelain
advertising figure, in the
form of a woman in
typical early 20thC
dress, 11½in (30cm) high.
£900-1,000 *Bea*

A mushroom shape
teapot and lid.
£100-120 *PCh*

Cross Reference
Egg cups
Teapots

Devon & Torquay

A teapot.
£16-25 *JO*

A cup and saucer.
£8-10 *JO*

Various small jugs, 2½ to
3½in (6.5 to 9cm) high.
£6-9 each *JO*
Mustard pots.
£4-8 each *JO*

A jug with a yacht design.
£16-20 *JO*

A two-handled mug, with
a rooster.
£18-25 *JO*

A pepper pot.
£6-8 *JO*

Bowls.
£5-10 each *PAC*

A hat pin holder.
£18-22 *JO*

A pin tray.
£4-6 *JO*

A jam dish.
£10-15 *JO*

A pair of candlesticks.
£38-45 *JO*

Doulton

In 1815 John Doulton invested £100 in a partnership in a small stoneware pothouse in Lambeth, which then traded as Jones, Watts & Doulton. Amongst the earliest characters manufactured were Nelson, Wellington and Napoleon, the forerunners of today's world famous range of Doulton commemorative and caricature stonewares. His son Henry, who joined the firm in 1835, encouraged free expression amongst his artists, the most famous of whom include George Tinworth, Hannah and Florence Barlow, Arthur Barlow, Frank Butler, Eliza Simmance and many others who created the first generation Doulton figures.

A figure of an elephant, in brown and mottled grey, c1930, 4in (10cm) high.
£220-260   *TP*

A rare trial edition.

A pair of Penguin bookends, 7in (18cm) high.
£100-140   *TP*
Commissioned during 1987 for Penguin books as a promotional item only and not for sale to the public.

Animals

A bulldog, World War 1, c1918, 6½in (16.5cm) high.
£160-220   *TP*

Character dogs, 3½in (9cm) high.
£35-50 each   *TP*

Dog models were discontinued in 1985.

l. A collie, 'Ashstead Applause', 5in (12.5cm) high.
r. A boxer, 'War Lord of Mazelaine', 6½in (16.5cm) high.
£85-110 each   *TP*

A French poodle.
£35-50   *TP*

DID YOU KNOW?___
In 1902 Doulton received the Royal Warrant.

A cockerel teapot, c1940, 6in (15cm) high.
£110-140   *TP*

Character Jugs

Jimmy Durante, 1985-86.
£40-60   *TP*

Scaramouche, 2nd Version, 1987.
£70-100   *TP*

Modelled by Stanley James Taylor for a limited edition of 1,500.

Friar Tuck, 1951-60.
£160-200   *TP*

Captain Hook, 1965-71.
£240-290   *TP*

John Barleycorn, 1934-60.
£60-80   *TP*

The first character jug designed by Charles Noke.

George Harrison and Paul McCartney, 5½in (14cm) high.
£15-20 each   *TP*

l. Anne Boleyn, 4½in (11cm) high.
r. Catherine of Aragon, 4½in (11cm) high.
£10-15 each   *TP*

l. Father Christmas with holly wreath handle.
£130-170
r. Father Christmas with candy cane handle.
£700-900   *TP*

Produced in limited editions for U.S.A. Television promotions.

l. Toby Philpot, 1939-69.
r. John Peel, 1940-60, 2in (5cm) high.
£30-45 each   *TP*

l. Dick Turpin, 1960-80,
3in (7cm) high.
£30-40
r. Pied Piper, 1957-80.
£40-50 *TP*

Simple Simon, 1953-60.
£250-300 *TP*

l. The Falconer.
r. Rip Van Winkle, 4½in
(11cm) high.
£10-15 each *TP*

In current production.

Lord Nelson.
£175-225

St. George.
£100-150 *Bon*

Figures

Chloe, HN1470, 1931-49, 6in (15cm) high.
£140-170 *TP*

Biddy Penny Farthing, 1938, 9in (23cm) high.
£40-60 *TP*

l. Lambing Time, 1938-80, 9½in (24cm) high.
r. Votes for Women, 1978-81, 10½in (26cm) high.
£80-110 each *TP*

Pantalettes, HN1362, 1928-38, 8in (20cm) high.
£180-220 *TP*

l. The Cavalier, 1976-82, 10in (25cm) high.
£70-100
r. The Captain, 1965-82, 9½in (24cm) high.
£90-120 *TP*

l. Janet, HN1537, 6in (15cm) high.
£40-60
r. Camille, HN1586, 1933-49, 7in (18cm) high.
£220-270 *TP*

Royal Doulton

Mantilla, 1974-79, 12in (30cm) high.
£120-150 *TP*

A Royal Doulton three-handled stoneware commemorative mug, Lord Nelson.
£140-160 *MGM*

A Royal Doulton loving cup, commemorating the Coronation of King George VI and Queen Elizabeth, designed by Charles Noke and Harry Fenton, No. 507 of a limited edition of 2,000.
£300-350 *Bea*

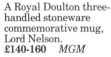

DOULTON WARES

Doulton marks – abbreviations

o.u.m.	– oval updated mark
o.m.	– oval mark, dated
c.m.	– circular mark
r.m.	– rosette mark
r.m. & e.	– rosette mark and England
d.l.e.	– Doulton Lambeth England
d.s.l.	– Doulton Silicon Lambeth
d.s.p.	– Doulton & Slaters Patent
c.m.l. & c.	– circle mark, lion & crown
c.m. & l.	– circle mark and lion
r.d.e.	– Royal Doulton England
s.c.m.	– slip-cast mark
i.c.f.m.	– impressed circular faience mark
r.d.f.	– Royal Doulton Flambé
b.r.m. & c.	– Burslem rosette mark & crown

A Royal Doulton teapot, slip decorated under the Kingsware glaze, with silicon mounts.
£120-150   *PGA*

A Royal Doulton Tower of London jug, limited edition.
£450-500   *HP*

H.M. Elizabeth II, base inscribed Peggy Davies 1953 Royal Doulton, 4in (10cm) high.
£300-350   *CSK*

A Royal Doulton stoneware teapot.
£350-400   *PGA*

Miscellaneous

A pair of silicon ware vases, late 19thC.
£15-20   *CAC*

A tankard, signed Noke, produced 1930, 5in (12.5cm) high.
£40-70   *TP*

A cup, saucer and plate, in green, silver and white, c1933.
£65-75   *BEV*

A graduated set of 3 Lambeth stoneware Queen Victoria commemorative jugs, impressed marks, 6 to 9in (15 to 23cm) high.
£100-150

The White Hart Inn at Southwark, from Pickwick Papers, 1937-60, 5½in (14cm) high.
£70-90   *TP*

Oliver Twist, 1936-60, 6in (15cm) high.
£70-90   *TP*

A Kingsware tobacco jar, engraved 'Oundle School Jan 17, 1922', body cracked, printed marks.
£50-60

A Lambeth stoneware jug, body cracked, impressed marks.
£50-60   *Bon*

FURTHER READING
Eyles Desmond and Dennis Richard, *Royal Doulton Figures*, London 1978.
Eyles Desmond, *Royal Doulton 1815-1965*, London 1965.

> **Cross Reference**
> Egg cups
> Drinking
> Teapots

73

Maling Ware

The Maling family business flourished for 200 years and their products remain a symbol of the tradition of pottery making in Tyneside.

At first only brown earthenwares were made, but later Maling produced creamwares and white pottery with transfer printing, particularly for commercial use, such as jam and marmalade pots, druggist jars and sanitary ware. It was these white wares which contributed to Maling's fortune. Changes in fashion were also accommodated, and were influenced by the artistic styles of Art Nouveau and Art Deco.

The Company was sold to Hoults Pottery in 1947, but retained the Maling name, and post-war production thrived. The Maling factory was finally closed in 1963, and the buildings converted to a furniture repository.

Dating Maling ware can be difficult as over 40 different marks were used throughout production, some simultaneously, and patterns remained in use for long periods.

A ginger jar, in pink lustre with embossed flowers, c1954, 7in (18cm) high.
£115-135 *JBO*

A pot with lid, with spring flowers, 4½in (11cm).
£45-65 *JBO*

A lustre ware vase, with Daisy pattern, c1935, 8in (20cm) high.
£250-350 *JBO*

A lustre ware jardinière, with Daisy pattern, c1935, 9in (23cm) diam.
£250-350 *JBO*

A pair of candlesticks and a tray, in columbine green lustre.
£65-75 *JBO*

Two plates with rural scenes, c1936, 11in (28cm) diam.
£125-150 each *JBO*

Staffordshire

Cottages

A thatched roof cottage, c1840.
£70-90 *JO*

A windmill, c1860, 8in (20.5cm) high.
£100-120 *JO*

A house with blue roof, c1855, 6in (15cm) high.
£120-140 *JO*

Bank, c1845, 4½in (11cm) high.
£70-90 *JO*

A watch holder, reputed to be the front of Drury Lane before the fire.
£85-100 *RBE*

A house with swans, c1850.
£50-90 *JO*

These were made over a long period of time, as the price reflects.

A clocktower spill vase, c1860, 11in (28cm) high.
£110-160 *JO*

A house with a tower, c1855, 9½in (24cm) high.
£140-160 *JO*

A thatched roof cottage, c1860, 6in (15cm) high.
£120-140 *JO*

A cottage, c1845, 4in (10cm) high.
£120-140 *JO*

A house with bower, c1855, 10in (25.5cm) high.
£110-130 *JO*

General

A castle, c1845.
£60-80   *JO*

A castle, c1845, 6in
(15cm) high.
£110-140   *JO*

A blue and white dolls
dinner service, by
F. Morley, comprising 28
pieces, c1850.
£550-600   *MAN*

A turkey plate, with blue
transfer decoration
depicting hares in a rural
landscape, damage to
rim, 20½in (51cm).
£180-200   *WIL*

A castle with grape
vines, c1850, 8in (20.5cm)
high.
£130-150   *JO*

A mug, 19thC.
£30-40   *MAN*

Figures

Girl with dog and rabbit.
£85-95   *RBE*

A gardener.
£75-100   *RBE*

DID YOU KNOW?

Rare Figures: Books and guides often describe items
as 'rare' or 'common', but it is more important to
know whether the figure is collectable. Some
collectable 'common' figures are better investments
than 'rare' and unwanted figures. After all they may
be rare because no-one wants them!

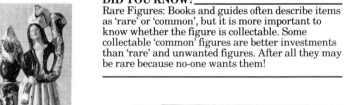

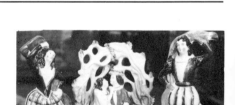

l. and r. A pair of
gardeners, restoration to
the top of one pillar, 8in
(20.5cm).
£125-150
c. Musician in arbour,
9in (23cm) high.
£85-95   *RBE*

l. and r. Pair of dancers,
Carlotta Grisi,
restoration to nose, 8½in
(22cm) high, Pierrot,
damaged.
£100-120
c. Lorenzo and Jessica in
arbour, by Thomas Parr.
£90-120   *RBE*

BUYING VICTORIAN STAFFORDSHIRE FIGURES

Victorian Staffordshire figures have for several years proved to be a good investment, as well as forming an interesting collection. To obtain the best results only good quality figures should be purchased and the surest way is to purchase from dealers who specialise in Staffordshire figures. Such a dealer will be prepared to back his judgement of age and quality with a money back guarantee if proved wrong.

1. Inspect the goods and ask about restoration; restored figures should be marked as such.
2. Find out if the figures are named or recognisable; ask for proof of identity.
3. Look for good crisp moulding, good colouring and consider the overall 'appeal' of the figure.

l. Man with dog.
£75-85
c. Farmer and girl spill holder, some restoration, 9in (23cm) high.
£80-100
r. Man with basket, chip restored on basket, 9in (23cm) high.
£55-65   *RBE*

Hunter on Horse.
£135-155   *RBE*

A Victorian figure.
£85-95   *RBE*

A Crimean group.
£100-125   *RBE*

A pair of royal children with dogs and pets.
£175-195   *RBE*

Possibly Jack of Jack and Jill.
£75-85   *RBE*

Christmas Evans, legs cracked, c1855, 14in (35.5cm) high.
£600-800   *CSK*

An equestrian figure of Sir Robert Peel, repaired, c1850, 12½in (31.5cm) high.
£900-1,200   *CSK*

Rival.
£125-150   *RBE*

Col. Sir George de Lacy Evans, c1854, 13in (33cm) high.
£700-750   *CSK*

Wesley in pulpit, small chip in base, restored, 11in (28cm) high.
£125-145   *RBE*

A zebra with lustre stripes, ear missing, c1860, 8in (20.5cm) high.
£70-100   *OSc*

A spill vase with swans.
£85-95   *RBE*

A bottle and screw stopper modelled as Mr. Punch, restored, c1840, 8in (20.5cm) high.
£350-400   *CSK*

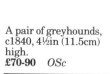

A theatre figure, c1855, 10in (25.5cm) high.
£95-120   *RBE*

l. Birds and nest spill vase.
£45-55

r. Babes in wood spill vase.
£75-85   *RBE*

A pair of greyhounds, c1840, 4½in (11.5cm) high.
£70-90   *OSc*

Children's Ceramics

Children's pottery and porcelain is becoming a very popular area for collectors. The plates, bowls and cups, etc., were often designed as teaching aids to spelling and reading. Alphabets featured as well as figures and animals; the most interesting, however, are the wonderful proverbs and sayings to assist early nursery education and moral upbringing.

A Welsh plate with sponged border and cockerel design, late 19thC.
£100-120 *AP*

A plate with raised dog design, 18thC.
£150-170 *AP*

A baby's plate, 6½in (17cm) diam.
£10-12 *AL*

Mugs depicting animals.
£90-130 each *AP*

A Welsh sponged ware cup, with bird pattern, c1880.
£30-40 *AP*

A Wedgwood Peter Rabbit mug, 3in (7.5cm) high.
£10-15 *AL*

A Staffordshire child's plate, printed and coloured with a couple before a blacksmith, some damage, c1840, 6in (15cm).
£80-100 *Bon*

A mug with sheep decoration, early 19thC.
£90-110 *AP*

Mid-19thC plates.
£65-85 *AP*

A brown transfer printed plate, The Defender, 19thC.
£28-30   CAC

A plate with flowered border and transfer printed picture, late 18thC.
£130-150   AP

A Royal Doulton plate, 6½in (17cm) diam.
£10-12   AL

A plate depicting a swan.
£120-130   AP

A pair of plates, early 19thC.
£160-180   AP

A Welsh plate with embossed border.
£70-80   AP

A plate with green and yellow flowered border, early 19thC.
£60-70   AP

A Wedgwood Beatrix Potter plate, 6in (15cm) diam.
£10-12   AL

A Staffordshire money box, c1840, 7in (18cm).
£750-800   DL

A plate with horse decoration, early 19thC.
£80-90   AP

Named plates.
£65-95   AP

Commemorative Ware

Mugs

Admiral Lord Nelson, c1805, 3½in (9cm) high.
£275-325 *LR*

A creamware mug with Queen Caroline, c1821, 3½in (9cm) high.
£225-275 *LR*

A creamware mug depicting the arms of the Orange Order, c1825, 3½in (9cm) high.
£200-250 *LR*

An electioneering mug, 'Bell and Victory', c1826, 4½in (11.5cm) high.
£250-300 *LR*

A mug with busts of Russell and Brougham, 'Champions of Reform', c1832, 4in (10cm) high.
£100-125 *LR*

George V and Queen Mary's Silver Jubilee, May 1935.
£15-20 *VB*

George V and Queen Mary's Coronation, 1911.
£20-25 each *VB*

'Peace' — World War 1914-18.
£18-22 *VB*

George VI and Queen Elizabeth's Coronation, May 1937.
£8-12 *VB*

George V and Queen Mary's Silver Jubilee, 1935.
£16-20 *VB*

A Doulton Lambeth three-handled loving cup, by Frank Butler, dated 1881, impressed marks, 6in (15cm) high.
£260-300 *Bon*

Limited editions — Princess Anne appointed The Princess Royal. The Death of the Duchess of Windsor.
£20-25 each *BC*

Queen Elizabeth II, Coronation 1953.
£4-6 *VB*

Jugs

Queen Caroline, c1820.
£220-250 *LR*

A Prattware jug,
Wellington at Waterloo,
c1815, 6½in (17cm) high.
£325-350 *LR*

Memorial to Queen
Caroline, c1821, 6in
(15cm) high.
£320-380 *LR*

Queen Caroline, c1821,
6in (15cm) high.
£300-330 *LR*

George IV's visit to
Scotland, 1822, 6in
(15cm) high.
£325-375 *LR*

William and Adelaide's
Coronation, c1830, 6in
(15cm) high.
£220-250 *LR*

Francis Bagnall, the
inner base with Reform
and William IV
Coronation, 1833, 5in
(12.5cm) high.
£175-225 *LR*

A stoneware jug,
Coronation 1902.
£65-75 *P*

A commemorative jug,
'Marquis of Wellington
in the Field of Battle',
early 19thC, 5½in (14cm)
high.
£65-75 *PCh*

A Doulton stoneware
loving cup, Silver
Wedding 1888.
£220-250 *P*

An Art Deco design
portrait jug, slight
fading, 1937.
£70-80 *P*

A stoneware jug,
inscribed 'Mortlock . . .
HRH Prince of Wales,
November 9th, 1879', the
base marked F.E.L.
£280-300 *P*

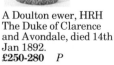

Death of Edward VII,
inscribed with dates on
the reverse.
£40-50 *P*

A Doulton ewer, HRH
The Duke of Clarence
and Avondale, died 14th
Jan 1892.
£250-280 *P*

Flatware

William III of Orange,
6½in (17cm).
£60-90 *LR*

A Collection of Nursery
plates.
£170-300 *P*

Princess Charlotte
memorial dish, c1817,
8in (20.5cm).
£75-95 *LR*

l. Coronation
1902.
£70-90
c. HRH Prince
of Wales
Investiture,
1911.
£80-100
r. Death of
Edward VII,
chipped.
£30-40 *P*

The marriage of Victoria
and Albert, 1840, 7in
(18cm) diam.
£200-250 *LR*

Duke and Duchess of
Edinburgh, Royal
Wedding 1874.
£130-150

Crown Ducal plates:
Coronation 1937.
£45-55
Royal Visit to the United
States, 1939.
£40-60 *P*

Royal Visit to Burnley,
1886.
£180-200 *P*

Cross Reference
Tins

A pair of Royal Doulton
plaques, Coronation
1902.
£120-150
A Royal Copenhagen
plate with silhouette of
Princess Alexandra,
1914.
£130-150 *P*

Miscellaneous

Princess Charlotte
memorial bowl, c1817,
6in (15cm) diam.
£180-220 *LR*

A Queen Victoria's
Jubilee teapot, c1897,
6in (15cm) high.
£80-120 *LR*

A brown glazed pottery
vase, with a silhouette
portrait of George III,
replacement foot, 10½in
(26.5cm) high.
£250-300 *P*

l. and r. Staffordshire
portrait busts of William
IV and Adelaide.
£800-900
c. A biscuit porcelain
bust of Frederick, Duke
of York, printed beehive
mark, Saml. Alcock &
Co., Cobridge,
Staffordshire.
£220-250 *P*

l. A Royal Staffordshire
water jug, printed with
2 maps of the world,
inscribed to base 'Emu.
Australian Wines', 1937.
£35-45
c. A Wedgwood jug,
Silver Jubilee 1935, 8in
(20cm).
£100-120
r. A Doulton loving cup,
In Memoriam, c1936.
£90-100 *P*

A white glazed jug,
modelled as a caricature
of Mrs. Thatcher, 1983,
4in (10cm).
£8-10 *Bon*

FURTHER READING
Balston, Thomas. *Staffordshire Portrait Figures of the Victorian Age*. London 1958.
Bemrose, Geoffrey. *Nineteenth Century English Pottery and Porcelain*. London 1952.
Haggar, Reginald G. *English Pottery Figures, 1660-1860*. London 1947.
Mackay, James A. *Commemorative Pottery and Porcelain*. London 1971.
Mountford, Arnold R. *Staffordshire Saltglazed Stoneware*. London 1971.
Pugh, P. D. Gordon. *Staffordshire Portrait Figures and Allied Subjects of the Victorian Era*, London 1971.
Read, H. *Staffordshire Pottery Figures*. London 1929.

A pottery loving cup,
Prince Edward of York's
birth, 1894.
£280-300
TRH Duke and Duchess
of York, July 1899.
£80-100
A Doulton Lambeth
statue, '1910, Edward
VII'.
£190-220
A Copeland gin flask,
Coronation 1911,
inscribed Andrew Usher
& Co., Distillers,
Edinburgh, 10in (25cm)
high.
£50-80 *P*

Cups & Saucers

A cup, saucer and plate set with pink and gilt decoration, plate 5in (12.5cm).
£25-35   *CAC*

A Copeland cup and saucer.
£35-45   *MAN*

A cup and saucer with rural scenes on a green ground, saucer 6in (15cm).
£75-100   *MAN*

Copeland, marked, cup 2½in (6cm) high.
£50-60   *MAN*

A hand painted cup and saucer, with gilt decoration, saucer 5½in (14cm).
£15-25   *MAN*

Dresden Wolfsohn, saucer 3in (7.5cm).
£50-60   *MAN*

A cup and saucer with deep yellow ground, marked.
£60-70   *MAN*

Davenport, with gold decoration, saucer 6in (15cm).
£25-30   *MAN*

Meissen in white with gilt trim, cup 2½in (6cm) high.
£40-45   *MAN*

A cup and saucer with pastel shades, saucer 6in (15cm).
£25-35   *MAN*

Fairings

Ready to Start.
£30-60 pair *PVH*

I am off with him and I am starting for a long journey.
£40-60 pair *PVH*

Nursery Rhymes —
Little Red Riding Hood,
Dick Whittington, Little
Boy Blue and Little Bo
Peep.
£30-40 each *PVH*

Hark Tom Somebody's coming.
£120-160
Five o'clock tea.
£30-50
Good Templars.
£80-100 *PVH*

To Epsom, damaged hence
£200-250
Perfect.
£500-600 *PVH*

Necessity Knows no Law
and Let us do Business
together.
£30-50 each *PVH*

*Variety of caption is more
important than the age of
the pieces, and must be in
perfect condition.*

Family cares.
£20-30 pair
The Orphans.
£100-120 *PVH*

Champagne Charlie is
my name.
£100-150 *PVH*

Attack and Defeat.
£160-180 pair *PVH*

The Old Welsh Spinning
Wheel and The Welsh
Tea Party, German,
c1895.
£30-40 each *PVH*

Going, Going, Gone and
Which is prettiest.
£30-50 each *PVH*

Courtship and Marriage.
£150-200 *PVH*

The spoils of War and Tug of War.
£160-180 pair *PVH*

Pluck and The decided Smash.
£160-180 pair *PVH*

Please Sir, what would you charge to christen my doll?
£120-150
If you please, Sir.
£150-200 *PVH*

A mouse! a mouse! and An awkward interruption.
£50-100 each *PVH*

Kiss me quick and The power of love.
£60-80 each *PVH*

Three o'clock in the morning and Returning at one o'clock in the morning.
£30-50 each *PVH*

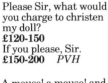

Shall we sleep first or how? and Twelve months after marriage.
£40-60 each *PVH*

Some contributors to Punch.
£200+ *PC*

If youth knew! and If old age could.
£300-350 pair *PVH*

The attentive Maid.
£150-200 *PVH*

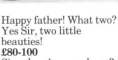

Happy father! What two? Yes Sir, two little beauties!
£80-100
Sir, where's your gloves? if you think to go out with me.
£150-180 *PVH*

Can you do this grandma.
£80-100 *PVH*

The last in bed to put out
the light, c1870.
£40-60 each   *PVH*

*The candles have been
deliberately snapped off
because of the superstition
'holding a candle to the
Devil'.*

Favourable opportunity
and Now Ma'rm say
when.
£50-80 each   *PVH*

Robbing the (male) mail
and knight of labor.
£50-80 each   *PVH*

The night cap and Oh!
What a difference in the
morning.
£50-80 each   *PVH*

Returning at one o'clock
in the morning.
£30-50   *PC*

A dressing table and an
altar.
£15-30 each   *PVH*

For three legs! I'll charge
2d. and Alone at last.
£30-50 each   *PVH*

Two different views.
£200-250
An awkward
interruption.
£90-120   *PVH*

Dressing tables, the centre one with silver paper mirror.
£15-30 each *PVH*

God save the Queen.
£80-100 *PVH*

Pin Boxes

Daisy design pin boxes.
£30-60 *PVH*

A clock.
£40-60 *PVH*

Two couples.
£25-35 *PVH*

Pin boxes.
£35-55 *PVH*

MAKE THE MOST OF MILLER'S
Condition is absolutely vital when assessing the value of any item. Damaged pieces appreciate much less than perfect examples. However, a rare, desirable piece may command a high price even when damaged.

Animals.
£25-35 *PVH*

Children in bed.
£15-30 each *PVH*

Mother and daughter,
and The Chess Players.
£30-60 each *PVH*

Two children on chairs
and Mr. Punch.
£30-60 each *PVH*

Two little girls seated.
£30-60 each *PVH*

Child asleep, hand
painted, 6½in (16.5cm)
high.
£30-60 *PVH*

A lady and gentleman
and children with swans.
£20-30 each *PVH*

Three dressing tables.
£40-50 each *PVH*

The child's prayer and
According to the rule.
£30-50 each *PVH*

Watch, painted red,
Faith Hope and Charity
and painted seal.
£40-60 each *PVH*

Child with dog, 7½in
(19cm) high.
£30-60 *PVH*

Figure pin boxes.
£30-50 *PVH*

Spill Holders

Paddling his own canoe.
£30-50 *PVH*

Spill holders.
£20-50 each *PVH*

Match Strikers

Three match strikers.
£20-30 each *PVH*

Small figures sitting on
chamber pots, 2in (6cm)
high.
£30-60 each *PVH*

Three match strikers.
£20-30 each *PVH*

FURTHER READING
Bristowe, W. S., *Victorian China Fairings*, London
1971.
Godden, Geoffrey, *Antique China and Glass under
£5*, London 1965.
Interest in fairings has grown since the publication of
this book. Nevertheless it is still useful.

Goss China

The prices given here are for perfect examples only. Any cracks, chips, faded crests, or even rubbed gilding, can halve the value on smaller models. Most firing flaws occurring during production do not affect value unless they are exceptionally noticeable. Ten years ago damaged items used to be discarded by collectors and dealers, but in the last few years there has been an increasing market for substandard wares amongst those who like to pay less for their collections. Remember not to pay perfect prices for imperfect pieces, about quarter to half of perfect price for moderate damage or restoration is acceptable.

Goss Brading Stocks with matching arms.
£250   *G&CC*

Melon teapot.
£35   *G&CC*

Melon cup and saucer with Bagware tea plate.
£10 each   *G&CC*

Stratford-on-Avon church font.
£35   *G&CC*

Cottage pottery nut tray.
£25   *G&CC*

Welsh Lady teapot.
£75   *G&CC*

Range of Goss models.
£7-10 each   *G&CC*

Goss Ann Hathaway's cottage, Shottery.
£90   *G&CC*

Bust of John Milton.
£165   *G&CC*

Goss Royal Commemoratives.
£18-45 each   *G&CC*

Shakespeare's House, Stratford-on-Avon, nightlight.
£160-200   *G&CC*

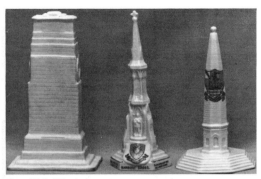

Goss Third Period
buildings — Cenotaph.
£25-45
Banbury Cross.
£75
Richmond Market Cross.
£50 *G&CC*

Unusual Durham
Sanctuary knocker mug.
£40-125 *G&CC*

Goss Melrose cup.
£40-75 *G&CC*

Carmarthen coracle.
£20-40 *G&CC*

Goss Whitby Ammonite.
£25-45 *G&CC*

Eddystone
Lighthouse.
£20-35 *G&CC*

Goss Egyptian mocha
cup with British Empire
Exhibition 1925
decoration.
£15 *G&CC*

North Foreland
Lighthouse.
£50-75 *G&CC*

Stornoway Highland
milk crogan.
£8-30 *G&CC*

Oxford Ewer with
matching arms.
£10-30 *G&CC*

Manx spirit measure.
£9-30 *G&CC*

Robert Burns' Cottage
nightlight.
£185-200 *G&CC*

Jersey fish basket.
£11-20 *G&CC*

Saffron Walden covered
urn.
£17-40 *G&CC*

Peterborough Tripod
matching.
£15-20 *G&CC*

Cheddar cheese, yellow
or white.
£25-30 *G&CC*

A selection of Domestic
Goss.
£10-18 *CCC*

A collection of named
models.
£14-40 *CCC*

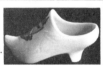

Dinant wooden shoe.
£20-50 *G&CC*

Crests which can add value
A basic vase which might be worth £5 could have a
coat-of-arms worth infinitely more. A Queen Victoria
Golden Jubilee commemorative, for example, is
worth £45. So take a closer look at the decoration on even
the plainest of Goss pots and see what you can find.
To identify the exact price of a piece, take the value from
*The Concise Encyclopaedia and 1989 Price Guide to Goss
China* and the value of the crest or decoration from *Goss
China, Arms Decorations and Their Values,* both by
Nicholas Pine (available from Milestone Publications,
62 Murray Road, Horndean, Hants. PO8 9JL.
(Tel: Horndean 597440.)

What has always seemed a paradox is that the
prettiest, daintiest cottages, for example, Anne
Hathaway's, are the most common and least valuable,
and the most attractive crests are usually the least
valuable. This is because they sold better at the time and
therefore are more common now. The least likely looking
crests and shapes are often found to be the valuable ones.

Types of crest and decoration which add value include:
nobility, ecclesiastical, educational, foreign,
commemorative, transfer printed views, butterflies,
flora and fauna, Masonic, flags, verses and words — in
all there were over 7,000 different coats-of-arms and
decorations produced on Goss china

Selection of Goss
transfers.
From £25-85 *G&CC*

Crested China

What to collect?

The endless variety and numerous themes produced by crested manufacturers in the Potteries (1880-1930) provide the collector with a choice of over 10,000 different shapes.

Buildings can look impressive in a cabinet, especially when they include bridges, windmills and clock towers. Animals, either comical or realistic, continue to hold their value, and still, new ones are coming to light. Novelty shapes such as watering cans, milk churns and tiny cheese dishes are good fun as are the quaint and rather vulgar comical pepper pots with faces, black boys in various scrapes, fat ladies on scales, seaside whelks, yachts and paddle steamers. *Crested China* by Sandy Andrews (Milestone) is a beautiful tome detailing all the shapes made, in their themes, and reveals the history of the pottery which made each.

The most collected theme is First World War military china, with its battery of ambulances, array of tanks, guns and ammunition, hats and figures, of Tommy driving a steamroller and with a machine gun. What seems to the eye as being valuable such as a fairly big Mark 1 tank, is often under £25, whereas an insignificant looking little grenade could fetch five times this amount. In order to locate exact prices, see *The 1989 Price Guide to Crested China* by Nicholas Pine (Milestone) and for those in search of a detailed, illustrated listing of all WW1 heraldic china *Take Me Back To Dear Old Blighty* by Robert Southall (Milestone). Both books available from Milestone Publications, 62 Murray Road, Horndean, Hants. PO8 9JL. Tel: Horndean 597440.

It is still possible to find a piece not recorded and possibly valuable. The crested china factories left no records of what they produced, and previously unrecorded models appear daily.

Arcadian jockey on racehorse, some colouring.
£65 *G&CC*

Arcadian St Paul's Cathedral.
£14-25 *G&CC*

Crested personalities, various manufacturers.
£15-45 each *G&CC*

Selection of Crested cats.
£8-45 each *G&CC*

Ever popular sports items.
£5-40 each   *G&CC*

A range of timepieces.
£10-20   *G&CC*

Carlton truck of coal.
£15-20   *G&CC*

Carlton motorcycle and sidecar.
£75   *G&CC*

Carlton treadle sewing machine.
£25
and spinning wheel.
£18   *G&CC*

Miniature cheesedishes.
£5-8   *G&CC*

Musical instruments —
Willow guitar.
£10
Florentine grand piano.
£15
Willow banjo.
£10   *G&CC*

Arcadian lion.
£12-15   *G&CC*

Two Blackpool models, Big Wheel and Tower.
£10-20   *G&CC*

Arcadian crocodile.
£75   *G&CC*

Take a seat! Assortment of chairs, various factories.
£10-85   *G&CC*

Try these for size! Shoes from several potteries.
£7-12   *G&CC*

Military Crested China

Grafton HMS Iron Duke.
£85 *CHA*

Carlton armoured car.
£100 *CHA*

Arcadian airship.
£15
and Shelley Zeppelin.
£65 *CHA*

Grafton aeroplane.
£65 *CHA*

Grafton Tank HM
Landship Crème-de-
Menthe.
£25 *CHA*

Carlton HM Whippet
tank.
£135 *CHA*

Carlton British anti-
aircraft motor.
£120 *CHA*

Arcadian Tommy
throwing hand grenade.
£150 *CHA*

Arcadian bugler boy.
£135 *CHA*

Carlton Old Bill, Bruce
Bairnsfather character
£70 *CHA*

Carlton French 75 field
gun with sights.
£35 *CHA*

Arcadian HMS Queen
Elizabeth battleship.
£35 *CHA*

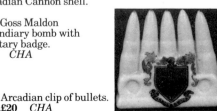

Goss 6in British shell.
£20 *CHA*

Arcadian Cannon shell.
£4
and Goss Maldon
incendiary bomb with
military badge.
£75 *CHA*

Arcadian clip of bullets.
£20 *CHA*

Jugs

Mason's Ironstone
Japan pattern jugs, the
tallest 6½in (16cm) high.
£60-130 each *OMH*

*More valuable than the
Imari pattern.*

A creamware jug, with
printed decorations,
restored, mid-19thC, 8in
(20cm) high.
£60-100 *WIL*

Mason's Ironstone Imari
pattern jugs, the tallest
8½in (21cm) high.
£50-120 each *OMH*

A Chinese chocolate pot,
with terracotta and gilt
enamelling over
underglaze blue, damaged,
Qianlong, 5½in (14cm)
high.
£120-150 *WIL*

A parian jug, c1885.
£35-60 *CAC*

An English jug with
harvest scenes, 19thC,
8½in (21.5cm).
£60-80 *CAC*

An English stoneware
jug, inscribed 'Presented
by the inhabitants of
Yeovil and its vicinity in
testimony of their
approval of the conduct of
the Mudford troop of the
Yeomanry Cavalry
during the riots in that
town in 1831', below 'To
Mr. G. Midlane', 9½in
(24cm) high.
£550-600 *Bon*

A caricature jug, printed
with cock fighting scene,
the cock with a head of
Henry Hunt, with
satirical verses, 4½in
(11.5cm) high.
£450-500 *Bon*

An earthenware spirit
jug and stopper, printed
in sepia with portrait
busts of H.M. King
George V and the R.Hon
H. H. Asquith, on a blue
ground, 11in (28cm).
£320-350 *Bon*

A Prattware jug,
moulded and decorated
in colour glaze on both
sides with bust portraits
of Queen Caroline, with
satyr mask lip, 6in
(15cm) high.
£260-300 *Bon*

Devon & Torquay

A 19thC jug, 8in (20cm)
high.
£45-55 *CAC*

Two jugs, with seagull
design, 3 to 6in (7.5 to
15cm) high.
£6-20 each *JO*

Jug inscribed 'Good
Luck'.
£9-12 *JO*

Cross Reference
Commemorative
Clarice Cliff
Spongeware

Lustreware

A Sunderland jug depicting Cotton Spinners Friendly Society, coloured with enamels, inscription on reverse, c1810, 5in (12cm) high.
£250-300 *LR*

A rare silver lustre jug, black printed with the bust of John Jones of Yestrad, and inscription, 6in (15cm) high.
£600-650 *Bon*

A copper lustre goblet and jug with raised painted decoration, goblet 4½in (11cm) high.
£20-30 *OMH*

A Sunderland pottery pink lustre jug, 7in (18cm) high.
£400-450 *Bon*

Three copper lustre jugs with painted design.
£40-60 each *PAC*

Painted designs are more valuable.

A copper lustre teapot with painted decoration, 8in (20cm) high.
£45-60 *OMH*

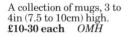

A collection of mugs, 3 to 4in (7.5 to 10cm) high.
£10-30 each *OMH*

LUSTRE

Lustre is a shiny surface produced by coating the pottery with a metallic pigment, generally copper or silver, but occasionally gold or platinum, which by means of a reducing atmosphere in the kiln, is not allowed to oxidise.

An Adam's silver lustre hair tidy, 20thC.
£20-30 *CAC*

Three jugs with blue bands, tallest 6in (15cm) high.
£35-50 *OMH*

Miniature Pottery

l. A jug, Stiff & Sons, London, 'Walkers Dairy Sloane Street', c1870, 3in (7.5cm) high. **£40-50**
c. A Doulton Lambeth jug, 1½in (4cm). **£40-50**
r. A pair of Doulton Lambeth, salts, 1½in (4cm). **£40-50** *MAN*

Three pieces of Staffordshire green pottery, unmarked, 19thC.
Teapot. **£40-50**
Jug and vase.
£15-20 each *MAN*

A Wedgwood jasper ware teapot in pink, 2in (5cm).
£15-25 *MAN*

A very rare Rockingham teapot, 2½in (6cm) high.
£500-600 *MAN*

A brown glazed teaset, including 6 cups and saucers, possibly Derbyshire, 19thC.
£130-150 *MAN*

A Crown Staffordshire tea tray, with 2 cups and saucers, a jug and sugar basin, c1900, tray 6in (15cm) wide.
£100-125 *MAN*

A commemorative cup and saucer.
£20-30
A cup and saucer, possibly Spode, 19thC.
£90-100
A Staffordshire cup and saucer.
£90-100
A Staffordshire cup and saucer, marked Adderleys, c1900.
£40-50 *MAN*

l. A saltglaze barrel, 19thC, 2½in (6cm) high.
£45-55
r. A Royal Doulton bottle, 2in (5cm) high.
£40-50 *MAN*

Cross Reference
Cups and Saucers
Egg Cups
Mugs
Jugs

A Worcester tyg, 2in (5cm) high.
£55-65 *MAN*

A mug transfer printed in puce, 19thC, 2in (5cm) high.
£30-40 *MAN*

A rare bust of the Rev. John Wesley, c1800, 5in (12cm) high.
£400-450 *LR*

A Davenport blue and white tureen, cover and stand, 19thC.
£85-95 *MAN*

Mugs

A German souvenir mug, c1900.
£5-12 *CAC*

A Continental mug, 20thC.
£2-5 *CAC*

A Royal Crown Derby two-handled mug, 2in (5cm).
£110-130 *MAN*

Blue transfer ware half pint measures, 4in (10cm).
£30-50 *AL*

A potato stamped mug, 19thC.
£95-110 *AP*

A blue transfer ware Imperial Pint mug, 19thC, 4in (10cm).
£35-45 *CAC*

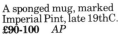

A mug, c1875.
£10-20 *CAC*

A sponged mug, marked Imperial Pint, late 19thC.
£90-100 *AP*

Pot Lids

Printing on ceramics was perfected c1840. One result was the use of the process to produce pictorial lids for small pots containing many domestic items, including ointments, cosmetics and comestibles such as meat paste. These lids were produced in quantity between 1840 and the end of the 19th Century. The most collectable are the early flat tops (1845-50) and the convex tops of 1860-75. Later lids tend to lack the strong colours and light texture of the early examples. Beware of post 1900 re-issues which can usually be detected by lack of crazing.

Bear Subjects

Bear with Valentines.
(11)
£1,800-2,400 *P*

Arctic Expedition in search of Sir John Franklin. (17)
£400-500 *P*

The Ins. (15)
£100-150
The Outs. (16)
£100-150 *P*

Polar Bears. (18)
£100-140 *P*

All but Trapped. (20)
£1,000-1,400 *P*

Bear attacked by Dogs.
(2)
£500-700 *P*

About 400 pot lid designs have been identified. These have been documented and numbered by A. Ball in his invaluable reference work *Price Guide to Pot Lids* which all collectors should possess. The listing which follows contains a representative selection of the pot lids most likely to be encountered by the general collector. The number refers to the listing system devised by Mr Ball in his book.

No. Description
1. Alas! Poor Bruin.
   £80-100
2. Bear attacked by Dogs.
   £500-700
3. Bear's Grease Manufacturer, lettering on marbled border.
   £2,000-3,000
4. Bear Hunting.
   £150-200
5. Bears Reading Newspapers.
   £600-700
9. Bears at School.
   £80-100
11. Bear with Valentines.
    £1,800-2,400
15. The Ins.
    £100-150
16. The Outs.
    £100-150
17. Arctic Expedition.
    £400-500
18. Polar Bears.
    £100-140
20. All but Trapped.
    £1,000-1,400
21. Pegwell Bay.
    £600-800
24. Lobster Fishing, damaged.
    £80-120
25. Pegwell Bay, Lobster Fishing.
    £100-120
27. Belle Vue Tavern.
    £200-230
29. Belle Vue Tavern.
    £220-250
30. Belle Vue without bay window.
    £70-100
31. Shrimpers, damaged.
    £60-80
32. S. Banger, Shrimp Sauce Manufacturer.
    £300-400
33. Shrimping.
    £60-80
34. The Dutch Fisherman.
    £1,000-1,200
35. Still Life – Game.
    £100-120
37. Ramsgate, Farmyard Scene.
    £60-80
38. Landing the Fare – Pegwell Bay.
    £50-60
41. Royal Harbour.
    £50-60
42. Royal Harbour, Ramsgate.
    £40-50
43. Nelson Crescent, Ramsgate.
    £80-100
45. Walmer Castle.
    £50-60

No. Description
48. Pretty Kettle of Fish.
   £75-95
49. Lobster Sauce.
   £40-50
52B. Shell.
   £45-55
53. Examining the Nets.
   £50-60
55. Landing the Catch.
   £30-40
60. The Net-Maker.
   £200-250
62. Foreign River Scene.
   £50-60
63. The Shrimpers.
   £40-60
64. Sea Nymph and Trident.
   £200-250
65. Swiss Riverside Scene.
   £60-90
66. Dutch River Scene.
   £100-120
76. Charge of the Scots Greys at Balaklava.
   £120-140
78. Fall of Sebastopol.
   £120-140
97. The Bride.
   £120-150
98. An Eastern Repast.
   £100-120
101. The Mirror.
   £100-120
106. Lady with Hawk.
   £90-100
107. Lady with Guitar.
   £60-70
110. Lady Fastening Shoe.
   £150-200
111. Lady Brushing Hair.
   £160-200
114. The Matador.
   £350-450
116. Jenny Lind.
   £1,200-1,500
118. The Trysting Place.
   £70-100
119. The Lovers.
   £60-90
123. Musical Trio.
   £80-100
139. Crystal Palace, Interior.
   £260-300
143. Dublin Industrial Exhibition 1853.
   £90-110
144. International Exhibition 1862.
   £150-180
145. L'Exposition Universelle de 1867.
   £75-100
149. England's Pride.
   £125-155
153. The Late Prince Consort.
   £75-85
156. Napoleon III and Empress Eugenie.
   £100-120
157. Albert Edward, Prince of Wales and Princess Alexandra, on their marriage 1863.
   £75-100

Pegwell Bay

Pegwell Bay. (23)
£600-800   *P*

Lobster Fishing, damaged. (24)
£50-100   *P*

Belle Vue Tavern. (29)
£220-250   *P*

Shrimping. (33)
£60-80   *P*

The Dutch Fisherman. (34)
£1,000-1,200   *P*

Ramsgate, Still Life Game. (35)
£100-120   *P*

Ramsgate, Farmyard Scene. (37)
£60-80   *P*

Royal Harbour, Ramsgate. (42)
£40-50   *P*

Nelson Crescent, Ramsgate. (43)
£80-100   *P*

The Net-Maker. (60)
£200-250   *P*

Personal Subjects

Lady Fastening Shoe.
(110)
£150-200   *P*

Lady Brushing Hair.
(111)
£160-200   *P*

The Lovers. (119)
£60-90   *P*

Jenny Lind, J. Grossmith
& Co. Newgate St,
London, hairline crack.
(116)
£900-1,200   *P*

The Trysting Place. (118)
£70-100   *P*

Musical Trio. (123)
£80-100   *P*

DID YOU KNOW?
- Earliest types had black and white lids advertising Bear's Grease as a hair dressing.
- Principal makers were F. & R. Pratt & Co. c1847-88, and T. & J. Mayer.
- The technique of colour transfer-printing was perfected by Jesse Austin, an engraver and artist employed by F. & R. Pratt.

Exhibition Subjects

Dublin Industrial
Exhibition 1853. (143)
£90-110   *P*

International Exhibition
1862. (144)
£150-180   *P*

No.	Description
159.	Wellington with Cocked Hat. £1,500-2,500
160A.	Wellington with clasped hands. £100-140
166.	Balaklava, Inkerman, Alma. £250-300
167A.	Admiral Sir Charles Napier C.B. £220-250
168.	The Allied Generals. £90-100
170.	Sir Robert Peel. £200-230
171.	Peabody. £80-120
172.	Harriet Beecher Stowe. £700-1,100
174.	The Blue Boy. £80-100
175.	Dr. Johnson. £30-50
176.	Buckingham Palace. £90-120
179.	Drayton Manor. £50-80
180.	Windsor Park, Returning from Stag Hunting. £120-150
181.	Sandringham. £60-80
183.	New Houses of Parliament, Westminster. £190-250
185.	St. Paul's Cathedral and River Pageant. £90-120
188.	Strathfieldsaye. £70-110
189.	Westminster Abbey. £200-250
192.	St. Paul's Cathedral. £150-200
193.	Charing Cross. £80-100
195.	New Houses of Parliament. £100-150
201.	Trafalgar Square. £40-60
202.	Holborn Viaduct. £60-80
205.	The Thirsty Soldier. £60-80
206.	Embarking for the East. £60-80
209.	Sebastopol. £60-75
210.	The Battle of the Nile. £55-75
211.	Meeting of Garibaldi and Victor Emmanuel. £50-60
214.	The Volunteers. £90-120
216.	The Redoubt. £500-600
219.	War. £35-45
220.	Peace. £40-50
221.	Harbour of Hong Kong. £50-60

No. Description
222. Ning Po River.
    £80-100
223. Rifle Contest, Wimbledon 1864.
    £50-60
224. Wimbledon, July 1860.
    £45-55
226. Shakespeare's Birthplace – Exterior.
    £40-50
227. Shakespeare's Birthplace – Interior.
    £30-60
228. Anne Hathaway's Cottage.
    £50-60
229. Holy Trinity Church.
    £80-100
233. May Day Dancers at the Swan Inn.
    £30-50
236. The Parish Beadle.
    £90-110
237. The Children of Flora.
    £70-80
240. The Village Wedding.
    £20-30
241. Our Home.
    £100-150
245. The Enthusiast.
    £40-50
248. Chiefs Return from Deer-stalking.
    £90-100
249. Dangerous Skating.
    £50-70
250. Fair Sportswoman.
    £40-60
253. Snapdragon.
    £70-90
257. A Race or Derby Day.
    £30-50
258. The Skaters.
    £70-90
259. The Game Bag.
    £40-50
261. Pheasant Shooting.
    £30-50
263. Children Sailing Boats in Tub.
    £70-90
264C. Six Dogs.
    £400-450
265. Good Dog.
    £50-60
266. Contrast.
    £60-70
267. Feeding the Chickens.
    £50-60
269. Deerhound Guarding Cradle.
    £130-160
270. The Begging Dog.
    £70-90
272. Both Alike.
    £45-65
273. Country Quarters.
    £70-80
277. The Skewbald Horse.
    £60-70
289. The Sea Eagle.
    £80-100
309. The Faithful Shepherd.
    £60-80
314. The Breakfast Party.
    £90-100

Portrait Subjects

England's Pride. (149)
£125-155   *RBE*

Albert Edward, Prince of Wales and Princess Alexandra, on their marriage 1863. (157)
£75-100   *P*

Sir Robert Peel. (170)
£200-230   *P*

Peabody. (171)
£80-120   *RBE*

The Allied Generals. (168)
£90-100   *RBE*

Historic Buildings

St. Paul's Cathedral and River Pageant. (185)
£90-120   *P*

Strathfieldsaye. (188)
£70-110   *P*

Westminster Abbey. (189)
£200-250   *P*

New Houses of Parliament, Westminster, damaged. (183)
£160-200   *P*

Buckingham Palace.
(176)
£90-120   *P*

L'Exposition Universelle
de 1867. (145)
£75-100   *P*

St. Paul's Cathedral.
(192)
£150-200   *P*

New Houses of
Parliament. (195)
£100-150   *P*

War & Geographical Subjects

Embarking for the East.
(206)
£60-80   *RBE*

Sebastopol. (209)
£60-75   *RBE*

Meeting of Garibaldi and
Victor Emmanuel. (211)
£50-60   *RBE*

Balaklava, Inkerman,
Alma. (166)
£250-300   *RBE*

General

Windsor Park, Returning
from Stag Hunting. (180)
£120-150   *P*

Wimbledon, July 1860.
(224)
£45-55   *RBE*

Rifle Contest,
Wimbledon 1864. (223)
£50-60   *RBE*

The Quarry, damaged.
(352)
£60-80   *RBE*

No.	Description
315.	Cattle and Ruins. **£50-70**
318.	The Old Water Mill. **£50-60**
319.	The Queen, God Bless Her. **£50-70**
322.	The Rivals. **£75-85**
323.	The Dentist. **£100-120**
324.	The Farriers. **£50-60**
325.	The Shepherdess. **£50-60**
327.	The Times. **£40-60**
328.	Uncle Toby. **£30-50**
329C.	The First Appeal. **£50-60**
331.	Strasbourg. **£40-50**
334.	The Trooper. **£50-70**
337.	The Flute Player. **£30-50**
340.	On Guard. **£40-60**
341.	The Fisher-boy. **£50-70**
347.	Tam O'Shanter. **£90-110**
348.	Peasant Boys. **£50-70**
351.	Preparing for the Ride. **£50-70**
352.	The Quarry. **£100-150**
358.	Little Red Riding Hood. **£60-80**
359.	The Red Bull Inn. **£50-70**
361.	The Wolf and the Lamb. **£40-60**
365.	The Waterfall. **£60-80**
397.	Tyrolean Village Scene. **£40-60**

Spongeware

Spongeware or spatterware was made in the 19th Century — mainly in the Staffordshire Potteries, but it is possible to find examples of Scottish and Welsh designs.

Bright colours were sponged on through a stencil, the design was often supplemented with painting. The more detailed patterns were applied with potato stamps.

The most unusual decorations are those with animals and birds and these are much sought after by collectors. The pea hen is a design that is very collectable in America.

A sponged bowl with stylised flowers and leaves, probably Scottish, mid-19thC.
£100-120 *AP*

A sponged bowl with pink and grey decoration, early 19thC.
£65-75 *AP*

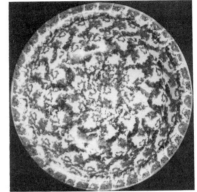

A blue and white sponged bowl, similar to American style, mid-19thC.
£100-120 *AP*

Bowls

A potato printed bowl with stylised tulips in red and green, mid-19thC.
£65-75 *AP*

A bowl with marble effect sponged pattern, early 19thC.
£50-60 *AP*

A potato printed bowl, with pink and green flowers, mid-19thC.
£60-70 *AP*

A fluted bowl, early 19thC.
£140-160 *AP*

A potato printed bowl, with design of birds, early 19thC.
£60-70 *AP*

A sponged bowl, with unusual design in pink, blue and green, early 19thC.
£120-130 *AP*

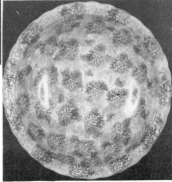

A potato printed bowl with stylised tulips and leaves, mid-19thC.
£140-150   *AP*

A potato printed bowl with blue rope border and pink and white flowers, mid-19thC.
£65-75   *AP*

A sponged bowl with blue potato print border and pink butterflies, mid-19thC.
£70-80   *AP*

A bowl with yellow and blue sunflower border, possibly Scottish, mid-19thC.
£90-100   *AP*

A potato printed and painted bowl, with pink flowers and blue painted lines, mid-19thC.
£55-65   *AP*

A potato printed bowl with sponged central decoration, mid-19thC.
£90-100   *AP*

A potato printed bowl, mid-19thC.
£45-55   *AP*

A potato printed bowl with double handles, damaged, mid-19thC.
£60-70   *AP*

A sponged bowl with a design of a lion and a bird, early 19thC.
£130-150   *AP*

A bowl with potato printed design of swagged bows and flowers, 19thC.
£60-70   *AP*

A potato printed bowl with pink and white flowered border, mid-19thC.
£45-55   *AP*

A blue and white potato printed bowl, mid-19thC.
£50-60   *AP*

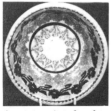

A potato printed and sponged bowl, possibly Scottish, mid-19thC.
£110-120   *AP*

A potato printed bowl, slight damage, 19thC.
£20-30   *AP*

A Welsh potato printed bowl.
£65-75   *AP*

A sponged bowl with design of potato print leaves in blue and grey.
£100-120   *AP*

108

A sponged bowl, early
19thC.
£45-55 *AP*

A sponged bowl with a
rare design of pink
elephants and pale green
border, c1810.
£250-270 *AP*

A potato printed bowl,
mid-19thC.
£65-75 *AP*

Plates

A potato printed plate
with unusual design in
pink, green, red, black
and yellow, early 19thC.
£90-100 *AP*

A blue and white
sponged plate, early
19thC.
£65-75 *AP*

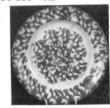

A child's plate with
painted and potato
printed flowered border,
mid-19thC.
£90-100 *AP*

A potato printed plate,
with pink and green
flowers, mid-19thC.
£50-60 *AP*

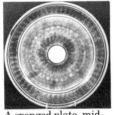

A sponged plate, mid-
19thC.
£90-100 *AP*

A pair of potato printed
plates, mid-19thC.
£220-250 *AP*

A bright green sponged
plate, early 19thC.
£75-85 *AP*

Carpet Bowls

A carpet bowl with pink
and white sponged
pattern, mid-19thC.
£60-70 *AP*

A carpet bowl with
sponged pattern, marked
Made in Scotland,
mid-19thC.
£80-90 *AP*

A carpet bowl, with
yellow, pink, and green
decoration, mid-19thC.
£50-60 *AP*

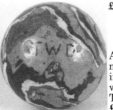

A carpet bowl with blue,
green and red decoration,
late 19thC.
£60-70 *AP*

A carpet bowl with
marble effect decoration
in pink, green, blue and
white, with initials
TWD, late 19thC.
£75-80 *AP*

109

Dishes

A sponged dish, mid-19thC.
£130-140 *AP*

A small dish with potato printed pattern, late 19thC.
£60-70 *AP*

A blue and white sponged meat dish, mid-19thC.
£120-130 *AP*

A potato printed dish, mid-19thC.
£80-90 *AP*

A Scottish blue and white potato print dish.
£100-110 *AP*

A potato printed dish, mid-19thC.
£110-130 *AP*

A potato printed dish, mid-19thC.
£100-120 *AP*

Jugs

A potato printed jug, with blue, green and red design, early 19thC.
£100-120 *AP*

A potato printed jug, with blue and green design, mid-19thC.
£70-80 *AP*

A large sponged jug, with blue and white pattern, mid-19thC.
£140-160 *AP*

A jug with blue and green sponged design, c1800.
£120-130 *AP*

A large potato printed jug, mid-19thC.
£130-140 *AP*

A sponged jug in blue and white, mid-19thC.
£75-85 *AP*

A sponged jug with pink, green and blue pattern, early 19thC.
£120-130 *AP*

A jug with potato printed pattern, mid-19thC.
£160-170 *AP*

A small jug with black sponged pattern.
£60-70 *AP*

A small sponged jug, with pink and green pattern, early 19thC.
£100-120 *AP*

Miscellaneous

A sponged gravy boat, late 19thC.
£90-100 *AP*

A mustard pot with potato printed pattern, 19thC.
£60-70 *AP*

A sponged mustard pot with lid, early 19thC.
£70-80 *AP*

A blue and white sponged pepper pot, mid-19thC.
£70-80 *AP*

A blue and white sponged salt pot, early 19thC.
£65-75 *AP*

Mugs

A potato printed mug, mid-19thC.
£90-110 *AP*

MAKE THE MOST OF
MILLER'S
Price ranges in this book reflect what one should expect to *pay* for a similar example. When selling, however, one should expect to receive a lower figure. This will fluctuate according to a dealer's stock, saleability at a particular time, etc. It is always advisable, when selling, to approach a reputable specialist dealer or an auction house which has specialist sales.

A potato printed mug with pink border and chequerboard pattern, mid-19thC.
£90-110 *AP*

A potato printed mug with flower pattern, late 19thC.
£40-50 *AP*

A potato printed mug, early 19thC.
£65-75 *AP*

A potato printed mug, in blue, white and pink, mid-19thC.
£70-80 *AP*

A potato printed mug, early 19thC.
£60-70 *AP*

111

Teapots

Art Deco

An aeroplane teapot, white with chrome decoration.
£200-250 *PGA*

A Carlton ware Australian pattern teapot, scarce pink ground colour, c1930.
£80-120 *PGA*

A Susie Cooper Kestrel shape teapot, c1930.
£65-75 *PGA*

A Grimwades Royal Winton teapot and stand.
£140-160 *PGA*

Belleek

A teapot in the form of a shell, c1930.
£200-250 *PGA*

A shell and coral teapot, First Period.
£300-400 *PGA*

A tea kettle, First Period.
£350-400 *PGA*

A teapot in the form of a sea urchin, with lustre glaze, c1880.
£400-450 *PGA*

Clarice Cliff

A Clarice Cliff Bones the Butcher honey glaze teapot, 1931.
£500-600 *PGA*

A rare Clarice Cliff Stamford shape teapot, based on Edouard Benedictus' original design, House and Bridge pattern, c1931.
£650-750 *PGA*

A Clarice Cliff trial teapot, never put into production, known as Nautilus or Snail, Rhodanthe pattern, 1935.
£650-750 *PGA*

A Clarice Cliff cockerel teapot, c1930, and child's chick pot, c1932.
£450-550 each *PGA*

A Clarice Cliff Rhodanthe pattern conical shaped teapot, c1934.
£220-250 *PGA*

A Clarice Cliff 'Teepee' teapot, designed by Betty Silvester, base marked 'Greetings from Canada', 1952.
£450+ *PGA*

DID YOU KNOW?
This varied selection of teapots is only part of a large collection started by Paul Gibbs some 15 years ago. He was intrigued by the various shapes and novel designs, and instead of selling them, decided to form a 'small' collection.
There are now over 500 in his collection! On view in Conway.

Doulton

A teapot designed by Eliza Simmance, painted in soft glaze to resemble an oil painting.
£250-300 *PGA*

A Royal Doulton Bunnykins teapot, designed by Barbara Vernon, c1930.
£75-85 *PGA*

A stoneware teapot, with rabbit design by Hannah Barlow, 1873.
£550-600 *PGA*

A 'Devil' teapot, attributed to Mark Marshall, c1890.
£250-300 *PGA*

Majolica

A Minton monkey teapot, impressed marks, c1875.
£850+ *PGA*

A J. Holdcroft, Staffordshire, teapot in the form of a chinaman on a coconut, the head forming the lid, c1870.
£650-750 *PGA*

A Holdcroft majolica teapot, modelled as a bird on a nest, with separate stand, c1870.
£850-950 *PGA*

An Isle of Man three-legged teapot, the man astride a branch.
£500-550 *PGA*

Beware of German copies which are worth considerably less.

Moorcroft

A Moorcroft Macintyre Florianware teapot, in blue poppy design, c1903.
£450-500 *PGA*

A Moorcroft moonlit blue landscape design, made for Liberty's, c1925.
£750-800 *PGA*

Moorcroft globular teapot, decorated in the orchid pattern.
£250-350 *PGA*

Frederick Rhead

An Intarsia design teapot, designed for the Wieman factory, c1890.
£450+ *PGA*

A 'cosy' pot, in the Trellis pattern, Bursley ware, with tube liners, marked, c1925.
£75-85 *PGA*

Foley earthenware Intarsia political caricature teapots, c1900.
£550-650 each *PGA*

The Weiman factory was taken over by Shelley.

113

James Sadler & Sons

Car teapots, one with nursery figures, with registration No. OKT 42, c1930.
£45-150 *PGA*

Locomotive teapot, c1930.
£120-150 *PGA*

Wild West teapot, milk jug, and sugar basin, c1930.
£120-150 *PGA*

Father Christmas, c1939.
£75-100 *PGA*

Shelley

A Harmony dripware teapot, c1934.
£65-85 *PGA*

A nursery teapot in the form of a tent, designed by Hilda Cowhan, c1928.
£300-350 *PGA*

A nursery teapot in the form of a duck, designed by Mabel Lucie Attwell, c1930.
£250-300 *PGA*

A nursery teapot in the form of a mushroom house, designed by Mabel Lucie Attwell, c1926.
£200-250 *PGA*

Wedgwood

A white stoneware 'dry body' teapot, c1817.
£150-200 *PGA*

The catalogue price when new — 1s (5p).

A three colour jasper ware teapot, 19thC, 5in (12.5cm) high.
£400-500 *PGA*

The three colour decoration makes this a rare pot.

A smear glaze tobacco leaf pattern teapot, late 18thC.
£300-350 *PGA*

A teapot with Egyptian motifs, Battle of the Nile period, c1815.
£450-500 *PGA*

Worcester

A blue and white teapot, late 18thC, 5in (12.5cm).
£350-400 *PGA*

A rare melon-shaped teapot, with applied leaf decoration, impressed wheel and crown mark, c1880.
£300-350 *PGA*

A rare marine subject teapot, finely modelled with fronds and coral handle, c1875.
£750-850 *PGA*

A rare teapot with reticulated decoration, c1895.
£650-750 *PGA*

The outer wall of a double wall vessel was hand pierced, and proved extremely difficult to fire successfully.

Miscellaneous

A Capodimonte Naples teapot, with typical relief decoration in baroque style, 19thC.
£250-350 *PGA*

Brighton Electric Sea Railway teapot, 'Need a steady hand drinking your tea on this form of transport', German, c1910.
£120-150 *PGA*

A barge novelty teapot, with double spout, South Derbyshire, late 19thC.
£150-200 *PGA*

A black Jackfield type earthenware heart-shaped teapot, with gilt embellishment, 19thC.
£75-100 *PGA*

A Newhall silver shape chinoiserie pattern teapot, c1820.
£350-400 *PGA*

A Harley ware lozenge shaped teapot, c1805.
£400-450 *PGA*

A Paris teapot, c1810, gold decoration, 4in (10cm).
£350-400 *PGA*

A 'Cadogan' teapot, filled from the bottom via long internal tube, no need for a lid, c1820.
£125-150 *PGA*

A Studio pottery, Castle Hedingham 'Cadogan' style teapot, marked, 10in (25.5cm) high.
£300-350 *PGA*

A Castle Hedingham teapot with chinaman finial, late 19thC.
£375-400 *PGA*

An S.Y.P. pot, 'Simple Yet Perfect', patented by the Earl of Dundonald, c1906.
£85-100 *PGA*

When the teapot is placed on its side the tea is separated from the leaves; when righted the tea is ready to pour. The makers claimed it was to safeguard the nervous and digestive systems by separating the tea leaves from the water before the injurious element called tannin has time to do its devilish work!

A barge teapot from Church Gresley, Derbyshire, decorated with applied flowers and birds, dated 1888, 15in (38cm) high.
£250-300 *PGA*

Elephant and boy teapots,
l. Japanese enamelled and gilded, c1930.
r. English 'Sabu' pot, by Colclough China, Longton, c1930.
£45-85 each *PGA*

A German earthenware begging dog teapot.
£65-85 *PGA*

A Crown Ducal, A. G. Richardson, black cat set, c1910.
£90-120 *PGA*

A Carlton ware novelty pig teapot, the tail forming the handle.
£65-85 *PGA*

A 'Biggles' bi-plane teapot, with green glaze, c1930.
£65-85 *PGA*

A Devonmoor, Newton Abbot, grotesque Simple Simon teapot, the school cap forming the lid, c1930.
£65-85 *PGA*

A novelty Humpty Dumpty teapot, in yellow with gold trim, marked Lingard Rd. 830102.
£65-85 *PGA*

A cannon teapot, Geo. Clews, Tunstall, c1930, 7in (18cm) high.
£75-95 *PGA*

A Paragon nursery teapot, designed by J. Robinson, c1925.
£125-150 *PGA*

A Lingard & Co., Old Lady Who Lived in a Shoe teapot.
£85-100 *PGA*

A Goss Welsh lady teapot, c1920.
£80-100 *PGA*

A cottage teapot.
£25+ *PGA*

A multi-coloured rooster teapot, Staffordshire, c1930.
£65-75 *PGA*

A sponged ware miniature peahen pattern teapot, Staffordshire, 19thC.
£350-400 *PGA*

Three cat teapots, English and Continental, from 1910.
£35-85 *PGA*

A honeycomb teapot, with bee finial, c1930.
£65-85 *PGA*

A figural teapot 'Ye Daintee Laydee', as purchased by Queen Mary, c1930.
From £25 *PGA*

Character

A rare Royal Doulton 'Sairey Gamp' teapot, designed by Harry Fenton, c1939.
£700+ *PGA*

Toby teapots.
£85-125 *PGA*

Beswick character teapots, 'Sairey Gamp' and 'Dolly Varden'.
£65-85 each *PGA*

Beswick Dickensian novelty teapots, c1930.
£65-85 *PGA*

Four miniature Dickensian character teapots, 2in (5cm) high.
£25-35 each *PGA*

A Toby teapot, picked out in lustre, by Charles Allerton, Longton, c1910.
£85-100 *PGA*

A Mr Pickwick teapot.
£55-65 *BEV*

A Royal Worcester Aesthetic Movement teapot, signed Budge, inscribed on the base 'Fearful consequences through the laws of natural selection and evolution of living up to one's teapot'.
£1,200-1,500 *PGA*

A Doulton 'Old Charley' teapot, modelled by Harry Fenton, 1939.
£800+ *PGA*

The outbreak of World War II resulted in very few of these pots being sold.

117

Toby Jugs

The most desirable Toby jugs were made by Ralph Wood, but most of the factories produced them in quite substantial quantities. Some claim the title honour for Sir Toby Belch of 'Twelfth Night', and others Uncle Toby in 'Tristram Shandy' by Sterne. It is more likely, however, that the character was inspired by the print published in 1761 of Toby Philpot illustrating the popular song 'The Brown Jug'.

There are many varieties for the collector: The Night Watchman, The Drunken Parson, Prince Hal, Hearty Good Fellow, Admiral Jarvis, Martha Gunn, etc. On these early jugs, crisp modelling, good colouring and any unusual features all increase value. Many limited editions depicting characters from the First World War and later Churchill were produced, and their rarity leads to reasonably high prices today.

A Toby jug, 6½in (16.5cm) high.
£80-110   *JO*

Hearty Good Fellow, 12in (30.5cm) high.
£100-150   *JO*

The Snuff Taker, 9in (23cm) high.
£80-140   *JO*

A Toby jug, c1800, 4in (10cm) high.
£70-90   *JO*

Nelson, 12in (30.5cm).
£130-180   *JO*

The Squire, 11in (28cm) high.
£240-300   *JO*

A collection of Toby jugs.
£70-250   *JO*

Thin Toby, 7½in (19cm) high.
£120-140   *JO*

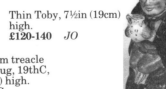

A Rockingham treacle glazed Toby jug, 19thC, 10in (25.5cm) high.
£85-100   *OSc*

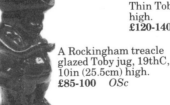

Hearty Good Fellow Toby jugs, 9in (23cm) high.
£85-100
The larger one by Ralph Wood, 11in (28cm) high.
£100-300   *OSc*

FURTHER READING
Bedford, John, *Toby Jugs*, London 1968.
Eyles Desmond, *Good Sir Toby: The Story of Toby Jugs through the Ages*, London 1955.
Price, R. K. *Astbury, Whieldon and Ralph Wood Figures and Toby Jugs*, London 1922.
Mount, Sally, *Price Guide to 18th Century English Pottery*, Woodbridge 1972.

Vases

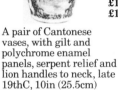

Clarice Cliff, Newport Pottery Bizarre vases.
£190-220 pair
£130-150 *SWO*

An Ault pottery vase, attributed to Christopher Dresser, moulded on each side with the face of a grotesque fish in green against moulded foliage, moulded mark and numbered 457, 7in (18cm) high.
£70-100 *CSK*

A pair of Cantonese vases, with gilt and polychrome enamel panels, serpent relief and lion handles to neck, late 19thC, 10in (25.5cm) high.
£170-200 *WIL*

A Wedgwood majolica vase, with dragon support, 19thC, 9in (23cm) high.
£85-95 *PCh*

A Belleek porcelain vase, coloured with a turquoise enamel in varying depths, printed factory marks, 8in (20cm) high.
£200-300 *Bon*

A white pottery vase by Keith Murray, slight damage, 8in (20.5cm) high.
£145-155 *VDB*

When perfect.
£200+ *VDB*

A Pilkington's Lancastrian vase, by Charles Cundall, impressed marks, artist's monogram and date code for 1912, 11in (28cm) high.
£220-300 *CSK*

A Carter, Stabler and Adams Poole vase, painted in red, green, mauve and blue with stylised leaves, flowers and birds in flight, reserved against a grey ground, impressed marks, painted in blue NT and IY, 11½in (29cm) high.
£450-500 *P*

An early stoneware vase, the unglazed exterior with bands of painted decoration, impressed Carter & Co. Poole, 8in (20cm).
£100-120 *C*

A Rookwood stoneware vase, painted in browns, amber and green with 3 wild roses, the base impressed with R.P. mark and number 611D, 8½in (21cm) high.
£300-350 *C*

A Mintons Secessionist vase, covered in mustard yellow and turquoise glazes, with green and brown piped slip decoration of stylised trees, the base printed Mintons Ltd., No. 1 with impressed 712, 8½in (23cm) high.
£200-250 *C*

A Bennett vase, likened to Charlotte Rhead, c1930, 8in (20cm) high.
£80-100 *BEV*

A Royal Doulton stoneware vase, impressed marks, 12in (30.5cm) high.
£140-160 *C*

Cross Reference
Glass

General

Chamber Pots

A chamber pot.
£60-80   *CB*

A Minton pottery
turquoise and white
chamber pot, with gilt
rim, c1880.
£80-100   *CB*

A floral Corona ware
chamber pot.
£40-60   *CB*

An English chamber pot,
richly decorated in gilt,
c1800.
£80-120   *CB*

A Henry Alcock & Co.,
chamber pot.
£40-60   *CB*

Parian Ware

Ariadne and the panther,
12in (30.5cm) high.
£230-280   *CB*

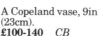

A pair of Minton figures
of Autumn and Spring,
14in (35.5cm).
£240-260   *CB*

A Copeland vase, 9in
(23cm).
£100-140   *CB*

A Minton figure of
Temperance, 20in (51cm)
high.
£650-750   *CB*

DID YOU KNOW?____
Miller's Collectables
Price Guide is designed
to build up, year by year,
into the most
comprehensive reference
system available.

Miscellaneous

A Wedgwood & Co., wash set, decorated in a design by George Logan, with motif in yellow, white and black on a blue ground, printed marks, jug 12in (30.5cm) high.
£700-750 *CSK*

A Wilkinson's jam pot and spoon, c1930.
£6-10 *CAC*

A Bournes pottery spirit flask, the reverse impressed Denby & Codno Park, 8in (20cm).
£420-450 *Bon*

Spill vases, c1860.
£5-10 each *CAC*

A Staffordshire beaker, black printed with a bust of Hunt, pink lustre border, some damage, 3in (7.5cm) high.
£320-350 *Bon*

A Moorcroft toilet set, comprising 2 scent bottles and a powder box, decorated with irises in blue, white and pink, impressed marks, signed in blue, bottles 6in (15cm) high.
£350-400 *CSK*

A Continental porcelain match holder, 4½in (11cm) high.
£140-180 *Bon*

A blue and white pap boat, 19thC.
£15-30 *OSc*

A Paragon china plate, printed in brown with a portrait medallion of Neville Chamberlain, 1938, 9in (23cm) diam.
£180-220 *Bon*

A Staffordshire blue printed wall plaque, with portrait of Gladstone, 14in (35.5cm) diam.
£40-80 *Bon*

Coca-Cola

A key ring, c1980.
£2-4   *PC*

A shop advertising sign.
£65-75   *PC*

A coat hanger, c1966.
£45-55   *PC*

A tin tray, c1914.
£45-55   *PC*

Three glasses.
Under £1 each   *PC*

Fridge magnets, c1980.
£2-4 each   *PC*

A baseball cap.
£6-8   *PC*

A pencil sharpener.
£2-4
A miniature bottle.
£7-10
A tin.
£4-8   *PC*

Souvenir cups, c1980.
£1-2 each   *PC*

An advertising sign,
c1960, 24in (61cm).
£65-75   *PC*

An ashtray, c1970.
£8-10   *PC*

An advertising sign,
c1950.
£20-30   *PC*

A lighter.
£10-15
A money box.
£4-5
A radio.
£6-8   *PC*

An American badge,
pre-war.
£18-20   *PC*

A selection of cans, c1974.
Under £1 each *PC*

A bottle opener, c1940.
£10-15 *PC*

A display bottle in gold
sprayed glass, c1958.
£15-20 *PC*

A record, c1970.
£2-4 *PC*

An ice bucket, c1960.
£15-20 *PC*

An enamel advertising
sign, c1950, 16 by 22in
(40 by 55cm).
£100-120 *PC*

A lighter, pre-war.
£15-20 *PC*

A camera in working
order, c1970.
£25-35 *PC*

A penknife, c1960.
£15-20 *PC*

Two belts.
£4-6 each *PC*

Miniature trays with
box, c1978.
£10-15 *PC*

A Frisbee, c1978.
£20-25 *PC*

*Very rare as they were
made without permission
from Coca-Cola.
Consequently very few
survive as most of them
had to be destroyed.*

A lampshade, c1960.
£20-25 *PC*

A bottle opener, pre-war.
£10-15 *PC*

123

Corkscrews

Metal corkscrews.
£3-8 each *TM*

Corkscrews with turned
wooden handles.
£4-5 each *MAN*

A rack corkscrew with
worn brush.
£75-85 *AD*

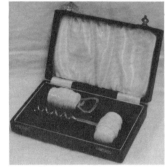

A bone handled
corkscrew.
£65-75 *AD*

A turned handle
corkscrew with brush.
£25-35 *AD*

A reverse thread
corkscrew.
£25-35 *AD*

An ivory barrel shaped
opener and corkscrew, in
case.
£90-100 *PCh*

Wooden handled
corkscrews.
£3-5 each *MAN*

Wooden handled
corkscrews.
£3-5 each *MAN*

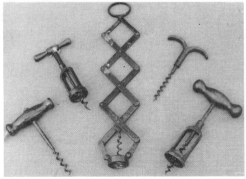

Mappin & Webb silver
plate bottle openers,
original box, c1930.
£45-55 *BEV*

A John Loach's patent
brass corkscrew, with
royal coat-of-arms, ivory
handle, 2 internal spikes
and Archimedean screw
worm, lacks brush.
£800-900 *P*

A collection of
corkscrews.
£10-30 each *TM*

Wooden handled
corkscrews.
£12-15 each   *MAN*

Metal corkscrews.
£3-10 each   *MAN*

A metal corkscrew.
£12-15   *MAN*

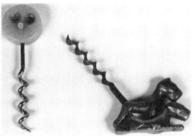

Novelty corkscrews.
£3-10 each   *MAN*

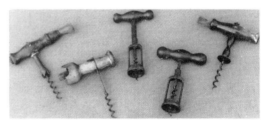

A collection of
corkscrews.
£10-20 each   *TM*

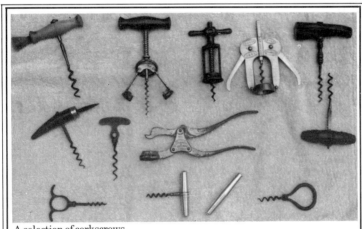

A selection of corkscrews,
with wooden or bone
handles or all metal.
£5-15 each   *MOR*

Corkscrews with
brushes.
£12-20   *MAN*

A spirally fluted
corkscrew, with mother-
of-pearl handle, maker's
mark DF, 18thC.
£400-450   *P*

A combined corkscrew
and bottle opener, The
M.G. Car Company,
Oxford.
£15-20   *FAL*

Dolls

Bisque

Bisque is porcelain at the 'biscuit' stage of manufacture, i.e. the paste is first fired, then left unglazed. Bisque was first used for dolls heads in France and Germany and the best examples usually date between 1860 and 1914. It is thought that the earliest bisque headed dolls were made for use as couturiers' models exhibiting the highest quality of dress and accessories. During the mid-1870s bisque dolls were produced to resemble babies and young children, the best of these bébés being produced by the most collectable (and expensive) manufacturers, e.g. Jumeau, Bru and Descamps.

The German doll makers, notably Armand Marseille, Heubach, Kammer & Reinhardt and Simon & Halbig, never quite achieved the quality of the best French dolls but they did export vast quantities all over the world.

l. A Jumeau bisque-headed bébé, stamped Tête Jumeau with Bébé Jumeau body sticker, damaged, 20in (50cm) high.
£1,300-1,600
r. A Jumeau bisque-headed lady doll, with mohair wig and kid body, incised 7, blue body stamp, damaged and worn, 19in (48cm) high.
£1,000-1,200   CNY

A bisque-headed bébé, with jointed wood and composition body, marked D and with red stamp Deposé Tête Jumeau and stamped in blue on body Bébé Jumeau Diplome d'Honneur, 17½in (44cm) high.
£2,000-2,400   CSK

A bisque three-faced doll's head, probably by Carl Bergner, 3in (7.5cm) high.
£450-550   CSK

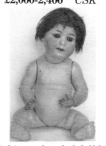

A bisque-headed doll by Heubach Köppelsdorf, 20½in (51cm) high.
£220-250   HCH

DID YOU KNOW?
The bisque dolls made by Huret of Paris always had double chins.

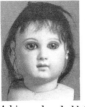

A bisque-headed bébé, with papier mâché and wood body, damage, stamped Jumeau Medaille d'Or Paris, marked EJ9, c1880, 23in (58cm) high.
£2,400-2,600   CSK

A bisque-headed character doll, wearing original clothes, marked S & H 1249 Dep. Santa 8 for Hamburger & Co., 19in (48cm) high.
£650-750   CSK

A bisque-headed character baby doll modelled as Princess Elizabeth, the composition body dressed in whitework dress and underwear, marked Porzellan Fabrik Burggrub Das Lachende Baby 1930-4, 19in (48cm) high.
£450-550   CSK

An Armand Marseille doll, c1905, 14in (35cm) high.
£50-65   Bon

A bisque-headed character baby doll, with composition body, marked J.D.K.16, 20in (50cm) high.
£400-500   CSK

A bisque swivel headed Parisienne, with Geslard body and bisque limbs, 14in (35cm) high.
£1,800-2,000   CSK

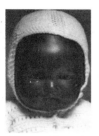

A brown bisque-headed baby doll, the bent limbed composition body dressed in pink and white, marked AM 341/8K, 20in (50cm) high.
£300-400   *CSK*

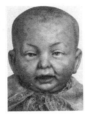

A bisque-headed character baby doll, in original clothes, marked 28K * R100, 10in (25cm) high.
£350-450   *CSK*

A bisque-headed character baby doll, slight damage, marked JDK, 14in (35cm) high.
£450-550   *CSK*

A bisque-headed character baby doll, slight damage, marked JDK, 14in (35cm) high.
£450-550   *CSK*

A bisque-headed child doll, the composition body dressed in cream silk with straw bonnet, marked 192 by Kestner, 18in (45cm) high.
£2,200-2,500   *CSK*

A bisque shoulder headed doll, with stuffed body, 16½in (41cm) high.
£250-350   *CSK*

A bisque-headed character child doll, the jointed wood and composition body dressed in green, marked JDK 260 48, 18in (45cm) high.
£500-600   *CSK*

A small bisque-headed baby doll by Armand Marseille, c1905.
£40-60   *Bon*

DID YOU KNOW?
The eyes for Jumeau dolls were made in a similar way to fine paperweights and the workers had first to serve a five year apprenticeship.

A selection of bisque-headed dolls, all about 17in (43cm) high.
£250-750 each   *CNY*

A bisque-headed character baby doll, marked PM 2314, 23in (58cm) high.
£200-300   *CSK*

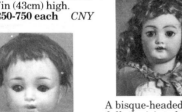

A bisque-headed child doll, the jointed wood and composition body in white with green velvet cape, damaged, marked S&H 1079 Dep.13 and red Wimpern stamp, 29in (73cm) high.
£450-550   *CSK*

A bisque-headed child doll, with jointed wood and composition body, marked Simon & Halbig K*R 46, 18in (45cm) high.
£350-450 *CSK*

A selection of bisque-headed dolls:—
From left to right:
By Jumeau, damaged, stamped and incised E11J, 23in (58cm) high.
£1,200-1,500
By Jumeau, repaired, 23½in (59cm) high.
£1,200-1,500
By Kestner, 23in (58cm) high.
£700-800
By Jumeau with Gesland stamp and sticker, incised 7, 21in (53cm) high.
£500-600 *CNY*

Character dolls

A bisque-headed clockwork walking doll, with metal feet, dressed in khaki uniform, marked S&H 1039 7 Dep, 16in (40cm) high.
£450-550 *CSK*

A Steiff soldier doll, wearing a grey felt uniform, probably Niederschlesisches Infantrie, buttons on soles of boots and in ear, c1915, 20½in (51cm) high.
£350-450 *CNY*

A composition doll modelled as Lord Kitchener, in original uniform, 19in (48cm) high.
£100-150 *CSK*

A cloth doll with moulded felt face, dressed in the uniform of the 17th Lancers, possibly Chad Valley, 18in (46cm) high.
£150-200 *CSK*

Felt

A painted felt child doll, from the 109 series by Lenci, c1927, 22in (55cm) high, in original box.
£350-450 *CSK*

A felt doll modelled as a soldier, marked with Steiff button in ear, c1910, 13in (33cm) high.
£600-700 *CSK*

A painted felt headed portrait doll, modelled as Prince Edward of Kent, marked with the Chad Valley label 1938, 14½in (36cm) high.
£300-400 *CSK*

A painted felt doll, dressed in the costume of Sicily, marked on foot by Lenci, c1941, 15in (38cm) high.
£200-300 *CSK*

A painted felt portrait doll, modelled as Princess Margaret Rose, with Chad Valley label, 16in (40cm) high.
£250-350   *CSK*

Composition

A composition shoulder headed doll, by Joel Ellis of the Co-operative Doll Co., 11in (28cm) high.
£200-250   *CSK*

Originally with clockwork mechanism enabling the doll to walk pushing a pram.

A composition headed portrait doll, marked Madame Alexander Sonja Henie, c1939, 18in (45cm) high.
£150-200   *CSK*

A painted felt portrait doll, modelled as Princess Elizabeth, by Chad Valley, 17½in (44cm) high.
£200-300   *CSK*

Googlie-eyed

A composition mask faced googlie-eyed doll, in original clothes, 9in (23cm) high.
£200-250   *CSK*

A composition mask faced googlie-eyed doll, 13in (33cm) high.
£250-350   *CSK*

A composition mask faced googlie-eyed doll, c1914, 10½in (26cm) high.
£350-450   *CSK*

These dolls were advertised as Hug Me Kiddies in 1914.

DOLLS

A bisque-headed googlie-eyed doll, in original clothes, marked SK 10, 7in (17.5cm) high.
£500-600 *CSK*

A bisque group of 2 googlie-eyed figures, in original hats, by William Goebel, 3½in (9cm) high.
£300-400 *CSK*

A googlie-eyed doll, eyes missing, small chip, marked 172-4, by Herdel Schwab & Co, 15in (38cm) high.
£2,200-2,500 *CSK*

Papier Mâché

A papier mâché headed doll, with white kid body and wooden limbs, in original clothes, c1840, 9in (22.5cm) high.
£120-150 *CSK*

A papier mâché headed doll, c1840, 11in (28cm) high.
£300-400 *CSK*

A papier mâché shoulder headed doll, carrying a wicker basket, 15½in (39cm) high.
£500-550 *CSK*

Wax-Headed

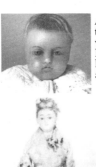

A poured wax baby doll, the stuffed body with wax limbs, possibly by Pierotti, 17in (43cm) high.
£250-300 *CSK*

A poured wax-headed child doll, eyes needing repair, c1810, 22in (55cm) high.
£550-650 *CSK*

Two wax shoulder-headed dolls, 24in (60cm) high.
£100-300 each *CEd*

A poured wax doll, the stuffed body with wax limbs, dressed in white baby gown and cream silk carrying cape and bonnet, the body marked with the oval Lucy Peck, Regent Street stamp, 20½in (52cm) high.
£500-600 *CSK*

Wooden

Small wooden peg dolls by Grödnertal, c1850, 1in (2cm).
£20-30 each *Bon*

A painted wooden Grödnertal doll, in rose silk dress, early 19thC, 5½in (14cm) high.
£450-550 *CSK*

Four dolls with carved wooden heads, made by the Door of Hope Mission in Shanghai, China, in original silk outfits, from 9½ to 12in (24 to 30cm) high.
£300-400 *CSK*

A turned and carved painted wooden doll, with gesso covering, probably taken from a shadow box, c1840, 13in (33cm) high.
£1,000-1,500 *CSK*

Other

Four bisque baby dolls, made in Germany.
£40-50 *CAC*

A pair of piano dolls, the faces painted on cloth, mounted on corks with fine straws enabling them to dance when piano is played, c1830, 2½in (6.5cm) high.
£300-350 *CSK*

A cloth doll, by Käthe Kruse, 18in (45cm) high.
£600-700 *CSK*

A pair of bisque headed dolls house dolls, 5in (12.5cm) high.
£175-200 *CSK*

FURTHER READING
Bateman, Thelma, *Delightful Dolls,* Washington 1966.
Bullard, Helen, *The American Doll Artist,* Boston 1965.
Coleman, Elizabeth A., *Dolls: Makers and Marks,* Washington 1963.
Coleman, Dorothy S., Elizabeth A. and Evelyn J., *The Collector's Encyclopedia of Dolls,* New York 1968.
Faurholt, Estrid and Jacobs, Flora G., *Dolls and Dolls Houses,* Tokyo 1967.
Fraser, Lady Antonia, *Dolls,* London 1963.
Gerken, Jo Elizabeth, *Wonderful Dolls of Wax,* Lincoln (Nebraska) 1964.
Hart, Luella, *Directories of British, French and German Dolls,* Oaklands (Calif) 1964-65.
Hillier, Mary, *Dolls and Dollmakers,* London 1968.
Johnson, A., *Dressing Dolls,* London 1969.
King, Constance, *Dolls & Dolls Houses,* London 1977.
Noble, J., *Dolls,* London 1968.
White, G., *Dolls of the World,* London 1962.
White, G., *European and American Dolls,* London 1966.

Dolls Houses

A painted wooden dolls house with 2 separated storeys, together with furniture and 3in (7.5cm) high bisque doll, Nuremberg, late 19thC, 21in (52.5cm) high.
£300-400 *CSK*

A painted wooden box-type dolls house, with furniture and other German pieces, 35in (88cm) high.
£300-400 *CSK*

A painted wooden box-type dolls house, 25in (63cm) high.
£350-450 *CSK*

A Victorian dolls house, 20½in (51cm) wide.
£300-350 *AP*

A painted wooden dolls house, containing 4 pieces of Dinky furniture and metal fireplace, 16in (40cm) wide.
£250-350 *CSK*

A child's wooden toy theatre, with 9 standing figures, Nuremberg, 28in (70cm) wide.
£200-300 *CSK*

A modern dolls house, containing 7 pastel painted rooms and staircase, c1930, 30½in (76cm) wide.
£500-700 *CNY*

A matchstick dolls house, 10½in (26cm) square.
£20-30 *AL*

A dolls house with 4 rooms, electric lighting, made for charity, c1920.
£400-450 *CAC*

A French painted wooden toy stable, 18in (45.5cm) high.
£150-200 *CSK*

A painted wooden dolls house, opening to reveal 5 rooms with hall and staircase, with 4 metal fireplaces, including kitchen range and nursery fire, 43in (109cm) high.
£700-750 *CSK*

A painted wooden box-type dolls house, by Silber and Fleming, 13in (32.5cm) high.
£100-150 *CSK*

A wooden dolls house, with white painted 'Gothic' details and brass pediment, opening to reveal 2 rooms, each with 2 fireplaces and green painted walls, 23in (58cm) high.
£1,000-1,500 *CSK*

Dolls House Furniture

A late Georgian yellow japanned metal dolls house bath, 3in (7cm) wide, together with other miscellaneous items.
£100-150 *CSK*

A quantity of dolls house furniture.
£330-380 *CSK*

A dolls mahogany half tester bed, 23in (58.5cm) and doll.
£250-300 *CSK*

A set of varnished dolls house furniture.
£300-350 *CSK*

A set of simulated satinwood dolls house furniture, the chairs upholstered in pale blue silk, some damage.
£300-400 *CSK*

A dolls house gas fire and coal fire.
£15-25 *CAC*

An enamelled metal bathroom suite.
£50-60 *CAC*

133

DOLLS HOUSES

A miniature grand piano, probably Viennese, late 19thC, 3in (7.5cm) long.
£200-300 *CSK*

A group of Waltershausen dolls house furniture.
£750-850 *CSK*

Dolls House Equipment

A selection of accessories, the gloves 2½in (6cm) long.
£280-300 *CSK*

A selection of dolls house pieces.
£2-10 *CAC*

A miniature teaset.
£25-30 *VB*

Dolls house china ware.
£20-25 *CAC*

A turned and painted wooden dolls dinner service, in original box, German.
£550-650 *CSK*

A German turned and painted wooden dolls house tea service, in cream and blue gold leaf design, early 19thC, in original bentwood box.
£350-400 *CSK*

A late Georgian brass
and steel firegrate, 4in
(10cm) wide, together
with pewter dish covers
and tin chamber light.
£400-500 *CSK*

A Victorian brown and
white transfer ware part
tea service, with the
Cinderella pattern.
£20-40 each piece *MAN*

Dolls Prams

A c1910 model, larger
than the others.
£95-130 *PWA*

A c1910 model.
£55-65 *PWA*

A late Victorian coach
built dolls pram, with
2 seats and foot well, the
4 wheels with rubber
tyres.
£350-450 *HSS*

A c1900 model, in green.
£60-85 *PWA*

A wooden dolls pram,
28in (71cm) long.
£350-400 *CSK*

A c1920 model, 3½in
(9cm) wide.
£50-60 *PWA*

A 1930 model, 4in (10cm)
high.
£40-50 *PWA*

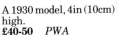

Drinking

Advertising

A Spode Bell's Whisky bottle, c1950.
£5-10 *CAC*

A Williams & Humbert sherry figure.
£50-60 *CHA*

A rubber figure advertising Guinness, c1960.
£20-30 *COB*
A Guinness tortoise, c1935, 3½in (9cm) long.
£40-60 *BEV*
A toucan, c1950.
£35-55 *COB*
A Carltonware toucan, c1935.
£200-250 *BEV*

A Royal Doulton figure of 'The Old Crow' for Bourbon, c1960, 13in (32cm) high.
£90-130 *TP*

A Royal Doulton Grouse Liqueur whisky bottle, 10in (25cm) high.
£30-40 *TP*

Beakers

A pair of horn beakers with silver tops, 18thC, 4in (10cm) high.
£35-45 each *CAC*

Horn beakers, 4in and 5in (10cm and 12.5cm) high.
£10-15 each *OSc*

A collapsible beaker, in a leather case.
£8-10 *VB*

A horn beaker, 6in (15cm).
£30-35 *CAC*

Cocktails

An Art Deco glass cocktail set, with gilt decoration.
£200-300 *CSK*

A cocktail set, the silver plated sticks with cherry tops, c1930.
£50-60 *BEV*

A silver plate cocktail shaker with measures, c1930.
£150-200 *BEV*

A cocktail set including silver Martini sticks with clips, c1933.
£100-140 *BEV*

A cocktail set, c1930, in original box.
£30-50 *BEV*

A cocktail and cheese set with Bakelite handles, c1930, in original box.
£35-55 *BEV*

A silver plate and Bakelite cocktail recipe holder, with recipes, 4in (10cm) high.
£65-75 *BEV*

A set of cocktail sticks, c1930.
£35-45 *BEV*

A cocktail shaker and silver plated goblets, c1935.
£175-225 *BEV*

Cross Reference
Corkscrews
Glasses
Wine Labels

Ice Buckets

A pair of silver plate champagne buckets by Mappin & Webb, with the Dorchester Hotel motif, c1935.
£450-500 *BEV*

A W.M.F. spiral pattern champagne bucket, c1895.
£350-450 *BEV*

A chrome and black Bakelite champagne/ice bucket, with lid, c1930.
£125-175 *BEV*

An Art Deco cocktail cabinet, with chrome fittings, 17in (43cm) wide, on wooden stand.
£550-650 *P*

Egg Cups

Collectable egg cups are primarily fun
items, mostly available for less than £5.
We have endeavoured here to include the
most collectable areas, some of which,
particularly commemorative ware and
Victorian character faces, are likely to
prove good value for the future. Older egg
cups, as can be seen in *Miller's Antiques
Price Guide,* especially Spode, Copeland
and Worcester, are valuable but don't be
deterred as a Clarice Cliff or a Martinware
piece can still easily be discovered.

Egg cups advertising
Robertson's Jams,
Guinness and McVitie's
Digestive Biscuits.
£10-15 each   *PC*

Esso advertising egg cup.
£5-10   *COB*

Animal egg
cups.
£3-6 each
PC

Children's
characters.
£3-5 each
PC

Sooty is particularly
sought after.
£5-10 each   *PC*

A white porcelain egg cup.
£5-7 *AL*

A selection of animal egg cups.
£3-6 each *PC*

A pottery egg cup.
£4-6 *AL*

5 Spode egg cups.
£15-20 *CAC*

Victorian faces.
£15-18 each *BEV*

Children's characters.
£3-5 each *PC*

Egg cups on stand, c1930.
£10-15 *CAC*

A multi-sized egg cup.
£4-6 *AL*

Caricatures.
£6-8 each *PC*

A pair of egg cups.
£3-4 *AL*

EGG CUPS

Various egg cups.
£4-6 each *PC*

A Ladybird pattern
German egg cup.
£3-5 *PC*

A Poole Pottery egg cup.
£2-4 *CAC*

Transfer ware egg cups.
£4-5 each *AL*

Commemorative.
l. & c. Coronation
Edward VIII, 1937.
r. Silver Jubilee, 1935.
£6-10 each *PC*

Oriental egg cups.
£3-5 each *PC*

A plastic egg cup with
wooden brick egg cup.
£3-5 each *PC*

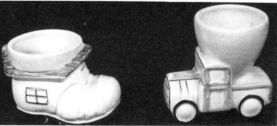

Novelty egg cups.
£3-5 each *PC*

Transfer ware egg cups.
£4-5 each *PC*

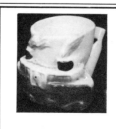 

Boat, with whistle.
£30-35
Aeroplane.
£3-5 *PC*

140

Wooden egg cups, c1950.
£3-5 each *PC*

A Devon & Torquay
Pottery egg cup.
£6-8 *JO*

An egg cosy, c1950.
£5-10 *PC*

Silver plated egg cups.
£4-6 *VB*

A Martinware egg cup
set, 7in (18cm) diam.
£600-700 *VDB*

Oriental, c1900.
£3-5 each *PC*

A selection of egg cups.
£3-5 each *PC*

Oriental egg cups.
£4-6 each *VB*

A lustre egg cup.
£4-5 *AL*

Also refer to *Miller's
Antiques Price Guide
1989*
p.108 Coalport egg cup.
£30-40
p.110 Chamberlain's
Worcester egg cup, in
yellow and gilt, c1800.
£250-300

Cross Reference
Ceramics
Glass
Toys
Treen

EPHEMERA
Autographs

Actors & Actresses

Nijinsky.
£600-900   *N*

SARAH BERNHARDT

Sarah Bernhardt.
£140-180   *N*

Rudolf Valentino.
£550-850   *N*

EILLE NORWOOD AS "SHERLOCK HOLMES"

Eille Norwood as
Sherlock Holmes.
£40-60   *N*

*Eille Norwood is
almost unknown, but the
fact that he was
portraying Sherlock
Holmes makes the picture
valuable.*

BELA LUGOSI

Bela Lugosi, signed in
red (blood?).
£150-250   *N*

MARILYN MONROE

Marilyn Monroe.
£800-1,200   *N*

Deanna Durbin.
£20-30   *N*

Tallulah Bankhead.
£20-30   *N*

Errol Flynn, signed by
secretary.
Under £1   *N*

Joan Crawford.
£16-22   *N*

DID YOU KNOW?

The main value of an autograph is directly related to
the content, especially letters, etc.

* Especially sought after, e.g. Composer/musician
  = few bars of music, artist = sketch/doodle.
* Autographed Ephemera — signatures on
  cheques, receipts, bills, etc.
* Signed copies of books.
* Autographed letter (A.L) written in hand of
  person concerned.
* Letter (signed) (L.S).
* Autographed document (A.Docs), wills, etc.
* Document signed (D.S) State documents, etc.
* Typewritten letter (T.L)
* Autographed photos and postcards.

Stan Laurel and Oliver Hardy.
£375-450 *N*

Sir Lawrence Olivier and Vivien Leigh.
£120-180 *N*

Humphrey Bogart and Lauren Bacall.
£800-1,200 *N*

Marlene Dietrich.
£20-30 *N*

Bette Davies.
£15-20 *N*

Orson Welles.
£30-50 *N*

Bing Crosby.
£30-40 *N*

Robert Donat.
£20-30 *N*

Military

U.S. Army Commission, signed U.S. Grant.
£450-650 *N*

Montgomery of Alamein.
£50-80 *N*

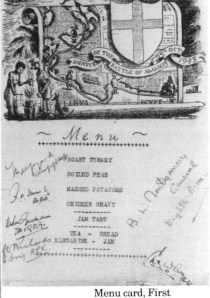

Menu card, First Anniversary of the battle of El Alamein. A scarce menu in itself.
£150-200 *N*

American

Ronald and Nancy Reagan, signed commemorative postcard, 1982.
£40-60   *N*

Dwight Eisenhower.
£140-180   *N*

Mark Twain.
£400-600   *N*

Harry Houdini.
£300-400   *N*

Music

DID YOU KNOW?
A New York waiter collected autographs by writing to celebrities at the beginning of their careers. In 1960, Woody Allen replied: 'As I am a new act, I do not as yet have professional photos. In fact, it was only recently that I acquired an autograph.'

Louis Armstrong.
£120-180   *N*

Fats Waller.
£200-300   *N*

Giacomo Puccini.
£300-400   *N*

The Beatles.
£150-250   *N*

Royalty

Queen Victoria.
£800-1,200   *N*

George V and Queen Mary.
£200-400 each   *N*

DID YOU KNOW?
Every signature is an autograph but not every autograph is a signature!

Prince Edward's Christening, signed by Philip.
£400-700   *N*

Sporting

Jack Dempsey.
£40-60 *N*

Babe Ruth.
£550-750 *N*

W. G. Grace.
£100-140 *N*

Signed photograph of
Don Bradman's 40th
birthday cake, Lords,
1948.
£10-15 *PC*

Max Baer.
£20-30 *N*

General

George Bernard Shaw, a
specially bound Malvern
Festival programme.
£300-500 *N*

Albert Schweitzer.
£200-300 *N*

A leather autograph
book, with drawings.
£5-15 *CAC*

FURTHER READING
Benjamin, Mary A., *Autographs: A Key to Collecting,*
New York 1946.
Charnwood, Lady, *An Autograph Collection,* London
1930.
Munby, A. N. L., *The Cult of the Autograph Letter in
England,* London 1962.

The British Antarctic
Expedition 1907-1909.
£300-500 *N*

Beer Mats

Although beer mats are very collectable, many collections having tens of thousands of examples, they are not, generally, very expensive. Most beer mats have no particular value, being only worth what another collector is prepared to pay.

A collection from obsolete breweries, pre-war.
£2-5 each   *RS*

A collection from current breweries, post-war.
Under £2 each   *RS*

A collection of obsolete breweries beer mats, post-war.
£4-6 each   *RS*

A collection of very rare obsolete breweries beer mats, post-war.
£4-6 each   *RS*

A collection from current breweries, pre-war.
£2-5 each   *RS*

Four rare beer mats from obsolete breweries, pre-war.
£5-10 each   *RS*

A collection from obsolete breweries, post-war.
£2-5 each   *RS*

Commemorative mats,
1948-53.
£1-2 each   *RS*

A collection of various
designs, 1950-60s.
Under £1 each   *RS*

A commemorative beer
mat, Coronation 1953.
£1-3   *RS*

A rare war-time issue,
1939-45.
£3-5   *RS*

Various shapes, 1950-
60s.
under £1 each   *RS*

DID YOU KNOW?
The first beer mats were produced by Watney's
Brewery in 1922 to advertise their Pale Ale.
In 1960 Chris Walsh from Coventry placed an
advertisement for beer mats in *Exchange and Mart*.
The response was so tremendous that the British
Beer Mat Society was formed and is still thriving
today.

Various shapes, 1950-
70s.
Under £1 each   *RS*

A jig-saw of 4 mats.
Under 50p each   *RS*

A set of 4 Guinness Irish
universities, and
5 'British Pastimes',
c1960.
Under 30p each   *RS*

Kentish beer mats.
Under £1 each *RS*

Two beer mats and
2 cocktail mats, c1987.
Under £1 each *RS*

Two cartoon mats, c1961.
£1-2 each *RS*

Mansfield humorous
mats, 1978.
Under 10p each *RS*

Cork beer mats.
£3-5 each *RS*

Two giant mats for jugs,
c1967.
Under 50p each *RS*

Six rare Mac's second set
of vintage cars, c1959.
40p each *RS*

Six 'Black Country
Traditions', c1984.
Under 10p each *RS*

Two humorous mats.
Under £1 each *RS*

Books

A Louis Wain paperback annual, 1908, cover slightly damaged.
£30-40   *N*

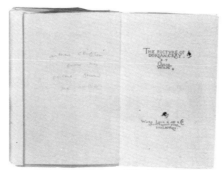

The Picture of Dorian Gray, by Oscar Wilde, first edition, first issue with misprint on p.208, inscribed by the author, original parchment backed boards, slight damage, Mason 328, London 1891.
£500-800   *P*

The Happy Prince and other Tales, by Oscar Wilde, second edition, inscribed and signed by author, illustrated by W. Crane and J. Hood, original boards, soiled, Mason 315, 1889.
£800-1,200   *P*

Seven publicity leaflets by W. Heath Robinson.
£120-150   *ONS*

A song folio, with accompaniment for piano or organ by favourite composers, c1883.
£5-10   *MB*

The Works of George Eliot, 24 volumes, cabinet edition, Edinburgh and London, 1878-85, bound by Riviere & Son in later half morocco, slight rubbing.
£500-800   *CSK*

The Sphinx, Oscar Wilde, first edition, inscribed and signed, illustrated in green and red by Charles Ricketts, slight damage, Mason 361, 1894.
£2,000-3,000   *P*

Eighteen poems by Dylan Thomas, first edition, inscribed on front endpaper with caricature, 1945.
£800-1,000   *P*

Just So Stories, by Rudyard Kipling, first edition, some damage, 1902.
£300-400   *CSK*

Bound volume of The Florist, c1860.
£150-350   *PC*

Price depends on condition and the number of colour plates. Many volumes, although in good condition, have some plates missing. Other volumes are magazines bound together and these are not so valuable.

FURTHER READING

Carter, John, *The ABC of Book Collecting,* London 1964.
Muir, Percy, *English Children's Books,* London 1954.
Spielman, P. E., *Catalogue of the Library of Miniature Books,* London 1961.

Comics and Annuals

Annuals and comics are today more widely collected than ever before, and in some instances very high prices have been achieved.

Jumble sales and second-hand book shops are always good sources for bargains. Compulsive hoarders may be surprised to find that their collections of nostalgic comics and annuals in their lofts and attics are now highly desirable.

Bobby Bear's Annual, 1935.
£8-10 *HE*

Daily Express Children's Annual, No. 4, with pop-up pictures, 1935.
£20-30 *HE*

Annuals

Gulliver's Travels Music Album, 1939.
£5-6 *HE*

Buffalo Bill Annual, 1951.
£4-6 *HE*

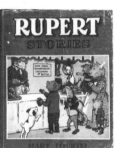

Rupert Stories, 1950.
£12-15 *HE*

Not as collectable as Rupert annuals.

T.V. Century 21 Annual, 1966.
£6-8 *HE*

T.V. Comic Annual, undated, c1955.
£3-4 *HE*

Beano annual, 1955.
£30-35 *HE*

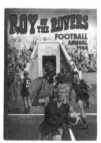

Roy of the Rovers Football Annual, 1958.
£7-9 *HE*

Dandy annual, 1960.
£15-20 *HE*

School Friend Annual, 1956.
£2-3 *HE*

Pinky and Perky Annual, 1964.
£2-3 *HE*

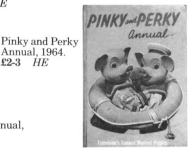

Eagle Annual, 1965.
£3-5 *HE*

Playbox Annual, 1951.
£2-3   *HE*

Fireball XL5 Annual,
1965.
£8-12   *HE*

Stingray Annual, 1966.
£5-7   *HE*

The Broons 1985 and Oor
Wullie 1986 annuals,
popular in Scottish
newspapers, drawn by
Dudley Watkins.
£2-3 each   *HE*

Comics

Tiny Tots, 1939.
£2-3   *HE*

Tiger Tim's Weekly,
1937.
£2-3   *HE*

Rupert annual, 1967.
£4-7   *HE*

*Rupert annuals are very
desirable, in some
instances reaching
several hundreds of
pounds.*

The Hotspur, 1947.
£1-2   *HE*

Rainbow, 1949.
£1-2   *HE*

The Wizard, Jan 1950.
£1-2   *HE*

Film Fun, 1954.
£2-3   *HE*

Knock-Out, c1945,
scarce war-time issues.
£4-6 each   *HE*

The Rover, 1950.
£1-2   *HE*

Chips, 1953, black type
face on pink paper.
£1-2   *HE*

The Topper, 1955.
£1-2   *HE*

151

EPHEMERA/COMICS

Eagle No. 1, 1950.
£50-75 *HE*

Express Weekly, 1959.
£1-2 *HE*

Girl 1956, companion to Eagle.
£1-2 *HE*

Lion 1956.
£1-2 *HE*

Sun 1955.
£1-2 *HE*

The Beano, Dec 1958.
£3-4 *HE*

T.V. Fun, 1958.
£1-2 *HE*

Cowboy comics, c1950.
£2-3 *HE*

The Dandy, 1956.
£1-2 *HE*

Boy's World, First issue 1963.
£2-3 *HE*

The Beano, December 1959.
£3-4 *HE*

The Beano, No. 1,000, September 1961.
£3-4 *HE*

The Dandy, 1962.
£1-2 *HE*

The Victor, 1968.
Under £1 *HE*

Comet 1957.
£1-2 *HE*

The main nostalgia period at the moment is the late 1950s.

Pow! 1968.
Under £1 *HE*

Tiger 1964.
Under £1 *HE*

Smash! 1969.
Under £1 *HE*

Smash! 1966, reprints of American Marvels.
Under £1 *HE*

Boys' World, 1963.
Under £1 *HE*

School Stories

Valiant, 1970.
£1-2 *HE*

The Magnet, orange and blue cover, No. 1467, 1936.
£7-10 *PC*

The Magnet, mauve cover, No. 1663, 1939.
£5-8 *PC*

Cigarette Cards

Beauties

A selection of cigarette
cards by J. & F. Bell Ltd,
1887, FR-G.
£20-30 each *N*

Cigarette cards originated in the United States as stiffeners for the newly introduced cigarette pack. It is generally accepted that the oldest surviving card dates from the late 1870s, being issued in the States by Marquis of Lorne cigarettes. This card now has an honoured place in New York's Metropolitan Museum.

Early examples were printed on one side only, but by the mid-1880s descriptive matter was usually to be found on the reverse of the picture. The tobacco 'wars' at the end of the 19th Century resulted in the production of millions of often superbly produced cards designed to persuade smokers to change — or remain faithful to — their brand. The period up to the First World War is therefore a fruitful and often rewarding period for the serious collector, though later issues of the twenties and thirties are currently showing a somewhat disappointing return on investment.

Allen & Ginter —
World's Beauties, second
series.
£40-50 set *P*

Ardath Tobacco Co.,
manufacturers of State
Express and Ardath
cigarettes, a series of 50
cards entitled 'Who is
this?'.
10-30p each
£10-15 set *MS*

Taddy's Actresses —
Harriet Vernon, 1897.
£30-40 each *N*

Glass & Co. Actresses —
S. Arnoldson, slight
creasing, G.
£15-20 each *N*

GLOSSARY
Conditions
EX — Excellent
MT — Mint
VG — Very Good
F — Fine
G — Good
FR — Fair
P — Poor
VR — Varying Condition
Where sets or part sets are indicated, this does not necessarily imply that the set is complete.

Godfrey Phillips —
Beauties, c1898.
£30-50 each *WIN*

Wills's Cigarettes — a
set of 25 cinema stars,
second series, 1928.
£8-10 the set *WIN*

Richmond Cavendish —
Beauties, c1905.
£20-32 each *WIN*

Godfrey Phillips —
Actresses, Series C,
slight creasing, G.
£25-35 *N*

Hignett Bros.
— Pretty
Girls, 1900, P-G.
£35-45 *N*

Kinnears Actresses,
Esme Beringer.
£25-35 each *N*

Lambert & Butler —
Actresses and their
autographs, Ellen Terry
1898.
£30-50 each *N*

Hignett's — Actresses,
slight damage, FR-G.
£35-45 *N*

Fauna

Wills's Cigarettes — a
series of 50 dogs, 1937.
£5-10 set *WIN*

DID YOU KNOW?_____

Important points to consider when pricing cigarette
cards.
* Condition is all important, even if a card is very
  highly catalogued, any damage will significantly
  reduce the value. The more valuable the card, the
  more critical the condition.
* A premium is paid for complete sets.
* Fashion — of the many and varied subjects
  covered by cigarette card issues, some are always
  popular, i.e. military, cricket and railway interest,
  whereas others are popular for shorter periods.

155

EPHEMERA/CIGARETTE CARDS

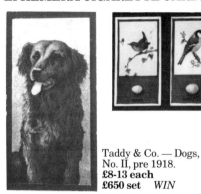

Taddy & Co. — Dogs,
No. II, pre 1918.
£8-13 each
£650 set   *WIN*

Godfrey Phillips & Co. —
British Birds and their
Eggs, series of 50, 1936.
£10-20 set   *MS*

Franklyn Davey & Co. —
5 Birds, 1896, FR-G.
£70-90   *N*

Players — An album of
50 game birds and wild
fowl, c1927.
£8-20 set   *WIN*

Godfrey Phillips & Co. —
Animal Studies, a series
of 30, 1936.
£4-5 set   *WIN*

Heraldic

Wills's Cigarettes — A
series of 25 Arms of
Universities, May 1923.
£15-25 set   *WIN*

Kensitas — silk cigarette
cards, British Empire
flags, 1933.
£12-24 set   *WIN*

Kensitas — silk cigarette cards.
from £1 each *MS*

These have increased in price over the last year.

Wills's Cigarettes — A set of 50 Borough Arms, 1905.
£10-20 set *WIN*

Military

E. Robinson & Sons — Medals and decorations, slight adhesion marks:
l. Victoria Cross
c. Royal Red Cross
r. Albert Medal
£30-40 each *N*

Dobson Molle & Co. — V.C. Heroes, 1916, FR-G.
£100-150 set *N*

Wills's Cigarettes — Waterloo set, in excellent condition.
£1,800-3,500 *N*

This set remained unissued because we were allies of France in 1915. The key card in the set of 50 was Napoleon.

157

John Player & Sons —
Regimental uniforms, a
set of 50.
£14-18 set   *MS*

Edwards Ringer & Bigg
— Easter Manoeuvres,
c1897.
£200-225 each   *N*

W. & F. Faulkner —
Grenadier Guards, 1899,
FR-G.
£25-35   *N*

Salmon & Gluckstein
Ltd. — Heroes of the
Transvaal War, P-G.
£45-55   *N*

W. A. & A. C. Churchman
— Boer War Generals,
1901, MacDonald,
Coalville, Plumer, G-VG.
£15-20   *N*

Cohen Weenan — Home
and Colonial Regiments,
G-VG.
£26-32   *N*

Royalty

Glass & Co. — British
Royal Family, Queen
Victoria, slight damage,
about G.
£10-15 each   *N*

Taddy & Co. — Royalty
series, 1902.
£8-10 each   *WIN*

Wills's — Unissued
series, the Life of H.M.
King Edward VIII, a set
of 50, VG-EX.
£200-300 set   *P*

Kinnear Ltd. — Royalty,
Duke of York, 1897,
G-VG.
£8-12 each   *N*

Sporting

John Player & Sons — A
series of 40 Racing
Caricatures.
£4-6 set   *MS*

Taddy — Famous
Jockeys, G+.
£80-120 set   *P*

John Cotton — Golf
strokes, series A-B,
mainly VG.
£50-70 set   *P*

A series of 50 famous footballers issued with Ardath Cork and State Express 333.
£5-7 set *MS*

SOUTH AFRICAN CRICKET TEAM, 1907.

TOD. SLOAN.

Kinnear Ltd. — Jockeys, with owners name.
£8-12 each *N*

Singleton & Cole — Footballers, 1905.
£5-10 each *N*

J. W. HEARNE MIDDLESEX

S. D. SNOOKE.

Taddy & Co. — South African Cricket Team, 1907.
£25-40 each *WIN*

SALMON & GLUCKSTEIN'S HIGH CLASS Cigarettes

Cohen Weenan — Cricketers, a set of 25, VG.
£50-70 set *P*

Salmon & Gluckstein — Owners and Jockeys series of 6, G+.
£50-80 set *P*

WILLS'S CIGARETTES

YORKSHIRE CRICKET Vanity Fair. 1ˢᵗ Series Nº 2

Wills's — Vanity Fair, first series 1902, slight damage, G-EX.
£50-70 *N*

FLOWERS NOTTS

Wills's — Cricketers, 1896, G.
£15-20 each *N*

KINNEAR'S HANDICAP CIGARETTES

Kinnear Ltd. — Australian Cricket Teams, some damage, otherwise G.
£25-35 each *N*

CHICAGO

F. JONES, CHICAGO.

A.T.C. — Baseball Series, some wear, mainly G.
£7-12 each *P*

DID YOU KNOW?
* During the wages strike in the cigarette industry in 1920, Taddy's owner, Gilliate Hatfield, was so upset that his workers had joined the strike that he closed the company down and destroyed all the records.
* Mardin, Son & Hall, Printers of Bristol, part of the Imperial Tobacco Co., printed all cigarette cards. Bombed in 1940, all printing plates were destroyed so unable to repeat series.
* Records kept by Lunn Cigarette Card Co. from 1920-1940.

159

Transport

A collection of Players automobile cigarette cards, in 1d album, compiled 1936.
£7-8   *FAL*

Hignett Bros. — Yacht, Britannia, slight damage, G.
£18-24   *N*

Carreras — original artwork for a series of 50 Famous Airmen and Airwomen, watercolours, 8 by 4in (20 by 10cm).
£700-1,200   *N*

A set of 50 cards, entitled Speed, 1938.
£3-6 set   *WIN*

H. Y. Archer & Co., a series of 50 famous ships issued by R. & J. Hill Ltd.
£6-8 set   *MS*

General

Franklyn Davey — Types of Smokers, G-VG.
£18-25   *N*

A.T.C. — A series of cards from various songs, VR.
£100-140 set   *P*

Cope Bros. — Chinese series, slight adhesion marks, generally G.
£40-50   *N*

John Sinclair — World's Coinage, a set of 50 cards, VG.
£200-250 set   *P*

Ogdens, a branch of the Imperial Tobacco Co. — a series of 50 cut-out cards called Children of All Nations, c1924.
£10-20 set *MS*

B.D.V. Cigarettes — large silk card of Sir Edward Carson.
£2-3 each *MS*

B.D.V. Cigarettes — large silk card of President Wilson.
£2-3 each *WIN*

A set of old Inns, 1936.
£20-40 set *WIN*

Gallaher — A set of 25 cards of Views in North of Ireland, slight damage, otherwise VG.
£300-400 *P*

Wills's — Musical Celebrities, 8 original withdrawn cards from the second series, v. rare, VG-EX.
£400-600 *P*

Players — Everyday Phrases, by Tom Brown, 1900, a set of 25, slight damage, VG-EX.
£80-120 set *N*

Players — a set of 25 cards of the Treasures of Britain.
£12-20 set *WIN*

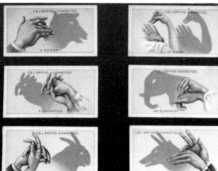

F. & J. Smith, Imperial Tobacco Co. — a series of 25 shadowgraphs.
£3-5 each
£50-100 set *MS*

FURTHER READING

Bagnall, Dorothy, *Collecting Cigarette Cards,* London 1965.
Bagnall, Dorothy, *Catalogue of British Cigarette Cards 1888-1949,* London 1975.
For further information, send sae to:
The London Cigarette Card Company Ltd.
Sutton Road
Somerton
Somerset
TA11 6QP

Greetings Cards

Birthday Cards

A card with glitter and
verse, late 19thC.
£2-3   *PC*

A Victorian card, the tab
at the bottom pulls to
reveal mottos under each
picture.
£10-12   *PC*

A Very Happy Birthday.
£4-5   *WIN*

Birthday Greetings.
£1-2   *WIN*

Hearty Greetings.
Under £1   *WIN*

Picture frame greetings
card.
50p-£1   *PC*

Inspirational card, early
20thC.
50p-£1   *PC*

A sampler envelope with message.
£2-3 *PC*

Blessings.
£2-3 *WIN*

Good Tidings.
£1-2 *WIN*

Christmas Cards

A Merry Christmas to you.
£1.50-2 *WIN*

Christmas Blessings.
£4-5 *WIN*

DID YOU KNOW?
The first Christmas card made its appearance in 1843 when Henry Cole asked J. C. Horsley RA to design a greetings card for his friends. Horsley designed a three-fold card showing a happy festive family group flanked by side panels depicting "Feeding the hungry and clothing the naked". About a thousand were produced by line engraving and then hand-coloured. They sold at a shilling each (a tidy sum then). De la Rue reprinted this card, using chromolithography, in 1887.

A Christmas card with an owl.
£3-4 *WIN*

Easter

Jesus Christ is Risen Today.
£5-6 *WIN*

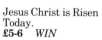

Easter Greetings, c1900.
£1.50-£2 *WIN*

Hearty Easter Greetings.
£3.50-4 *WIN*

Greetings card from Paris.
£3-4 *WIN*

General

Best New Year Wishes.
£3-4 *WIN*

Portrait greetings card.
£1-2 *WIN*

Valentines

A valentine card with gold embossed border and hand coloured inset.
£25-35   *IMA*

A valentine card with black border and hand coloured stencil in centre, printed and published by Wrigley, Manchester, c1850.
£30-35   *IMA*

A valentine card with raised lace border in white and pale blue satin with coloured painted scrap in the centre, was perfumed.
£30-40   *IMA*

A Valentine card in the form of a sampler on silk ribbon, 1865.
£5-8   *PC*

Valentine card with verse.
£5-6   *VB*

DID YOU KNOW?
St. Valentine, the Christian martyr beheaded on 14th February, 270 AD, was renowned for his chastity!

DID YOU KNOW?
The last great Valentine-sending era came briefly in the 1950s before rising postage costs put too high a price on love by mail.

Valentine card, probably American.
£20-25 each   *IMA*

A collection of unused Art Deco Valentine cards in original envelopes.
£40-50   *P*

'An Earnest Appeal' valentine card, with raised border, hand coloured centre illustration with 4 cabochon jewels.
£50-60 *IMA*

A valentine card with hand coloured centre, c1850.
£30-40 *IMA*

DID YOU KNOW?

Insults on Valentine's Day are nothing new — at the turn of the century scurrilous messages accused recipients of being spiteful, vain, flirtatious, miserly, ugly and scandalous! Not surprisingly, few of these have survived!

An insulting valentine card, tab makes head nod up and down.
£50-60 *IMA*

A valentine card with woven silk centre, dated 1874.
£15-20 *IMA*

A hand coloured lithograph valentine card.
£50-60 *IMA*

Valentine card, possibly American.
£25-30 *IMA*

A valentine card envelope and fold-over card, German.
£20-25 *IMA*

FURTHER READING

Lee, Ruth W., *A History of Valentines,* London 1953.
Staff, Frank, *The Valentine and its Origins,* London 1969.

Music Covers

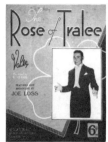

Selection of 1930s sheet music.
£1-2 each   *PC*

Musicals between 1946 and 1949.
50p-£1 each   *PC*

Song album with music, c1937.
50p-£1   *PC*

Sheet music, 1945, Harry Leader and his orchestra.
50p-£1   *PC*

Advertising Postcards & Posters

Many successful and popular posters were reproduced on postcards. All the examples illustrated here are postcards and priced as such. The original posters, when available, can be as much as ten times more than the postcard price.

Meckumfat Poultry Food, VG to Ex.
£15-20 *N*

Faulder's Chocolates, VG to Ex.
£30-40 *N*

Cobra Polish, boot boy and maid VG to Ex.
£16-22 *N*

Camp Coffee, c1910, VG.
£20-30 *N*

Apollinaris

"POLLY" AND SCOTCH

Mineral Water, Apollinaris, by Ludlow, VG.
£16-22 *N*

Park Drive Cigarettes, Ex to MT.
£20-30 *N*

Fry's Cocoa and Chocolate, G to VG.
From £15-35 each *N*

SAVORY
- THE CIGARETTE -

Savory, The Cigarette, by Hassler, 1923, VG to Ex.
£30-40 *N*

Lucerna Chocolate, slight crease, G.
£20-30 *N*

Brown & Polson's Cornflour, G to VG.
£25-35 *N*

Persil, VG.
£18-25 *N*

Cross Reference
Posters
Postcards
Ephemera General

Posters

Most posters pre-dating 1939 have a value; the subject is all important. Particularly collectable are transport themes (see Cross Reference) and advertising household products. Posters of artistic merit and those which have since become advertising milestones are also desirable.

Rarity and damage can affect values drastically. The most common posters must be in pristine condition to demand good prices.

Aynho Station, G.W.R., c1886.
£30-40   *COB*

Grand Evening Soiree, c1889.
£30-40   *COB*

Peak Frean & Co. poster, c1890.
£80-90   *COB*

Notice, c1905.
£40-50   *COB*

The Church Army Huts, Open to All, on linen.
£12-15   *ONS*

Army Boxing, 1938.
£10-15   *COB*

Evening News, November 27th 1939.
£10-15   *COB*

A Mercedes Benz poster showing military vehicles and planes, 13 by 9½in (33 by 24cm), framed and glazed.
£60-100   *CSK*

Air France to South America, c1954.
£70-80   *COB*

Lend to Defend the Right to be Free, c1940.
£15-20   *COB*

Cunard White Star – New York World's Fair, c1939.
£14-20   *COB*

Cross Reference
Aeronautica
Advertising Postcards
Railway
Shipping

Wartime Posters

At The Front!
£120-150 *ONS*

There's Room for You,
Enlist Today.
£70-80 *ONS*

Remember the
'Lusitania', c1915.
£70-80 *COB*

Bad Form in Dress,
poster on linen.
£60-80 *ONS*

If the Cap Fits You, Join
the Army Today.
£30-40 *ONS*

Follow Me! Your Country
Needs You.
£80-100 *ONS*

National Service,
Women Clerks wanted.
£160-200 *ONS*

Life-Boat Day, Tuesday,
May 1st 1917.
£50-70 *ONS*

Nearest Army Recruiting
Office, 1914-18.
£8-10 *COB*

Enlist Today – Lord
Kitchener, on linen.
£50-70 *ONS*

Missing! To the Sisters of
the Red Cross.
£60-100 *ONS*

'Daddy, what did you do
in the Great War?'
£250-300 *ONS*

Who's Absent? Is It You?
on linen.
£60-70 *ONS*

Women are working Day
and Night to Win the
War, linen poster.
£80-100 *ONS*

Are You in This?
£130-150 *ONS*

Don't, a poster published by the National Organising Committee, on linen.
£40-60 *ONS*

Roll of Honour, poster on card, 16 by 13½in (41 by 34cm).
£30-40 *ONS*

Single Men Show your Appreciation, poster on linen.
£55-75 *ONS*

Your King and Country Need You.
£80-100 *ONS*

Come Along Boys, Enlist Today, poster with Welsh text.
£80-100 *ONS*

Subscribe to the 5½% Loan, on linen, 38 by 26in (96 by 66cm).
£110-120 *ONS*

War Savings, by Norma Wilkinson.
£45-55 *COB*

Posters by Norma Wilkinson are very much sought after

Lord Kitchener Says: poster on linen.
£90-100 *ONS*

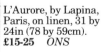

Pour La France, Versez Votre Or, damp stained, 47 by 32in (118 by 80cm).
£15-25 *ONS*

L'Aurore, by Lapina, Paris, on linen, 31 by 24in (78 by 59cm).
£15-25 *ONS*

Victory, 1915.
£45-55 *COB*

Serbia's Defender, Bomb Thrower of Fourteen, poster on linen.
£60-80 *ONS*

Emprunt National, Souscrivez, on linen, 47 by 32in (118 by 80cm).
£70-90 *ONS*

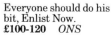

Everyone should do his bit, Enlist Now.
£100-120 *ONS*

He's Happy and Satisfied Are You?
£60-80 *ONS*

Programmes

Concert

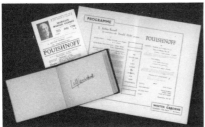

Programme for Winter
Garden, Margate, for
Pouishnoff concert, with
autograph, 1949.
£10-20 *PC*

Two programmes for
Winter Gardens,
Margate, the Cyril Smith
programme autographed,
1948.
50p-£2 each *PC*

Programmes from Eileen
Joyce concerts, one
autographed, 1947.
£10-15 *PC*

Moiseiwitsch at the
Royal Albert Hall, 1951.
50p-£1 *PC*

Programme from
Beniamino Gigli Spring
Tour, 1953.
£2-5 *PC*

Promenade Concert,
Diamond Jubilee Season,
1954.
£2-3 *PC*

Theatre

An autographed
programme from the
Hippodrome, Margate,
with Brian Rix among
the cast.
£5-8 *PC*

Programmes from the
Shakespeare Memorial
Theatre, Stratford-upon-
Avon, Festival of Britain
year 1951.
50p-£1 each *PC*

*Richard Burton starred
as Henry V.*

Programme from Globe Theatre, with William Franklyn, 1966.
50p-£1 *PC*

Programme from Whitehall Theatre, Gala Show, starring among others Julie Andrews, Tommy Trinder, Winifred Attwell and Beatrice Lillie, in aid of the Jamaica Hurricane Relief Fund, 1951.
£2-3 *PC*

Programme from Chiswick Empire for The Merry Widow, starring Eve Lister, 1948.

Programme from Duchess Theatre for The Deep Blue Sea by Terence Rattigan starring Peggy Ashcroft and Kenneth More, 1952.
£1-2 each *PC*

The Mousetrap, with Richard Attenborough, 1953.
£1-2 *PC*

Programme for The Mousetrap, 1973, with photograph taken by Angus McBean.
£1-2 *PC*

Sleuth, 1971.
50p-£1 *PC*

Theatre programmes from the St. James's Theatre and Apollo Theatre, c1950.
£1-2 each *PC*

Two programmes from the Garrick Theatre, c1951.
£2-3 each *PC*

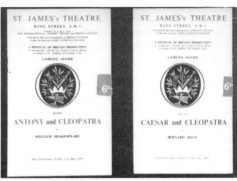

Programme from the Aldwych Theatre for A Streetcar Named Desire, 1950, signed by Bonar Colleano, with autograph of Lawrence Olivier and Vivien Leigh.
Programme **£5-10**
Autograph **£150-200**
PC

Programmes for Antony and Cleopatra and Caesar and Cleopatra, starring Lawrence Olivier and Vivien Leigh, 1949.
£1-2 each *PC*

The first Whitehall farce, 1946.
£2-3 *PC*

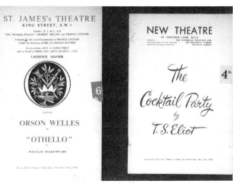

Programmes from the St. James's Theatre and New Theatre, c1950.
£1-2 each *PC*

Programme from the Theatre Royal, Haymarket, for Lady Windermere's Fan, c1948.
£1-2 *PC*

The Love of Four Colonels, 1952.
50p-£1 *PC*

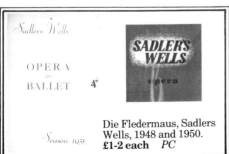

Die Fledermaus, Sadlers Wells, 1948 and 1950.
£1-2 each *PC*

Danny Kaye at the London Palladium, 1948.
50p-£1 *PC*

Sid Field's Harvey, with inset London Theatre Guide for February 1949.
50p-£1 *PC*

Programme autographed by Richard Murdoch, Kenneth Horne and Maurice Denham, 1949.
£5-8 *PC*

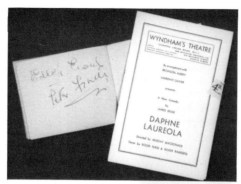

Programme from Wyndham's Theatre, for Daphne Laureola, c1950.
£1-2 *PC*

Programme from Folies Bergere, 1950.
£4-6 *PC*

First London production of Oklahoma! 1949.
50p-£1 *PC*

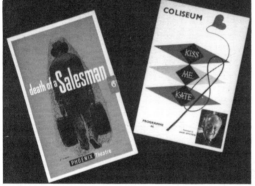

Two theatre programmes, c1950.
£1-2 each *PC*

Programme from the Adelphi Theatre, 1949.
£1-2 *PC*

Brigadoon, 1949.
50p-£1 *PC*

Sporting

Spurs v. Dortmund, 1951.
£1-2 *PC*

England v. France Rugby Union programme, 1949.
50p-£1 *PC*

Coronation Ascot race card, first day, 1953.
£1-2 *PC*

Lord's Victory Test, England v. Australia, July 1945, completed scorecard.
£12-25 *PC*

Stevengraphs

* Stevengraphs are silk-woven pictures, produced by Thomas Stevens of Coventry during the second half of the 19thC.
* Stevens produced silk-woven bookmarks as early as 1862, but the Stevengraph as we know it was launched at the York Exhibition on 7th May 1879.
* First 2 subjects were the London and York Royal Mail Coach and a celebration of Stephenson's 60 mph locomotive.
* Main subject headings are:
  – Landscape Views
  – Sporting Scenes
  – Historical Scenes
  – Portraits
  – American Interest.

Stevengraph entitled For Life or Death.
£60-70 *Bon*

A Stevengraph, Dick Turpin and Black Bess.
£60-90 *PC*

A pair of Stevengraphs.
£65-95 each *PC*

Stevengraph entitled Are You Ready?
£60-70 *Bon*

A pair of Stevengraphs.
£80-120 each *PC*

A selection of Stevengraphs.
£40-70 each *PC*

Two sporting Stevengraphs, The Start and The Finish.
£60-70 each *Bon*

DID YOU KNOW?

Originally Stevengraphs were available in the standard size of 6 by 2in (15 by 5cm) and unframed at a cost of one shilling. However for 2/6d (12½ new pence) they could be purchased in a gilded 'Oxford' frame.

Scripophily

Bank Notes

Government of Ceylon,
100 rupees, GVF, 1945.
£100-150   *P*

Bank of Nassau,
unissued 4/–, EF, 1905.
£100-120   *P*

Bermuda, £5, GVF, 1947.
£160-180   *P*

Complete collection of
advertising note design
types, EF, 1921-78, from
the Bankers Almanac.
£300-350   *P*

$100 note with error,
inverted serial numbers,
EF, 1977.
£100-110   *P*

Bank of Nassau,
unissued £1, in blue with
central picture of Queen
Victoria, EF.
£130-150   *P*

The Royal Bank of
Canada, $20, VF, 1938.
£200-250   *P*

Commercial Bank of
Australia, £1, damaged,
F, 1923.
£200-300   *P*

Ceylon, £5 unissued, EF.
£100-120   *P*

Bulgaria, 500 leva
Srebro, VF to GVF.
£100-120   *P*

Royal Bank of Canada,
$100, marked, GVF,
1920.
£500-550   *P*

Four specimen bank
notes, Hong Kong &
Shanghai Banking
Corporation, $5 and
$500, EF, $10 and $100,
EF-UNC, 1900.
£300-450   *P*

Hong Kong & Shanghai
Banking Corporation, $5
and $10 specimen note,
EF, 1900.
£280-300 each   *P*

El Banco Italo-Oriental,
100 pesos specimen note,
EF, 1889.
£130-160 *P*

Japan, 1 yen, GF to VF,
1878.
£180-200 *P*

Mexico, Banco de
Guanajuato, GVF,
50 pesos.
£100-120 *P*

Bank of New South
Wales, £1 specimen, by
C. Skipper & East for
Auckland, stained, GVF.
£100-120 *P*

Bank of New Zealand,
£5, GF, 1921.
£180-200 *P*

National Bank of New
Zealand, £5, GF, 1926.
£200-250 *P*

Reserve Bank of New
Zealand, £50, repaired,
VG.
£100-150 *P*

El Banco de Espana,
25 pesetas, damaged,
GF, 1893.
£100-120 *P*

El Banco de Espana,
1,000 pesetas, GF.
£120-150 *P*

Turkey, Banque
Imperiale Ottomane,
50 livres, damaged, G to
VG, 1908.
£100-120 *P*

Barclays Bank, Trinidad,
$100, VF, 1937.
£230-250 *P*

Barclays Bank, Trinidad,
VF, $20.
£200-230 *P*

Southern Rhodesia, £5,
VF, 1944.
£230-250 *P*

Siege of Mafeking, £1,
1900, no centre crease,
therefore GVF to EF.
£550-650 *P*

Portugal, 100 escudos,
damaged, VG to F, 1918.
£100-120 *P*

DID YOU KNOW?
Initials used to describe the condition of notes:

UNC = Uncirculated; clean, crisp as issued.
EF = Extremely fine; clean, but with traces of folds.
VF = Very fine; minor folds and creases, signs of a little wear.
F   = Fine; creased and worn but still clear.
Fair = A note which has seen a great deal of use.

British Bank Notes

Exchequer Bill for £10 issued in 1697, with many endorsements on back, F.
£500-600   *P*

Union Bank, £5, VF to GVF, 1920.
£90-120   *P*

Bank of England, £1, missing prefix and serial numbers, GVF, 1948.
£100-150   *P*

Bank of England, £100 note, GVF, 1938.
£450-500   *P*

Bank of England, Manchester, £5, GVF, 20 November 1916.
£300-350   *P*

Bank of England, £10, EF, 16 April 1915.
£400-450   *P*

Bonds, Stocks & Shares

American Express Co. certificate for 4 x $500 shares, signed, uncancelled, repaired on reverse, F to VF, 1865.
£330-350   *P*

Holyford Copper Mining Co. Ltd, certificate for 5 shares, embossed seal, 1864.
£20-25   *GKR*

The Great Republic Gold & Silver Mining Co. of Virginia, £50 bond, vignettes of Queen Victoria and Abraham Lincoln, VF, 1867.
£120-140   *P*

International Nickel Company of Canada, certificate for 10 shares.
£6-8   *GKR*

Lehigh Coal & Navigation Co, certificate for 100 shares.
£6-8   *GKR*

Wisconsin Investment Co. certificate for less than 100 shares, c1931.
£6-8   *GKR*

Kineton Gas Light, Coal & Coke Co. Ltd. certificate for one £2 share, 1863.
£15-20   *GKR*

City of Philadelphia, 6% Loan, bond for $500, F to VF, 1871.
£30-50 *P*

Brown, Bailey & Dixon Ltd. certificate for one share, red seal, 1873.
£15-20 *GKR*

United States Lines Inc. certificate for less than 100 shares, c1931.
£10-12 *GKR*

The Stepney Spare Motor Wheel Ltd, 1911, Poor to VF.
£20-30 *P*

The Newcastle Chilled Shot Company Ltd. certificate for £5 share, 1876.
£15-20 *GKR*

Whitehead Aircraft (1917) Ltd, ordinary 1/– and £1 shares, Poor to VF.
£170-200 *P*

Dewey & Almy Chemical Co. certificate for less than 100 shares.
£7-9 *GKR*

A collection of 170 bonds and share certificates, including Canadian North Pacific Fisheries Ltd. and Grand Trunk Railway, Poor to VF, 1902-30s.
£150-180 *P*

National Patent Salt Co. 10 x £20 shares, on vellum, VF to EF, 1838.
£120-£50 *P*

Twenty Well Stone & Brick Co. Ltd. 1871.
£15-20 *GKR*

The National Cotton Spinning Co. of Bulgaria Ltd, certificate for Ordinary shares, 1907.
£10-12 *GKR*

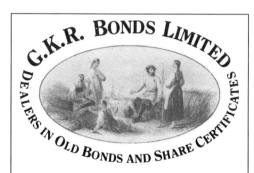

179

Tattershall & Conningsby Gas & Coke Co. certificate for one £10 share, embossed seal, 1860.
£20-25 *GKR*

The Imperial Mercantile Credit Association Ltd. certificate for five £50 shares, 1864.
£20-25 *GKR*

The Lands Allotment Co. Ltd. signed by Jabez Spencer Balfour, 1877.
£25-30 *GKR*

Railways

Shrewsbury & Hereford Railway Co. £20 share, 1846, VF.
£60-80 *P*

The Wharfdale Railway Co. £15 share, VF, 1840.
£70-90 *P*

Chicago, Brazil & Ohio River, Railroad and Coal Co. bond for £20/$100, 1881.
£35-40 *GKR*

Southern Railway Co. certificate for 10 shares, c1935.
£8-10 *GKR*

Ten Bond and Share certificates, including Brazil Railway Co. £200 Debenture, 1912, Fair to VF.
£60-80 *P*

Windsor & Annapolis Railway Co. Ltd. bearer warrant entitlement to 25 x $20 shares, Poor to Fair, 1868.
£120-140 *P*

Baltimore & Ohio Railroad Co. certificate for less than 100 shares.
£7-10 *GKR*

Choctaw, Oklahoma & Gulf Railroad Co. certificate for 100 shares, Preferred stock, c1902.
£8-10 *GKR*

Illinois Central Railroad Co. certificate for 100 shares, c1960.
£5-8 *GKR*

FURTHER READING
Robin Hendy, *Collecting Old Bonds and Shares*, London 1978.

General Ephemera

The British Worker,
General Strike, 1926.
£8-20 *PC*

Prudential Insurance
Policy.
50p-£1 *PC*

Miniature Daily Mail,
New Year, 1923.
£1-2 *PC*

Christening tract dated
1894, 6 by 4in (15 by
10cm).
£2-3 *CAC*

Soldier's Book and
miscellaneous papers,
WW1.
£1-10 *PC*

*Condition very important
as well as regimental
connection.*

Post Office Savings Bank
deposit book 1891.
£1-2 *PC*

Miniature newspapers
produced by the Daily
Express to commemorate
astronaut Neil
Armstrong walking on
the moon, 21st July 1969.
£1-2 each *PC*

Our Gracious Queen,
1837-1897, by Mrs. O. F.
Walton.
£20-40 *PC*

Official Souvenir
Programme, Coronation
of King George VI and
Queen Elizabeth.
£8-12 *PC*

Embossed picture cards
from the Religious Tract
Society.
£1-2 each *PC*

Hand painted Brownie badges.
£20-30 *VB*

Advertising ephemera, advertising Clarke's Buffalo Cakes, VG.
£15-20 *N*

Theatre postcards, large letters, G to VG.
£30-50 *N*

Raphael Tuck postcard to make into dolls house furniture, cut-outs, VG to EX.
£200-300 *N*

Menu from Half Litre Car Club Dinner Dance, 1952, plus card, guest of Mr. Peter Collins.
£18-25 *PC*

Two Liebig Menu cards.
£20-30 each *N*

Advertising Magazine give-away, good VR.
£5-10 *N*

Scraps

Victorian scraps, complete sheet of 8, VG.
£20-30 *N*

Victorian scraps.
£12-18 *N*

Comedy Frogs, complete sheet of 9, G to VG.
£15-20 *N*

Fans

The folding fan is said to have originated in China, and was brought to Europe by the early Portuguese explorers in the 16thC. France soon became the centre for manufacture. Fans within their original cases or boxes are very much sought after.

A Flemish fan with ivory sticks, carved and pierced with figures, scrolls and baskets, the guards applied with carved mother-of-pearl, the chicken skin leaf painted with Flora, c1720, 11in (28cm).
£750-850 *P*

A fan with carved, pierced ivory sticks, painted with chinoiserie cartouches, the vellum leaf painted, probably North Italian, c1730, 10in (25.5cm), in a brown papier mâché box.
£600-700 *P*

A fan with Italian carved ivory sticks, the leaf painted with a hunting party, probably German, c1700, 11½in (29.5cm), in a brocade box.
£500-600 *P*

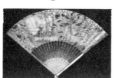

A chinoiserie fan, the ivory sticks pierced with scrolls and painted, c1730, 10in (25cm), and a papier mâché box.
£900-1,000 *P*

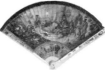

A painted and gilded ivory brisé fan, probably Dutch, c1730, 8½in (21cm).
£550-650 *P*

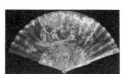

A French fan, the mother-of-pearl sticks carved and pierced, the vellum leaf painted with Minerva greeted by the Muses, c1760, 11½in (29.5cm).
£450-500 *P*

A ballooning fan, the saxe blue leaf painted in white with hot air balloons, with wooden sticks, c1783, 11in (28cm).
£200-300 *CSK*

Probably commemorating the ascent of Mm. Charles and Robert in 1783.

A French fan with carved, pierced and silvered ivory sticks, the silk leaf painted and decorated with coloured foil, spangles and tamboured metal thread, c1770, 11in (27.5cm).
£150-200 *P*

A French printed revolutionary commemorative fan, Les Municipalites ou les Moeurs Corigees, with wooden sticks, c1789, 11in (28cm).
£400-600 *CSK*

A French fan with sticks of carved, pierced, silvered and gilt tortoiseshell decorated with medallions, the leaf painted with Solomon and the Queen of Sheba, c1770, 10in (25.5cm).
£550-650 *P*

A Chinese ivory brisé fan, painted with landscapes, c1770, 10½in (25.5cm).
£400-500 *P*

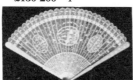

A Chinese ivory brisé fan, carved and pierced with birds and flowers, c1780, 10in (25cm).
£300-350 *P*

A French fan with elaborately carved ivory sticks, with painted chicken skin leaf, c1760, 11½in (29cm).
£2,200-2,500 *P*

A printed and painted fan with bone sticks, damaged, early 19thC.
£18-20 *VB*

A Chinese Macau fan, with black and gilt lacquer sticks, the leaf decorated with figures of ivory and silk appliqué, c1830, 11in (27.5cm), and a box.
£80-100 *P*

A French fan, the leaf a hand coloured etching, wooden sticks, c1740, 10½in (26.5cm).
£250-300 *P*

A French fan, with carved and pierced ivory sticks designed with butterflies and flowers, the leaf painted, c1760, 10½in (27cm).
£200-250 *P*

FANS

A Victorian black
feather fan.
£15-25 *CAC*

A Chinese tortoiseshell
brisé fan, carved and
pierced both sides, c1840,
7½in (19cm).
£250-300 *P*

A printed fan, Eventail
Cycliste, the leaf a
chromolithographic map
of Paris, stamped 119024
depose, with wooden
sticks printed with title,
damaged, late 19thC,
10in (25.5cm).
£150-200 *CSK*

A fan with carved pierced
ivory sticks, the decoupé
paper leaf applied with
gilt paper spangles and
painted with a central
cartouche, c1770, 10½in
(27cm), and a papier
mâché box labelled
Thomn. Clarke, Fan
Maker, N143 Leadenhall
Street, London.
£400-500 *P*

A Chinese black and gilt
lacquer brisé fan, c1840,
9½in (24cm).
£450-550 *P*

A Chinese fan with ivory
sticks, the painted leaf
decorated on both sides
with ivory and silk
appliqué, c1850, 11in
(27.5cm), in original
black and gilt lacquer
box with interior glass
lid.
£450-500 *P*

A French painted fan,
signed M. Dumas, the
verso painted with
rocaille and signed
Duvelleroy, the mother-
of-pearl sticks carved,
pierced and gilt, backed
with mother-of-pearl,
repaired, late 19thC,
10½in (26.5cm).
£400-600 *CSK*

A North European fan,
with carved, pierced,
painted and gilt ivory
sticks, possibly Austro-
German, c1750, 11in
(28cm).
£550-650 *P*

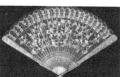

A Chinese silver gilt
filigree fan, with blue,
green and yellow
enamelled decoration,
c1840, 7½in (18.5cm).
£550-650 *P*

A French fan designed as
a peacock, with carved
pierced horn sticks with
piqué work, the silk leaf
painted and applied with
sequins, signed
A. Tomasse, the reverse
inscribed Duvelleroy,
c1900, 10in (25.5cm), in a
box labelled Duvelleroy,
ll Bould. de la Madeleine
Anciennement Passage
des Panoramas.
£350-400 *P*

A fan with mother-of-
pearl sticks, carved and
gilded with entwined ivy,
with Brussels bobbin
lace leaf, signed
S. Drinot, c1890, 13in
(33cm), in box labelled
J. Duvelleroy, London,
167 Regent Street.
£350-450 *P*

A fan with carved,
pierced mother-of-pearl
sticks, the leaf of Brussels
bobbin lace, backed with
gauze, c1880, 12in
(30.5cm), in a box.
£600-700 *P*

A French fan with
carved, pierced and
gilded mother-of-pearl
sticks, the gilt metal
guards decorated in high
relief with cherubs and
scrolls, the leaf with
hand coloured
lithograph, c1860, 10½in
(26cm).
£300-400 *P*

A Japanese ivory brisé
fan with black, red and
gold lacquer decoration,
c1870, 11in (28cm).
£1,700-2,000 *P*

A fan with mother-of-
pearl sticks, the initial
guard applied with gold
monogram MD, the leaf
of Brussels point de gaze,
the guard inscribed
Buissot, Paris, late
19thC, 13in (32.5cm), in
original box labelled
E. Buissot, Fabrique
d'Eventails, 46 Rue des
Petites, Paris.
£350-400 *P*

A pierced horn brisé fan,
decorated with inset cut
steel, painted on both
sides, early 19thC, 6½in
(16cm).
£1,500-2,000 *P*

A South American white feather fan, with turned bone handle, c1870, 12½in (31.5cm), in original box labelled Melles M & E Nattie Fleuristes, 46 Rue de Ouvider, Rio de Janeiro.
£150-200 *P*

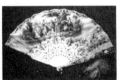

A hand painted ivory fan.
£55-65 *MAN*

A hand painted satin and ivory fan.
£35-45 *MAN*

A painted silk fan.
£30-40 *VB*

A Chinese fan with carved, pierced, painted and gilt ivory sticks, backed with mother-of-pearl, the paper leaf painted, c1800, 13½in (33.5cm), in a framed and glazed case.
£750-850 *P*

A fan with carved, pierced, painted and gilt bone, the silk leaf painted with a Spanish scene, c1900, 10in (25.5cm).
£220-250 *P*

An ivory fan.
£25-35 *MAN*

A black satin fan with gold decoration.
£25-30 *MAN*

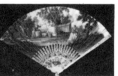

An ostrich feather fan, with tortoiseshell sticks.
£55-65 *VB*

A North European fan, the ivory sticks carved and pierced with birds, the leaf painted with a rural landscape, c1740, 11½in (28.5cm), in a black shagreen box.
£350-400 *P*

A wooden fan trimmed with satin, lace and sequins, in original box.
£75-85 *MAN*

A Brussels lace and mother-of-pearl fan.
£50-60 *VB*

A Regency ivory fan.
£20-25 *VB*

FURTHER READING
Armstrong, Nancy, *A Collector's History of Fans,* London 1974.
Fan Guild, *Fan Leaves,* Boston 1961.

An ostrich feather fan.
£35-45 *MAN*

An embroidered fan, with fitted lacquered box.
£40-50 *VB*

A lace fan with painted wood sticks.
£30-35 *VB*

A painted and dyed feather fan.
£15-20 *VB*

An Italian fan with carved ivory sticks, c1780, 11in (27.5cm).
£400-500 *P*

Fishing

Reels

A Hardy Silex Jewel casting reel, post-war, restored, 4in (10cm).
£40-60 *JMG*

An Alex Martin Thistle fly reel, copy of the Hardy Perfect, with ball-bearings, unscrewing faceplate, left hand drum lock screw, 3½in (9cm).
£30-50 *JMG*

A brass reel with embossed fishing scene on back and front, brass knob on crank for winding, unknown origin, 19thC, 2½in (6cm).
£30-50 *JMG*

An Ogden Smith Exchequer trout fly reel, double reverse tapered white composition handle, red agate lineguard, restored to mint condition, 3in (7.5cm).
£30-50 *JMG*

A Hardy Perfect all brass fly reel, c1896, 2½in (6cm).
£500-600 *JMG*

A Young's Beaudex salmon fly reel, c1955, 4in (10cm), in unused and boxed condition.
£30-50 *JMG*

A Hardy Longstone sea reel, unperforated drum face, 4in (10cm).
£30-50 *JMG*

A Hardy wide drum salmon fly reel, with rare silent check, c1930, 4in (11cm).
£150-200 *JMG*

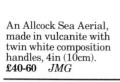

An Allcock Sea Aerial, made in vulcanite with twin white composition handles, 4in (10cm).
£40-60 *JMG*

A rare French fixed spool bait-casting reel, the Croizix, made during World War II, with undulating spool for distribution of the line.
£40-60 *JMG*

A Hardy Spitfire Perfect fly reel, lacquered bright finish, c1942, 3in (7cm).
£100-130 *JMG*

A Hardy Silex reel in
brass and blued steel,
c1900, 4in (10cm).
£30-50 *JMG*

A Hardy Princess fly
reel, with green handle
and anodised green
finish, brass drum latch
holder, c1950, 3½in
(9cm).
£30-50 *JMG*

A small fly reel with
unusual large
perforations, black
handle, c1914, 3in
£15-25 *JMG*

A Carter Centabrake
reel, black drum face,
light aluminium case,
brass drag control, c1914,
3in (7cm).
£15-20 *JMG*

The Allcock-Stanley
fixed spool casting reel,
c1930.
£25-35 *JMG*
*Introduced by Allcocks
about 1930 for about
£1.10s.0d. as a lower
price range item.*

An American Magic
side-winder reel, c1945,
4in (10cm).
£20-30 *JMG*

A Percy Wadham 'The
Cowes' (Isle of Wight)
bait casting reel,
gunmetal and ebonite,
with ivorine knob for
giving kick start to spool,
c1910, 4in (10cm).
£40-60 *JMG*

A rare Scottish vintage fishing tackle
dealer, c1924, with a deep knowledge
of old reels, grey beard, ruddy-ish
patina, and a most generous nature
towards owners of fine tackle;
buys up to £300   *JMG*

I am keen to buy the very best reels, particularly
those made by Hardy before 1939. Other
desired piscatoriana: ingenious fly boxes and
cabinets, catalogues, line driers, and all the
fishing gadgets.

**Overseas antique dealers please note that I can
supply and deliver brass and wooden reels for you.**

Write or call:

Jamie Maxtone Graham

<table>
<tr><td>LYNE HAUGH</td><td>Telephone:</td></tr>
<tr><td>Lyne Station</td><td>(07214) 304</td></tr>
<tr><td>Peebles EH45 8NP</td><td>(Visits by</td></tr>
<tr><td>Scotland</td><td>appointment only)</td></tr>
</table>

A Hardy Silex Multiplier,
turned ivorine brake
handle and brass oil pipe
on back, c1924, 3in (7cm).
£80-120 *JMG*

A Hardy Cascapedia
salmon fly reel, nickel
silver rims, vulcanite
side, unused and mint
condition, c1932, 3in
(7.5cm).
£1,000-1,500 *JMG*
*Smallest and rarest size,
only 12 made.*

A Hardy Uniqua wide drum salmon fly reel, horseshoe drum latch, c1930, 3½in (9cm).
£30-50 *JMG*

A Hardy Perfect brass faced salmon fly reel, face engraved with rod-in-hand trade mark, 4½in (11cm).
£170-190 *CSK*

A Hardy St. George multiplying salmon fly reel, with notched brass foot, ebonite handle and smokey agate line guide, fitted with line, 3½in (8.5cm).
£140-160 *CSK*

A rare fixed spool side-casting reel, by Howell of Birmingham, The Howban, twin brown plastic handles, 3 side grips, c1945.
£15-25 *JMG*

A Perfect trout fly reel, restored to mint condition, c1950, 3in (8cm).
£30-50 *JMG*

A fly reel with telephone latch, copper wire drum core, 3in (7.5cm).
£25-35 *JMG*

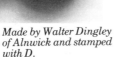

Made by Walter Dingley of Alnwick and stamped with D.

A Hardy Bros. Silex No. 2 alloy spinning reel, 4½in (11cm).
£50-70 *CEd*

A pike trimmer from Lake Windermere, red and white cork bearing owner's name, c1880, 4in (10cm).
£20-30 *JMG*

A bait casting reel, with unusual oak drum core, London, c1900, 4in (10cm).
£30-50 *JMG*

A Hardy Bros. 1896 pattern Perfect reel, all brass with ivorine handle, 4in (11cm).
£300-400 *CEd*

A Hardy Bros. Perfect reel, all brass with ivory handle, 4½in (12cm).
£250-350 *CEd*

A C. Farlow & Co. Ltd. brass faced alloy reel, 4½in (11cm).
£100-150 *CEd*

Miscellaneous

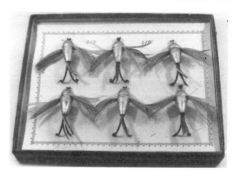

A Pegley-Davies anglers' knife, main blade broken, poor condition, c1945.
£5-10   *JMG*

A box of Hardy sprats, boxed for use as spinning baits, in original box, c1916.
£8-10   *JMG*

A collection of flies made for sale to U.S.A. by Murdoch of Redditch.
£10-20   *JMG*

A Gut Cast Box and a tin.
£5-10   *AL*

An important collection of Hardy's Anglers' Guides, catalogues and supplements from 1906 to 1977, in original wrappers, totalling 37 items.
£1,500-2,000   *CEd*

A stuffed and mounted pike, in natural riverbed setting, contained within glazed ebonised wood case, 52½in (132cm) long.
£250-350   *CSK*

FURTHER READING
Maxtone Graham, Jamie, *Best of Hardy's Angler's Guides*, Peebles, Scotland 1982.
Maxtone Graham, Jamie, *To Catch a Fisherman*, Peebles, Scotland 1984.
Maxtone Graham, Jamie, *Fishing Tackle of Yesterday*, Peebles, Scotland 1989.

The Compleat Angler's lamp, patented, c1928.
£40-60   *JMG*

A silver prize cup, won by a fishing lady, in Essex, c1910.
£12-15   *JMG*

GLASS

Cranberry Glass

A ruby glass jug with gilt trim, 4in (10cm) high.
£50-60 *CB*

A cranberry glass tumbler with painted decoration, 5in (12cm) high.
£30-45 *CB*

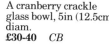

A cranberry glass sweetmeat dish, with fluted edges, 6in (15cm) diam.
£40-55 *CB*

A cranberry trailed bowl and dish, Stevens & Williams, bowl 5in (13cm) diam.
£40-55 *CB*

A cranberry quilted glass posy bowl, 4in (10cm) high.
£70-80 *CB*

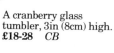

A cranberry glass basket bowl, 8½in (21cm) high.
£80-100 *CB*

A cranberry glass jug, 6½in (16cm) high.
£90-100 *CB*

A cranberry speckled glass jug, 7in (17.5cm) high.
£75-95 *CB*

A cranberry crackle glass bowl, 5in (12.5cm) diam.
£30-40 *CB*

A cranberry glass tumbler, 3in (8cm) high.
£18-28 *CB*

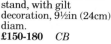

A cranberry glass cake stand, with gilt decoration, 9½in (24cm) diam.
£150-180 *CB*

A Victorian cranberry glass oil lamp with facet stem, 8½in (21cm) high.
£140-170 *CB*

A cranberry glass bracelet.
£20-30 *CB*

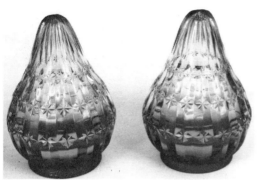

A pair of cranberry cut glass shades, 7in (17.5cm) high.
£80-120 *CB*

A cranberry glass jam pot, with silver plated spoon and lid, 3½in (9cm) high to lid.
£40-50 *CB*

A cranberry glass jug with silver top and handle, 6½in (16cm) high.
£150-170 *CB*

A cranberry carafe and tumbler, 6½in (16cm) high.
£75-85 *CB*

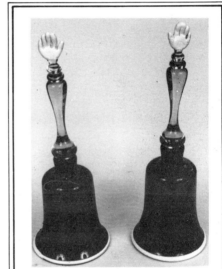

A pair of cranberry glass bells, with unusual white glass hands and footrim, 12½in (31cm) high.
£300-380 *CB*

A cranberry glass jug and bowl, jug 4in (10cm) high.
£80-100 *MAN*

A cranberry glass sweetmeat bowl, with white glass trailing, 3in (7.5cm) high.
£60-70 *CB*

A pair of cranberry vases, 8½in (21cm) high.
£90-120 *CB*

A cranberry glass cruet and silver plated stand, 6½in (16cm) high.
£80-100 *CB*

Cloud Glass

Cloud glass is a term used to describe the range of glassware produced between 1922 and 1940 by the Gateshead company of George Davidson & Co. The first colour used was purple and this was followed by red, orange and green between 1929 and 1934. There are a variety of effects documented, mainly produced by using a combination of the basic colours. A complete range of glass products was manufactured providing an interesting and varied field for collectors.

A pair of vases:
l. Red, 6in (15cm) high.
£70-80
r. Green, 7½in (19cm) high.
£25-35   *BEV*

A tortoiseshell custard cup, with 'frog' for flowers.
£30-40   *BEV*

A green dish, 14½in (36cm) wide.
£45-55   *BEV*

l. A red dressing table bowl, 5in (13cm) high.
£75-85
r. A red candlestick, 2½in (6cm) high.
£45-55   *BEV*

A topaz vase, 6½in (16cm) high.
£90-100   *BEV*

A tortoiseshell ashtray with matchstick holder.
£25-35   *BEV*

A purple bowl, 9½in (24cm) wide.
£30-40   *BEV*

For use as a fruit bowl or flower holder.

A tortoiseshell vase, 8½in (21cm) high.
£45-55   *BEV*

A topaz bowl, 12in (30cm) wide.
£85-95   *BEV*

An amber tortoiseshell bowl on stand, 8in (20cm) high.
£55-65   *BEV*

A blue bowl, 8½in (24cm) wide.
£45-55   *BEV*

The flower holder is referred to as a 'frog'.

A plate, 9in (22.5cm).
£20-30   *BEV*

A purple vase, 11in (28cm) high.
£65-75   *BEV*

DID YOU KNOW?___
Red and grey are the rarest colours, the most collectable and therefore the most expensive.

A blue jug, 8in (20cm) high.
£80-90 *BEV*

A green posy holder.
£25-35 *BEV*

A green bowl with 3 feet, 7in (18cm) high.
£70-80 *BEV*

A blue salad bowl, 7½in (19cm) diam, with servers.
£90-100 *BEV*

A purple tray with bowls.
£15-30 *BEV*

Monart & Vasart Glass

A Monart glass vase, with blue green enamels, 14in (35.5cm) high.
£350-450 *SC*

A Strathearn glass vase, in red brown colours, 8in (20.5cm) high.
£30-50 *SC*

A Monart vase with pink swirls on green and white, 7½in (19cm) high.
£120-150 *SC*

A Vasart vase, in shades of orange, 8in (20cm).
£35-45 *SC*

A Monart vase, green with red, 11in (28cm) high.
£200-250 *SC*

A Monart vase, grey blue with gold flecks, 7½in (19cm) high.
£100-150 *SC*

A Monart bowl, with silver flecks on an orange base, 14in (35.5cm) diam.
£200-250 *SC*

A Strathearn glass bowl, with blue green swirl design, 12in (30.5cm) diam.
£50-70 *SC*

A Monart veined glass vase in blue and purple, 9½in (24cm) high.
£350-450 *SC*

DID YOU KNOW?
* Ysart glass made only by Salvador and his sons Paul, Vincent, Augustine and Antoine.
* Monart produced at Moncrieff Glassworks in Scotland from 1924-1939.
* Early pieces uncased, often textured surface and lustred finish.
* After 1929 all pieces cased in crystal.
* Pontil usually left on the base, after being smoothed down, later production had a ground footring.
* Approximately 300 shapes produced in a wide variety of colours, with red the rarest, orange and green the most common.
* All free hand-blown with no moulds used.
* Vasart produced independently by Salvador, Augustine and Vincent Ysart.
* Mostly pastel shades made.
* Acid-etched signature 'Vasart' used from 1946-1956.
* Paper label replaced signature from 1956-1964.
* Strathearn Glass took over Vasart in 1965, pieces have a leaping salmon seal impressed in pontil.

Nailsea Glass

A looped bellows flask,
mid-19thC.
£60-100 *BAL*

Three Nailsea style scent
bottles, c1860, 2½ to 3in
(5 to 7.5cm).
£90-100 each *Som*

A green bell with ribbed
body, mid-19thC.
£90-130 *BAL*

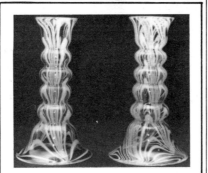

A pair of Nailsea looped
candlesticks, mid-19thC.
£100-150 *BAL*

A ruby pipe with opaque
rim, mid-19thC.
£90-120 *BAL*

A Nailsea glass carafe,
8in (20cm) high.
£80-110 *CB*

A wrythen Bristol blue
bugle, early 19thC.
£150-200 *BAL*

THIS IS A PRICE GUIDE _____
NOT A PRICE LIST
The price ranges quoted indicate the *average* price a
purchaser should pay for similar items. However,
there are many other factors which should be taken
into account when assessing the value of a piece.
These include:
Condition
Rarity of design or pattern
Size
Colour
Provenance
Restoration
If sought after
When buying or selling, remember that prices can be
greatly affected by condition. Unless otherwise
stated all goods illustrated are of good saleable
quality, and the price ranges reflect this. Pieces
offered for sale in exceptionally fine or in poor
condition may reasonably be expected to be priced
considerably higher or lower than the estimates
quoted here.

A Nailsea double gimmel
flask, white opaque
trailing.
£75-95 *CB*

A Nailsea glass lamp,
11in (28.5cm) high.
£120-150 *CB*

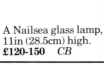

Three pale green Nailsea glass hats, 19thC.
£60-80 each *BAL*

Two Nailsea glass hats: r. Rare deep amber
l. Pale green. bowler hat.
£60-80 **£100-150** *BAL*

A glass frigate with pilot boat, under a glass dome, mid-19thC.
£130-180 *BAL*

A Nailsea glass display of 3 spun glass birds under dome, 19thC, on wooden base, 17in (42cm) high.
£180-200 *HOD*

A pair of Bristol blue bells, mid-19thC.
£230-280 *BAL*

Rolling Pins

A Nailsea glass rolling pin, 15½in (39cm) long.
£30-60 *CB*

A Nailsea black glass rolling pin, c1800.
£50-70 *BAL*

DID YOU KNOW?

* Glass rolling pins in use from late 17thC.
* Earliest examples plain, in very heavy, coarse glass.
* End of 18thC Nailsea glassworks produced more decorative examples.
* At the turn of the century deep Bristol blue glass pins were produced.
* Early 19thC bottle green and opaque white pins became popular, followed by ruby, turquoise and amethyst.
* Dated commemorative pins are more valuable, as are pictorial ones.
* Hollow pins often used to keep salt in and hung over the fireplace to keep salt dry!

Powell Glass

The Whitefriars factory was established in 1680 and moved to Harrow in the late 19thC, under the direction of James Powell. High quality hand-blown glass was produced in crystal clear colours. Some very fine drinking glasses from this early period can still be found.

Barnaby Powell, a relative, was a notable designer in the 1930s of ribbon vases with banding.

Liberty and Gallé, in fact, bought Powell glass, which was enamelled for their own use.

The advent of the digital thermometer brought about the closure of the factory in 1980.

A Webb amethyst bowl, 10in (25.5cm) diam.
£80-100 *SWa*

An Art Nouveau vase moulded as a flowerhead, with looped stem, in clear and frosted green glass, 9in (23cm) high.
£170-200 *CSK*

A red glass vase, c1940, 8in (20cm) high.
£70-90 *SWa*

An amber glass bowl, 12in (30.5cm) diam.
£85-95 *SWa*

An amber vase with white flecks, c1930, 6in (15cm) high.
£35-45 *SWa*

An amber heavy glass vase, later Powell, 8in (20cm) high.
£50-60 *SWa*

An amethyst vase, c1930, 8½in (21.5cm) high.
£85-95 *SWa*

An amber glass vase, 3½in (9cm) high.
£30-40 *SWa*

MAKE THE MOST OF MILLER'S
Just like *Miller's Antiques Price Guide*, Miller's Collectables Price Guide will be completely different each year. Each edition will contain new photographs and no photograph will be repeated.

196

Decanters

A Georgian decanter with moulded stopper, 12in (30cm).
£80-130   *CB*

A pair of Georgian cut glass decanters, 9in (23cm).
£350-500   *CB*

l. and r. A pair of decanters, with flute cutting, target stoppers, c1810, 8½in (21.5cm).
£550-650

c. A decanter with mushroom stopper, c1810, 8½in (21.5cm).
£150-200   *Som*

A pair of club shaped spirit decanters, with band of egg and tulip engraved decoration, c1780, 9½in (23.5cm).
£180-200   *Som*

Cut glass decanters.
£30-50 each   *VB*

A Bristol green carafe, c1860, 8in (21cm).
£80-100   *CB*

A Victorian liqueur decanter with 4 glasses.
£20-40   *CAC*

An Art Deco glass decanter, 8in (19.5cm), with 6 glasses.
£320-350   *P*

An Art Deco glass decanter, 10in (25cm), with 5 glasses.
£420-450   *P*

A Bristol green engraved decanter, 10in (25cm).
£150-200   *CB*

A decanter, 7½in (19cm), and 2 glasses, with red trailing decoration.
£80-120   *CB*

A German Art Nouveau claret jug, with silver plated trim.
£240-260   *BEV*

An Art Nouveau W.M.F. metal mounted green glass claret jug, 14½in (36cm).
£750-850   *CSK*

197

Drinking Glasses

l. A tumbler, early
19thC, 2½in (6cm) high.
£20-35
r. A Lynn tumbler, 3in
(7cm) high.
£80-100   CB

*The factory in King's
Lynn was in existence for
about 10-12 years only
and therefore Lynn glass
is very collectable.*

A Georgian glass.
£25-30   VB

A Victorian etched glass.
£5-8   CAC

Two English wrythen ale
glasses, c1760, 5in
(12.5cm) high.
£30-40 each   CB

A selection of jelly
glasses:
l. A set of 8, c1870, 5in
(12cm).
£185-200
c. Star cut, 4½in (11cm).
£12-18
r. Ale glass with lemon
squeezer base, 5½in
(14cm) high.
£30-50   CB

Two Georgian glasses.
£20-40 each   VB

A pair of Victorian
rummers, with rough
pontil mark, 5½in (14cm)
high.
£50-60   AL

A turquoise opaline
goblet with gilt
decoration, 6½in (16cm).
£150-180   CB

A cut glass, c1850.
£30-40   VB

A champagne flute,
c1850.
£22-25   VB

A pair of rummers.
£25-35 each   VB

A collection of small
Victorian glasses.
£7-9   VB

Hyacinth Vases

A pair of peach blown
hyacinth vases.
£80-100 *CB*

A vaseline glass hyacinth
vase, 9in (23cm) high.
£40-50 *CB*

A pair of amber hyacinth
vases.
£65-75 *CB*

A hyacinth vase.
£6-10 *VB*

An amber hyacinth vase
with enamelled flower
decoration.
£30-40 *CB*

A vaseline glass hyacinth
vase.
£45-55 *CHA*

An amethyst hyacinth
vase.
£10-20 *AL*

An amethyst hyacinth
vase with fluted top.
£35-50 *CB*

A blue hyacinth vase.
£15-20 *AL*

A turquoise blue
hyacinth vase.
£35-45 *CB*

A pair of cranberry glass
hyacinth vases.
£100-150 *CB*

Hyacinth vases.
£30-40 *CB*

A turquoise blue
engraved hyacinth vase,
with registration mark.
£45-65 *CB*

Two green hyacinth
vases.
£10-20 each *LAM*

Dark blue and gold
hyacinth vases.
£10-20 each *AL*

199

Perfume Bottles

Three silver-topped perfume bottles:
l. Edwardian, plain glass, 3in (7.5cm).
£70-80
c. Victorian, ruby glass, 2½in (6cm).
£100-120
r. Victorian, amber glass, 2½in (6cm).
£90-100   *MAN*

A selection of display perfume bottles for department stores filled with coloured water, by Lanvin, Christian Dior and Guerlain.
£10-25   *ZIG*

A handbag perfume bottle in Bakelite case, metal decoration, c1940.
£15-20   *ZIG*

Three Victorian perfume bottles.
£95-105 each   *MAN*

Evening in Paris perfume and powder cream in original box, c1930.
£25-35   *ZIG*

l. An Edwardian cut glass bottle with silver top, 4½in (11cm).
£100-110
r. A cut glass bottle with silver top, 8in (20cm).
£85-100   *MAN*

Three scent bottles.
£50-150   *Tri*

A Guerlain Jicky bottle, made in France.
£12-15   *ZIG*

A bird cream perfume holder, unnamed.
£7-10   *ZIG*

Two modern green glass perfume bottles, with silver trim, 4in (10cm).
£30-40 each   *MAN*

A pair of heavy cut glass scent bottles, with silver mounts, London 1887, in presentation case.
£130-150   *PC*

DID YOU KNOW?
Older perfume bottles do not have plastic on the inside of the rim.

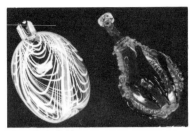

Two glass flasks.
£40-70 *MAN*

l. Lalique perfume bottle
with perfume, made for
Coty, in original box.
£15-20
r. Baccarat perfume
bottle, for Roger &
Gallet, in original box.
£15-20 *PAT*

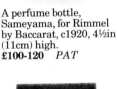

A perfume bottle,
Sameyama, for Rimmel
by Baccarat, c1920, 4½in
(11cm) high.
£100-120 *PAT*

An Eau de Cologne bottle
and contents, in original
box.
£20-25 *PAT*

*Label intact which
increases value.*

A perfume bottle,
Narcisse Noir by
Baccarat, c1925, 2½in
(6cm) high.
£90-100 *PAT*

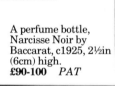

A textured and frosted
glass perfume bottle and
powder bowl, in original
box.
£40-50 *PAT*

Belle du Jour made for
Atkinsons, no signature
but possibly Lalique,
c1925, 6in (15cm) high.
£100-120 *PAT*

A selection of small
perfume bottles.
£2-10 *ZIG*

*Label necessary to be
valuable.*

DID YOU KNOW?
Miller's Collectables
Price Guide is designed
to build up, year by year,
into the most
comprehensive reference
system available.

Evening in Paris
perfume, in Bakelite egg,
c1930.
£35-40 *ZIG*

201

General

Celery Vases

A cut glass celery vase, with turn-over rim, 7in (18cm) high.
£80-110 *CB*

A cut glass celery vase, with scalloped rim, 10in (26cm) high.
£40-60 *CB*

Engraved glass celery vases, 9½in (24cm) high.
£50-80 *CB*

Custard Cups

Custard cups.
£5-9 each *VB*

A set of 8 custard cups, 3in (7.5cm) high.
£100-120 *CB*

A custard cup, with polished pontil, 3½in (9cm) high.
£15-25 *CB*

Victorian '2d lick' ice cream glasses.
£7-10 *VB*

Bowls

A green glass jug and basin set, with enamel and gilt decoration, basin 4in (10cm) diam.
£65-85 *CB*

A Russian blue glass globular bowl, with dark green overlay, faceted and thumb cut decoration, etched mark to base for the Imperial Russian Glass Factory, early 20thC, 6½in (16.5cm) high.
£120-140 *WIL*

A pink pearl glass bowl and dish, 3in (7.5cm) high.
£25-30 *MAN*

A set of trailed glass coloured finger bowls, with dishes, bowl 5½in (14cm) diam.
Dishes and bowls
£20-25 each piece *CB*

Eye Baths

A selection of eye baths.
£4-7 each *AL*

Four eye glasses.
£10-15 each *CB*

A selection of eye baths.
£5-16 each *AL*

Fairy Lights

Glass fairy lights, plain, coloured and blue.
£2-7 *AL*

A Continental painted flask, with later silver gilt top, 9in (23cm) high.
£200-300 *CB*

Flasks

A Continental engraved flask, c1790, 5in (12.5cm).
£40-80 *CB*

A Continental engraved flask, c1790, 5½in (14cm) high.
£85-95 *CB*

Jugs

A Victorian engraved jug, with celery handle, 7½in (19cm) high.
£30-40 *CB*

An English glass jug, c1840, 8in (20.5cm) high.
£150-170 *CB*

A cut glass jug, c1920, 7in (18cm) high.
£35-45 *CB*

'Mary Gregory' Glass

This is a term used by collectors to describe the design. It is believed to have been created by a Mary Gregory, working in a Boston, U.S.A. factory who copied Bohemian designs from 1850 onwards. These designs depict Victorian children enamelled in white or pink/white.

A pair of dishes, 3½in (9cm) wide.
£40-50 *CB*

Three opaline glass vases, 4½ to 5in (11.5 to 12.5cm) high.
£30-50 each *CB*

A green glass jug with gilt rim, 6in (15cm) high.
£50-65 *CB*

A powder bowl, in pink and white, 4½in (11.5cm) diam.
£60-80 *MAN*

A cranberry glass jug, 6in (15cm).
£75-85 *CB*

A cranberry glass.
£45-55 *CB*

Salts

Three English glass
salts, with square bases,
c1825.
£20-40 each   *CB*

A pair of heavy glass
salts, 3in (7.5cm) high.
£25-50   *CB*

A pair of glass salts, 2½in
(6cm) high.
£30-50   *CB*

Spangled Glass

A vase, two layers of
glass sandwiching silver
flecks, 4in (10cm).
£40-60   *CB*

A casket, 4½in (11.5cm)
wide.
£280-300   *CB*

Posy holder, with red
interior.
£18-25 each   *MAN*

Stourbridge Glass

Stourbridge glass is from a large group of
factories in and around Stourbridge in
Worcestershire and in the 19thC were the
most important factories in England for
the production of fine table glass and
decorative glass. Many types of glass were
produced, including cased, decorated flint
glass, Venetian style filigree glass and
cameo glass.

A jug in milky pink
colour, 6½in (16.5cm)
high.
£75-95   *MAN*

Glass stirrup cups in the
shape of boots, 4in
(10cm).
£40-55 each   *CB*

A vase, 8in (20.5cm) high.
£85-95   *MAN*

Rinsers

A rinser, 3½in (9cm)
high.
£22-25 *MAN*

A rinser, 5in (12cm)
diam.
£12-15 *MAN*

A Georgian rinser, 4in
(10cm) high.
£35-40 *MAN*

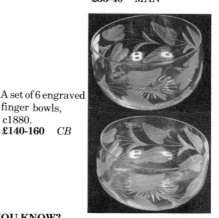

A set of 6 engraved
finger bowls,
c1880.
£140-160 *CB*

A Georgian rinser, 4½in
(11cm) diam.
£20-25 *MAN*

A double lipped cut glass
rinser, c1830.
£25-35 *CB*

Vaseline Glass

DID YOU KNOW?
A Rinser or Cooler is a glass bowl used for cooling
wine glasses – the stem rested in the lip leaving the
bowl in the cold water.
   Finger bowls were sometimes referred to as rinsers
– after eating shellfish, for example, it was necessary
to rinse your fingers.

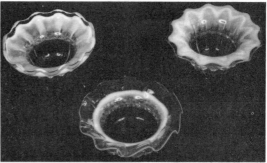

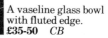

Three vaseline glass
sweetmeat dishes.
£40-55 *CB*

A tall Victorian vaseline
glass epergne, 20in
(50cm).
£280-350 *CB*

A tall vaseline lily vase
with folded foot, 23½in
(59cm) high.
£320-400 *CB*

> **Cross Reference**
> Hyacinth Vases

A vaseline glass bowl
with fluted edge.
£35-50 *CB*

Art Nouveau Glass

A Loetz glass vase, covered with a green/purple iridescence on a yellow ground, 8½in (22cm) high, with wooden base.
£500-600 *CSK*

A Loetz glass vase, covered with a network of silvered iridescent designs over light and dark green glass, 7in (18cm) high.
£1,400-1,800 *CSK*

Miscellaneous

A Gateshead glass, 1870.
£10-15 *CAC*

An Austrian glass vase, c1890.
£10-20 *CAC*

A medicine glass, c1910.
£5-10 *CAC*

A Lalique seal (cachet), with initial engraved on the base, c1940, 4in (10cm) high.
£100-120 *PAT*

A Scottish glass basket.
£10-15 *CAC*

FURTHER READING

Ash, D., *How to Identify English Drinking Glasses and Decanters*, London 1962.
Bickerton, L. M., *Eighteenth Century English Drinking Glasses,* 1986.
Brooks, J., *The Arthur Negus Guide to British Glass,* 1981.
Charleston, R. J., *English Glass*, 1984.
Davis, D. C., *English and Irish Antique Glass*, 1964.
Dodsworth, R., *Glass and Glassmaking*, 1982.
Elville, E. M., *Collector's Dictionary of Glass*, 1961.
Harden, D. B. and others, *Masterpieces of Glass*, British Musuem 1968.
Hughes, G. B., *English Glass for the Collector*, 1958.
Wilkinson, O. N., *Old Glass*, 1968.
Wills, G., *Country Life Pocket Book of Glass*, 1966.

Hairdressing & Hatpins

Hairdressing

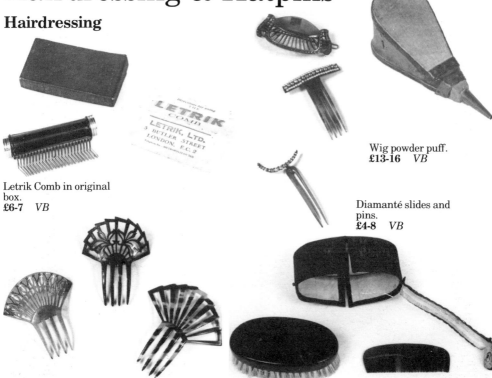

Letrik Comb in original box.
£6-7 *VB*

Wig powder puff.
£13-16 *VB*

Diamanté slides and pins.
£4-8 *VB*

Tortoiseshell and celluloid combs.
£7-9 *VB*

A travelling hair brush, comb and mirror set.
£9-12 *CAC*

Hatpins

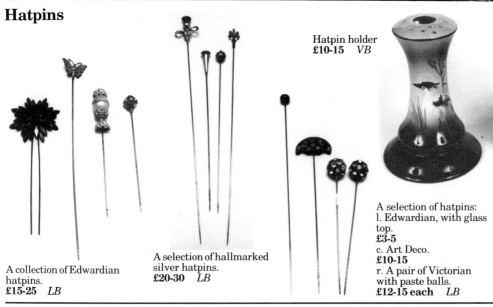

Hatpin holder
£10-15 *VB*

A collection of Edwardian hatpins.
£15-25 *LB*

A selection of hallmarked silver hatpins.
£20-30 *LB*

A selection of hatpins:
l. Edwardian, with glass top.
£3-5
c. Art Deco.
£10-15
r. A pair of Victorian with paste balls.
£12-15 each *LB*

Horse Brasses & Harness

The origins of horse brasses are lost in time, many of the basic designs representing pagan and early religious symbols, i.e. the Sun, Moon and Stars and The Cross. Other collected areas are farming subjects, especially horses and the harvest, heraldic crests and a variety of inanimate objects, bells being popular.

Commemorative brasses continue to be highly collectable.

Horse Brasses

An old martingale.
£100-140 *SAD*

19thC martingales.
£150-175 *SAD*

l. A brass face piece on leather.
£40-50
r. A cast face piece.
£35-45 *SAD*

A horse shoe face piece.
£35-40 *SAD*

A selection of horse brasses.
£20-30 *SAD*

An Invicta horse brass, late 19thC.
£40-50 *SAD*

A selection of brasses.
£20-30 *SAD*

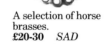

l. Club design.
£35-45
r. Of gypsy origin.
£15-25 *SAD*

Two pony brasses.
£5-8
£10-15 with leather
SAD

Top. Early pressed brass
fleur-dy-lys.
£30-35
l. and r. Old cast brass.
£25-30 *SAD*

Two heart designs.
£20-25 *SAD*

A selection of old brasses.
£15-25 *SAD*

Harness

A pair of unusual brass
bridle decorations.
£35-45 *SAD*

l. Two-bell swinger with
plume.
£55-65
r. Three-bell terret with
plume.
£60-65 *SAD*

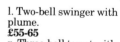

A bell swinger and a
three-bell terret.
£35-50 each *SAD*

Two brass decorations on
old leather.
£20-35 each *SAD*

A pair of swingers on oak bases, and a fly terret.
£25-35 each   *SAD*

A very fine three-bell swinger.
£50-60   *SAD*

An early plume, 6in (15cm) high.
£25-35   *SAD*

Two commemorative decorations:
l. Victorian penny on brass rosette, 3in (7.5cm) diam.
£8-12
r. Coronation wall plaque, 1953.
£12-15   *SAD*

A two-bell terret on bell, with red, white and blue plume.
£60-65   *SAD*

FURTHER READING

Brears, Peter C. D., *Horse Brasses*, 1981.
Brown, R. A., *Horse Brasses — Their History and Origin*, 1963.
Evans, G. E., *The Horse in the Furrow*, 1960.
Hartfield, George, *Horse Brasses*, 1965.
Hughes, G. B., *Horse Brasses*, 1956.
Richards, H. S. *All About Horse Brasses*, Birmingham 1943.
Vince, John, *Discovering Horse Brasses*, 1968.

Inkwells

A pair of Georgian silver plated inkwells, with unused ink.
£55-65   *MB*

A Victorian ladies inkwell, 3in (7cm) high.
£30-40   *MB*

A Victorian cut glass inkwell.
£25-35   *MB*

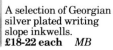

A selection of Georgian silver plated writing slope inkwells.
£18-22 each   *MB*

211

INKWELLS

A pair of matching inkwells with brass tops, 2in (5cm) high.
£50-60 *MB*

Inkwell and match holder.
£9-13 *VB*

An Edwardian inkstand, engraved with Royal Crown and Cypher and underneath: To Mr. Joseph Duveen for services rendered during the Coronation, 1902, by J. B. Carrington, 11½in (29cm) wide, 40oz.
£1,200-1,400 *P*

A silver plated calendar inkwell, 4in (10cm) diam.
£30-35 *AL*

Victorian inkwells for writing slopes.
£20-25 each *MB*

A Victorian cast iron inkwell, 5in (12.5cm) diam.
£20-30 *OSc*

A Liberty pewter inkwell with stylised plant decoration, 6in (15cm) diam.
£150-200 *ST*

A gilt and enamel inkwell, possibly Indian.
£20-25 *MB*

Glass inkwells.
£3-10 *VB*

An Esterbrook inkwell in Art Deco style, in black Bakelite with glass and chrome trim, c1930.
£25-35 *OR*

An Art Deco inkwell, 6½in (16cm) high.
£100-150 *PAT*

A Continental ceramic and gilt inkwell, with seal and candle, 5½in (14cm) high.
£30-40 *PAT*

A Lalique glass inkwell.
£1,000-1,200 *HP*

An ormolu and white onyx inkwell, c1920, 7½in (19cm) high.
£100-120 *PAT*

A bronze inkstand, 16in (40cm) wide.
£400-600 *CSK*

Travelling inkwells.
£10-20 *VB*

Travelling inkwell, 2in (5cm) square.
£40-50 *AL*

Travelling inkwell.
£15-20 *VB*

Jewellery

Bracelets

A selection of amber
Bakelite bracelets.
Under £20 each   *ZIG*

A selection of green
Bakelite jewellery.
Under £25 each   *ZIG*

A selection of Art Deco
bracelets.
£6-22   *ZIG*

A jade and silver gilt
bracelet.
£75-85   *SAD*

An amber Bakelite
bracelet, set with glass
stones.
£90-100   *ZIG*

Persian bracelets, with
painted miniatures.
£50-60 each   *SAD*

Brooches

Bakelite brooches.
£15-20   *ZIG*

A Victorian silver bird
brooch, with ruby eye
and diamanté, 1in
(2.5cm).
£25-35   *SAD*

A silver brooch with
Cairngorm stone.
£35-45 *SAD*

A Victorian silver and
turquoise scarab brooch.
£20-30 *SAD*

A Victorian hair brooch.
£35-45 *SAD*

A Victorian silver bird.
£20-25 *SAD*

A selection of Art Deco
Bakelite clips.
£10-18 *ZIG*

A Victorian micro-mosaic
brooch, c1880, 1in
(2.5cm).
£380-400 *LG*

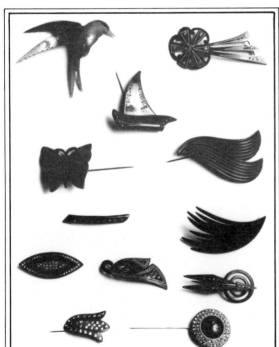

Various millinery pins.
£14-18 *ZIG*

H.M.S. Edinburgh, in
silver.
£28-35 *SAD*

A Victorian 9ct gold
brooch.
£35-45 *SAD*

DID YOU KNOW?___
Mizpah is a Jewish word
meaning 'The Lord
watch between Thee and
Me'.

A selection of brooches,
in silver filigree, brass
and paste.
£4-11 *VB*

Various brooches.
£3-9 *VB*

Bead Flowers

Bird brooches.
£8-14 *VB*

A beadwork brooch.
£5-7 *VB*

French carved horn
brooches, c1880-1930.
£30-40 *ZIG*

MAKE THE MOST OF
MILLER'S
Price ranges in this book reflect what one should
expect to *pay* for a similar example. When selling,
however, one should expect to receive a lower figure.
This will fluctuate according to a dealer's stock,
saleability at a particular time, etc. It is always
advisable, when selling, to approach a reputable
specialist dealer or an auction house which has
specialist sales.

1930s bead flowers.
£1-2 *VB*

Cuff Links

A cuff link set and tie clip.
£20-25 set *ZIG*

A cuff link set.
£12-15 *ZIG*

Necklaces

A Norwegian silver gilt
and green enamel
necklace, signed on every
link sterling J. Tostrup.
£110-120 *SAD*

A Chinese silver, coral
and turquoise necklace.
£35-45 *SAD*

Rings

A gold mounted blue and
white jasper necklace,
with 26 waisted beads,
probably Wedgwood,
early 19thC, 17½in
(44cm) long.
£2,000-2,500 *C*

A turquoise and white
sapphire ring.
£35-45 *SAD*

A silver and ivory
eternity ring.
£20-30 *SAD*

A 9ct gold chrysoprase
ring.
£40-50 *SAD*

Lockets

Miscellaneous

A jade charm.
£10-15 *SAD*

A Victorian brass and
gilt double locket.
£18-25 *SAD*

A silver locket.
£35-45 *SAD*

Ivory earrings, c1930.
£20-25 *SAD*

Kitchenalia

Advertising

Sunlight Flakes soap box.
Under £5 *WHA*

O-Cedar liquid polish.
Under £5 *WHA*

Margerison's Golden Windsor soap.
Under £5 *WHA*

Lady Gay Ballroom Floor Polish, unopened.
Under £5 *WHA*

Pea Flour, for strong nourishing gravy and soups.
Under £5 *WHA*

National Dried Milk.
Under £5 *WHA*

Ceramics

A sultana jar, 6in (15cm) high.
£15-20 *AL*

Maypole Dairy milk measure, 6in (15cm) high.
£30-35 *AL*

An egg coddler, 4in (10cm).
£5-7 *AL*

Harris's Clotted Cream container, 'This valuable product highly esteemed for its delicacy with Fruits, Pastry, Jams, Puddings, Coffee, Salads, Fish, Vegetables etc., gives richness of flavour unapproachable, also greatly used for whisking by dissolving in milk. This nourishing article has been most successfully employed in case of debility and consumption for which it is highly commended by the Faculty', 5in (12.5cm) high.
£5-10 *AL*

An ice cream cone server, 5in (12.5cm) high.
£5-10 *AL*

Kent's Patent milk saver.
£5-10 *AL*

The 'Blériot' Pie Divider.
£15-20 *AL*

BROWN&POLSON'S
RaisingPowder
Makes Shortbread
Crisp and short
And more easy of
digestion.
"PAISLEY FLOUR"
TRADE MARK

Shortbread
Is deliciously crisp,
short and easy of digestion
if made with
Raisley
The SURE raising powder
Made by Brown&Polson, Ltd.
and as reliable as
their Corn Flour

Shortbread dishes.
£10-15 each *AL*

A Grimwade's 'Quick
Cooker' pie dish, 9in
(23cm) diam.
£15-20 *AL*

A stone hot water bottle.
£6-10 *WHA*

Sidney's patent
measuring jug, pale blue
pottery Ironstone,
Edward Walley, 7½in
(19cm) high.
£15-20 *AL*

A Staffordshire pottery
'New Milk' pail, crack to
base, early 20thC, 12in
(30.5cm).
£85-95 *WIL*

A Forfar blue
transferware pie dish.
£20-30 *AL*

A Priests of Cardiff
spittoon.
£25-30 *WHA*

A Weetabix cereal dish.
£10-15 *AL*

Pie Funnels

A pie funnel, 4cm.
£35-45 *MAN*

Crown pottery pie funnels, 3 and 4in (7.5 and 10cm) high.
£5-7 *AL*

A pie funnel.
£4-6 *AL*

An elephant pie funnel.
£7-10 *AL*

Cutters

A set of cutters.
£7-10 *WHA*

A set of cutters, with brass plaque J. Bennington, 97 Jermyn Street, St. James's, London, 9in (23cm) wide.
£10-15 *AL*

A pig biscuit cutter, 7in (18cm) wide.
£5-10 *AL*

Tin pastry cutters.
£8-10 *AL*

Pastry cutters, in case.
£10-15 *AL*

Lighting

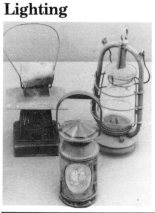

Various oil lamps.
£15-30 *TM*

An early oil lamp, 6½in (16.5cm) high.
£10-12 *WHA*

An oil lamp, 6½in (16.5cm) high.
£10-15 *SAD*

KITCHENALIA

Tin Openers

A German tin opener, marked 'Clou', 6in (15cm).
£2-5 *AL*

A tin opener, 6in (15cm).
£2-5 *AL*

Cast iron bulls head tin openers.
£12-15 *NM*
The first openers were produced for opening corned beef tins.

A wooden handled opener, 9in (23cm).
£1-2 *AL*

A bulls head tin opener.
£12-15 *AD*

A fish can opener, 5in (12.5cm).
£7-9 *AL*

A wooden handled tin opener, 6in (15cm).
£1-2 *AL*

Rolling Pins

An Allinson's flour rolling pin.
£20-25 *AL*

A rolling pin with Hovis on the handle.
£10-15 *AL*

A 'Coombs Eureka Flour' pottery rolling pin.
£20-25 *AL*

A Victorian rolling pin.
£18-20 *WHA*

Wooden Items

A collection of wooden spoons.
Under £5 *WHA*

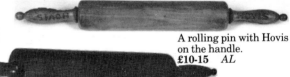

Butter pat.
£4-6 *WHA*

A softwood four-section spice box, each bearing transfer label, early 19thC, 7in (18cm).
£50-100 *WIL*

A butter churn.
£45-55 *WHA*

An oak cutlery box.
£65-75 *WHA*

Clothes pegs.
£5-7 *AL*

Meat tenderisers.
£4-5 each *WHA*

Two scoops, 3½ and 6in
(9 and 15cm).
£25-30 *AL*

Miscellaneous

An enamel half pint
measure for shellfish.
£5-10 *AL*

A garden seed container,
6½in (16.5cm) high.
£60-70

Cross Reference
Treen
Scales and Balances
Egg Cups
Ceramics
Teapots
Spoons
Tools
Metalware

Bread Boards & Knives

'Be Thankful' bread board.
£25-35 *AL*

'Long Life and Happiness' wedding gift bread board.
£25-35 *AL*

A Victorian commemorative bread board.
£30-35 *AL*

A bread knife, engraved 'Not a cold corner in the house, thanks to Mr. Therm'.
£7-10 *AL*

'Staff of Life' bread board.
£20-30 *AL*

Carved wooden handled bread knives.
£20-25 *AL*

A Joseph Rodgers & Sons bread knife, 13in (33cm).
£30-35 *AL*

Bread knives, with silver plate handle and parian handle.
£20-30 *AL*

Ivory handled bread knives.
£20-25 *AL*

Chicken Nests

Highly decorated chicken nests were produced in the 19thC. The nests were placed on the sideboard and filled with warm water in which boiled eggs were kept until ready to be eaten. Earthenware and glass nests were kept in the larder and used for storing fresh eggs.

White pressed glass hen and nests, with red and yellow decoration, 6 and 8in (15 and 20cm).
£65-75 each   *MAN*

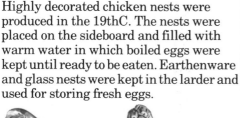

A brown glazed pottery cockerel on nest, marked Kensington, 8½in (21.5cm) wide.
£35-45   *MAN*

A dark green glazed pottery hen, 8in (20.5cm) wide.
£40-50   *MAN*

An English blue glazed pottery hen on nest, 10in (25.5cm) wide.
£50-60   *MAN*

A pressed glass transparent chicken, 10in (25.5cm) wide.
£50-60   *MAN*

A yellow pressed glass nest, 6in (15cm) wide.
£35-45   *MAN*

A pressed glass hen on nest, turquoise blue, 6in (15cm) wide.
£40-50   *MAN*

Gadgets

An American brass kettle whistle, 4in (10cm) high.
£30-35   *AL*

Household Wants Indicator, 13½ by 11½in (34 by 29cm).
£25-30   *AL*

A wooden coffee grinder.
£15-20   *WHA*

A butter churn, 13in (33cm) high.
£20-25   *AL*

A Danish bread slicer.
£30-40   *WHA*

A collection of nut crackers.
£3-4 each   *AL*

Two cherry stoners.
£25-30   *AL*

An early garlic press, 10in (25.5cm) long.
£15-20   *AL*

An early lemon squeezer, 10in (25.5cm).
£15-20   *AL*

A Standard Royal Icing set, with original box.
£12-15   *WHA*

Knife Rests

Knife rests were used to protect table
linen from carving and other implements,
and there are many examples to be found,
usually in glass or metal.

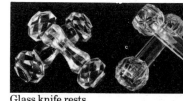

Knife rests.
£7-9 *VB*

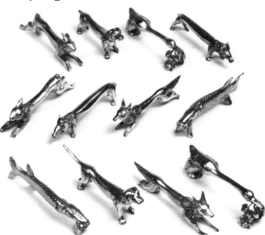

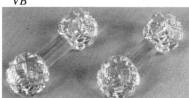

Glass knife rests.
£7-8 *VB*

A set of 12 Art Deco
metal knife rests, in
original fitted box.
£330-350 *CSK*

Glass knife rests.
£7-8 *VB*

Pewter knife rests.
£16-20 *VB*

Glass knife rests.
£9-10 *VB*

Knife rests.
£3-8 *VB*

Moulds

Two copper jelly moulds,
5in (12.5cm) high.
£90-120   *OSc*

A selection of Victorian
copper moulds.
£25-35 each   *PC*

Victorian copper
miniature fish moulds.
£30-40 each   *PC*

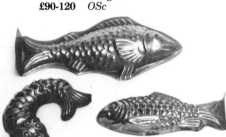

A selection of Victorian
copper miniature
moulds, 1½ to 2in (4 to
5cm) high.
£30-40 each   *PC*

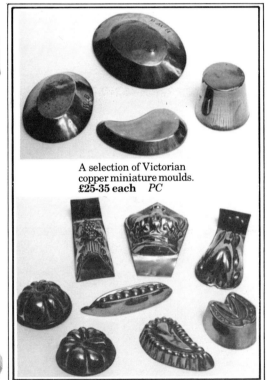

A selection of Victorian
copper miniature moulds.
£25-35 each   *PC*

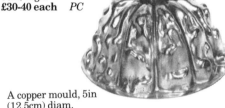

A copper mould, 5in
(12.5cm) diam.
£25-30   *PAC*

Plain copper jelly moulds.
£19-25 each   *AL*

Jelly moulds, 3 and 5in
(7.5 and 12.5cm) high.
£8-12   *AL*

Jelly mould sets.
£30-120 per set *MAN*

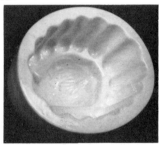

A pair of Wedgwood jelly moulds, marked, 3½in (8.5cm) wide.
£55-65 each *MAN*
A white glazed mould, 4½in (11.5cm) high.
£8-10 *MAN*

A copper and tin jelly mould, 7½in (19cm) wide.
£60-70 *AL*

A jelly mould, 2in high.
£125-150 *MAN*

A Wedgwood jelly mould, marked, 4in (10cm) wide.
£55-65 *MAN*

A set of 3 Shelley jelly moulds, 2½in (6cm) high.
£12-15 *MAN*

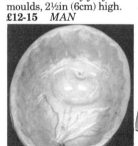

A Wedgwood jelly mould with smear glaze, 3½in (8.5cm).
£75-85 *MAN*

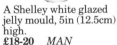

A Shelley white glazed jelly mould, 5in (12.5cm) high.
£18-20 *MAN*

Two ceramic jelly moulds, 6in (15cm) wide.
£20-25 each *AL*

Glass jelly moulds.
£7-8 each *AL*

Wooden pork pie moulds.
£14-16 each *WHA*

A pottery blanc-mange
mould.
£15-20 *AL*

A Royal Pudding Mould
with lid, 6in (15cm) diam.
£10-15 *AL*

A plain blanc-mange
mould.
£35-40 *AL*

A shaped Brown &
Polson blanc-mange
mould.
£15-20 *AL*

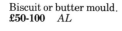

Biscuit or butter mould.
£50-100 *AL*

A German soap mould.
£35-40 *WHA*

A wooden butter mould,
3½in (9cm) diam.
£50-100 *AL*

A pie mould, 7in (18cm)
wide.
£100-120 *MAN*

Biscuit or butter moulds.
£50-100 *AL*

Luggage

A Louis Vuitton suitcase,
fitted with
compartments, 28in
(71cm) wide.
£450-500 *CSK*

A ladies leather
travelling companion
case, fully fitted with
silver topped containers.
£1,200-1,500 *PC*

A collection of Louis
Vuitton luggage, covered
with 'LV' material, all
numbered.
£300-1,100 each *CSK*

A leather hat box, with
fitted interior, and a top
hat, late 19thC.
£125-150 *PC*

A leather collar box.
£17-20 *MB*

An Asprey's picnic set,
the tan leather covered
case with hinged lid,
containing 6 place
settings, containers and
jars, c1930, 30in (76cm)
wide.
£5,000-6,000 *C*

METALWARE
Brass

Miscellaneous

A duck letter holder, 6in (15cm) long.
£75-150 *PC*

A vesta box with chalcedony eyes, striker on base.
£100-120 *PAT*

Letter holders in the form of hands, marked J.E. Ratcliffe, Birmingham, 4 and 6in (10 and 15cm) long.
£50-100 each *PC*

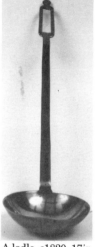

A ladle, c1820, 17in (43cm).
£30-40 *OSc*

A milk churn cover.
£75-100 *AL*

A Georgian shoe horn, 10in (25cm) long.
£30-35 *SAD*

An early Georgian pestle and mortar, 3in (7.5cm).
£65-75 *SAD*

A balance for weighing sovereigns, by Wilkinson, c1840, 4in (10cm) long.
£45-55 *SAD*

Cross Reference
Candlesticks

Fenders

A Regency fender, on bracket feet.
£280-320 *CEd*

A Victorian serpentine fender, on bun feet, 51in (128cm).
£650-750 *CEd*

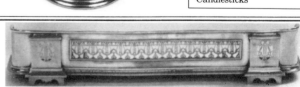

A late Regency pierced and engraved fender, on black cast iron plinth, 57in (143cm).
£750-850 *CEd*

Bronzes

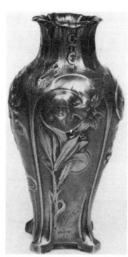

An Art Nouveau Susse
Frères gilt bronze vase,
cast from a model by
Becker, with inscriptions
'Printemps, Ete,
Automne, Hiver',
impressed marks, 9in
(23cm) high.
£600-650 *CSK*

An Art Deco patinated
green bronze figure, cast
from a model by
M. Guiraud Riviere, on
marble base, base
inscribed M. Guiraud
Riviere, 18½in (47cm)
high.
£1,750-2,000 *CSK*

A cold painted bronze
figure of a dancer, cast
from a model by Lorenzl,
inscribed, 26in (66cm).
£2,000-2,500 *CSK*

A bronze figure of a
grenadier, by G. E.
Wade, cast in 2 parts,
musket missing, stamped
by manufacturer
H. Luppens & Co., 1889,
23in (58cm) high.
£500-550 *C*

A French bronze model of
a reeve, on an oval
naturalistic base, signed
J. Moigniez, 19thC, 7½in
(19cm).
£450-500 *C*

A bronze figure of a
panther, signed on base
M. Prost, founder's
marks Susse Fres. Edits.
Paris, base chipped,
14½in (47cm) wide.
£850-900 *C*

A bronze sculpture,
'Source d'Or', inscribed
and signed E. Wante,
10½in (25.5cm) high.
£900-1,000 *C*

A French bronze statue
of 'L'Industrie Moderne',
signed on side of pedestal
Charley Perron, late
19thC, on mottled green
marble base, 25in (63cm).
£500-550 *C*

A Georgian bronze wool
weight, cast with the
Royal Armorial bearings,
and initials 'G.R', 6½in
(17cm) high.
£700-750 *Bea*

Austrian cold painted bronze figures of 2 dogs, 3 and 2in (7.5 and 5cm) and a painted metal group of 2 lambs.
£160-200 *CSK*

A Viennese bronze portrait bust of a young girl, signed Strasser and dated 1894 on marble plinth, 16½in (42cm).
£550-600 *C*

A French bronze relief of a lion, signed Barye, 19thC, 16in (41cm) wide.
£525-550 *C*

Door Plates

A copper finger plate, possibly Georgian, hand crafted.
£5-20 *VF*

Art Nouveau finger plates
£5-20 each *VF*

Finger plates.
£5-20 each *VF*

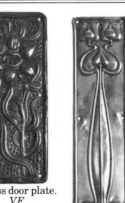

A brass door plate.
£5-20 *VF*

A Victorian brass finger plate, hand made.
£5-20 *VF*

Art Nouveau copper finger plates.
£5-20 *VF*

General Metalware

Britannia Metal

A tobacco box, c1840, 4in (10cm) high.
£60-80 *OSc*

An engraved teapot.
£26-32 *WHA*

A teapot.
£24-30 *WHA*

Cast Iron

Nut crackers, raise the tail to open the mouth, c1900.
£40-60 *DL*

A pair of boot scrapers, 14in (35.5cm).
£150-170 *CSK*

A pair of late Victorian brackets, 10 by 9in (25.5 by 23cm).
£35-45 *VF*

A painted door stop, Mr. Punch, 30in (76cm).
£50-80
Unpainted **£30-50** *OSc*

Firemarks

Westminster Insurance, lead, policy No. 26424.
£300-350 *P*

A boot scraper.
£100-120 *CSK*

British Fire Office.
£300-350 *P*

Pewter

A warming dish, 9in
(23cm) diam.
£150-180 *AL*

Spoons.
£5-7 each *SAD*

A tappit hen, 17thC.
£600-800 *PC*

Cross Reference
Writing accessories
Spoons

A pewter seal, 3½in
(9cm) high.
£35-45 *SAD*

DID YOU KNOW?_____
Pewter is an alloy of tin, with either lead or copper, or
sometimes both, added.
  The darker the pewter the higher the lead content.
The more silver grey the higher the tin content.
Britannia metal is an alloy of tin and antimony.

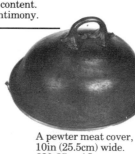

A pewter meat cover,
10in (25.5cm) wide.
£20-25 *AL*

A quart measure, Star &
Crown, Goudhurst, 6in
(15cm) high.
£250-300 *PC*

*The hostelry is now
known as The Star and
Eagle.*

A Victorian tankard,
engraved with initials
and name underneath.
£55-65 *SAD*

A measure, engraved
W. Lewis, 5in (12.5cm).
£45-55 *SAD*

A marked pewter
tankard, 5in (12.5cm)
high.
£55-65 *SAD*

Silver

A Victorian teaset,
Chester 1898, 34oz.
£550-600 *WIL*

A hot water jug, Charles
Stuart Harris & Son,
London 1934, 8in
(20.5cm), 10.25oz gross.
£165-185 *CSK*

A George III mazarine,
probably John Parker
and Edward Wakelin,
London 1775, 13in
(33cm), 15.25oz.
£330-350 *CSK*

A silver and enamel
picture frame, William
Hutton & Sons, stamped
with maker's marks and
London hallmarks for
1903, 8in (20.5cm) high.
£900-1,000 *C*

A George III inkstand,
with glass inkwells,
maker C.S.H, London
1776, 19oz.
£620-650 *WIL*

A Guild of Handicrafts
porringer, designed by
C. R. Ashbee, the handle
set with oval cabochon
chrysoprase, stamped
G. of H. and London
hallmarks for 1902, 7in
(18cm) wide, 136gms.
£950-1,000 *WIL*

A matching pair of
George III sauceboats, by
Daniel Smith and Robert
Sharp, c1760, 27oz.
£1,300-1,500 *P*

An Art Deco bowl, hand
wrought showing
hammering to interior,
no marks, 18oz approx.
£150-200 *WIL*

A George IV engine
turned vinaigrette,
Samuel Pemberton,
Birmingham 1820, 1½in
(4cm), in contemporary
red morocco case with
label 'Belonged to Lady S
Reeve'.
£160-180 *DN*

Trinket trays.
l. Late Victorian, H.H. &
S., Birmingham, 1900,
10in (25.5cm), 8oz.
£165-185
r. Edwardian Art

Nouveau, engraved with
registration No., Moss &
Company, Birmingham
1907, 12½in (32cm),
11.25oz.
£280-300 *CSK*

DID YOU KNOW?
Vinaigrettes are beautifully made small boxes
designed to hold a small sponge primed with
aromatic spices.

237

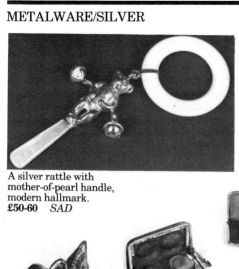

A silver rattle with
mother-of-pearl handle,
modern hallmark.
£50-60 *SAD*

A selection of mother-of-
pearl silver bladed fruit
knives.
£12-25 each *VB*

Sovereign holders.
£12-15 each *VB*

A pill box, 1½in (4cm)
long.
£75-85 *SAD*

A sovereign case,
Chester 1824, 1¼in
(3cm).
£65-75 *SAD*

Tongs, Peter Bateman,
c1791, 5½in (14cm).
£40-50 *SAD*

Ladies shoe horns.
£40-50 *PGA*

A carriage with cherubs,
Cheshire, 1898, 4in
(10cm).
£65-75 *SAD*

A button hook.
£15-25 *PC*

A Sheffield pen knife,
1931.
£25-35 *SAD*

A pin cushion, 2in (5cm).
£60-70 *SAD*

An early Victorian
child's rattle.
£250-300 *SAD*

Cross Reference
Button hooks

DID YOU KNOW?
DUTY MARK
From 1st December, 1784, an extra mark appeared
on silverwares. It was a profile of a head of George III
and indicated that the new tax imposed on silver had
been paid. Both the tax and the Duty Mark were not
abolished until 1890.

A Victorian hallmarked brush.
£20-25   *PC*

Dressing table items.
Box.
£100-130
Bottles.
£20-30 each   *PC*

A bound almanac with purse at either end, 1793.
£20-25   *VB*

A selection of nut picks.
£1-8 each   *VB*

A swizzle stick, Birmingham 1935.
£22-25   *VB*

Silver pencils, by Mordan, c1900.
£9-15   *VB*

A pencil holder, Birmingham 1905.
£16-20   *SAD*

A cigar holder, 4in (10cm) long.
£35-40   *VB*

A pen wiper, Chester.
£18-25   *VB*

A silver handled seal breaker.
£15-17   *VB*

A cruet set.
£100-130   *PC*

Napkin holders, 1906.
£18-20 each   *VB*

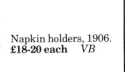

A sugar caster, 8in (20.5cm).
£45-65   *PC*

Cross Reference
Writing Accessories
Smoking

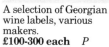

A selection of Georgian
wine labels, various
makers.
£100-300 each *P*

A selection of Victorian
and Georgian wine
labels.
£150-400 each *P*

A selection of Georgian
wine labels, various
makers.
£90-150 each *P*

Wine labels.
£150-250 *P*

Wine labels.
£130-160 *P*

Silver Plate

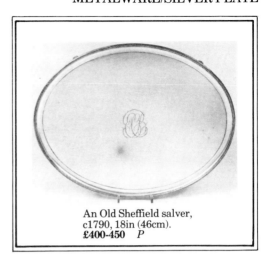

A neo-classical style
goblet, c1790.
£100-150   *P*

A salver, by J. Watson &
Son, c1835, 8½in (21cm)
diam.
£280-320   *P*

An Old Sheffield salver,
c1790, 18in (46cm).
£400-450   *P*

A pair of Sheffield plate
vases, with metal liners,
13in (33cm).
£220-250   *P[Re]*

A pair of Sheffield tongs,
1906, 4in (10cm).
£50-60   *SAD*

An egg cup.
£7-10   *AL*

A pair of Victorian grape
scissors, 5½in (14cm).
£20-30   *SAD*

A coaster.
£70-90   *PC*

A whistle, 3½in (9cm).
£2-5   *SAD*

A teaset, impressed
marks 'The Cube Tea Pot
Robert Johnsons patents
Gt. Britain 110951
U.S.A., 1380066, Napper
Davenport Birmingham
England'.
£250-300   *CSK*

A Regency candlestick,
marked, 7½in (19cm).
£55-65   *SAD*

An Art Deco muffin dish,
12in (30.5cm) wide.
£100-150   *PC*

Cross Reference
Egg cups

MILITARIA

Badges

Badges and buttons are very popular areas for the militaria collector. Most readily available are examples from this century, especially World War II. Buttons are often sold at auction in bagged lots, sometimes providing a sought after specimen at a reasonable price.

Brass cap and helmet badges can be found dating back to the mid-19thC, before that date there were few standard regimental badges, although sometimes a king's crown would be used on belt buckles and shoulder plates; the pattern of the crown is a valuable aid to dating.

l. Machine gun corps.
£4-6
c. The Queen's Regiment (Royal West Surrey).
£3-4
r. Royal Air Force.
£1-2 *CHA*

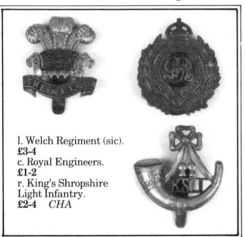

l. Welch Regiment (sic).
£3-4
c. Royal Engineers.
£1-2
r. King's Shropshire Light Infantry.
£2-4 *CHA*

l. South Staffordshire Regiment.
£3-4
c. Manchester Regiment, pre-1923.
£3-4
r. The Green Howards, The Princess of Wales Own Yorkshire Regiment.
£3-4 *CHA*

l. Royal Corps of Signals.
£1-2
c. The Royal Sussex Regiment.
£3-4
r. Royal Artillery.
£1-2 *CHA*

Durham Light Infantry
£3-4 *WAL*

Royal Marines Light Infantry.
£5-6 *WAL*

Disbanded in 1922.

Royal Army Medical Corps.
£1-2 *WAL*

Cameron Highlanders.
£3-4
The Gordon Highlanders.
£3-4
The Highland Light
Infantry.
£3-4   *CHA*

Lapel badges.
£1-2 each   *WAL*

WWI Comrades badge.
£1-2   *WAL*

The National Union of
Women's Associations.
£1-2   *WAL*

Royal West Kent
Regiment.
£3-4   *WAL*

DID YOU KNOW?
Following a dreadful incident in London during the
First World War, when a lady pressed a white
feather into the hand of a soldier who had been
discharged due to appalling wounds received in
action for which he had won the Victoria Cross, it was
decided to institute a simple lapel badge inscribed
'For King and Empire – Services Rendered'.

£1-2   *WAL*

Women's Royal Army
Corps, WWII.
£5-6   *WAL*

The Life Boys.
50p-£1   *WAL*

DID YOU KNOW?
Miller's Collectables
Price Guide is designed
to build up, year by year,
into the most
comprehensive reference
system available.

ARP lapel badge, silver.
£2-3
Metal **£1-2**   *WAL*

W.V.S.
50p-£1   *WAL*

Cross Reference
Police

Metropolitan Special
Constabulary.
£2-3   *WAL*

Shoulder – Belt Plates

Scots Fusilier Guards, pattern worn until 1855.
£220-250 *CSK*

Royal Scots Fusiliers.
£55-65 *CSK*

6th (1st Warwickshire) Regiment of Foot officers.
£140-160 *CSK*

2nd Royal Tower Hamlets Militia (Queen's Light Infantry).
£220-250 *CSK*

56th Bengal Native Infantry.
£140-160 *CSK*

27th Enniskillen Regiment of Foot.
£200-220 *CSK*

The Black Watch (Royal Highlanders).
£140-160 *CSK*

Gordon Highlanders.
£160-180 *CSK*

72nd (Duke of Albany's Own Highlanders).
£120-140 *CSK*

Seaforth Highlanders.
£135-145 *CSK*

Black Watch.
£165-185 *CSK*

26th (Cameronians).
£165-185 *CSK*

Helmet Plates

The King's (Liverpool Regiment).
£80-100 *CSK*

19th Lancashire Rifle Volunteer Corps.
£200-220 *CSK*

Army Ordnance Corps.
£60-80 *CSK*

1st Volunteer Battalion, The Suffolk Regiment.
£120-140 *CSK*

DID YOU KNOW?

Always try and buy buttons and badges from a reputable dealer. Even these less expensive collectable items have suffered from the attentions of forgers and fakers. Be particularly wary of restrikes and reproductions.

Hampshire Regiment.
£80-100 *CSK*

Duke of Wellington's (West Riding Regiment).
£110-120 *CSK*

Somerset Light Infantry.
£80-120 *CSK*

Queen's Own (Royal West Kent Regiment).
£80-120 *CSK*

Buttons

Royal Welch Fusiliers.
50p-£1 *WAL*

The Royal Scots.
50p-£1 *WAL*

The Oxfordshire &
Buckinghamshire Light
Infantry.
50p-£1 *WAL*

The Royal Highlanders.
50p-£1 *WAL*

The North Staffordshire
Regiment.
50p-£1 *WAL*

Queen's Royal Regiment.
50p-£1 *WAL*

l. Royal West Surrey
Regiment.
r. Royal Warwickshire
Regiment.
50p-£1 each *WAL*

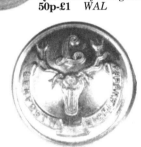

The Seaforth
Highlanders.
50p-£1 *WAL*

The East Surrey
Regiment.
50p-£1 *WAL*

Duke of Wellington's
West Riding Regiment.
50p-£1 *WAL*

l. Wiltshire Regiment.
r. Sherwood Foresters.
50p-£1 each *WAL*

The Worcestershire
Regiment.
50p-£1 *WAL*

The Cameronians.
50p-£1 *WAL*

Cross Reference
Buttons

DID YOU KNOW?
Dating British buttons is straightforward. After
1767 the regimental number was embossed on all
buttons (which were generally of pewter). Pewter
buttons were not finally replaced by brass ones until
mid-19thC. These early buttons are valued at £10
each and more. Brass buttons with the 'county'
regimental titles are priced generally from 50p to
£1.50 depending on condition and rarity. General
Service buttons, R.A., and R.E., etc., are 10-15p each.

Bayonets

An early triangular socket bayonet, stamped 54, blade 14in (35.5cm), and a Brown Bess triangular socket bayonet, marked S. Hill, blade 15½in (39cm).
£30-40   *WAL*

A US M1917 bayonet, a 1907 SMLE bayonet, plated mounts, in scabbard, blade surface rust, and an Export M 1899 Mauser bayonet, in brass mounted scabbard.
£60-80   *WAL*

A Japanese Type 30 bayonet, hooked quillon, in steel scabbard, an Argentine 1891 sword bayonet in steel scabbard, and a Czech M1924 bayonet in scabbard.
£55-65   *WAL*

A brass hilted P 1825 Baker bayonet, with triangular tapering blade, inspection stamp at forte, some pitting and damage, blade 17in (43cm).
£170-200   *WAL*

A French Chassepot bayonet, engraved 'Mre D'Armes De Chatt Spbre 1874', in steel scabbard, scabbard minor pitting, blade 22½in (57cm), and another with no inscription.
£25-35   *WAL*

A German M 1898/02 Pioneer bayonet, saw backed blade, marked with crown and 'Erfurt', issue marks for 1903, cleaned, areas of light pitting, grips minor wear, blade 17in (43cm).
£100-120   *WAL*

A scarce Elcho bayonet, spatulate saw backed blade, knight's head mark, diced black leather grips, steel mounts, cleaned, light age rust, grips shrunk, blade 19½in (50cm).
£200-250   *WAL*

A French 1842 sabre bayonet, engraved on backstrap 'Mre Imple De Chatt Juin 1866 S.B. Mge 1842', in dark blued steel scabbard, slight blade marking, blade 22½in (57cm).
£45-55   *WAL*

A 1903 SMLE bayonet, by Sanderson, inspection marks, also stamped crown 'ER', in scabbard, and three Spanish bayonets, in scabbards.
£70-100   *WAL*

A Martini Henry 18/5 pattern saw backed bayonet, knight's head maker's mark, inspection stamps, steel mounts, diced black leather grips, cleaned, some pitting, grips slightly shrunk, blade 18in (46cm).
£80-100   *WAL*

An SMLE No. 7 Bowie bladed bayonet, in scabbard.
£25-35   *WAL*

A Chinese Type 53 folding bayonet, a Nazi K98 bayonet, a Spanish M 1941 Bolo bayonet in scabbard and a Czech M 1924 bayonet in scabbard.
£45-55   *WAL*

A French 1866 Chassepot bayonet, engraved on backstrap 'Mre Natle De St Etienne Obre 1870' in steel scabbard, scabbard some dents and light pitting, blade 22½in (57cm), and a similar, marked 'Mre D'armes de Chatt Obre 1873, light marking, no scabbard.
£25-30   *WAL*

247

Medals

Military General Service, 1793, bar Fort Detroit, 41st Foot.
£950-1,000 *WAL*

Military General Service, 1793, bar Chateauguay, HMS Warrior.
£900-1,000 *WAL*

Military General Service, 1793, bar Chrystler's Farm, 49th Foot.
£950-1,000 *WAL*

Military General Service, with 13 clasps, James Coates, Cpl. 40th Foot.
£2,000-2,200 *C*

Very rare with 13 clasps.

Naval General Service, 1793, bar Boat Service 14 Dec. 1814.
£550-650 *WAL*

Waterloo Medal, 1815, John Berwick, Private 7th Hussars, re-named, hence lower value.
£100-150 *P*

Army of India, 2 bars, Bhurtpoor, Ava, Punjab, 1849, 2 bars, Chilianwala, Goojerat to Maj Williams 45th Bengal, Native Infantry.
£1,000-1,200 *WAL*

From l. to r. Group of Five, Cabul 1842, Maharajpoor Star 1843, Sutlej for Moodkee, bar Ferozeshuhur, Punjab, no bar, Indian Mutiny, 1 bar, Delhi, Punjab claw re-affixed, contact pitted.
£350-400 *WAL*

Indian Mutiny, Victoria Cross, pair to Pte R. Newell, 9th Lancers.
£8,000-9,000 *WAL*

Conspicuous Gallantry Metal, Ashanti Medal, bar Coomassie, to D. Driscoll, Leading Seaman.
£1,300-1,500 *WAL*

Order of the Bath, Meeanee Hyderabad, 1843 to Capt Conway, 22nd Regt.
£2,500-3,000 *WAL*

G.S.M. China, J. H. Skinner, 2nd Sick Berth Steward, HMS Centurion (750 to ship).
£50-60 *CHA*

South Africa 1853, D. D. Beck, 7th Dragn. Gds, GVF, minor nicks, 7th Dragoon Guards, present during 1846/7, 16 officers, 152 ORs.
£150-180 *WAL*

British South Africa Company medal for Matabeleland 1893, bar Rhodesia 1896, Trooper W. Nettlefold, Raafs Column, EF.
£160-200 *WAL*

South Africa 1853, W. Nash, 7th Dgn Gds, VF, with edge knock.
£110-150 *WAL*

I.G.S. 1854, 1 bar Umbeyla, Lieut. E. C. Davidson, 71st Highlrs, GVF, with miniature, no bar.
£150-200 *WAL*

South Africa Medal, 1877-79, Sgt. J. Connors, 88th Foot, 1/Connaught Rangers, with bar, 1877-8-9.
£100-120 *CHA*

Three medals to Mr. John Langford Smith, British Consul at Amoy, China, 1900, one clasp Relief of Pekin, China, Governor of Szechuan Gold Medal, and China, Emperor Kuang-hsu Silver Medal.
£900-1,000 *C*

Pair: South Africa 1877/79, bar 1879, I.G.S. 1854, 1 bar Burma 1887-89, 2nd Lieut. Capt. P. T. Armitage, 2-24th Foot, VF.
£450-500 *WAL*

South Africa 1877-79, no bar, 2363 Pte. A. Davis, 2-24th Foot, EF.
£100-120 *WAL*

D.S.O. Victorian, Ashanti Star 1896, East and West Africa Bar 1897-98, Ashanti Medal Bar Kumassi to Capt. Armitage 3rd South Wales Borderers.
£2,000-2,500 *WAL*

East and West Africa 1887-1900, 2 clasps, Witu August 1893 and Juba River 1893, E. Richardson, A.B., HMS Blanche, minor edge bruising, F.
£1,400-1,600 *C*

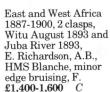

Victorian Long Service and Good Conduct, Army, Drummer F. Golding, 2/7 Foot, R. Fusiliers.
£30-40   *CHA*

Victorian Long Service and Good Conduct, Navy, Ldg. Stoker John Bowden, HMS Belleisle.
£35-45   *CHA*

1. Egypt 1880-1889.
2. Order of the Osmenieh.
3. Order of the Medjidig.
4. The Khedive Bronze Star to Interpreter J. Hewgill.
£250-300   *CHA*

Egypt 1882-89, Pte. H. G. Falgo, 12th Coy Comm. & Trans. Corps. with brass, Suakin 1885, Tofrek.
£70-80   *CHA*

Abyssinian Medal, 1867-68, Gnr. T. Donnelly, G. Bty, 14th Bde. Royal Artillery.
£125-150   *CHA*

Military G.S.M. 1793-1814, James Broom, 84th Foot, with bar, Nive.
£185-195   *CHA*

India G.S.M. 1895-1902, Pte. W. Doney, 2/R Sussex Regt. with bars, Punjab Frontier 1897-98 Tirah 1897-98.
£50-55   *CHA*

The Unique Officially Impressed Bronze Crimea Medal, The Captain's Dog HMS Leopard, not fitted with suspension, edge bruising, nearly very fine.
£500-600   *C*

ROMSEY MEDAL CENTRE

MEMBERS OF THE O.M.R.S. and LAPADA

Leading Medal Dealers with International Experience

We wish to purchase:
Individual Campaign Medals, Orders
Decorations, Groups and Collections

Telephone (0794) 512069
or write
Romsey Medal Centre
101 The Hundred, Romsey
Hampshire S051 8BY

---

*Medal Collectors can usually find interesting
items amongst our displayed stock, at
The Romsey Medal Centre*

*Or alternatively an enquiry or wants list will
be dealt with on a personal basis*

Three D.C.M. Victorian issue, Q.S.A, 5 bars, K.S.A both date bars, 1957 Serjt. Maj. F. Kingsley W. York Regt, D.C.M. for action at Spion Kop, GVF and VF.
£600-650   *WAL*

Three Cape of Good Hope General Service medal, Q.S.A. 3 bars, Cape of Good Hope L.S & G.C., VF.
£450-500   *WAL*

Three South Africa 1877-79, Cape of Good Hope, Q.S.A. 3 bars, VF.
£180-200   *WAL*

I.G.S 1895, 5 bars, GVF.
£140-180   *WAL*

Pte. J. Hetherington, 1899-1902, 14th Co. Imp. Yeo. Northumberland, with 5 bars.
£30-35   *CHA*

Pte G. B. Pearson, Kings Own Scottish Borderers, British War medal and Victory medal.
£6-10   *CHA*

A.C.I.A.L. Hall Royal Air Force, General Service Medal, with Kurdistan bar.
£90-135   *CHA*

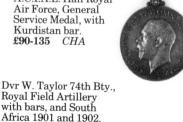

Dvr W. Taylor 74th Bty., Royal Field Artillery with bars, and South Africa 1901 and 1902.
£40-50 pair   *CHA*

Pte J. Jones, Cape Mounted Rifles with bar, 1899-1902.
£25-30   *CHA*

The Edward Medal in bronze for Industry, bravery award to George Edward Thorpe.
£325-425 *CHA*

S.S. 3672 A.B. J. D. Hill, Naval General Service Medal, 1915-1962, H.M.S. Fox, with bar Persian Gulf 1909-14.
£40-50 *CHA*

Pte H. M. Wilson 1st Btn.B.N Rly. Vol. Rifle Corps, George V, Volunteer Long Service.
£20-25 *CHA*

Capt J. Line, Royal Flying Corps, Air Force Cross George V group.
£500-600 *CHA*

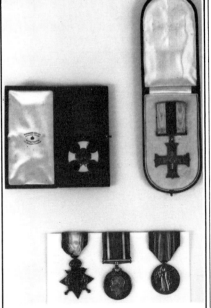

Cpl J. Mousdale, 126th Bty, R.F.A., Military Medal, George V.
£30-40 *CHA*

Maj A. H. Brown, Royal Engineers, D.S.O., Military Cross, 1914 Star, British War Medal, Victory Medal, killed in action 22nd March 1918.
£600-750 *CHA*

A scarce Lincolnshire Regimental medal awarded for Gallantry in Ireland, 1921, reverse inscribed '2nd Lieut:L.Morley-Turner for Gallant Conduct in Ireland 29th Sept:1920', GVF.
£275-300 *C*

German Iron Cross, 2nd class, 1914.
£8-14 *CHA*

253

Distinguished Flying
Cross, Geo VI issue,
reverse lower arm
engraved 1944, GVF.
£200-250 *WAL*

D.S.M. Geo VI, 1939-45
star, Atlantic star with
France & Germany bar,
War medal (all named
C/Jx 420245 N. Lambert
A.B. R.N), GVF. D.S.M.
£250-300 *WAL*

Distinguished Flying
Medal, Geo. VI, 526603
Sgt. C. J. Adair R.A.F.,
GVF., recipient in
No. 101 squadron.
£270-300 *WAL*

G.S.M. 1918, 1 bar
Northern Kurdistan
(L.A.C.) 1939-45 star,
Africa star, War, R.A.F.
L.S. & G.C. George VI
first type, King Feisal's
War medal with bar,
363300 Sgt. J. G.
Whiddon R.A.F. Average
VF., G.S.M. a rare bar.
£400-450 *WAL*

D.S.M., Geo V admirals
bust, Sea Gallantry
medal 1854, 'In Saving
Life at Sea' Geo V issue,
'B.W.M., Victory' (SA
2708 A. Elsome 2nd Hd.
R.N.R. 'Cygni' Aux
Patrol 1917, gallantry
medal engraved 'Alfred
Elsome 'Lord
Charlemont' 19th April,
1918', BWM and Vic as
SA2708 A. Ellsome Skr
R.N.R) VF.
£530-560 *WAL*

U.S.A. Purple Heart, for
wounds.
£17-22 *CHA*

M.M., George VI first
type, 1939-45 star, F & G
star, Defence and War,
6139267 Pte E. Wyeth.
E. Surr. R. all named,
GVF.
£230-250 *WAL*

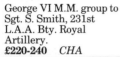

George VI M.M. group to Sgt. S. Smith, 231st L.A.A. Bty. Royal Artillery.
£220-240 *CHA*

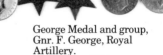

George Medal and group, Gnr. F. George, Royal Artillery.
£450-750 *CHA*

Sgt R. Nicol, Royal Air Force, General Service Medal, bar Malaya Campaign Service

Medal, Bar Borneo, R.A.F. Long Service and Good Conduct medal.
£50-80 *CHA*

National Fire Brigade Association, Defence Medal, N.F.B.A. Long Service Medal, Far Exemplary Fire Service Long Service, Fireman V. G. Houghton, West End, Hampshire Brigade.
£30-35 *CHA*

Pte B Cox, R.A.O.C., G.S.M. with bar Malaya.
£10-16 *CHA*

Volunteer Decoration, Queen Victoria overseas type, 1896, reverse engraved 'Captn. B.H. Skelton, 2nd Bn. B.B. & C. 1 Ry Volr. Rifles', GVF.
£240-270 *WAL*

R.N.V.R. Decoration, George VI first type, un-named, reverse dated 1942, NEF.
£70-90 *WAL*

R.N.V.R. Decoration, Eliz. II issue, un-named reverse dated 1957, EF.
£80-100 *WAL*

Efficiency Decoration, Eliz. II issue, with Army Emergency Reserve bar, dated 1958, un-named, EF.
£70-90 *WAL*

Efficiency Decoration, with 'T & A.V.R' bar brooch, 1952, un-named, EF.
£70-90 *WAL*

Meritorious Service Medal, Eliz. II issue, 2nd type, 1070679, W.O. Cl.1, D. F. Wright, R.E., EF.
£60-80 *WAL*

Observer J. C. Thomson,
Royal Observer Corps,
Long Service Medal,
ER II.
£25-35   *CHA*

Gnr H. L. Robinson,
Royal Artillery,
Campaign Service Medal
1962, with bar Northern
Ireland.
£15-20   *CHA*

Sgt L. J. Sharples,
R.E.M.E, African
General Service Medal,
1902, with bar Kenya.
£40-50   *CHA*

Act F Sgt. E. Leese,
Royal Air Force, with
bar.
£90-110   *CHA*

Pte D. J. Rousen, South
Wales Borderers,
Campaign Service
Medal, 1962, with bars.
£50-60   *CHA*

Orders

The Commander of the
Order of the British
Empire, C.B.E.
£80-90   *CHA*

Prussian Order of the
Crown Grand Cross,
Breast Star.
£1,200-1,500   *WAL*

Commander of the
Legion of Honour, Third
Republic, in gold.
£180-220   *CHA*

Mecklenburg-Schwerin
Order of the Wendian
Crown, Grand Cross.
£1,600-2,000   *WAL*

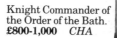

Knight Commander of
the Order of the Bath.
£800-1,000   *CHA*

Prussian Order of the
Black Eagle Grand
Cross, Breast Star.
£2,000-2,400   *WAL*

Pistols

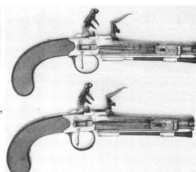

A brass barrelled flintlock blunderbuss pistol, engraved Liverpool, signed J. Parr, 8in (20cm) long.
£800-1,000   *P*

A 38 bore flintlock boxlock pocket pistol, engraved H. Nock, London, restored, c1800, 6in (15cm) overall.
£75-100   *WAL*

A brass framed and barrelled boxlock flintlock cannon barrelled pocket pistol by Barbar, some age wear, c1775, 6in (15cm).
£260-300   *WAL*

A pair of flintlock boxlock pistols, signed Grice, London, barrels 5in (13cm).
£900-1,200   *P*

A four-barrelled .30 rimfire Derringer, signed Tipping & Lawden, Sharps Patent, 7.5cm barrel.
£350-400   *P*

A cannon barrelled boxlock flintlock pocket pistol, by G. Devillers of Liège, some damage, c1765, 6½in (17cm).
£100-150   *WAL*

A flintlock long sea service pistol, 12in (30cm) long.
£550-600   *P*

A 20 bore flintlock travelling pistol, by I. Ward, restored, c1800, barrel 10½in (26.5cm).
£160-200   *WAL*

A decorative Turkish flintlock pistol, 18in (45.5cm).
£40-60   *WAL*

A .22(L.R) Model 18-2 combat masterpiece double action revolver, by Smith & Wesson, No. K766714, with 4in (10cm) barrel, nitro proof, with a leather holster and belt.
£160-180   *CSK*

A .450 double-action No. 4. Webley-Pryse 6-shot service revolver, retailed by Army & Navy C.S.L., No. 81112, barrel 5½in (14cm), in fitted oak case, engraved J. G. Woldrige Gordon, Sutherland Highlanders.
£350-400   *CSK*

Powder Flasks

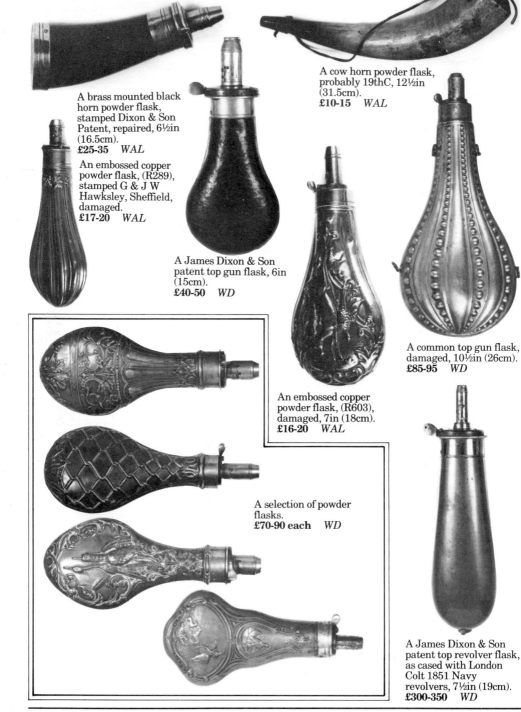

A cow horn powder flask, probably 19thC, 12½in (31.5cm).
£10-15 *WAL*

A brass mounted black horn powder flask, stamped Dixon & Son Patent, repaired, 6½in (16.5cm).
£25-35 *WAL*

An embossed copper powder flask, (R289), stamped G & J W Hawksley, Sheffield, damaged.
£17-20 *WAL*

A James Dixon & Son patent top gun flask, 6in (15cm).
£40-50 *WD*

A common top gun flask, damaged, 10½in (26cm).
£85-95 *WD*

An embossed copper powder flask, (R603), damaged, 7in (18cm).
£16-20 *WAL*

A selection of powder flasks.
£70-90 each *WD*

A James Dixon & Son patent top revolver flask, as cased with London Colt 1851 Navy revolvers, 7½in (19cm).
£300-350 *WD*

Swords

A 1796 type Light Cavalry officer's sabre, by Andrews, 9 Pall Mall, engraved, with William IV cypher, 32½in (82cm) with engraved steel mounted leather scabbard.
£330-350 *P*

A French Napoleonic Light Cavalry officer's sabre, blade engraved, blade damaged, 33½in (85cm), in brass scabbard with steel shoe.
£350-400 *P*

A Scottish basket hilted backsword, with fishskin covered grip, late 18thC, 33½in (84.5cm).
£400-450 *P*

A Scottish basket hilted backsword, with fishskin covered grip, late 18thC, 31in (78.5cm).
£300-350 *P*

A Victorian 1821 pattern Light Cavalry officer's undress sword, by J. Jos. Barlow Litchfield, worn, 33½in (85cm), with steel scabbard.
£110-150 *WAL*

A Georgian 1796 pattern Infantry officer's sword, blade 32½in (82cm), and black leather scabbard.
£120-140 *WD*

A German Nazi officer's dress dagger, by Alcoso, Solingen, WWII, 10½in (27cm), also Nazi armband.
£100-150 *WIL*

A Naval officer's fighting sword, blade 25in (63cm), in engraved brass mounted leather scabbard.
£1,500-2,000 *P*

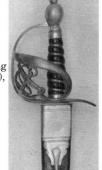

A Victorian 1822 pattern Infantry officer's sword, by Wilson, Lombard Street, some damage, curved blade 32in (81cm), in leather scabbard with copper mounts.
£30-50 *WAL*

A Royal Naval Volunteer's cutlass.
£450-550 *WAL*

Uniforms

An officer's short-tailed coatee of the Royal Flintshire Militia, by J. Quenby, Winchester, c1801.
£1,000-1,200   *CSK*

An officer of the 2nd Life Guards uniform items, with label to Colonel Sir A. D. Neeld, Bart.
£1,500-2,000   *CSK*

An officer's short-tailed scarlet coatee, the gilt buttons with the letters LEV.
£400-450   *CSK*

An officer's blue full dress tunic of the Staffordshire Yeomanry (Queen's Own Royal Regiment), full dress pouch and lace pouch belt.
£350-400   *CSK*

An officer's full dress uniform of the 10th Royal Hussars.
£1,400-1,600   *CSK*

A short-tailed scarlet coatee, dark blue facings, silver lace and white metal ball buttons, bearing the letters NCDY.
£300-350   *CSK*

A Rifle Volunteers, probably 4th Norfolk Rifle Volunteer Corps, Bugle-Major's uniform, cap adapted, c1872.
£220-250   *CSK*

A trooper's uniform of the City of London Yeomanry, Rough Riders, worn.
£70-100   *WAL*

An RAF Flight Lieutenant's tunic, added Air Gunners and WWII medal ribbons.
£45-55   *WAL*

Headgear

A French Kepi.
£25-35 *WAL*

An Italian Fascist officer's black fez.
£35-45 *WAL*

An Imperial German/Bavarian staff officer's pickelhaube, c1890.
£1,300-1,500 *GW*

An officer's blue cloth spiked helmet, bearing a K.C. plate of the Queen's Royal West Surrey Regiment.
£300-350 *CSK*

A Prussian feldmutze, field service cap, for Jager Battalion, moth holes, WWI.
£30-40 *WAL*

An officer's peaked forage cap of The Northumberland Fusiliers, chin strap missing and moth holes.
£130-150 *WAL*

A Nazi Paratrooper's steel helmet, lining and chinstrap replaced from another helmet.
£50-100 *WAL*

An officer's blue side cap of The Royal Dragoons.
£75-85 *WAL*

An officer's peaked cap of The Royal Dragoons.
£75-85 *WAL*

A khaki linen Wolseley pattern helmet.
£40-50 *WAL*

A brass skull only of a fireman's helmet, reinforced, c1900.
£25-35 *WAL*

A Nazi Wehrmacht steel helmet, chinstrap missing.
£50-100 *WAL*

General

Drums

Rope-tension side drums, 4th (Carms.) Bn. The Welch Regiment, 5th Battalion, The Welch Regiment, 2nd Battalion, Royal Fusiliers, City of London Regiment, 23rd Service Battalion, Royal Fusiliers.
£200-300 each *CSK*

A composite German drum of Landsknecht form, stamped Kaltenecker & Sohn, München, tabs missing, cord replaced, 15in (38cm) diam.
£400-450 *CSK*

Shoulder Scales

A pair of white metal shoulder scales.
£80-100 *CSK*

East Lothian Yeomanry, gilt chain shoulder scales.
£30-40 *CSK*

1st Life Guards and 1st Royal Dragoons, heavy brass scales.
£80-100 *CSK*

Lothians and Berwickshire Yeomanry, a pair of ornate gilt shoulder scales.
£40-50 *CSK*

Royal Navy, Vice Admiral's pair of epaulettes.
£40-50 *CSK*

1st Royal Guernsey Light Infantry Militia, an officer's pair of scales, rank badge of Lieutenant-Colonel.
£180-200 *CSK*

Sporrans

Gordon Highlanders, an officer's white hair sporran.
£150-180 *CSK*

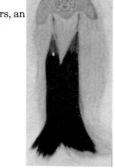

Queen's Own Cameron Highlanders, an officer's Victorian grey hair sporran.
£100-150 *CSK*

Sashes

Grenadier Guards, a Drum Major's sash, embroidered with trophy of arms, Royal Crest, regimental grenade and 34 battle honours, ending with France and Flanders 1914-18.
£800-1,000 *CSK*

Royal Scots Fusiliers, a Drum Major's sash, embroidered with grenade badge, St. Andrew and Cross and with battle honours including Sebastopol.
£300-350 *CSK*

Accoutrements

William IV 3rd Dragoon Guard sabretache, V.R. pouch and belt.
£2,000-2,500 *WAL*

15th Hussar officer's leopard skin shabraque.
£850-950 *WAL*

General

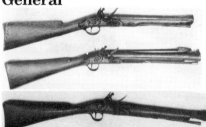

Brass barrelled flintlock blunderbusses.
£400-800 each *P*

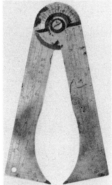

Royal Bucks Hussars, officer's dress items.
£800-1,000 *CSK*

An Indian rampart gun, with two-stage 44in (110.5cm) iron barrel, stepped pan, stamped 544 at breech and decorated with pennant device, mounted on an iron peg swivel mount, approx 1in (2.5cm) bore.
£100-150 *CSK*

A brass gunner's calliper, signed on one arm M. Berge, London, 12in (30.5cm).
£400-450 *CSK*

A Scottish silver mounted dress dirk, blade by Macleod, College St. Edin'r, 14in (35.5cm).
£320-350 *P*

A shell case tie pin, Battle of Ypres.
£8-10 *MB*

Musical

Gramophones

A mahogany single spring Monarch gramophone, by the Gramophone Company Limited, with Gramophone Co. Exhibition soundbox and Morning Glory horn, with original maroon paintwork, rusted and varnished, 1909.
£400-450   *CSK*

A Star Model 50 external horn talking machine, with bevel drive double spring motor in mahogany case, 10in (25.5cm) turntable, tone arm with internal volume control, tube for waste needles at side, winder and nickel plated flower horn.
£500-550   *CSK*

A gramophone in the form of a miniature grand piano with Thorens soundbox, gooseneck tone arm and internal horn emerging at keyboard, in mahogany case on paired tapered legs with casters, 54in (137cm) long.
£600-650   *CSK*

An HMV mahogany Intermediate Monarch horn gramophone, with single spring motor, winder, HMV Exhibition soundbox and mahogany horn, c1911, 18in (46cm) diam, case re-finished.
£700-750   *CSK*

An HMV Model 203 cabinet gramophone, No. 2030000042, with self-lubricating motor, 5A soundbox and re-entrant tone chamber enclosed by doors, the mahogany case with gilt internal fittings, tone arm refinished.
£2,200-2,600   *CSK*

A Tyrela cabinet gramophone in mahogany case with replacement tone arm, Thorens soundbox and internal horn enclosed by door, 22in (56cm) wide.
£200-250   *CSK*

A Gramophone &
Typewriter Limited
Senior Monarch
gramophone, in oak case
with carved mouldings,
fluted corner columns,
triple spring worm drive
motor, 12in (30.5cm)
rocking turntable, G & T
Exhibition soundbox and
repainted Morning Glory
horn, c1907, 23in
(58.5cm) diam.
£100-150   *CSK*

A Deccalian mahogany
table gramophone with
Salon soundbox, Decca
tone arm and bowl-in-lid
reflector and G.C.L. 'Hall
Mark' motor, c1923.
£140-160   *CSK*

DID YOU KNOW?
Wurlitzer jukeboxes were built like tanks.
Warehousemen found the best way to break them up
was to hoist them up to the loft and push them out!

A Gramophone &
Typewriter Ltd., Style
No. 6 gramophone in
panelled oak case with
bevel drive motor, plated
bedplate, Concert
soundbox, travelling arm
and brass horn with
leather elbow, c1901.
£1,000-1,200   *CSK*

Phonographs

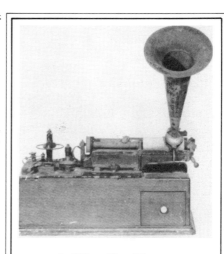

An Edison Concert
Opera phonograph,
No. 4298, with Diamond
A reproducer and
traversing mandrel in
oak case, lacks horn and
lid, repainted.
£450-550   *CSK*

An Edison Fireside
phonograph, Model A
No. 25426, with K
reproducer and Fireside
horn, rusted, crane and
36 wax cylinders in
cartons.
£500-550   *CSK*

An Edison Class M
electric phonograph, now
with 2 and 4 minute
pulley, C & H
reproducers, recorder
and 14in (35.5cm) brass
belled witch's horn, in
oak case with accessories
drawer and North
American Phonograph
Co., patent plate,
damaged.
£1,000-1,500   *CSK*

Oriental

A Chinese soapstone lion and cub figure, 2½in (6cm) high.
£25-35 *CBA*

An ivory figure of Buddha, 3in (8cm) high.
£35-45 *CBA*

A Chinese soapstone figure, 4in (10cm) high.
£70-80 *CBA*

A Chinese jade figure of the God of Longevity, 19thC, 3in (7.5cm).
£90-100 *CBA*

A Chinese soapstone figure, 3in (7.5cm) high.
£20-30 *CBA*

A Chinese soapstone monkey, 3in (7.5cm) high.
£15-20 *CBA*

A Chinese silver and brass box, 3½in (9cm) high.
£70-80 *CBA*

An Indian ivory figure, 6in (15cm) high.
£90-100 *CBA*

Two miniature soapstone animals, 1½in (4cm).
£5-10 *CBA*

A carved bone shrine, 3in (8cm) long.
£20-30 *CBA*

An ivory carving of a Chinaman holding Guanyin, 3in (8cm) high.
£275-325 *CBA*

A bronze young lady, 19thC, 6in (15cm) high.
£70-90 *CBA*

A Japanese ivory okimono of 2 figures, with wine and fish, 19thC.
£250-280 *GEN*

A soapstone figure, 6in (15cm) high.
£25-35 *CBA*

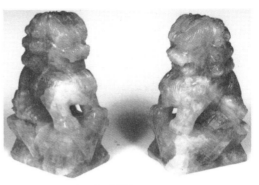

A pair of Chinese rose quartz Dogs of Fo, 6in (15cm) high.
£170-200 *CBA*

A green jade carving of a dog and pup, 18thC.
£160-190 *GEN*

A green jade two-handled bowl, on wooden stand, 19thC.
£180-200 *GEN*

A Chinese bronze duck, 6in (15cm) wide.
£110-130 *CBA*

A set of 4 Kutani plates, 5in (12.5cm).
£30-50 *CBA*

A Chinese bronze vase, 8in (20cm) wide.
£80-100 *CBA*

A red agate carving on a wooden stand, 19thC.
£380-400 *GEN*

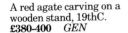

A Chinese ginger jar, 7in (18cm) high.
£60-80 *CBA*

A Chinese porcelain water dropper, 19thC, 4½in (11cm) high.
£140-160 *CBA*

A Japanese lacquer vase, 5in (12.5cm) high.
£15-25 *CBA*

A spill vase and
container.
£20-30 *OSc*

Two early models in lard
or fat-stone, 18thC.
£30-40
Softer than soapstone.

Two spill vases, 6in
(15cm) wide.
£20-30 *OSc*

A Satsuma cup and
saucer, 8in (20cm) wide.
£12-15 *CBA*

An Oriental carved ivory
card case, the front
depicting Napoleon's
house.
£450-500 *GD*

A spill holder, 10in
(25cm) wide.
£50-60 *OSc*

A pair of copper menuki,
formed as lobsters,
unsigned, 18th/19thC.
£200-300 *C*

Cross Reference
Card Cases

A Japanese ivory card
case, with carved
portraits and pierced
decoration.
£240-280 *GD*

A Chinese village scene,
6in (15cm) high.
£60-80 *OSc*

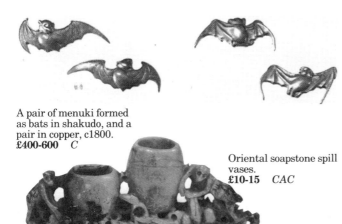

A pair of menuki formed as bats in shakudo, and a pair in copper, c1800.
£400-600 *C*

Oriental soapstone spill vases.
£10-15 *CAC*

A carved amber coloured soapstone group of a diety with a dog of Fo at his feet, incised signature, 19thC, 8in (20cm) wide.
£400-500 *CDC*

Snuff Bottles

A Chinese snuff bottle, 18thC.
£50-70 *GEN*

Snuff Bottles:
Soapstone. **£125-150**
Jade. **£175-225**
Ivory. **£130-160**
Soapstone. **£50-75** *PC*

A cloisonne snuff bottle, 19thC.
£120-140 *GEN*

A glass snuff bottle, painted in colours on the inside, signed, 19thC.
£125-150 *GEN*

A Chinese glass snuff bottle with blue decoration, 19thC.
£70-90 *GEN*

A Chinese carved agate snuff bottle, 19thC.
£170-200 *GEN*

Netsuke

An ivory netsuke in the form of a seated man, 1in (3cm) high.
£175-200 *CBA*

A wood netsuke of terrapins in a basket, signed Chuichi (Tadakazu), damaged, c1900, 2in (4.5cm) wide.
£700-900 *C*

A wood okimono style netsuke of Hanasaka-Jiji, signed Ryukei, 19thC, 2½in (6.5cm) high.
£1,300-1,500 *C*

A wood netsuke of a rat, with dark horn eyes, unsigned, 19thC, 1½in (4cm) high.
£800-1,000 *C*

A Japanese ivory netsuke of a man and children, 19thC.
£150-170 *GEN*

An ivory netsuke of a baying deer, 18thC.
£170-200 *GEN*

A wood netsuke of Ran-Ryo-O, the actor, wearing a mask with ivory teeth, some damage, 19thC, 2in (5.5cm) high.
£400-600 *C*

A wood netsuke of a group of apes, signed Ryoichi (Yoshikazu), 19thC, 1in (3cm).
£550-650 *C*

An ivory netsuke of Ebisu, signed Tamemitsu, 19thC, 1in (3cm) high.
£600-800 *C*

A Japanese ivory netsuke, signed, 19thC.
£240-260 *GEN*

A wood netsuke of a snake and a tortoise, signed Ryoichi (Yoshikazu), slight chip, 19thC, 1½in (3.5cm) wide.
£700-900 *C*

A wood netsuke of Oni and an old woman, signed Ryukei, late 19thC, 1½in (4cm) high.
£400-600 *C*

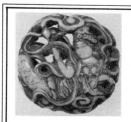

Two unsigned ivory netsukes, early 19thC.
£450-650 each *C*

Textiles

A panel of Chinese silk, embroidered in coloured silks, 19thC, 82in (208cm) high, joined.
£400-600 *P*

A pair of Chinese sleeve bands of ochre silk, embroidered in colours, 19thC.
£100-150 *P*

A Chinese shawl of ivory silk embroidered in coloured silks, with macramé fringe.
£150-200 *P*

A Chinese coverlet of black silk embroidered in gold thread and coloured silks, 68in (174cm) square, lined.
£700-900 *P*

Tsuba

An iron tsuba, signed Nara Masayoshi, 18thC, 3½in (8.5cm).
£350-450 *C*

An iron Migakiji tsuba, signed Yukiyoshi, c1800, 3in (7.5cm).
£250-350 *C*

A Mokkogata iron tsuba, signed Komai sei, late 19thC, 3in (7.5cm).
£3,000-4,000 *C*

A Mokkogata iron tsuba, signed Komai sei, late 19thC, 3in (7.5cm).
£3,000-3,500 *C*

A Mokkogata iron tsuba, with dark brown patina, decorated with comic masks, gilt rim, signed Komai sei, late 19thC, 3in (7.5cm).
£3,000-4,000 *C*

271

Papier Mâché

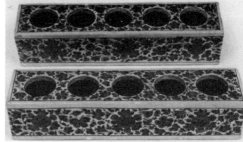

A pair of papier mâché quails egg holders.
£25-35   *CAC*

A papier mâché writing slope, hand painted and inlaid with mother-of-pearl, with 2 silver plaques with presentation inscriptions, London marks.
£700-800   *MB*

A pair of Victorian papier mâché graduated trays, stamped Jennens and Bettridge, London, Birmingham, 25 and 19in (63.5 and 48cm) wide.
£400-500   *CSK*

A papier mâché hand painted chinoiserie note rack, 19thC, 6in (15cm) high.
£55-65   *MB*

A Russian papier mâché box, the hinged cover painted with figures riding in a troika pulled by 3 horses, 5in (12.5cm) wide.
£150-200   *CSK*

A papier mâché owl, 4½in (11cm) high.
£25-35   *CAC*

A papier mâché photograph frame, with mother-of-pearl inlay and painted decoration, 3½ by 3in (9 by 7.5cm).
£20-30   *OSc*

Patch Boxes

Patch boxes,
l. deer.
£145-165

r. fox.
£250-300 *EUR*

Patch boxes depicting a
lady and a man.
£60-130 *EUR*

Two patch boxes,
l. Madonna and child.
£650-700

r. Rustic scene.
£150-170 *EUR*

Patch boxes,
l. Shakespeare.
£220-250

r. A drinker.
£325-350 *EUR*

French patch boxes,
l. Domestic scene.
£625-650

r. Le Tableau Magique.
£175-225 *EUR*

Two patch boxes
depicting a rural scene
and card players.
£150-300 *EUR*

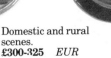

Two patch boxes.
£125-175 *EUR*

Domestic and rural
scenes.
£300-325 *EUR*

Johe Rase Jean Jean and
L'Agrement de la Chasse.
£65-85 each *EUR*

Photographs

Albumen Prints

K. Ogawa, Japan, an album of 50 hand-tinted albumen prints, 1880s.
£550-650 *CSK*

Sommer, Stretton, Bourne, Paier, Pont and others, Switzerland, Italy, Gibraltar, Egypt, Ceylon, India, South Africa, 2 albums of 179 photographs, c1870.
£300-400 *CSK*

Shanghai architecture and Chinese portraits, an album of 64 prints, late 19thC.
£400-500 *CSK*

F. M. Sutcliffe, 'Alice and Roger', 'Holding Hands', 'Man with muck cart' and 'Colts Foot', 4 albumen prints, late 19thC.
£250-450 *CSK*

Eduard Baldus, Farnham Maxwell Lyte and others, Photographic Views in France, 38 prints, early 1860s.
£1,500-1,800 *CSK*

Gustave Le Gray, The Harbour, Sète, albumen print, 12 by 16in (30.5 by 40.5cm), late 1850s.
£3,500-4,500 *CSK*

Bourne, Penn, Sache, Lawton, Miller, F. Beato, Sebah, Zangaki, The Middle and Far East, Asia, Russia, Europe, Madeira and the Canary Islands, an album of 177 prints, c1865.
£2,200-2,500 *CSK*

Burmese portraits, architecture and topography, an album of 34 prints, 1880s.
£500-600 *CSK*

Sebah, Hammerschmidt, Bourne, Skeen & Co., Kurkdjian and others, the Middle East, South Africa, Asia and Far East, approx. 115 photographs, c1880.
£200-300 *CSK*

Guglielmo Pluschow, Nude Studies, stamped on reverse, c1900.
£200-300 *CSK*

Baron Wilhelm Von
Gloeden, attributed,
2 albumen prints, c1900.
£350-450 *CSK*

Carleton E. Watkins,
Vernal Fall, 300ft,
Yosemite, an albumen
print, 16 by 20½in (40 by
51cm), early 1860s.
£700-800 *CSK*

J. Laurent, Frith, Naya,
Sommer & Behles, Brogi,
Pozzi and others, Spanish
and Italian architecture,
an album of approx. 80
prints, 1870s, 12½ by
16in (31.5 by 40.5cm).
£100-150 *CSK*

Melbourne and environs,
an album of 60 prints,
6 by 8in (15 by 20.5cm),
c1885.
£600-700 *CSK*

Thomaso Cuccioni,
Rome: architecture,
sculpture and frescoes,
25 albumen prints, 13 by
18in (33 by 46cm), c1855.
£600-700 *CSK*

Anon, possibly Beato,
Nagasaki, Yedo, Osaka
and Kobe, 7 prints, 8½ by
11in (21.5 by 28cm),
c1865.
£350-450 *CSK*

Anon, possibly Charles
Percy Pickering, New
South Wales, an album
of 15 prints, 14 by 10in
(35.3 by 25.5cm), 1870s.
£1,000-1,400 *CSK*

John Burke, Afghan War
1878-79, Peshawur
Valley Field Force, an
album of 102 prints.
£1,000-1,200 *CSK*

Charles Negre, Imperial
Asylum, Vincennes,
general view with coach,
an albumen print, 13 by
17½in (33 by 44cm),
1859.
£450-550 *CSK*

Carleton E. Watkins,
4 views of Yosemite, 16
by 20in (40 by 51cm),
early 1860s.
£500-600 *CSK*

Reuben Mitchell,
Photographic Album
containing 12
photographs with
natural clouds,
landscapes and places of
historical interest, late
1860s, 11 by 9in (28 by
23cm).
£600-700 *CSK*

Reuben Mitchell,
photographic views in
Bolton and
neighbourhood, John
Booth, 1868.
£450-550 *CSK*

PHOTOGRAPHS

Marville (S. Pont),
Reclining nude, c1860,
6 by 8in (15 by 20.5cm).
£300-350 *CSK*

Anon, possibly Anderson,
The Colosseum with
Meta Sudans and Arch of
Constantine, Temple of
Saturn, and Temple of
Vespasian, and Temple
of Paestum, framed,
c1860, 3 albumen prints.
£500-600 *CSK*

Joseph Cundall,
Highlanders, 1856, 9½
by 7in (24 by 18cm).
£220-250 *CSK*

Carleton E. Watkins,
Cliff House and Seal
Rocks, San Francisco
Bay, print mounted on
card, c1860, 16 by 20in
(41 by 51cm).
£1,000-1,200 *CSK*

Charles Aubry, Flower
still life, c1860, 14½ by
10½in (37 by 27cm).
£160-200 *CSK*

Philip Henry Delamotte,
Photographs executed
expressly for the Crystal
Palace Art Union, 1859,
with 13 albumen prints,
9½ by 7½in (24 by 19cm).
£400-450 *CSK*

Charles Marville,
Chapelle du College de
St. Dizier, a mounted
albumen print, c1860, 14
by 10in (35 by 25.5cm).
£200-250 *CSK*

Bisson Frères, Facade
detail, 1850s, 17½ by
13in (44 by 33cm).
£175-200 *CSK*

Gelatin Prints

Margaret Bourke-White,
'In a Korean village a
wife, mother and
grandmother lament the
death of their boy', c1940,
11 by 14in (28 by 35.5cm).
£500-550 *CSK*

Baron Adolf de Meyer,
Still life with parasols,
hat stands and flowers,
after 1914, 7½ by 9in (19
by 23cm).
£220-250 *CSK*

Albert Hiller,
Californian missions and
landscape, pictorial
photographs, 58 gelatin
silver prints, c1920, 10 by
14 (25.5 by 35.5cm).
£100-150 *CSK*

Francis Bruguiére, New York Theatre Studies, 8 gelatin silver prints, c1930.
£550-650   *CSK*

Heinz Loew, Corsets, 3 gelatin silver prints, c1925.
£550-650   *CSK*

Bill Brandt, Nude, July 1960, printed early 1970s, 23 by 27½in (58 by 70cm).
£800-900   *CSK*

Sacha Stone, Lady painting numbers, c1920, 7 by 8½in (18 by 21.5cm).
£400-450   *CSK*

Albert Renger-Patszch, Untitled, metal castings, c1930, 9 by 7in (23 by 18cm).
£500-550   *CSK*

Man Ray, Robert Winthrop Chanler, 1929, 10½ by 8in (26 by 20.5cm).
£100-150   *CSK*

Bill Brandt, Coach party, Royal Hunt Cup Day, Ascot, 1930s, printed early 1970s, 24 by 28in (61 by 71cm).
£200-250   *CSK*

Cecil Beaton, H.R.H. Princess Margaret, H.R.H. Princess Marina, H.R.H. Princess Alexandra and H.M. Queen Elizabeth, 33 gelatin silver prints, c1950.
£400-450   *CSK*

Cecil Beaton, Andy Warhol and Candy Darling, 1969, 7½ by 9in (19 by 23cm).
£220-250   *CSK*

Willy Prager, Girl on beach, c1930, 9½ by 7in (24 by 18cm).
£250-350   *CSK*

Man Ray, R. Rosselini, H. Langlois, Jean Renoir, c1940, 6½ by 9½in (17 by 24cm).
£300-350   *CSK*

PHOTOGRAPHS

F. M. Sutcliffe, A bit of news (at Robin Hood Bay), a toned gelatin silver print, 1880s, 8½ by 6½in (21 by 15cm).
£400-450 *CSK*

Robert Doisneau, Hell, c1950, 15 by 12in (38 by 30.5cm).
£750-800 *CSK*

Mr. Mendenhall, Photos of San Francisco Earthquake for Government record by Mr. Mendenhall of the Geodetic Survey 1906, 41 gelatin silver prints, 1906, each 3½ by 4½in (9 by 11.5cm).
£850-950 *CSK*

20 Chiaroscuros by Count Zichy, an album of 21 gelatin silver prints, c1948, 12 by 10in (30.5 by 25.5cm).
£850-950 *CSK*

Bill Brandt, Cocktails in a Surrey Garden, 1930s, printed 1980s, 12 by 10½in (30.5 by 26cm).
£400-450 *CSK*

Robert Frank, Mother and child, c1950, 9 by 13½in (23 by 34cm).
£1,800-2,000 *CSK*

Paris postcard album of erotic studies, containing 105 gelatin silver prints, c1900, each 5½ by 3½in (14 by 9cm).
£400-450 *CSK*

Herbert G. Ponting, The potter at his wheel, Japan, a brown toned gelatin silver print, 1902-5, 13 by 19in (33 by 48cm).
£300-350 *CSK*

Count Zichy, Celebrity and society portraits commercial and personal photographs, 8 albums containing 300 gelatin silver prints and colour prints, c1950, each 10 by 8in (25.5 by 20.5cm).
£250-300 *CSK*

Salt Prints

EM.PEC, possibly E. Pecquerel, Arles -1851, salt print from waxed paper negative, 1851.
£350-400 *CSK*

Roger Fenton, Homer T.85, salt print, 12 by 9in (30.5 by 23cm).
£600-650 *CSK*

278

Miscellaneous Prints

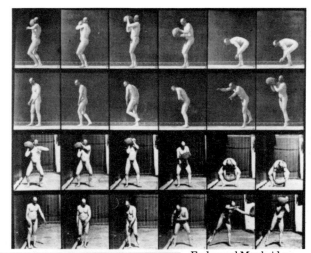

Robert Demachy, Senta Chretien, an oil transfer print, after 1910, 6 by 5in (15 by 12.5cm).
£170-200   *CSK*

Eadweard Muybridge, Animal Locomotion, men, 11 photogravure prints, 9½ by 12in (24 by 30.5cm) and 6 by 18in (15 by 45.5cm).
£450-550   *CSK*

Photographic subjects, 7 stereo cards, 2 albumen, 2 gelatin silver prints, and 3 half-tone prints, 1850-early 1900.
£110-150   *CSK*

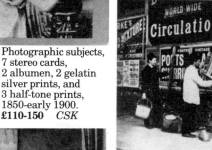

Martin Gerlach, Festons und Decorative Gruppen Nebst einem Zieralphabete aus Pflanzen und Thieren, Volumes I-IV, with 141 photogravure plates, late 19thC.
£150-200   *CSK*

A & J Bool and Henry Dixon, Old London, 43 carbon prints, 1876-1886, 7½ by 8½in (19 by 22cm).
£1,000-1,200   *CSK*

John Thomson, Street Life in London, with 37 woodburytypes, 4 by 3in (10 by 7.5cm), 1878.
£1,800-2,000   *CSK*

Photography studios, apparatus and stereo viewers, 4 stereo cards and 2 cartes de visite, c1860.
£300-350   *CSK*

Grundy, Elliott, Guerard and others, rural scenes and genre including painters studios, 62 stereo cards, 24 hand-tinted, 1850-60.
£140-160   *CSK*

Anthony Osmond-Evans, Portrait of Mother Theresa, R-type colour print, 20 by 16in (51 by 40.5cm), 1987.
£200-250   *CSK*

Pincushion Dolls

William Goebel was a notable manufacturer of pincushion dolls, which often featured roses on the bodices.

Kessler & Dressel pincushion|dolls.
£250-300 *PWA*

Marie Antoinette.
£250-300 *PWA*

Chocolaterie.
£250-350 *PWA*

A William Goebel pincushion doll, with roses on bodice, 4in (10cm) high.
£200-250 *PWA*

The swimmer, 3in (7.5cm) high.
£150-180 *PWA*

A Kessler & Dressel pincushion doll, 4in (10cm) high.
£200-220 *PWA*

An Art Deco pincushion doll, 5in (12.5cm) high.
£200-250 *PWA*

A selection of Art Deco models.
£85-200 each *PWA*

A googlie eyed doll.
£180-250 *PWA*

Two figures, 4 and 6½in
(10 to 16.5cm) high.
£30-50 *PWA*

A rare blackamoor doll,
4in (10cm) high.
£85-100 *PWA*

Jenny Lind by William
Goebel, 5in (12.5cm).
£80-100 *P*

A selection of small
figures, 1½ to 3½in (4 to
9cm) high.
£25-50 *PWA*

A William Goebel figure,
with original wig, 3½in
(9cm) high.
£180-250 *PWA*

Birds and insects, 1in (2.5cm) high.
£20-25 *PWA*

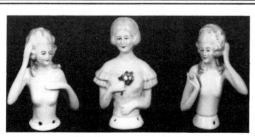

A selection of pincushion
dolls
£30-40 *PWA*

Mata Hari.
£200-250 *PWA*

Cross Reference
Dolls
Sewing
Toys

Playing Cards

Early playing cards were entirely hand-made, and it was only Royalty and the aristocracy who could afford to commission an artist to design and prepare a complete deck of cards. Popularity spread throughout Europe with the advent of wood block printing, stencilling and other printing methods.

Traditional suit signs, spades, clubs, hearts and diamonds, are used in England, France, many European countries and the U.S.A. The Spanish and Italians use swords, chalices, coins and batons whilst the Germanic countries use bells, hearts, acorns and leaves. All these 'ordinary cards' for each nation are referred to as 'standard packs'.

'Non-standard' decks are specially designed packs where the court cards have been changed to represent other figures or designs. Good examples of modern non-standard decks are where famous politicians are depicted on the court cards.

The Tarot Microscopique, 74 card pack, by B. Dondorf, c1900.
£280-300 *IC*

An American Victory pack, with Uncle Sam as the King of Hearts, the Joker depicts Hitler.
£65-85 *IC*

An early English Ace of Spades showing the tax due on a pack of cards, c1820.
£120-140 *IC*

Manuscript cards, King of Spades, c1860.
£110-130 *IC*

A can-can deck, published by Philibert, France, a limited edition, c1953.
£55-65 *IC*

A Belgian pack, showing allies on the court cards, World War I. Two versions:
The Bezique pack of 32 cards.
£60-80
Full Bridge pack of 52 cards.
£90-120 *IC*

Les Cartes a Rire, published in France, c1823.
£1,200-1,500 *IC*

These were produced with the specific purpose of satirising the contemporary newspapers.

A Belgian five-suited Bridge deck, the fifth suit being crowns, c1930.
£30-35   *IC*

A Belgian Great Mogul deck, 19thC.
£20-30   *IC*

Some low quality export packs were produced at the end of the 19thC still depicting single courts.

A Belgian 'Medieval' deck, in green and gold, 1880.
£110-130   *IC*

The Aztecs of Mexico, by Fournier of Spain, c1970.
£10-20   *IC*

A Piatnik Czech Heroes deck, the Jack of Acorns depicts Jan Zizka, 1930.
£50-60   *IC*

The Germans still use acorns, leaves, bells and hearts for their suits.

A Belgian Roxy advertising pack, c1960.
£15-20   *IC*

Collectors prefer packs where the Kings, Queens and Jacks are the smokers.

A hand drawn deck on hide with Spanish suit signs on the cards, late 1800s.
£75-100 each card   *IC*

Complete packs are very rare and a collector would be fortunate to obtain even one single card.

A Piatnik of Vienna large crown pattern pack, 1890.
£35-45   *IC*

An Austrian pack, with maker's name and tax stamp, 1878.
£375-400   *IC*

DID YOU KNOW?

One of the aids to dating playing cards is the method used to print them.

* Early hand painted cards are now extremely rare.
* Wood block engraving was used during the 18th Century into the 19th.
* Chromolithography used during the 19th Century.
* Most modern playing cards are now produced on the latest webb offset printing machinery.

Early cards were much wider than present day cards. Double-headed cards, although not unknown before, were not generally accepted until mid-19th Century.

PLAYING CARDS

Indian round, hand-painted cards, c1880, with decorative box.
£225-250 *IC*

Indian playing card packs often consisted of 96 or more cards.

Thomas de la Rue's 125th Anniversary pack, by Jean Picart le Doux, 1957.
£20-25 *IC*

White Star Line – a pack of playing cards, c1930.
£8-12 *PC*

P & O Playing cards, c1930.
£8-10 *COB*

The Worshipful Company of Makers of Playing Cards, limited edition commemorating the royal visit to Canada in 1906.
£75-85 *IC*

DID YOU KNOW?
Such was the addiction to card playing that the Earl of Sandwich refused to leave the table for meals, demanding bread and meat to be brought to him. Hence the sandwich!

The King of Diamonds from the Gibson Hunt deck, c1802.
£120-150 *IC*

Persian playing cards, known as 'As Nas', hand painted on papier mâché and hand lacquered, c1890.
£18-25 *IC*

A complete deck consists of 25 cards of 5 suits with 5 cards in each.

A classical Tarot pack, by J. M. Simon of Paris, reproduction.
£15-20 *IC*

The 'Grand Tarot Belline' was originally designed by Magnus Edmund in 1880, and reproduced in 1980.

A Geographic pack.
£480-500 *IC*

Many geographic packs have been produced in the last 200 years; one of the most colourful is Rock's 'Court Game of Geography' of 1839, the four suits being devoted to 4 continents.

A Joan of Arc Transformation pack, by J. G. Cotta, c1805.
£1,300-1,500 *IC*

J. G. Cotta was a bookseller in Germany who produced the earliest printed Transformation packs. He gave them away as Christmas gifts to his clients.

A Victorian burr walnut games box for Bézique, 7½in (18cm) square.
£230-250 *MB*

Playing cards never depicted spades on their designs as these were thought of as death cards.

Police

Handcuffs

A pair of handcuffs engraved 'Cranbrook'.
£30-40 *MIT*

A pair of early prison officers handcuffs, also used by the British for Boer War prisoners, with key.
£50-70 *MIT*

'Figure of Eight' handcuffs, also known as 'leading' handcuffs, c1800.
£35-40 *MIT*

A pair of women's or children's handcuffs, c1914.
£30-40 *MIT*

These handcuffs are made of lighter metal and the wrist size is smaller.

A pair of handcuffs made for use during World War II, dated 1943.
£10-15 *MIT*

A pair of Victorian leg irons, marked 'Sevenoaks'.
£100-120 *MIT*

A pair of modern patent police handcuffs, in use until 1968.
£10-15 *MIT*

A pair of first patent Metropolitan Police handcuffs, with key, c1829.
£200-220 *MIT*

Armbands

First World War armbands, with pewter badges.
£15-20 *MIT*

Metropolitan Police armbands, second patent, last worn in 1970.
£5-8 *MIT*

Headgear

A Superintendent's hat, c1902.
£50-60 *MIT*

A Peeler's hat from a county force, c1850.
£150-170 *MIT*

A Victorian patent helmet, Warwickshire, c1880.
£75-90 *MIT*

A Coventry Special Constable's hat, c1914.
£20-30 *MIT*

A Glamorgan force's helmet, c1914.
£80-100 *MIT*

A Cornwall Superintendent's hat, c1930.
£70-80 *MIT*

A Brighton Police blue cloth helmet, post 1902.
£20-30 *WAL*

Edinburgh Police Force, latest patented helmet used.
£40-50 *MIT*

A modern City of London helmet.
£30-50 *MIT*

A policewoman's hat, c1935.
£60-70 *MIT*

Truncheons

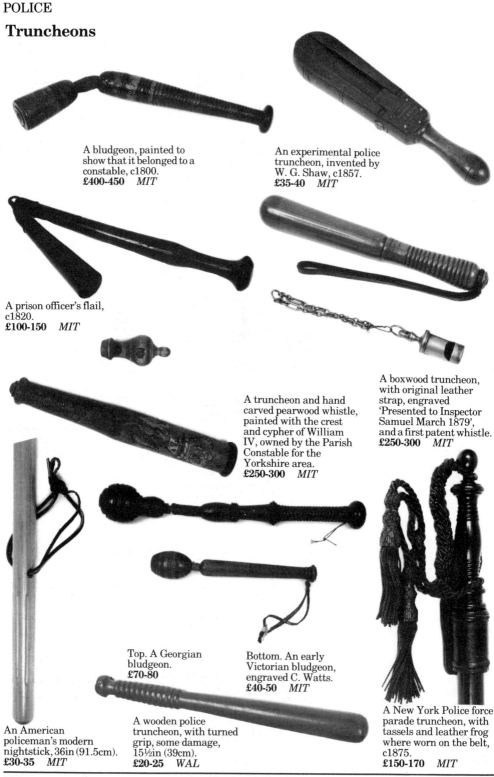

A bludgeon, painted to show that it belonged to a constable, c1800.
£400-450 *MIT*

An experimental police truncheon, invented by W. G. Shaw, c1857.
£35-40 *MIT*

A prison officer's flail, c1820.
£100-150 *MIT*

A boxwood truncheon, with original leather strap, engraved 'Presented to Inspector Samuel March 1879', and a first patent whistle.
£250-300 *MIT*

A truncheon and hand carved pearwood whistle, painted with the crest and cypher of William IV, owned by the Parish Constable for the Yorkshire area.
£250-300 *MIT*

Top. A Georgian bludgeon.
£70-80

Bottom. An early Victorian bludgeon, engraved C. Watts.
£40-50 *MIT*

An American policeman's modern nightstick, 36in (91.5cm).
£30-35 *MIT*

A wooden police truncheon, with turned grip, some damage, 15½in (39cm).
£20-25 *WAL*

A New York Police force parade truncheon, with tassels and leather frog where worn on the belt, c1875.
£150-170 *MIT*

Rattles

Two police rattles, c1820.
£100-120 *MIT*

A police rattle, as carried by the early nightwatchmen, c1800.
£30-35 *MIT*

Two early police rattles, c1900.
£60-70 *MIT*

Police nightwatchmen's rattles, c1800.
£30-35 *MIT*

Whistles

Police whistles.
£10-12 each
With chain.
£25-30 *MIT*

l. & c. Experimental police whistles.
£20-25
r. The Acme siren, with leather wrist strap.
£50-55 *MIT*

Pistols

A flintlock pistol, engraved Head Police Office, No. 8, c1800.
£400-500 *MIT*

A Birmingham Police force's percussion pistol, marked B, c1850.
£250-300 *MIT*

Posters

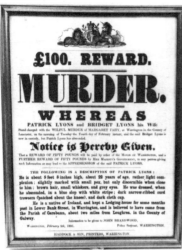

A police poster, dated 1851.
£100-140 *MIT*

Lanterns

A police or nightwatchmen's bull's-eye lantern, c1855.
£30-40 *MIT*

A candle lantern, with hook on the back to clip onto an overcoat belt, c1800.
£30-35 *MIT*

A police lantern, with changing colour lamp, c1920.
£15-20 *MIT*

A bull's-eye lantern, c1855.
£30-40 *MIT*

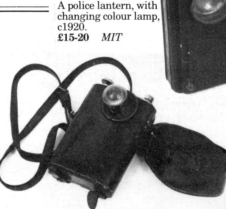

A police lamp with flashlight, in a pigskin case, c1920.
£50-70 *MIT*

A candle lamp with clip.
£25-30 *MIT*

Edged Weapons

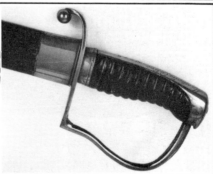

A Constable's sword, Marshalls Office, Mansion House, London, prior to 1838.
£200-250 *MIT*

Miscellaneous

A Royal Worcester kitchen pot, decorated in green and cream, c1875.
£100-130 *MIT*

Two original books on collecting truncheons.
l. 'Truncheons'.
£80-100
r. 'The History of Truncheons'.
£40-50 *MIT*

'The Policeman's Lot', a modern book on police collecting.

A King's Messenger's badge, with George IV cypher.
£500-550 *MIT*

A Good Service Medal presented by the Liverpool City Police to Inspector Birchall, c1931.
£30-40 *MIT*

A Reading Police Officer's belt, c1850.
£10-15 *MIT*

A Borough of Hartlepool Special Constable's medal, dated 1916.
£20-30 *MIT*

A Forfarshire Constable's badge, George IV.
£150-160 *MIT*

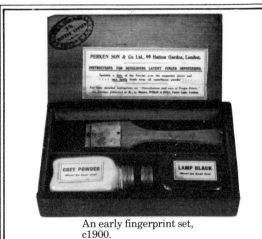

An early fingerprint set, c1900.
£30-35 *MIT*

A police station identification plate.
£50-100 *MIT*

FURTHER READING

Mitton, Mervyn A., *The Policeman's Lot*, London 1985.

Portrait Miniatures

Henry Monck, by N. Freese, fl. 1794-1814, in black papier mâché frame, 7cm high.
£450-550 *C*

A lady, by Charles Shirreff, b.1750, in gold frame, the reverse with gold monogram RJB on plaited hair, 7cm high.
£800-1,000 *C*

A pair of miniatures of John Alexander Wilson and Mary Anne Stewart Wilson, by Francis Hargreaves fl. 1810-54, one signed on reverse and dated 1829, with Liverpool address, with black wood frames, 9.5cm high.
£500-600 *C*

A gentleman, by George Engleheart, c1750-1829, with gold frame, 7cm high.
£900-1,000 *C*

James Lander, by John Field, 1772-1848, signed on obverse with No. 2 Strand, unbroken trade label No. 6 on reverse gold frame, 7cm high.
£200-250 *C*

A young girl, by George Engleheart, c1750-1829, the silver gilt frame with paste border, 4cm high.
£700-800 *C*

An elderly lady, by John Bogle, 1746-1803, signed with initials and dated 1786, gilt metal frame, 4.5cm high.
£800-900 *C*

A young lady by Miss Sophia Smith, fl. 1760-1769, signed with initials and dated 1769, gold bracelet clasp frame, the reverse erroneously engraved S. Shelley, 4cm high.
£500-600 *C*

A portrait of a gentleman, by George Engleheart, c1750-1829, with gold bracelet clasp frame, 3.5cm high.
£800-900 *C*

A gentleman, by Philip Jean, 1755-1802, signed indistinctly with initials, pierced scrolling gilt metal frame, 4.5cm high.
£400-450 *C*

A gentleman, by Thomas Richmond, 1771-1837, gilt metal frame, 7cm high.
£450-550 *C*

A gentleman, by John Comerford, 1770-1832, with gilt metal frame, 8cm high.
£600-650 *C*

A lady, by Andrew Robertson, 1777-1845, believed to be Mistress Macallister, with verre églomisé border, black wood frame, 7cm high.
£800-850 *C*

Andrew Robertson, a self portrait, 1777-1845, set in gold swivel brooch in chased foliate frame, the reverse with gold cupid, dog and harp in relief, 3cm high.
£5,500-6,500 *C*

Benjamin West, P.R.A., by Andrew Robertson, 1777-1845, the ormolu frame with beaded border, 8cm high.
£1,000-1,200 *C*

A French officer of Hussars, French School, c1806, gilt metal frame, 6cm high.
£550-650 *C*

An officer, by William Marshall Craig, fl. 1787-1827, gilt metal frame, 7.5cm high.
£800-900 *C*

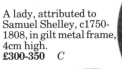

A lady, attributed to Samuel Shelley, c1750-1808, in gilt metal frame, 4cm high.
£300-350 *C*

A gentleman, by Andrew Robertson, 1777-1845, signed with monogram and dated (18)05, gilt metal mount, in fitted leather case, 8cm high.
£500-600 *C*

A gentleman, by Charles Robertson, 1760-1821, gold frame with plaited hair reverse, 6.5cm high.
£500-550 *C*

A gentleman, by Charles Shirreff, b.1750, signed on reverse and dated 1797, with Fort St. George, Madras, ormolu frame with chased border, 7.5cm high.
£400-500 *C*

Postcards

Art Nouveau

l. Basch, a rare card in good condition.
£20-50
This example in fair condition.
£8-10
r. Artist unknown.
£3-5   *P*

These cards show how condition can drastically affect prices — collectors prefer cards without handwriting.

Girls Heads, UB, MT, 2.
£20-30   *N*

C. Shand.
£4-8   *MS*

Elizabeth Sonrell, some foxing, adhesion mark to reverse, otherwise G, 2.
£20-30 each   *N*

An embossed and gilded silhouette postcard, fair.
£2-5   *P*

Raphael Kirchner

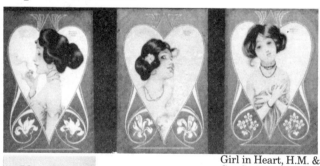

Tucks, girl in a car, 2709, pu, G.
£15-20   *N*

Girl in Heart, H.M. & Co., Series 123, G to VG.
£20-30   *N*

Bathing Belles.
Middle period.
£10-18
Early period.
£15-40
Bruton later period.
£5-10   *MS*

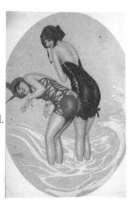

Four pastel studies of girls, early period, G+.
£20-30 each   *P*

Seven cards from Mikado series, some sl. crsing, little w.t.f.'s, early Japanese period, G.
£15-25   *P*

Alphonse Mucha

Czech, period colour art, about VG, 2.
£30-50 *P*

Relativity series, Czech period.
£18-25 *P*

Months of the Year, early period.
£40-70 *N*

Edwardian

Postcard.
40-80p *MS*

Gabrielle Ray, theatre
actress.
Under £1 *MS*

German scene.
50p-£1 *MS*

A French fantasy head,
c1910.
£8-12 *MS*

Edwardian postcards.
10-15p *MS*

Dancing girl with veil,
French, by Gayac.
£7-10 *MS*

Calendars

A. Asti, 1899, some
scuffing, G.
£25-35
C. Leandre, 1900, slight
scuffing, about VG.
£20-30

G. Maurice, 1897, slight
scuffing, about VG.
£20-30
L. Graner, 1898, slight
scuffing.
£16-22 *N*

Silk

Regimental.
£10-15   *MS*

Woven silk, Grants,
Queen Mary and George
V, G-VG.
£20-30   *N*

World War I silk cards,
French and Belgian.
Hearts and flowers.
£1-3

Woven silk, Knuffman
Volkeschlacht Leipzig,
UB, slight creasing,
otherwise VG.
£30-60   *N*

Disasters

Social History, railway
disasters.
£3-4   *P*

W. Gothard, Sharnbrook
rail disaster, G to VG.
£12-18   *N*

Tram smash, RP, Bury,
2 pin holes, otherwise G.
£5-8   *N*

H.M.S. Gladiator, a
collection of 65 cards in a
modern album.
£200-300   *P*

Fire Brigade

Fire Brigade, RP,
Gillingham, by Edgar,
small pin hole, G.
£20-30   *N*

Birmingham, RP, Fire
Brigade, VG to EX.
£18-25   *N*

Polar Expeditions

Wrench's Links with the
Empire, Series 3 No. 4,
with small c.d.s.,
Antarctic S.S. Discovery,
reverse pu. Christchurch
25th April, 1904, some
slight creasing, otherwise
G.
£100-130   *N*

Polar, b/w frame, pu
Norway 1902, VG.
£5-8   *N*

Railways

Railway station, RP, by
Brockland of
Windermere, VG.
£10-15 *N*

Railways, underground
poster, some scuffing, G.
£15-20 *N*

Railway underground,
G-Ex.
£5-7 *N*

Railway, French
advertising cards, VG.
£30-40 *N*

Transport

Motor Racing, 1903,
Gordon Bennett race
selection.
£2-3 each *P*

Aviation, R.P's aviators
and their planes, from
the Flying at Hendon
series, G-VG.
£3-5 *P*

Motor bus, RP, Fiat 16
seater, slight creasing, G.
£10-15 *N*

Motor bus, RP, London,
slight crease, G.
£15-20 *N*

Delivery vans,
RP, by
T.I.C., MT.
£16-22 *N*

Social History

Lifeboats, RP's, G.-VG.
£2-3 *P*

General interest.
£18-25 *MS*

Paris Vécu, A la Wallace,
about VG.
£20-30 *N*

Hop picking.
£2-3 *MS*

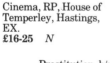

Cinema, RP, House of
Temperley, Hastings,
EX.
£16-25 *N*

Ox roastings, RP, G-VG.
£4-8 *P*

Trug basket making, RP,
EX.
£12-16 *N*

Prostitution, b/w, P.3,
VG.
£20-30 *N*

Mr. C. E. Fish.
£10-12 *MS*

*Died July 5, 1915, aged
75, for over 30 years in the
Ramsgate Lifeboat, on
service 365 times,
assisted to save 887 lives,
and helped to raise £25
for Lifeboat Fund.*

News vendor.
£8-12 *MS*

Empire Day, Retford,
1907.
£5-8 *MS*

Royalty

Duke and Duchess of Windsor.
£15-20

Proclamation of King Edward VIII.
£1.50-2.50   *MS*

The fact that postcards have been used makes little difference to the value.

Czar Nicholas II of Russia.
£7-10   *MS*

Russian royalty collectable.

Naval

England expects that every man this day will do his duty.
£1-3   *MS*

H.M.S. Niobe.
50p-£2   *MS*

Coded messages and mirror writing also collectable.

Humorous

Dental humour.
£5-6 *MS*

Seaside, comics and
similar.
50p-£2 *MS*

Modern

A comic card, over-
printed with town name.
50p-£2 *MS*

Film stars and pin-ups.
25-50p each *MS*

DID YOU KNOW?
When a plaque was unveiled in 1979 to mark the
birthplace of the famous saucy postcard artist
Donald McGill, a pair of Queen Victoria's white
drawers were used as the curtain!

Patriotic & Political

World War I butterfly girls with patriotic coloured wings, pub'd L. Geligne, Paris, G.
£1-3   *P*

Edward VII and Kaiser, UB, VG.
£8-12   *N*

Anti-Nazi, Dutch Edition caricatures of Montgomery, Eisenhower, Concentration Camp, Parade, FR-VG.
£20-25   *N*

Daily Express.
£8-10   *MS*

Patriotic propaganda, by Dudley Buxton.
50p-£1.50   *MS*

Nazi Germany

The victorious banners and standards of the German Army, by Gottfried Klein, G.
£15-20   *N*

Wilhelm Strienz, signed green pen, 23.7.44, G.
£16-22   *N*

Cards of Generals and Soldiers, unsigned £4-6.

Scenic

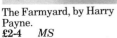

France, Chromo vignettes of Cirey et ses Environs, UB, G.
£2-3   *N*

The Farmyard, by Harry Payne.
£2-4   *MS*

Echaig Bridge, a 'Fairy Queen' postmark.
£10-15   *MS*

Miscellaneous

Louis Wain and Diabolo cards.
£8-15   *MS*

Butterflies, 48 unusual Japanese postcards, Nawa Entomological Factory credit on reverse, VG.
£25-35   *P*

Lovers, embossed, a set of 6, series 627, EX to MT.
£10-15   *N*

Phil May, Tucks No. 1771 complete, op. MT, 6.
£20-30   *N*

A Merry Christmas, chromo printed in rich colours.
£2-10   *MS*

Santa, chromo, slight corner wear, G+.
£20-30   *P*

Temperance Friendly Society.
£3-6   *MS*

Commonly used abbreviations.
Postcard Types:

apx.	=	approximate count
u.b.	=	undivided back
p.u.	=	postally used
n.p.u.	=	not postally used
RP	=	Real Photo
PP	=	Printed Photo
topo.	=	topographic
w.t.f.	=	writing to front
vig.	=	vignette
st. sc.	=	street scene
o.p.	=	original packet
pubd.	=	published
cnr. crs.	=	corner crease
a.c.m.	=	album corner marks

Marathon-Pentathlon, set of 6 in o.p., pubd. Prague 1912.
£40-60   *P*

FURTHER READING
Hill, C. W., *Discovering Picture Postcards,* Aylesbury, Bucks 1978.
Radley, C., *The Woven Silk Postcard,* Barking 1978.
Smith, J. H. D., *IPM Catalogue of Picture Postcards and Year Book 1989,* Hove 1989.
White, G., *Collecting Military Postcards,* Bristol 1987.

Cross Reference
Posters
Christmas cards
General ephemera

Posy Holders

A Victorian device for holding a posy of sweet smelling blooms, usually on the lapel, to mask unpleasant odours. Made in metal, the most sought after are in silver with intricate filigree work.

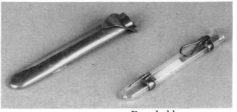

Posy holders.
£4-6   *VB*

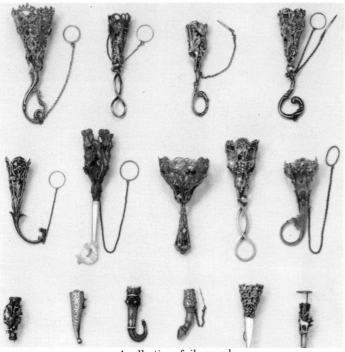

A selection of silver posy holders.
£30-130   *CSK*

A collection of silver and metal posy holders.
£100+   *CSK*

Five posy holders, l. to r. A Victorian posy holder, hallmarked for Birmingham 1863.
£140-160

A Victorian posy holder, stamped with butterflies.
£120-140

A Victorian posy holder, with filigree work.
£220-240

A Victorian posy holder, stamped with foliage and hounds, on a lattice work ground.
£110-130

A tulip shaped posy holder, engraved with flowers, foliage and scrollwork.
£160-180   *CSK*

Radios

A civilian wartime receiver, in standard case, medium wave only, c1944, 13½in (34cm) high.
£50-60 *OR*

Original price £12.3.4d.

A Murphy Radio Ltd., model AD94, c1940, 12½in (31cm) wide.
£125-150 *OR*

Original price £9.10.0d.

A Philco Radio & Television Corporation of Great Britain, People's set, c1936, 16in (40cm) wide.
£200-250 *OR*

Original price £6.6.0d.

An Ultra radio, model T401, by Ultra Electric Ltd., February 1946, 8in (20.5cm) high.
£40-60 *OR*

Original price £15.15.0d + P.T.

A rare Etronic model, 1945-7, 11½in (29cm) high.
£150-200 *OR*

A G.E.C. radio in light brown Bakelite cabinet, c1947, 11in (28cm).
£50-70 *OR*

A Majestic radio in brown Bakelite case, American, c1951.
£100-200 *OR*

A British Bush radio, DAC 90, with internal aerial, c1950, 11½in (29cm) wide.
£45-65 *OR*

Original price £12.1.8d.

A Bush radio, DAC 10, with programmable push buttons, 13in (32cm) wide.
£50-65 *OR*

Original price £14.16.0d.

A Marconi radio, Polish, c1935, 17½in (44cm) high.
£100-200   *OR*

A Mullard high fidelity set, with 3 separate chassis inside, 19in (48cm) wide.
£80-100   *OR*

Made for the Australian and New Zealand market.

A black speaker by Mullard, 'Pure Music', c1927, for use with early radios, 8in (20cm) diam.
£120-150   *OR*

Originally £6.6.0d.

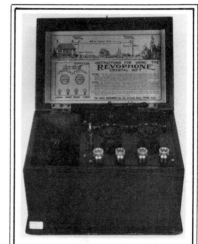

An Ekco AC 85 radio, in black and chrome, c1934, 12½in (31.5cm) wide.
£200-250   *OR*

E. K. Cole of Southend-on-Sea were the first company to produce entirely Bakelite sets, and to put the names of the stations on their dials.

Original price £13.13.0d.

A Kolster Brandes Ltd., model BM 20, c1950, 11½in (29cm).
£60-90   *OR*

A Revophone crystal set by Cable Accessories Co. Ltd., 1923, for use with headphone only.
£75-100   *OR*

Three televisions.
£15-20   *TM*

A collection of radios, tape recorders, record players, and a 'Cats Whisker' crystal radio receiver.
£20-40 each   *TM*

Railways

Coats-of-arms

Glasgow & South
Western Railway, green
garter with figures 789,
20in (51cm) square.
£200-220   *ONS*

Rhondda & Swansea Bay
Railway Company, 14 by
12in (35.5 by 30.5cm).
£100-120   *ONS*

Highland Railway
Company, 14 by 12in
(35.5 by 30.5cm).
£35-45   *ONS*

The North British
Railway Company, 16 by
15in (41 by 38cm).
£35-45   *ONS*

Stockton & Darlington
Steam Tramways Co.
Ltd., 16 by 15in (41 by
38cm).
£120-140   *ONS*

Manchester, Sheffield
and Lincolnshire
Railway Co., 12½ by 10in
(32 by 26cm).
£75-85   *ONS*

Cutlery & Crockery

A selection of G.W.R.
items.
£50-150   *ONS*

A selection of G.E.R.
items.
From £20-40   *ONS*

Silver plated items from
various railways.
£10-100 *ONS*

General

A tin hot water kettle,
inscribed L.N.E.R, and
3 oil cans, stamped
L.M.S., L.N.E.R. and
N.E.E., a G.W.R. No. 4
Midget Fire Appliance,
and a Caution Railway
Crossing metal sign.
£10-40 *ONS*

A plated trowel presented
to R. H. Prevost, Esq.,
May 21st 1900, in framed
box, 20in (51cm) high.
£300-350 *CSK*

A Continental brass and
metal paraffin vapour
warning lamp, with
stained red glass,
removable copper cap,
complete with burner,
inscribed No. 6225,
Luchaire, Ave Errad,
27 Paris, probably
S.N.C.F., 28in (71cm).
£200-250 *CSK*

Harness brasses.
£50-100 each *ONS*

Three L.N.E.R. white
metal paperweights,
original boxes.
£150-180 *CSK*

RAILWAYS

York Station, view from
the south showing
locomotives, overpainted
photograph, by F. Moore,
10 by 14½in (25.5 by
37cm).
£200-250   *ONS*

A London and South
Western Railway guide,
with leather cover.
£10-15   *PC*

L.Y.R. and L.M.S. signal
repeaters.
£50-80   *CSK*

Inkwells, stationery
racks, and an N.E.R.
single line block
telegraph instrument,
restored.
£10-60 each   *ONS*

Painted metal models of
express passenger
locomotives, supplied by
Locomotive Pub. Co., on
wood bases.
£350-400   *CSK*

Medallions

A collection of bronze and
silver plated medallions.
£20-100   *ONS*

A collection of bronze,
white metal and silver
plated medallions.
£15-40 each   *ONS*

Nameplates

City of Truro, a GWR
cast brass and steel
nameplate, from a
Badminton/Atbara class
locomotive No. 3717.
£4,000-6,000   *CSK*

A brass maker's plate,
16in (41cm) wide.
£450-500   *CSK*

Mounts Bay, a GWR cast
brass nameplate, from a
'Duke of Cornwall' class
locomotive No. 3273,
69in (175cm) wide.
£4,500-5,000   *CSK*

Penzance, a GWR cast
brass and steel
nameplate, from a 4–4–0
Bulldog class express
locomotive, No. 3377.
£3,000-4,000   *CSK*

A brass maker's plate,
with black lettering,
17½in (44cm) wide.
£650-700   *CSK*

Bosham, green and
white enamelled totem,
36½in (92cm) long.
£230-250   *CSK*

Tickets

A collection of Railway
tickets.
From £3-10 each   *ONS*

A collection of Railway
Season tickets and free
passes.
From £5-25 each   *ONS*

Railway Posters

H. G. Gawthorn,
Capacity-Mobility on the
LNER.
£200-250 *ONS*

Lawrence Bradshaw,
Kings Cross for Scotland.
£250-300 *ONS*

Frank Newbould,
Hamburg via Grimsby.
£200-250 *ONS*

H. G. Gawthorn,
Middlesbrough Dock.
£120-150 *ONS*

Graham Simmonds,
Holidays in Belgium.
£750-850 *ONS*

Anon, Lowestoft.
£100-150 *ONS*

To Edinburgh by
Pullman.
£600-700 *ONS*

Devonport, G.W.R.,
double royal, on linen.
£250-300 *ONS*

The Garden of England,
LBSCR, double royal, on
linen.
£150-200 *ONS*

Graham Simmonds,
Whitby, LNER.
£800-900 *ONS*

Gladys Peto, Outings on
the LNER.
£200-300 *ONS*

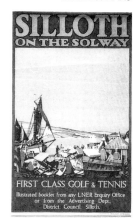

Leslie Carr, Silloth on
the Solway.
£50-100 *ONS*

Queen of Scots, All
Pullman.
£750-850 *ONS*

William McDowell,
Cross the Atlantic by
White Star, SR, double
royal.
£650-700 *ONS*

Vienna, via Harwich,
LNER.
£1,500-1,800 *ONS*

Frank Newbould, You
Always Dine Well on the
LNER.
£1,100-1,400 *ONS*

Margaret Bradley,
London/Paris Train
Ferry, 1939, double royal.
£300-400 *ONS*

It's Quicker by Rail,
GWR, LNER, LMS,
Southern, double royal.
£50-70 *ONS*

Rock & Pop Memorabilia

The Beatles

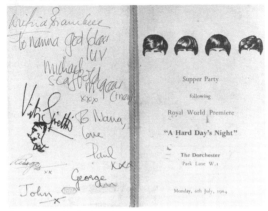

An autographed souvenir menu, July 1964.
£1,200-1,500 *CSK*

An autographed withdrawn butcher sleeve.
£1,700-1,800 *CSK*

An autographed hotel security pass from Doelen Hotel, Amsterdam, and an official Beatles Fan Club postcard.
£550-600 *CSK*

A contract from The Beatles last tour, March 1965.
£850-900 *CSK*

An autographed photograph of The Beatles in the Bahamas, creased, 1965.
£300-350 *CSK*

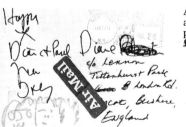

A John Lennon autographed picture postcard, 1971.
£300-350 *CSK*

An autographed Abbey Road cover photograph, mounted, framed and glazed.
£1,800-2,000 *CSK*

A signed publicity photograph of The Beatles, c1964, 9½ by 8in (24 by 20cm).
£400-450   *CSK*

A printed proof of an unissued version of the album cover Yesterday and Today, Capitol Records, 1966, framed and glazed.
£350-400   *CSK*

An autographed album cover, mounted, framed and glazed.
£350-400   *CSK*

An unpublished black and white photograph, signed by Valerie Wilmer, framed and glazed, image 11½ by 13in (29 by 33cm).
£300-400   *P*

A Yamaha FG-110 acoustic guitar, once the property of Paul McCartney, c1960.
£2,500-3,000   *P*

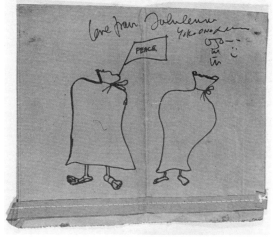

An autographed colour print photograph, 1963, window mounted, 9½ by 7½in (24 by 19cm).
£500-550   *CSK*

A John Lennon self portrait with Yoko Ono on a brown paper sack, c1969.
£1,800-2,000   *CSK*

An 'Old England' Apple wristwatch, unused, with original box and packaging.
£300-350   P

An unpublished photograph of The Beatles, with negative and copyright, 1965.
£1,200-1,500   CSK

A Dezo Hoffmann portrait photograph of The Beatles, 1964.
£150-250   CSK

An original sketch by John Lennon, framed and glazed.
£1,200-1,500   P

John Lennon's handwritten lyrics, and a colour photograph, c1970, framed and glazed.
£5,000-5,500   P

A black and white photographic print, 1967, mounted, framed and glazed.
£70-100   P

Forty-nine individually packaged Hofner/Selmer Beatles guitar strings, made by Selcol, unused.
£550-600   P

A cheque from Lennon Productions Ltd., to R. C. McKenzie, August 1971.
£1,000-1,200 *P*

A cheque from Lennon Productions Ltd., to the 'Freedom Fund', August 1971.
£1,500-2,000 *P*

The Rolling Stones

Two psychedelic posters, 1960s, framed and glazed.
£500-550 *CSK*

An autographed album cover, 1967, framed and glazed.
£400-450 *CSK*

A Philip Townsend group photograph, London 1963, printed later, framed and glazed.
£150-200 *CSK*

An NEMS promotional poster for a cancelled concert.
£250-300 *CSK*

A double sided acetate Road Runner/Diddley Daddy, I.B.C. Sound Recording Studios label, 1963.
£1,500-2,000 *CSK*

A set of autographs on a sheet of headed notepaper,
glazed.
£400-500 *P*

Elvis Presley

An autographed photograph of Priscilla and Elvis on their wedding day.
£400-450 *CSK*

An autographed song sheet, framed and glazed.
£500-550 *CSK*

A casual short-sleeved shirt, with fan club magazines.
£1,000-1,200 *CSK*

A large print of an oil painting by June Kelly, mounted, framed and glazed, 22 by 19in (58 by 48cm).
£700-800 *P*

An American in-house platinum disc for the 1977 LP 'Moody Blue', mounted with inscription plaque.
£1,100-1,300 *P*

A white one-piece stage suit, decorated with gilt studs, with matching cape lined in gold lame, 1972.
£26,000-30,000 *P*

Elvis Presley's gold plated cigar cutter, with snake design, c1970, 4cm.
£500-600 *P*

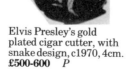

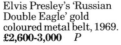

A page from an autograph book, and a machine print photograph of Elvis singing 'Hound Dog'.
£600-650 *CSK*

Elvis Presley's 'Russian Double Eagle' gold coloured metal belt, 1969.
£2,600-3,000 *P*

Presentation Discs

Cat Stevens, an
Australian presentation
gold disc, 'Teaser and the
Firecat', to Cat Stevens,
1972, on simulated wood
mount.
£850-950 *CSK*

Thompson Twins, two
presentation gold discs,
'Hold Me Now' 12in and
7in, with inscribed
plaque to David Simone,
1983, framed and glazed.
£200-250 *CSK*

Bill Medley/Dirty
Dancing, an R.I.A.A.
multi-platinum
presentation disc, to Bill
Medley, c1987.
£1,500-2,000 *P*

Frankie Goes to
Hollywood, a
presentation gold disc,
'Relax', to Martin
Cummings, 1984, framed
and glazed.
£350-400 *CSK*

Robert Plant, a
presentation gold disc,
'Shaken 'n' Stirred', to
Atlantic Records, framed
and glazed.
£450-550 *CSK*

Madness, a presentation
platinum disc,
'Absolutely', to Chris
Foreman, 1981, framed
and glazed.
£220-250 *CSK*

The Police, a
presentation platinum
disc, 'Outlandos
D'Amour', to Miles
Copeland, 1979, framed
and glazed.
£600-650 *CSK*

Heaven 17, a
presentation gold disc
'Penthouse and
Pavement', to Ian Craig
Marsh, 1982, framed and
glazed.
£120-150 *CSK*

Genesis, a presentation
gold disc, 'Invisible
Touch', to Atlantic
Records, framed and
glazed.
£400-450 *CSK*

Sting, an R.I.A.A.
presentation platinum
disc, 'Nothing But The
Sun', c1987.
£1,000-1,200 *P*

Michael Jackson

A quadruple presentation gold and platinum award for 'Thriller' to Freddy Demann.
£2,500-3,000   *CSK*

'Bad' L.P., and 12in single, and 'Man in the Mirror', 12in single, autographed.
£150-200 each   *P*

An autographed album 'Thriller', Epic Records, with an autograph note from Neil Tennant.
£500-600   *CSK*

Costume

Elton John, a straw boater, April 1985, mounted on a framed board.
£350-400   *CSK*

Cher, a leather and simulated leopard skin pillbox hat, signed.
£420-450   *P*

John Lennon's English military tunic, was made for 'Col Harrison', cWWI.
£2,200-2,500   *P*

E.L.O., a red satin promotional jacket for the 1979 LP 'Discovery', unused.
£70-100   *P*

Jimi Hendrix, an orange chiffon scarf, long sleeved stage shirt and wide brimmed, floppy hat.
£600-2,500 each   *CSK*

Posters

A decorative poster 'The First Annual Love Circus' at Winterland, promoting concert with Grateful Dead, framed and head glazed, c1967.
£75-80 *P*

A decorative psychedelic poster for the 'Middle Earth' club, mounted on card, c1967.
£80-100 *P*

Louis Jordan, an early concert advertising poster, c1948, framed and glazed.
£400-450 *CSK*

Psychedelia, a poster, 'Sunshine Superman', by Martin Sharp, framed and glazed.
£100-150 *CSK*

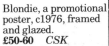

Blondie, a promotional poster, c1976, framed and glazed.
£50-60 *CSK*

A poster advertising a concert at the Saville Theatre, c1967, framed and glazed.
£450-500 *P*

T. Rex, a concert advertising poster for 'Electric Warriors', c1971, framed and glazed.
£220-250 *CSK*

Psychedelia, 'Blowing in the Wind', by Martin Sharp, framed and glazed.
£40-50 *CSK*

General

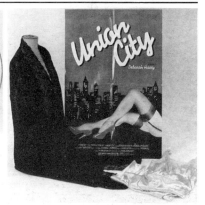

Phil Collins, an autographed drum skin.
£600-650 *CSK*

Jimi Hendrix, a collection of documents, receipts and invoices, c1969.
£1,400-1,600 *CSK*

Blondie, a full length peach satin 1930s style nightdress, black negligee, and poster, c1979.
£200-300 *CSK*

Keith Emerson's custom built keyboards.
£550-650 *CSK*

Elvis Costello, R. Hughes, a photographic silk screen print, numbered 643 of a limited edition of 750, c1980, framed and glazed.
£100-150 *CSK*

Al Jackson/Booker T and the M.G's, bronze trophies, c1971/2.
£250-300 each *P*

Bob Dylan, 'Tarantula', inscribed by the author.
£1,400-1,600 *CSK*

Buddy Holly and the Crickets, a page from an autograph book, c1958, framed and glazed.
£550-600 *CSK*

The Ronettes, an unpublished portrait photograph, c1962.
£100-120 *CSK*

Al Green, 15 original L.P's.
£450-500 *P*

An Ami 'Continental' Stereo jukebox, Model No. XJDB-100.
£950-1,000 *CSK*

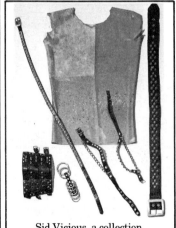

Sid Vicious, a collection of clothing.
£800-900 *CSK*

Elvis Costello and The Attractions, promotional poster.
£40-50 *CSK*

An American Seeburg jukebox, model 222, with 1960-70s records, 55in (140cm) high.
£700-800 *P*

Marmalade,
a Ludwig
drum skin, c1968,
framed and glazed.
£700-750   *CSK*

Sonny and Cher, a signed
letter from Richard
Nixon, 1972, laminated
onto a wooden plaque.
£500-550   *P*

Cliff Richard, a portrait
photograph, negative
and copyright.
£180-200   *CSK*

Bruce Springsteen, a
page of handwritten
lyrics for an unreleased
song, c1979.
£1,000-1,200   *P*

The Who

A page from an
autograph book, and a
photograph of the group,
c1968.
£400-500   *CSK*

'Magic Bus — The Who
On Tour', Decca DL
75064 album cover,
signed, c1974.
£320-350   *P*

A colour photograph of
Keith Moon, framed and
glazed.
£100-120   *CSK*

A Dezo Hoffmann
portrait photograph,
c1963.
£70-100   *CSK*

A photograph of The
Who performing on
'Ready, Steady, Go',
signed by all 4 members.
£200-250   *P*

A psychedelic poster, by
Byrd, for Tommy, some
damage, framed and
glazed, with letter of
authenticity stating that
this poster was once the
property of Keith Moon.
£400-450   *CSK*

Scales, Balances & Measures

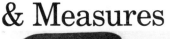

A pair of cast iron scales, with weights.
£50-60 *AL*

A brass Imperial yard, engraved Kilmarnock, County of Ayr, 1835, in a fitted mahogany case, a Burg of Ayr standard yard, in mahogany case, and a standard yard, in fitted mahogany case, 45in (114cm).
£220-250 *CSK*

A pair of brass faced spring scales, 24in (61cm).
£10-15 *AL*

A pair of postal scales, by Salter, 14in (35.5cm).
£50-60 *AL*

A pair of Salter's brass faced spring scales, 16in (40.5cm).
£45-55 *AL*

A gilt brass letter balance, late 19thC, 6in (15cm) wide.
£700-750 *CSK*

Three brass pocket balances.
£8-10 each *AL*

A gold coin balance and gauge, stamped S. Henry Inventor, by Royal Patent, for weighing a guinea, half guinea, and quarter, 18thC, case 5in (13cm) wide.
£400-500 *CSK*

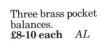

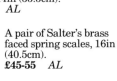

A set of collapsible
travelling scales, 19thC.
£300-400   *PC*

A selection of scales.
£30-40   *TM*

Measures

A set of 9 copper and
brass conical measures,
by W & T. Avery Ltd.,
London, each engraved
City of Glasgow, 1913,
the largest 13in (33cm).
£1,000-1,200   *CSK*

A set of 11 Imperial
measures, engraved
County of Ayr, and dated
1859/1879, the larger
measure by De Grave,
Short & Fenner, London,
20in (51cm) diam.
£2,500-3,000   *CSK*

Victorian wooden
measures, quart, pint
and ½ pint.
£20-30   *AL*

> **Cross Reference**
> Kitchenalia
> Scientific Instruments
> Tools

Weights

A pewter tankard, with
glass base, inscribed The
Vine, Tenterden, 4in
(10cm).
£60-80   *AL*

A set of brass weights by
De Grave & Co. Ltd.,
London, engraved Burg
of Renfrew, in fitted
mahogany case, 21in
(53.5cm) wide.
£1,200-1,500   *CSK*

A set of Burgh of Govan
brass weights.
£1,200-1,500   *CSK*

> **Cross Reference**
> Metalware

Scientific Instruments

Compasses

A dry card compass, the green card with silvered engraved ring on jewelled pivot, mounted in a lacquered brass bowl, signed J. Parkes & Son, Birmingham, with sight and sun shade mirror, mounted on gimbals and in mahogany part case, late 18thC, 11in (28cm).
£500-550   *CSK*

A gilt brass and silvered brass universal equinoctial compass dial, 18thC, signed Schreteger, in card case, 3½in (9cm), with maker's instructions.
£700-750   *CSK*

A Whitby jet sundial compass and others.
£3-35   *VB*

An 'improved' azimuth and surveying compass, by Somalvico & Co., 2 Hatton Garden, London, with instruction label mounted in oak case, 10in (25.5cm) high.
£600-650   *CSK*

Equinoctial Dials

A gilt brass equinoctial dial, signed on the underside of the compass box J.N. Hölderich Augsburg, 18thC, 2½in (6cm) diam.
£300-350   *CSK*

Drawing Sets

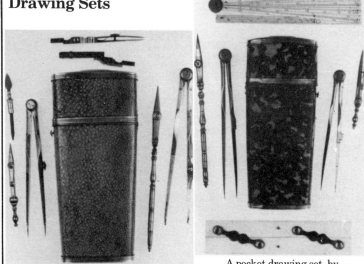

A pocket drawing set, by Dollond, early 19thC, case 7in (18cm).
£550-650   *CSK*

A pocket drawing set, by Backwell Senr. London, in silver mounted tortoiseshell case.
£500-550   *CSK*

A brass equinoctial inclining dial, signed on the hour ring, E.I. Dent, London, 19thC, 4½in (10.5cm).
£250-300   *CSK*

A brass universal equinoctial dial, signed Dollond, London, late 18thC, 5½in (14cm).
£550-600   *CSK*

Globes

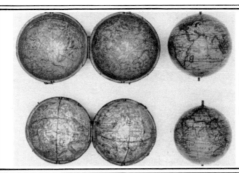

Pocket terrestrial globes, by J. Newton and Jas Wyld, 19thC.
£1,300-1,800 each *P*

A 4in (10cm) terrestrial globe, with label inscribed Globe Terestre J.L. & Cie Paris, late 19thC, 8in (20.5cm) high.
£400-450 *CSK*

A pair of 3in (7.5cm) Newton desk globes, mid-19thC, in mahogany cases.
£1,400-1,800 *P*

A 3in (7.5cm) terrestrial globe, inscribed Newton's New & Improved Terrestrial globe, published by Newton & Son, 66 Chancery Lane, London, in fitted domed mahogany case, damaged, mid-19thC, 4in (10cm) high.
£450-550 *CSK*

A Richard's chronosphere, the 6in (15cm) diam. terrestrial globe showing the ocean currents and undersea cables, the brass stand containing clockwork mechanism, late 19thC, 12in (30.5cm).
£800-900 *CSK*

A German 2in (5cm) instructional terrestrial globe, by J. G. Klinger, 19thC, in original card case.
£600-650 *CSK*

Mining Dials

A brass mining dial, signed on the compass dial Cail, Newcastle upon Tyne, No. 411, defective, early 19thC, 16in (40.5cm).
£200-250 *CSK*

A brass mining dial, signed J. Carpenter, Norwich, late 18thC, 10in (25.5cm) long.
£220-250 *CSK*

A lacquered brass mining dial, signed C. Osterland patent Freiberg, 19thC, 11in (28cm).
£550-650 *CSK*

Microscopes

A brass compound monocular microscope, signed on the shaped stand J.B. Dancer Optician Manchester, with accessories in fitted mahogany case, 19thC, 17in (43cm).
£550-650 *CSK*

A black enamelled, lacquered brass and satin chrome compound monocular microscope, signed Carl Zeiss, Jena, 49296, with accessories.
£700-800 *CSK*

A lacquered brass Cary-type monocular microscope, unsigned, in mahogany case, 19thC, 5in (12.5cm) wide.
£300-350 *CSK*

A lacquered brass Cary-type compound monocular microscope, unsigned, with accessories, in lined mahogany case, 19thC, 7in (18cm) wide.
£400-450 *CSK*

A brass compound monocular microscope, signed Watkins & Hill, Charing Cross London, with accessories, in mahogany case, 19thC, 11in (28cm) wide.
£400-450 *CSK*

A brass simple aquatic microscope, signed Banks inst. Maker to the Prince of Wales, 441 Strand, London, in fitted mahogany case, early 19thC, 8in (20.5cm) wide.
£200-250 *CSK*

A lacquered brass petrological microscope, signed Harvey & Peak, Beak Street, London W, with accessories, in fitted mahogany case, 16in (40.5cm) wide.
£400-500 *CSK*

Perpetual Calendars

A brass perpetual calendar/magnifying glass, unsigned, 18thC, 4.5cm diam.
£600-700 *CSK*

A German silver perpetual calendar, unsigned, 18thC, 2in (5cm) diam.
£700-750 *CSK*

A German silver perpetual calendar, unsigned, 18thC, 2in (5cm) diam.
£800-850 *CSK*

Spectacles

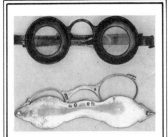

A pair of Georgian silver presentation turn-pin sides spectacles, engraved To D. Ritchie, in silver mounted tortoiseshell case, 5in (12.5cm) long.
£150-200 *CSK*

A pair of iron spectacles, 18thC.
£400-450 *P*

A pair of silver lorgnettes, Unite & Hilliard, Birmingham, 1825, lacking lenses.
£200-250 *P*

A selection of spectacles, c1870.
£40-80 each *BUR*

Sundials

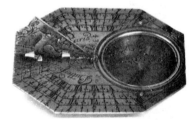

A Korean type brass pocket sundial, in rosewood case, 19thC, 4in (10cm).
£150-200 *CSK*

A German boxwood string gnomon diptych dial, late 18th/early 19thC, 4in (10cm).
£250-300 *CSK*

A brass dial, signed Butterfield A Paris, 18thC, 3in (7.5cm).
£550-600 *CSK*

A gilt brass and silver sundial, signed Johann Willibrand in Augsprung 48, late 17th/early 18thC, 2in (5cm).
£700-750 *CSK*

Telescopes

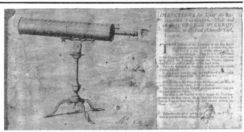

A collection of telescopes.
£100-200 each *P*

A lacquered brass 2¼in Gregorian reflecting telescope, probably by George Sterrop, damaged, mid-18thC.
£750-850 *P*

A three-draw vellum and brass 1½in (4cm) telescope, stamped Dollond, London, 18thC, 9in (23cm) long, closed.
£500-600 *CSK*

A brass 4in (10cm) reflecting telescope, signed James Innes 1796, with mahogany carrying case.
£500-600 *CSK*

A pair of Japanese 15 x 80 Nikko binoculars, grey painted with lens hoods.
£400-450 *CSK*

Theodolites

A lacquered brass theodolite, by J. B. Dancer, 19thC.
£550-650 *CSK*

A black enamelled and brass theodolite, by T. Cooke & Sons Ltd., London & New York, No. 13965, case 13½in (34cm) wide, with leather carrying strap.
£400-450 *CSK*

A black enamelled and lacquered brass transit theodolite, by Casella, London, No. 8028, in fitted mahogany case, 16in (40.5cm) wide.
£550-650 *CSK*

A brass theodolite, signed Pastorelli & Rapkin, London, with accessories and mahogany case, 19thC, 11in (28cm) wide.
£250-300 *CSK*

Thermometers

A brass water thermometer, unnamed.
£5-8 *JMG*

A mahogany bowfront thermometer, signed Troughton & Simms, London, slight damage, 19thC.
£500-600 *P*

Waywisers

A hand waywiser, signed W. Peplow, Wellington, Inventor & Maker, with 3½in (9cm) diam counter wheel and folding handle, 19thC.
£400-450 *CSK*

A mahogany waywiser, signed G. Adams, Fleet Street, London, early 19thC, the 32in (81cm) wheel with iron tyre.
£600-700 *CSK*

General

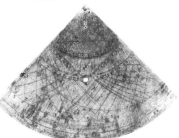

A boxwood quadrant, unsigned, early 18thC.
£450-500 *CSK*

A Daniels wet/dry bulb hydrometer, on fruitwood stand.
£60-80 *MB*

A brass and mahogany ship's inclinometer, c1930, 24in (61cm) high.
£50-75 *COB*

An oxidised brass sunshine recorder, by Casella, London, on adjustable base, 9½in (24cm) high.
£450-500 *CSK*

A barograph, by Short & Mason, London, in glazed mahogany case, 14in (35.5cm) wide.
£130-150 *WIL*

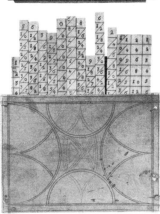

A set of boxwood Napier's bones, 3½in (9cm) wide, with letter of instructions, 18thC.
£3,000-3,500 *CSK*

A set of graduated rods formerly used for multiplication and division, based on a method invented by John Napier.

A brass Douglas's patent reflecting protractor, signed Cary, London patent 389, 6in (15.5cm) wide, in leather case, 19thC.
£400-450 *CSK*

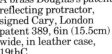

A brass graphometer, signed Lennel à la Sphére à Paris, dated 1778, with universal tripod attachment, in leather case, 8½in (21.5cm).
£700-750 *CSK*

```
Cross Reference
Barometers
```

A hard and soft cathode X-ray tube, the globe with printed legend by Cuthbert & Andrews, with vulcanite stand on wood base, 19½in (49cm) wide.
£300-350 *CSK*

FURTHER READING

Daumas, Maurice, *Scientific Instruments of the 17thC and 18thC and their Makers,* London 1972.
Herbert, Sir Alan P., *Sundials, Old and New,* London 1967.
Wynter, Harriet and Turner, Anthony, *Scientific Instruments,* London 1975.

Dental Instruments

A collection of dental instruments.
£5-10 each   *TM*

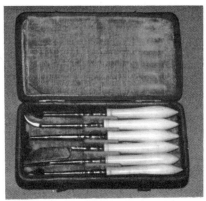

Dental scaling instruments, with ivory handles, c1830.
£200-250   *BUR*

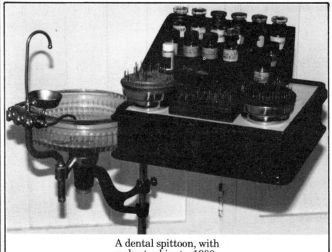

A dental spittoon, with walnut cabinet, c1900.
£300-400   *BUR*

A tooth key with adjustable claw, mid-19thC.
£140-160   *DBu*

An iron Pelican tooth extractor, with combination limb and 2 claws, 17thC.
£500-600   *CSK*

A walnut case of dental instruments, mid-19thC, 9½in (24cm).
£350-400   *CSK*

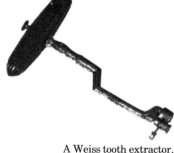

A Weiss tooth extractor, with ebony handle, mid-19thC.
£120-140   *DBu*

FURTHER READING
Bennion, Elizabeth, *Antique Medical Instruments,* London 1978.

Medical Instruments

Aspirators

An aspirator set, by Down Bros, c1890.
£60-80 *DBu*

A lacquered brass Portain's aspirator, by Arnold & Sons, London, complete in plush lined fitted mahogany case, late 19thC, 9½in (24cm) wide.
£200-250 *CSK*

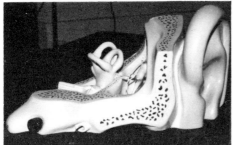

An aspirator set, for draining fluids, c1890.
£60-80 *DBu*

Ears & Eyes

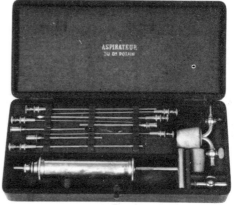

A French aspirator set, c1890.
£60-80 *DBu*

A French silver plated ear trumpet, c1880.
£180-200 *DBu*

A brass mounted tortoiseshell hearing aid, 19thC, 4in (10cm).
£160-200 *CSK*

A plaster model of an ear, for demonstration c1910.
£80-120 *BUR*

An ophthalmic instrument, c1895.
£60-80 *DBu*

A selection of glass eyes, c1900.
£15-20 each *DBu*

Enemas

A cylinder type enema pump for self-administration, c1880.
£80-100   *DBu*

A Maw pattern enema pump, with lacquered brass and ivory fittings, in fitted mahogany case, 19thC, 11in (28cm).
£400-450   *CSK*

Condition is important.

DID YOU KNOW?
Enema pumps were very fashionable in Victorian times. They were sometimes made of porcelain with scenes of steam trains printed on them, and also book shaped, to be kept in the library!

A cased enema set, made of pewter with ivory fittings, 19thC.
£80-100   *DBu*

General

A blood letting set, c1850, by Down Bros.
£500-600   *DBu*

A Fowler's phrenological head, 11in (28cm) high.
£550-600   *CSK*

A pewter Gibson medicine spoon, c1870.
£120-140   *DBu*

Invented by Gibson for giving medicine to children or mental patients.

A sputum blue glass bottle, Dr. Dettweiler, c1920.
£20-30   *DBu*

Doctor Bennett's percussor with ivory pleximeter, for diagnostic purposes.
£250-350   *DBu*

An articulated and sectioned human skull, late 19thC.
£550-600   *CSK*

An Italian waisted albarello, Castelli, damaged, early 18thC, 12in (30.5cm) high.
£220-250   *CSK*

A rosewood domestic medicine chest, by Savoury & Moore, with compartments for bottles, 2 trays with balance and other items, 19thC, 10½in (26.5cm).
£500-600   *CSK*

A Savona blue and white wet drug jar, spout repaired, glaze flakes, c1680, 7½in (19cm).
£350-400   *CSK*

A mahogany domestic medicine chest, with compartments for 12 bottles, the drawer containing pestle and mortar, the chest 7in (18cm) high.
£250-300   *CSK*

A mahogany domestic medicine chest, with fitted interior, 19thC, 9in (23cm) wide.
£350-400   *CSK*

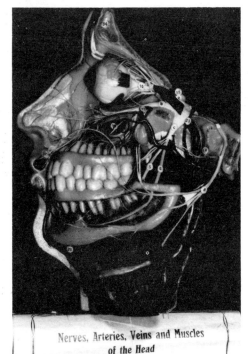

Nerves, Arteries, Veins and Muscles of the Head

A wax section of head and face, with descriptive leaflet, c1910.
£250-350   *BUR*

Staffordshire creamware jars and covers, Leeches jar 16in (40.5cm).
£450-500   *CSK*

Obstetric

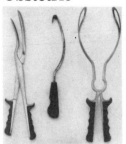

A pair of midwifery forceps of Anderson pattern, with ebony handles, by Brady & Martin, a blunt hook with rosewood handle and a pair of Simpson pattern craniotomy forceps.
£200-250 *CSK*

A pair of Sims speculum, silver plated on brass, c1890.
£30-50 each *BUR*

A brass single blade scarificator, in leather case, 18thC, 7cm wide.
£160-180 *P*

Perforators, c1890.
£60-80 *DBu*

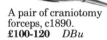

An obstetric instrument, c1860.
£80-100 *DBu*

A pair of craniotomy forceps, c1890.
£100-120 *DBu*

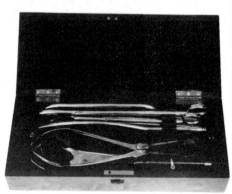

Obstetric forceps with wooden handles, c1790.
£150-200 *BUR*

Various obstetric instruments in a leather roll, c1850.
£300-400 *BUR*

A cased set of obstetric instruments, c1850.
£800-900 *DBu*

Rare to be found in a case.

A brass scarificator, by Allen & Hanbury, London, c1890.
£120-140 *DBu*

A pair of obstetric forceps, with ebony handle, c1890.
£100-120 *DBu*

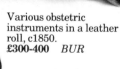

A French scarificator, nickel plate on brass.
£100-120 *DBu*

Stethoscopes

A monaural stethoscope,
c1895.
£80-100   *DBu*

Three stethoscopes,
19thC.
£100-350 each   *CSK*

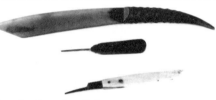

Georgian ivory handled
scalpels, and a Victorian
horn paper knife.
£12-15 each   *MB*

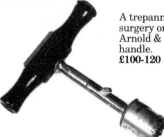

A trepanning saw, for
surgery on the skull, by
Arnold & Sons, ebony
handle.
£100-120   *DBu*

Surgical

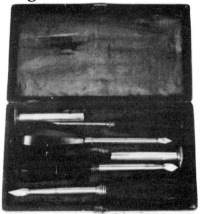

A trochlea and canula
set, with ebony handles,
in fitted case, c1860.
£130-150   *DBu*

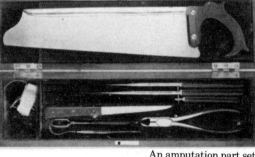

An amputation part set,
the Liston knives
stamped Z. Hunter, in
mahogany case, 19thC,
16½in (42cm) wide.
£400-450   *CSK*

A brass and steel spine
saw, 11in (28cm).
£110-150   *CSK*

Veterinary

A veterinary set with
horn handles, in leather
roll, c1890.
£120-140   *BUR*

A pair of haemorrhoid
forceps, with ivory blade,
c1900.
£60-80   *BUR*

FURTHER READING
Bennion, Elizabeth, *Antique Dental Instruments* and
Antique Medical Instruments, London 1978.
Wilbur, C. Keith, M.D., *Antique Medical
Instruments,* Pennsylvania, U.S.A.

337

Serviette Rings

A silver serviette ring.
£20-30 *MAN*

Serviette rings.
£3-11 *VB*

An ornate silver serviette
ring.
£45-50 *MAN*

Silver serviette rings.
£25-30 each *MAN*

Silver serviette rings.
£15-25 *PC*

Three plain silver
serviette rings.
£25-60 each *MAN*

A collection of ivory
serviette rings.
£3-25 each *AL*

Two small silver serviette
rings.
£20-30 each *MAN*

Silver serviette rings.
£30-40 each *MAN*

Two silver plated
serviette rings.
£10-12 each *MAN*

Wooden serviette rings.
£1-2 each *AL*

A silver serviette ring.
£30-40 *MAN*

Sewing Boxes & Cases

Two Georgian etuis with leather cases.
£200-250 each *PC*

A Louis XVI straw-work sewing box, with fitted interior, late 18thC, 10in (25cm) wide.
£300-400 *CNY*

An etui containing sewing articles.
£50-60 *VB*

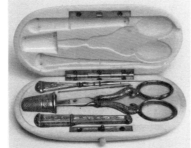

An ivory and gilt sewing case, 4½in (11cm) wide.
£80-120 *PC*

Cross Reference
Boxes

A Victorian needlework box, shaped as a house.
£250-300 *PC*

A Georgian gold etui, 3½in (9cm) long.
£150-200 *PC*

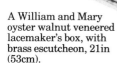

A William and Mary oyster walnut veneered lacemaker's box, with brass escutcheon, 21in (53cm).
£850-950 *WW*

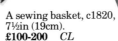

A sewing basket, c1820, 7½in (19cm).
£100-200 *CL*

Sewing Needles

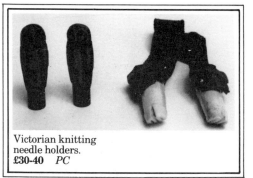

Victorian knitting
needle holders.
£30-40   *PC*

A Tunbridgeware needle
box and pin cushions.
£20-30   *PC*

A Georgian engraved
silver bodkin case.
£15-20   *PC*

A selection of silver
bodkins.
£20-30 each   *PC*

Three Georgian mother-
of-pearl needle cases.
£40-60 each   *PC*

A Baxter print case with
needle boxes inside.
£200-300   *PC*

A varied selection of
ivory needle holders.
£20-30 each   *PC*

Cross Reference
Treen

A Georgian fruitwood
pin poppet, 1¾in (2cm)
long.
£100-200   *PC*

Two vegetable ivory
carved needle holders.
£20-30 each   *PC*

FURTHER READING
Groves, Sylvia, *The History of Needlework Tools and
Accessories,* Devon 1973.
Longman, E. D. and Loch, S., *Pins and Pin cushions,*
London 1911.

DID YOU KNOW?
Threadneedle Street was originally known as
Threeneedle Street because of the three needles on
the Shield of Arms of the Worshipful Company of
Needlemakers.

Pin cushions

A selection of Georgian, Victorian and Edwardian pin cushions.
£40-50 *PC*

Prisoner-of-war bone pin cushions.
£20-30 *PC*

Two Victorian home-made emery cushions to remove rust from needles.
£10-15 *PC*

> **Cross Reference**
> Textiles

A brass humming bird clamp and pin cushion.
£100-150 *PC*

A horn, mother-of-pearl and blue velvet pin cushion clamp.
£70-90 *PC*

A Tunbridgeware pin cushion clamp.
£80-120 *PC*

Two pin cushion clamps, one with a drawer.
£80-120 *PC*

A pin cushion in the form of a sampler, possibly Georgian.
£100-150 *PC*

Two rosewood pin cushion clamps.
£25-35 each *PC*

DID YOU KNOW?
The term 'pin money' originated in France where it was customary for merchants to make a gift of pins to the wife or daughter of the person with whom they were doing business.

Sewing

General

A Georgian cut steel chatelaine, with needle box, note case, penknife, pencil, thimble, scissors and bodkin case.
£80-100 *PC*

A selection of waxers used for waxing thread, smallest 1in (2.5cm) high
£30-50 *PC*

A Georgian cotton reel holder with original ivory bobbins, 12in (30cm) high.
£80-100 *PC*

Bobbins used to go back to the shop to be re-wound.

A selection of thread winders in mother-of-pearl, ivory and wood.
£20-30 *PC*

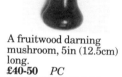

A fruitwood darning mushroom, 5in (12.5cm) long.
£40-50 *PC*

An ebony bobbin holder, 10½in (26cm) high.
£60-70 *PC*

A Georgian bobbin winder.
£80-120 *PC*

Cross Reference
Tartan ware

A tartan ware set of thimble holder, bodkin case and needle case, with original needles.
£50-70 *PC*

Cross Reference
Tartan ware
Tunbridgeware
Treen
Buttons
Buttonhooks
Toiletries

A fruitwood sewing
accessory, with pin
cushion and barrels
containing spools, late
19thC, 10in (25cm) high.
£140-160 *P*

Scissors

A leather case with
2 pairs of scissors,
marked RD 319401
Sheffield, c1880.
£10-15 *PC*

Tape Measure Holders

Rare holders in the form
of a carriage and a
watermill.
£40-50 each *PC*

A selection of steel
scissors.
£30-50 *PC*

Three varied tape
measure holders.
£10-40 each *PC*

Three tape measure
holders, in silver and
blue enamel, boxwood
and brass, and brass and
ivory.
£20-30 *PC*

An advertising tape
measure holder.
£15-20 *PC*

Three holders in ivory,
mother-of-pearl and
painted boxwood.
£15-25 *PC*

Cross Reference
Signs
Tins

Thimbles

Four Victorian thimbles
with Royal crests.
£70-80   *PC*

A thimble in original
case, commemorating
the birth of H.R.H.
Princess Royal on 21st
November 1840.
£60-70   *PC*

A selection of thimble
holders including one in
the shape of a teapot,
with a picture of
Tenterden on it.
£40-60   *PC*

Three gold thimbles.
£80-120   *PC*

Two silver thimbles, one
with amethysts and one
with turquoise stones.
£60-80   *PC*

*The bottoms of this type of
thimble used to be cut off
to make rings.*

A selection of thimble
holders, including a
silver bell with ivory
handle.
£30-40   *PC*

Four silver thimbles,
each set with a stone to
make it more hard-
wearing.
£60-80   *PC*

DID YOU KNOW?
The word thimble is derived from the Old English
thymel, meaning a thumb stall.

Three early silver
thimbles, 18thC.
£60-70   *PC*

Four thimble guards.
£40-60   *PC*

Shipping

A brass shipbuilder's plate, 1942, 17in (43cm) wide.
£35-40   *COB*

P. & O. Stewards' badges, c1950.
£10-15 each   *PC*

A ship's bell, c1913.
£600-650   *PC*

A stained oak ship's wheel, inscribed Brown Bros. & Co. Ltd. Rosebank Ironworks, Edinburgh, 1845, 36in (92cm) diam.
£100-150   *CSK*

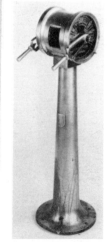

White Star Line ship's bell, Megantic Bridge Bell, c1922.
£800-1,200   *PC*

Queen Mary State Room telephone.
£100-150   *PC*

A vanity mirror from the Queen Elizabeth, c1940.
£5-10   *PC*

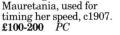

An hour glass from Mauretania, used for timing her speed, c1907.
£100-200   *PC*

A teak and brass binnacle with compass, gimbal mounting and cover, inscribed W. Ludolph, Wesermünde, Hamburg, 52½in (133cm) high.
£100-200   *CSK*

A brass ship's telegraph, inscribed John Bruce & Sons Ltd, Liverpool, 42in (107cm).
£200-300   *CSK*

Cunard Line

A cup and saucer from the First Class nursery on the Queen Mary, stamped Cunard White Star.
£20-25 *PC*

A Cunard Line soup bowl, c1850.
£40-60 *PC*

A Stratton powder compact in original box, c1969.
£15-20 *COB*

A tie pin from Queen Elizabeth II.
£10-20 *COB*

A waiter's tray.
£30-50 *PC*

A selection of china, from c1915 to 1987.
£30-40 each *PC*

Lifeboat and Raft rations tin from the Queen Mary.
£5-10 *COB*

A pewter pin tray from the Queen Mary.
£25-30 *COB*

A silver plated spoon from Queen Elizabeth II, in original box.
£4-6 *COB*

A medallion commemorating the last voyage of the Queen Elizabeth in 1968.
£40-45 *PC*

General

A North German Lloyd
sherry glass, c1900.
£30-40   *PC*

Mauretania launching
goblet, 1906.
£300-500   *PC*

*Possibly the only one in
existence.*

A ship's crest from H.M.
Yacht Britannia.
£10-15   *COB*

A Union Castle glass
ashtray.
£8-10   *COB*

A decorated egg in a
Union Castle Line egg
cup, c1900.
£30-35   *PC*

A beer can from Oriana,
c1985.
£1-5   *PC*

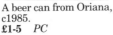

Cross Reference
Tins

A brass ashtray, R.M.S.
Aquitania.
£20-25   *COB*

A Huntley & Palmer
biscuit tin from the
Lusitania, 1907.
£100-150   *PC*

White Star Line

A silver plated salver
from the White Star Line.
£200-300 *PC*

A table light, c1910.
£50-55 *PC*

A cream jug, 1905, 3in
(8cm) high.
£20-40 *PC*

A blue and white dish,
1900, 8½in (21cm) wide.
£100-150 *PC*

A cigarette tin, 1909.
£30-40 *PC*

Titanic

S.S. Titanic sailor's cap
ribbon, reproduced today.
£6-8 *COB*

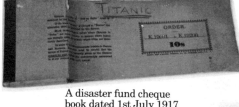

A disaster fund cheque
book dated 1st July 1917
to 1st October 1917.
£190-220 *COB*

A beer bottle from the
Titanic Brewery,
Burslem, Yorks.
£5-10 *PC*

*So named because of the
Titanic Captain's
Associations with
Burslem.*

A contemporary
watercolour drawing of
the R.M.S. Titanic
leaving Southampton,
April 12th 1912, sunk
April 15th 1912, signed
by J. Nicholson, 5 by
9½in (13 by 24cm),
unframed.
£120-140 *ONS*

Ephemera

Log Book and Journal for
H.M.S. Rambler, from
September 1880 to
March 1884 including
sketches.
£65-75 *WAL*

Shipping Identification
booklet, May 1913.
£45-55 *COB*

The Star Album of Naval Life

Postcard album, c1913.
£30-35 *COB*

The Navy List, April
1826.
£40-45 *COB*

P. & O. menu, Sydney to
London, R.M.S.
Moldavia, 1933.
£6-10 *COB*

A photograph of Jack
Buchanan who sailed on
the Queen Elizabeth,
1950s.
£25-30 *COB*

A Cunard menu from the
final voyage of R.M.S.
Queen Elizabeth, 6th
November 1968.
£6-8 *COB*

Cross Reference
Ephemera

Silver Jubilee Royal
Naval Review, Spithead,
16th July 1935, souvenir
programme.
£15-20 *COB*

Posters

Cunard Europe America,
by Odin Rosenvinge.
£500-600 *ONS*

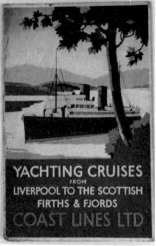

Yachting Cruises travel
brochure, 1937.
£8-12 *COB*

A Royal Mail travel
brochure for an autumn
cruise, 1936.
£12-15 *COB*

White Star Cabin to
Canada, S.S. Laurentic,
by Gordon Nicoll.
£300-350 *ONS*

Cross Reference
Posters

Allan Line to Canada,
c1910.
£200-250 *COB*

Hamburg-American
Line, June 1929.
£60-80 *COB*

Canadian Pacific poster,
c1913.
£300-350 *COB*

Cunard Line sailing list,
June 1933.
£10-15 *COB*

United States Lines to
New York.
£300-400 *ONS*

Rio de Janeiro, by Royal
Mail, by Kenneth
Shoesmith.
£250-300 *ONS*

White Star Line R.M.S.
Olympic, by M. B. Black
the largest British
steamer viewed from a
seaplane.
£500-600 *ONS*

S.S. United States, c1953.
£70-80 *COB*

United States Lines, S.S.
Leviathan, the largest
liner in the world, by
R. S. Pike Dorland.
£300-400 *ONS*

P.S.N.C. to South
America, by Kenneth
Shoesmith.
£250-350 *ONS*

White Star Line,
Liverpool to Australia
via Cape Town.
£250-350 *ONS*

Run Away to Sea, c1960.
£50-60 *COB*

Cunard White Star,
Queen Mary and Queen
Elizabeth, by Walter
Thomas.
£400-500 *ONS*

To Scandinavia from
New York via S.S.
Mauretania, 1924.
£40-50 *COB*

Wilson Line, c1901.
£80-90 *COB*

Signs & Advertising

Advertising

A painted plaster figure advertising North British Golf Balls.
£200-300   K

An ink bottle in the shape of a shell, the top containing marking ink, c1930.
£10-12   K

A Crosse & Blackwell strawberry conserve jar, with movable hands, 5in (13cm).
£10-15   AL

A Guinness brush, c1965.
£6-10   K

A promotional mirror, c1930.
£3-5   K

A ceramic bottle stand, 1960s.
£30-50   K

An enamel finished promotional thermometer for the film Some Like It Hot, showing Marilyn Monroe in the centre, c1959, 38in (98cm).
£4,500-5,000   P

An Art Nouveau cast metal figure, advertising Lifebuoy Soap, 28in (70cm) high.
£200-250   K

A small multi-coloured ceramic figure.
£40-50   K

A pottery storage jar with rich blue glaze, impressed lettering picked out in white, patent tap.
£250-300   K

A moulded hand painted Hennessy dog.
£50-60

A similar model with a puppy.
£60-100 *K*

A rare hand painted plaque.
£80-100 *K*

> **Cross Reference**
> Drinking

A hand painted rubber figure.
£20-30 *K*

A small figure with wooden base and plastic tankard, 1960s.
£15-30 *K*

An advertising pig.
£140-150 *WHA*

A miniature Wade figure of a drinker with tankard, 1970s.
£10-20 *K*

A gilded and painted cast metal figure by the London Art Advertising Metalwork Co.
£70-80 *K*

353

Signs

A multi-coloured transfer printed tin, Invincible Motor Insurance, in mint condition, c1936.
£30-50 *K*

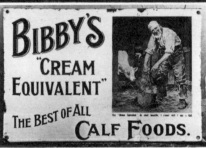

A small enamel sign, with sepia lithographic stencilled picture, small damage.
£150-200 *K*

A white metal vesta box with plastic coated print, c1910.
£20-30 *K*

Cross Reference
Tins

A blue, white and yellow finger plate, in fine condition.
£60-80 *K*

A metal enamelled advertising sign, 36in (92cm) wide.
£15-20 *WHA*

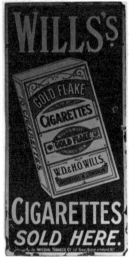

A promotional vesta box.
£10-15 *K*

An enamelled sign, yellow on dark blue, 27in (68cm) high.
£100-120 *K*

An enamel sign, 21 by 14in (53 by 35cm).
£50-55 *WHA*

An enamel sign, minor damage and staining, 30in (75cm) wide.
£150-200 *K*

An enamelled Oxo cube sign.
£10-15 *AL*

Smoking

An unusual gourd shaped cigarette dispenser.
£45-55 *MB*

A cigar cutter and holder in case.
£3-6 each *VB*

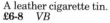

A leather cigarette tin.
£6-8 *VB*

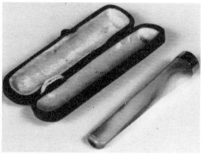

An amber and silver trimmed cigarette holder, original box.
£45-55 *MAN*

An Art Deco cigarette dispenser.
£150-180 *PGA*

A pearl cigarette holder with gold trim, 3in (8cm) long, original box.
£30-40 *MAN*

An amber and silver cigarette holder, 4in (11cm) long.
£25-35 *MAN*

A tortoiseshell cigarette holder, in original box, 5in (13cm) long.
£20-30 *MAN*

A Victorian cigar cabinet with cedar lining, 12½in (32cm) high.
£170-190 *MB*

A chrome and marble ashtray, with model aeroplane, c1934.
£65-75 *DEC*

An ivory cigarette holder, inlaid with rubies and pearls in gold, in original box stamped Newmans, 5in (13cm) long.
£110-130 *MAN*

Kensitas cigarette silks.
£1-2 each *VB*

A tobacco jar, 6in (15cm) high.
£15-20 *AL*

A Belgian chrome and Bakelite smoker's table, 29in (73cm) high.
£120-140 *DEC*

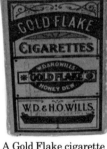

A Gold Flake cigarette packet.
£1-2 *FAL*

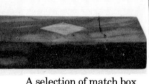

A Doulton Lambeth tobacco jar, 5in (13cm) high.
£30-35 *AL*

A selection of match box covers.
£5-12 each *AL*

Cross Reference
Boxes

A Victorian mahogany smoker's box, 15in (38cm) high.
£220-250 *MB*

An oak cigar box carved in the form of a kennel, with side drawer, 10½in (26.5cm) wide.
£600-700 *C*

A rare cranberry cigar holder, 5in (12.5cm) long.
£100-110 *CBA*

Player's cigarette tin.
£3-6 *WHA*

Cross Reference
Cigarette cards

A tin tobacco box made in
the Pontypool Factory,
c1780, 5in (13cm) wide.
£130-140 *CL*

Ashtrays by Grays, for
Dunhills, c1945.
£2-3 each *CAC*

Cross Reference
Tins

Pipes

A First Period
Watcombe, Torquay and
Devon clay pipe, c1880.
£20-25 *CBA*

A painted tin tobacco
box, c1850.
£80-120 *CL*

*The value of these boxes
depicting naked ladies
depends on quality and
appeal.*

A Prattware tobacco
pipe, 18thC.
£400-450 *P[Re]*

A treen pipe holder, 6in
(15cm).
£20-25 *AL*

Cross Reference
Treen

Lighters

A chrome table/hand
lighter, 5in (13cm) high.
£55-65 *DEC*

A chrome table lighter,
6in (15cm) high.
£45-55 *DEC*

A Ronson 'Touch Tip'
petrol fuelled table
lighter, U.S. Pat.
1986754, c1935, 6in
(15cm) long.
£500-600 *C*

A rocket table lighter
and ashtray, 11in (28cm)
high.
£85-95 *DEC*

SMOKING

A chrome table lighter,
4in (10cm).
£60-70 *DEC*

A chrome table lighter,
5in (13cm) high.
£35-45 *DEC*

A heavy chrome table
lighter, c1930, 5in (12cm)
high.
£35-45 *DEC*

A Falco automatic table
lighter in Bakelite, 5½in
(14cm).
£60-70 *DEC*

Match Strikers

A brass match striker
and stand.
£10-15 each *AL*

Match strikers.
£18-20 each *AL*

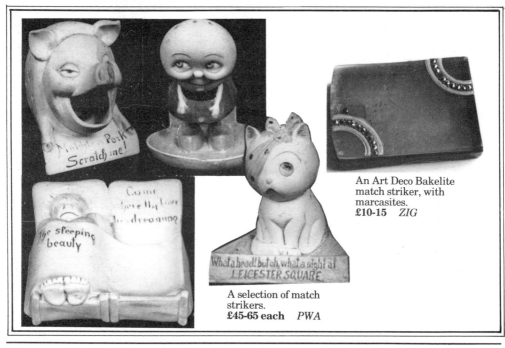

An Art Deco Bakelite
match striker, with
marcasites.
£10-15 *ZIG*

A selection of match
strikers.
£45-65 each *PWA*

Two match strikers.
£50-80 each   *PWA*

A Bakelite vesta case,
2½in (6cm) wide.
£12-15   *AL*

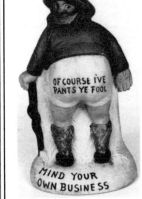

A match striker called
Pants, c1915.
£45-55   *PWA*

Three match strikers.
£10-16 each   *DEC*

Three Victorian vesta
boxes.
£25-30 each   *PC*

Silver match boxes were produced in a
variety of shapes including animals and
fruit. They were manufactured with great
skill, often incorporating a ring for
attachment to a watch chain. Small vesta
matches were popular during the 19th and
early 20th century, struck on a rasp end.

Three engraved silver
vesta boxes, c1920.
£40-50 each   *MAN*

A selection of silver vesta
cases.
£35-45 each   *MAN*

An Edwardian vesta case
of gilded metal.
£50-100   *MS*

Matchboxes

A selection of
matchboxes, including
some by Rigold and
Bergmann of Bombay,
scarce, G-VG.
£16-22 *N*

British Fusilier.
5p *KOL*

Pioneer matchboxes.
25p *KOL*

A set of 6 fish picture
matchboxes.
10p each *KOL*

Proof of Bryant & May
matchbox label, about
100 years old.
£2-3 each *KOL*

Cross Reference
Shipping

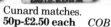

Cunard matches.
50p-£2.50 each *COB*

A selection of bookmatch
covers.
10p each *KOL*

*Bookmatch covers were
first produced more than
50 years ago.*

A selection of advertising matchbox labels.
5p each *KOL*

Morelands label with striker.
50p *KOL*

Two matchbox labels made in Europe, about 50 years old.
50p-£1 each *KOL*

A selection of new matchbox labels.
5p *KOL*

SMOKING/MATCHBOXES

An 80-year-old label.
35p *KOL*

Matchbox label, c1893.
£2-3 each *KOL*

Worth more with actual box.

Cross Reference
Advertising

Two matchbox labels, one with striker.
10p each *KOL*

Assorted matchbox labels.
10p each *KOL*

Label made in Sweden, c1890.
£1.50-2 *KOL*

A selection of labels from Israel, Sweden, Belgium and Great Britain.
10p each *KOL*

362

A selection of Swan Vestas labels.
25p each *KOL*

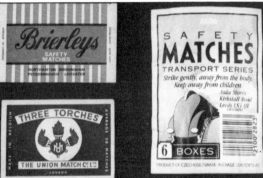

UPEC aircraft series of 25.
£1 the set *KOL*

Matchbox labels.
10p each *KOL*

Australian skillets.
5p each *KOL*

Packet label.
10p *KOL*

Cross Reference
Aeronautica

Austrian matchbox labels made in 13 different colours.
10p each *KOL*

Unused skillets.
10p each *KOL*

FURTHER READING
Newsletter of the British Matchbox Label & Booklet Society, obtainable from membership secretary, 3 Langton Close, Norwich.

Snuff Boxes

An agate and white metal snuff box, slight damage.
£30-40   *MS*

A French composition snuff box, commemorating a ballooning event, tortoiseshell lined, c1784, 3in (7.5cm) diam.
£175-200   *CL*

A George IV Scottish gilt-lined snuff box, with Italian micro-mosaic plaque of Pegasus, maker's or retailer's mark Home, Edinburgh, 1824, 3in (8cm).
£500-800   *C*

> **Cross Reference**
> Aeronautica

A wooden snuff box with wooden hinge, 3½in (9cm) wide.
£35-45   *SAD*

A Scottish horn snuff mull, with silver mounts, c1800, 4in (10cm) wide.
£80-100   *CL*

Snuff shoes.
£18-23   *VB*

A Victorian electro-plated snuff box, with garnets, 3in (7.5cm) wide.
£250-300   *P*

Burr elm snuff boxes, 3in (7.5cm) and 4in (10cm) wide.
£30-50 each   *CHA*

A George III amboyna wood snuff box, lined with gold and inscribed, 1819, 3½in (8.5cm) diam.
£500-600   *Bea*

A snuff shoe, 19thC.
£40-50   *PC*

A papier mâché snuff
box, with painted
caricature of an actor,
c1800.
£100-150   *CL*

A Victorian carved wood
snuff shoe, 3in (7.5cm)
long.
£60-80   *PC*

An early painted snuff
box, slight wear, c1770,
4in (10cm) diam.
£165-200   *CL*

*Earlier boxes more
expensive.*

A French pressed wood
snuff box, with
tortoiseshell lining, the
lid decorated with
Masonic motifs, early
19thC, 3in (8cm) diam.
£60-100   *CSK*

Pressed leather snuff box
with silver monogram,
2½in (6cm) wide.
£20-40   *CL*

A leather snuff box with
small silver monogram,
2½in (6cm) wide.
£20-40   *CL*

Cross Reference
Mauchline Ware

A Mauchline pen-worked
snuff box showing Menai
Straits, stamped 'Smith
of Mauchline', c1825, 3in
(7.5cm) wide.
£160-180   *CL*

A table snuff box, the
painted top depicting the
Death of Napoleon,
c1830.
£65-75   *CL*

A pressed leather snuff
box, with design of
Athena holding up the
head of Medusa, 4in
(10cm) long.
£70-80   *CL*

*These rare leather snuff
boxes are soaked in
lacquer to make them
hard.*

Spoons

A silver spoon engraved Teniers, 4½in (11cm) long.
£16-20 *MAN*

l. Plated spoon from Doncaster.
£12-15
r. Silver engraved spoon depicting York Minster.
£20-30 *MAN*

Three silver spoons, 4½in (11cm) long.
£12-15 each *MAN*

A selection of crested spoons from Jersey and Isle of Man.
£3-5 each *MAN*

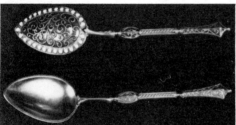

A pair of decorated gilt teaspoons, one blue, one green, 4in (10cm) long.
£15-20 each *MAN*

A silver teaspoon, engraved Bermuda J.W.
£12-15 *MAN*

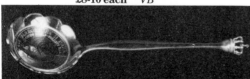

Silver shooting spoons, London 1913 and Birmingham 1917.
£8-10 each *VB*

Two silver teaspoons, 4½in (11cm) long.
£15-18 *MAN*

A silver commemorative spoon, engraved Queen Margarethe of Denmark 1972, made from a 10 krona coin, 6in (15cm).
£30-40 *MAN*

A Scottish Provincial silver spoon, possibly by John Heton, 1800, 5½in (14cm) long.
£15-20 *MAN*

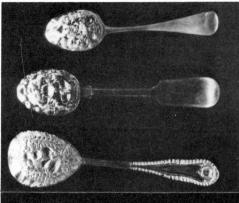

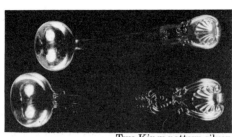

Two Kings pattern silver spoons.
£15-20 each *MAN*

A selection of silver spoons, smallest 4½in (11cm) long.
£10-20 *MAN*

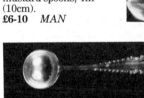

A pair of silver plated mustard spoons, 4in (10cm).
£6-10 *MAN*

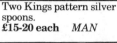

A silver plated spoon with bone handle, 7½in (19cm).
£12-15 *MAN*

Four silver sugar spoons, 4½-5in (11-12.5cm) long.
£12-15 each *MAN*

A pair of silver salt and mustard spoons.
£35-40 *MAN*

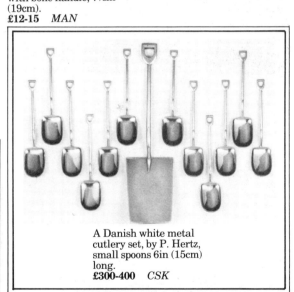

A Danish white metal cutlery set, by P. Hertz, small spoons 6in (15cm) long.
£300-400 *CSK*

A selection of gilt spoons.
£3-5 each *MAN*

A metal snake design salt spoon, 3½in (9cm).
£4-7 *MAN*

Silver mustard spoon.
£15-25 *MAN*

Caddy Spoons

A George IV caddy spoon
by Joseph Willmore,
Birmingham, 1822.
£110-130   *P*

George III spoon by
Matthew Linwood,
Birmingham, 1807.
£200-250   *P*

Engraved silver caddy
spoons.
£40-60 each   *MAN*

George III jockey cap
caddy spoon, c1800.
£250-280   *P*

George III spoon by
Matthew Linwood,
Birmingham, c1800.
£350-400   *P*

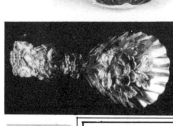

A Dutch silver caddy
spoon with hallmark.
£40-45   *SAD*

A silver caddy spoon.
£45-55   *MAN*

George III caddy spoon
by Josiah Snatt, 1805.
£350-400   *P*

George III spoon by
Josiah Snatt, 1808.
£120-140   *P*

A selection of vine leaf
caddy spoons.
£200-350 each   *P*

Two silver caddy spoons,
Birmingham, c1806.
£180-240 each   *P*

A George IV spoon,
engraved with crest, by
Paul Storr, 1821.
£450-500   *P*

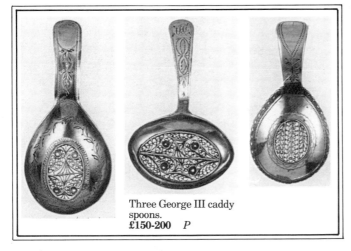

Three George III caddy
spoons.
£150-200   *P*

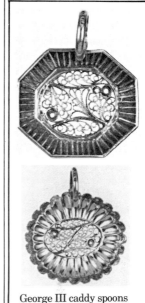

George III caddy spoons
with oval filigree panels.
£250-280   *P*

A George III Provincial
stamped out caddy spoon,
by J. T. Younge & Co,
Sheffield, 1809.
£100-150   *P*

A George IV Provincial
caddy spoon, by S. C.
Younge & Co, Sheffield,
1826.
£100-150   *P*

Two George III caddy
spoons.
£150-250   *P*

FURTHER READING_____
Norie, John, *An Illustrated Guide to Caddy Spoons*,
London 1988.

SPORT

Cricket

A clock with cricketing theme, 8-day movement with lever platform escapement, 8in (20cm) high.
£450-500 *CSK*

A cricket belt buckle and clasp with chain.
£30-40 *Bon*

A Staffordshire mug, with wicket-keeper Box, bowler Clarke, and batsman Pilch in white on blue ground, c1860, 4in (10cm) high.
£200-250 *CSK*

A yellow metal cravat pin, formed as a cricket bat and ball, stamped SS18, 2½in (7cm), cased.
£40-70 *Bon*

An Edwardian vesta case, stamped with a vignette of a cricket match, maker's mark indistinct, Birmingham 1907.
£300-400 *CSK*

A Doulton Lambeth stoneware cricketing jug, in brown, green and blue, cracked, 6in (15cm).
£200-300 *P*

An Australia Test cap of the 1924-25 series, label inscribed C.V. Grimmett in ink, slight wear to brim.
£260-300 *CSK*

A Victorian bright-cut vesta case, reverse engraved with a monogram H.J.C. Co. Ltd. Birmingham 1893, 2in (4cm).
£500-600 *CSK*

A Victorian vase shaped cup, with oval cartouches, one chased with a vignette of a game in progress, the other with an inscription, on ebonised wood plinth, Henry Wilkinson & Co, Birmingham 1882, 25in (63cm) high, 72oz free.
£1,500-2,000 *CSK*

Two bronze portrait busts of Geoffrey Boycott and Richard Hadlee, by Neale Andrew, both inscribed and standing on a mahogany base, 19in (48cm) and 16in (40cm) respectively.
£2,000-3,000 each *P*

A selection of Australian Test 1932-33 clothing, by Farmer's, Sydney, labelled C. Grimmett in ink.
From **£200-600 each**
CSK

An early cricketing print showing Miss Wicket and Miss Trigger, dated 1778, 10 by 14in (25 by 35cm), framed and glazed.
£400-500   *P*

An English School watercolour entitled Grand Cricket Match for One Thousand Guineas, late 18thC, 3 by 5in (8 by 12cm), framed and glazed.
£300-400   *P*

Cross Reference
Ephemera
Ceramics
Vesta Cases

A bronzed metal garniture, clock 11½in (29cm) high.
£400-500   *CSK*

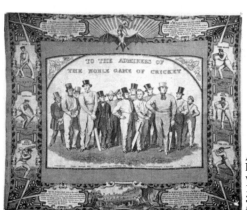

A commemorative cotton handkerchief printed with the England XI of 1847, 26½ by 32½in (66 by 81cm).
£300-400   *CSK*

Part set of 23 Player's cigarette cards, autographed by the subject, Australian Tourists 1934.
£200-250   *CSK*

371

Golf

Golf Balls

A Gourlay feather ball, stamped Wm Gourlay, size 25, mint condition.
£1,800-2,500 *CEd*

A fine feather ball by Allan Robertson of St. Andrews, with Allan in black.
£2,000-3,000 *Bon*

An unmarked feather ball.
£800-1,200 *Bon*

A hand hammered gutta golf ball, c1860.
£180-240 *CEd*

Eleven Hutchison bramble balls, marked 27, original box and tissue, minor paint chips, unused.
£600-700 *P*

A collection showing the development of the Silver King golf ball, all mounted in an ebonised case, 12 by 6in (30 by 15cm).
£200-300 *CEd*

A feather filled golf ball, size 32, stamped by W. & J. Gourlay and inscribed 32, in good condition, c1835.
£1,400-1,800 *CEd*

Two feather filled golf balls.
£900-1,400 each *CEd*

A metal mould for Kite golf balls.
£300-400 *CEd*

An alloy metal gutta golf ball mould and press, the mould with cross ridge pattern with Register No. 42, the press by G. B. Breeze of Glasgow.
£800-1,000 *CEd*

A feather filled golf ball, size 32, by W. & J. Gourlay, stamped W. & J. Go..., good condition, c1835.
£1,400-1,800 *CEd*

Golf Clubs

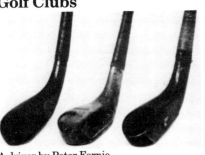

A driver by Peter Fernie.
£450-650   *CEd*

A club by McEwan &
Son, Musselburgh.
£250-350   *CEd*

A driver by John
Butchart.
£450-650   *CEd*

An Urquhart Patent
adjustable iron head club.
£300-400   *CEd*

A left handed rutter,
head stamped Wm. Park
Maker Musselburgh,
shaft stamped John
Wisden & Co. London
W.C., c1895.
£400-500   *CEd*

A boat shaped putter
with hickory shaft, by
Kempshall Mfg Co.
Arlington, N.J., c1903.
£100-200   *CEd*

A left handed lofter, by
Wm. Dunn, c1865.
£100-200   *CEd*

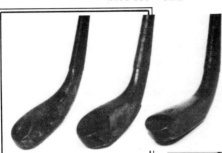

A Carrick rut iron, F. &
A. Carrick, Musselburgh,
shaft stamped John
Wisden, London, c1870.
£300-500   *CEd*

Three golf clubs:
l. Head stamped
T. Morris, shaft stamped
C. Brand, c1850.
£800-1,200

e. Head stamped R.
Forgan, c1870.
£400-600

r. A long nose brassie by
A. Patrick, stamped,
c1875.
£350-450   *CEd*

A hickory shafter roller
headed club, patented
July 1907.
£80-120   *CEd*

A mallet headed cross
head club, c1900.
£400-800   *CEd*

Left to right:
Anti-shank niblick.
Centre shafted wooden
head putter.
Bone attachment for
brass fittings.
Blade putter.
£20-30 each   *CEd*

A selection of clubs, late
19thC.
From **£400-1,400**   *CEd*

DID YOU KNOW?
A 'Baffy Spoon' is a term for a 19th Century wooden
golf club used for a lofted shot.

Golf Ephemera

A hand coloured print of
an advertisement in
Punch, 1931.
£20-25   *SAR*

Golfing picture.
£40-45   *SAR*

A coloured mezzotint by
W. A. Cox, 1923, of John
Taylor, after Sir John
Watson Gordon, in gilt
frame.
£50-80   *CEd*

Cartoon picture printed
on cloth.
£40-45   *SAR*

Golfing books by various
authors.
From **£50**   *CEd*

A selection of golfing
books by Horace
Hutchinson.
From **£50-200**   *CEd*

Golfing books, by
Bernard Darwin.
From **£50-350 each**
CEd

Golf Trophies

The MacGregor Cup, of the Ayrshire Professional Golfers Association, Birmingham 1906 hallmark, 7in (17.5cm) high, 20oz, with wood plinth.
£200-300   *CEd*

British Army of the Rhine, Inter-Divisional Golf Championships 1952.
£10-15   *SAR*

A silver trophy, Reading & S. Oxon Ladies Open Meeting, c1932.
£90-100   *SAR*

A silver replica golf challenge cup, Birmingham hallmark 1924, 12in (30cm) high, 17½oz.
£150-200   *CDC*

Golf General

Barometer.
£45-60   *SAR*

Three Royal Doulton Kingsware tankards, 5½in (14cm).
£200-300   *CDC*

A Royal Doulton Kingsware jug, 9½in (24cm).
£250-350   *CEd*

Ceramic figure.
£10-15   *SAR*

A Royal Doulton Kingsware pottery whisky flask, 8½in (21cm) high.
£250-300   *CEd*

Golfing mug.
£5-8   *SAR*

> **Cross Reference**
> Ceramics
> Doulton

Royal Doulton Toby jug, Golfer.
£20-25   *SAR*

A plate with golfing theme.
£22-25 *SAR*

A rare set of golf tiles, c1920.
£125-150 *SAR*

A bottle opener/horse brass.
£30-35 *SAR*

> **Cross Reference**
> Horse Brasses

A hand painted cocktail glass.
£17-20 *SAR*

Two bottle corks.
Left. Silver.
£45-50
Right. **£20-25** *SAR*

Bookmark.
£5-10 *SAR*

A crested golf club.
£14-18 *SAR*

A plate with original David Fisher design, from a limited edition of 25,000, Saxony 1987.
£15-20 *SAR*

A Royal Doulton tobacco jar with silver rim, c1920.
£230-250 *SAR*

Ashtray.
£25-30 *SAR*

A selection of golfing jewellery.
£18-35 each   *SAR*

A cold painted metal car mascot, of a golfer in the form of a dragonfly, early 20thC, 6in (15cm).
£450-500   *WW*

> **Cross Reference**
> Jewellery

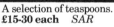

A silver cruet in the form of golf balls.
£90-100   *SAR*

> **Cross Reference**
> Spoons

A selection of teaspoons.
£15-30 each   *SAR*

A powder compact.
£23-25   *SAR*

Golfing cigarette lighter.
£5-15   *SAR*

A Stratton set of cuff links and tie pin, original box.
£15-20   *SAR*

A papier mâché advertising figure inscribed 'He played a Penfold', 20in (50cm) high, on wood stand.
£80-120   *Bon*

Sport General

A tapering cup with inscription 'National Flying Club presented by the Racing Pigeon, 2nd San Sebastian 1927 Chivers Bros. of Tunley, Velocity 773, 1575 Birds', 9in (22.5cm), 20.5oz.
£450-500 *CSK*

A boxing presentation belt, presented to R. C. Smerdon, Light Heavyweight Boxing Champion, 1911.
£200-250 *Bon*

A pottery tray printed in black and decorated in colours, showing 3 billiards players, with silver plated gallery, 14½in (36cm).
£150-250 *Bon*

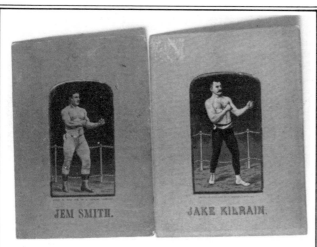

Two Stevengraphs of boxers, in original titled mount, 5 by 7in (13.5 by 17.5cm).
£80-120 each *Bon*

A Staffordshire pink ground enamel patchbox, entitled Set To, 1½in (3.5cm) wide.
£250-300 *CSK*

Three Welsh international football caps in green velvet.
£300-400 *CSK*

A pottery model of a footballer, probably Staffordshire, early 20thC, 13in (33cm) high.
£100-200 *CSK*

A selection of Football Association medals.
£200-250 *Bon*

A dark purple velvet
football cap, 1890-91.
£50-80 *Bon*

A child's cup and saucer.
£35-40 *SAR*

A pair of trophy oars,
with coats-of-arms and
crew names, dated 1875
and 1876.
£300-400 *CSK*

A pill box, the lid
polychrome, enamelled
with a 19thC tennis
player, import marks.
£350-450 *CSK*

A pair of trophy oars,
with coat-of-arms and
crew names, c1910.
£300-400 *CSK*

A papier mâché and
leather spectacle case,
with a portrait of Jenny
Lind and racehorses,
5½in (14cm) wide.
£40-60 *Bon*

An English pottery mug
printed in blue with the
names of winning horses
and jockeys since the
commencement of the
Derby, 4in (10cm).
£50-80 *Bon*

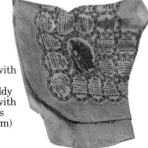

A printed silk scarf with
portrait of the 1960
Derby winner St Paddy
and Lester Piggott, with
details of the winners
since 1780, 34in (85cm)
square.
£30-40 *Bon*

Tea Caddies

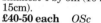

A George III rosewood
tea caddy with twin
canisters.
£200-250 *MB*

Inlaid tea caddies,
smallest 4 by 6in (10 by
15cm).
£40-50 each *OSc*

A George III kingswood
boxwood bound tea
caddy.
£240-280 *MB*

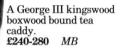

A George III twin
canister tea caddy in
satinwood with
rosewood inlay.
£275-325 *MB*

A Victorian rosewood tea
caddy with mother-of-
pearl and pewter inlay.
£170-190 *MB*

A Victorian rosewood tea
caddy.
£140-160 *MB*

A William IV tea caddy,
in rosewood and ebony.
£300-400 *MB*

A rosewood tea caddy
with original liner,
c1840.
£300-350 *MB*

An early Victorian
mahogany tea caddy,
with 2 sections.
£60-80 *MB*

A William IV mahogany
tea caddy, 12in (30cm)
wide.
£75-100 *PAC*

A William IV tea caddy,
with mother-of-pearl and
pewter inlay.
£180-200 *MB*

A George III satinwood
and marquetry box with
2 secret drawers inside,
6½in (16.5cm).
£1,100-1,300 *P*

A tea caddy painted to
simulate satinwood, the
cover with figures in a
landscape, early 19thC,
5½in (14cm) wide.
£300-400 *CSK*

A penwork tea caddy,
early 19thC, 10½in
(26.5cm) wide.
£400-450 *P*

A Regency papier mâché
tea caddy, needs
restoring, 6in (15cm)
high.
£20-25 *MB*

A Boulle work tea caddy
in red tortoiseshell and
engraved brass,
2 interior covers, 19thC,
9in (22.5cm).
£500-550 *DN*

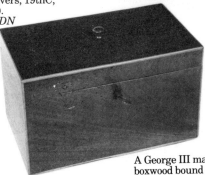

A George III mahogany
boxwood bound tea
caddy.
£120-160 *MB*

TEA CADDIES

A George III inlaid
mahogany tea caddy,
with shell inlay, 6½in
(16cm) high.
£250-350 *CNY*

A Victorian walnut
tea caddy, with
Tunbridgeware
decoration.
£120-140 *MB*

A William IV mahogany
tea caddy, with interior
compartment flanked by
twin canisters, 15in
(37cm) wide.
£400-450 *P*

Two Victorian walnut
tea caddies.
£120-140 each *MB*

A Prattware tea caddy
and cover, the moulded
figures picked out in
blue, orange, ochre and
green, cover restored,
c1790, 6½in (16.5cm)
high.
£300-400 *Bon*

A William IV rosewood
tea caddy with pewter
top.
£150-180 *MB*

A William IV rosewood
and burr oak tea caddy,
15in (37cm) wide.
£200-250 *MB*

Cross Reference
Treen

A Regency mother-of-pearl inlaid tortoiseshell tea caddy, with fitted interior, early 19thC, 5in (13cm) wide.
£450-550   *CNY*

Cross Reference
Papier Mâché

An early Victorian inlaid tea caddy.
£140-160   *MB*

A tortoiseshell and ivory tea caddy, with twin lidded compartments inside, early 19thC, 6in (14.5cm) wide.
£1,400-1,600   *P*

Regency tortoiseshell veneered tea caddies, enclosing twin lidded compartments, 8in (20cm) wide.
£400-450 each   *P*

A tortoiseshell veneered and pewter strung two-division tea caddy, early 19thC, 7½in (19cm) wide.
£200-300   *CSK*

A Regency fruitwood melon-shaped tea caddy, with mottled green body, 4½in (11.5cm) high.
£3,000-3,500   *C*

A tortoiseshell and ivory strung tea caddy, with silver monogram, lidded compartment within, damaged hinge, early 19thC, 6in (15cm) wide.
£800-900   *P*

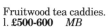

Fruitwood tea caddies.
l. **£500-600**   *MB*
r. **£900-1,000**   *C*

DID YOU KNOW?
* The earliest caddies were of porcelain and came from China.
* Silver caddies were used later and these should always have hallmarks, on both the caddy itself and the lid.
* In the 18thC wooden caddies appeared in the form of fruit, mainly apples and pears.

TEXTILES
Baby Clothes
Bonnets

A child's lawn bonnet with lace insertions.
£30-40 *LB*

An Edwardian crochet bonnet.
£25-30 *LB*

A Victorian lawn baby's bonnet, with hand tucked Ayrshire work.
£25-30 *LB*

A child's lace and silk ribbonwork bonnet.
£8-16 *CAC*

A Victorian lawn baby's bonnet, embroidered with lace trim.
£25-30 *LB*

A white linen bonnet with Hollie point lace trim, and bib with Brussels lace trim.
£200-250 *P*

Gowns

A Victorian hand embroidered Christening gown.
£140-150
A hand embroidered broderie anglaise cape, c1900.
£35-45 *CBA*

An Edwardian white lawn baby's dress.
£85-95 *LAM*

A Victorian Christening set consisting of a silk dress with pin tucks and embroidery, a carrying cape in lace trimmed with cotton voile, and a quilted satin cape trimmed with broderie anglaise.
£175-225 the set *LB*

Bags & Purses

A selection of purses in mother-of-pearl, beadwork and diamante decoration.
£10-20 each *VB*

A metallic thread bag.
£6-12 *CAC*

An Art Nouveau black evening bag.
£10-15 *LB*

A silk evening purse, c1920.
£10-15 *CAC*

Cross Reference
Beadwork

An Edwardian silk purse.
£10-15 *CAC*

A Victorian beadwork purse, mounted and framed.
£20-35 *CAC*

A beaded bag with tortoiseshell clasp, c1920.
£25-35 *LB*

Two misers' purses.
£7-10 *VB*

A coloured beaded purse/bag, 9in (22.5cm) wide.
£30-40 *CBA*

Costume
Dress

A Victorian lawn mob
cap with lace edging.
£15-20 *LB*

An Italian ecru
Buranowork cape, c1880.
£35-55 *LB*

A lady's summer spencer
of white lawn, c1815.
£150-200 *CSK*

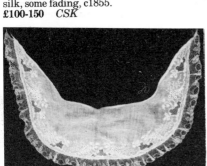

A silk chiffon dress with
beaded jacket, c1930.
£200-250 *LB*

A dress of raspberry pink
silk, some fading, c1855.
£100-150 *CSK*

An Edwardian silk dress
with bustle.
£125-150 *LB*

A Victorian lawn collar,
the edge hand
embroidered in lace.
£20-30 *LB*

A pair of Victorian
Brussels lace cuffs.
£30-40 *B*

A needlepoint collar,
probably Spanish, late
19thC, the fillings with
coronets, hearts and
dated 1636.
£350-450 *P*

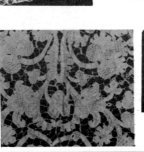

A fall cap of Brussels
point de gaze, 19thC.
£90-100 *P*

Flounces

A flounce of Brussels needlepoint appliqué, 19thC, 18in (46cm) wide.
£100-150 *P*

A flounce of Brussels bobbin and needlepoint appliqué, 19thC, 10½in (26cm).
£400-500 *P*

A muslin flounce, c1740, 53in (132cm).
£200-300 *P*

A flounce of Honiton lace, mid-18thC, 58in (148cm) long.
£260-300 *P*

Gloves

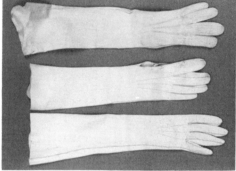

A pair of gloves from Cyprus, c1955.
£3-5 *CAC*

Three pairs of kid elbow-length gloves.
£5-10 each *CAC*

Lappets

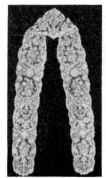

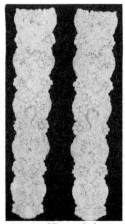

Veils

A pair of Brussels bobbin lace lappets, c1730.
£250-300 *P*

A pair of Brussels lace lappets, early 18thC.
£400-500 *P*

A veil of applied Brussels lace, 70in (176cm) square.
£150-200 *CSK*

A bridal veil of tamboured net, bordered with flowers.
£150-200 *P*

Household Linen

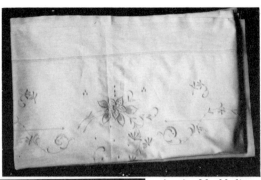

A white linen embroidered bedspread, with drawn thread work design, 100in (250cm) square.
£150-200 *LAM*

A pair of double linen sheets with blue embroidery.
£25-35 pair *LAM*

A selection of Victorian beaded milk jug covers.
£6-12 each *LB*

Two South German bobbin lace borders, 19thC, 3 and 4in (8 and 10cm) wide.
£160-200 *P*

A lawn cloth with Milanese lace border, 19thC, 46in (116cm) long.
£50-60 *P*

A set of 4 cream embroidered net curtains, 57in (144cm) wide.
£400-500 *P*

A selection of Edwardian doilies.
£3-7 each *LB*

An Italian cutwork and lace tablecloth, 18thC, 46in (115cm) square.
£175-225 *LB*

An Italian bobbin lace cover, 19thC, 133 by 94in (340 by 240cm).
£250-300 *P*

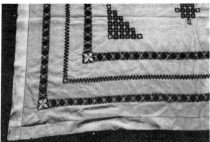

A linen tablecloth with drawn threadwork, 68in (172cm) square.
£120-150 *LAM*

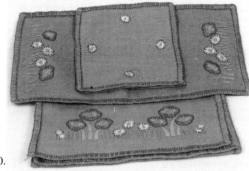

A duchess set, c1930.
£4-6 *CAC*

A heavy white cotton bedspread, early 19thC, 82 by 94in (210 by 240cm).
£90-150 *P*

A set of 7 linen mats embroidered with female figures, c1920, 8 by 5in (20 by 14.5cm).
£50-80 *CSK*

An Irish linen bedspread, 111 by 100in (284 by 254cm).
£250-300 *P*

A small table cloth with crochet work.
£15-25 *MAN*

A Victorian white linen tablecloth, with crochet inserts, 66in (165cm) square.
£100-150 *LB*

An Edwardian cloth with Chinese handwork set into crochet circles, 48 by 72in (120 by 183cm).
£100-150 *LB*

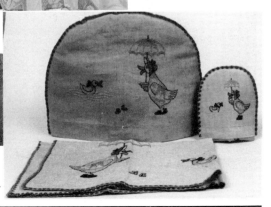

A child's tea cosy, egg cosy and tray cloth set.
£15-20 *CAC*

389

Beadwork

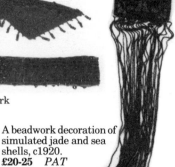

A piece of beadwork,
c1900, 15 by 6in (38 by
15cm).
£10-20   *CAC*

A Victorian jet beadwork
belt and cuffs.
£10-15   *CAC*

A beadwork decoration of
simulated jade and sea
shells, c1920.
£20-25   *PAT*

A Victorian bead bag
with ivory clasp and
handle.
£45-60   *LB*

Victorian beadwork
purse.
£25-30 *CAC*

A Victorian beadwork on
silk purse.
£30-40   *LB*

A piece of early
beadwork.
£10-15   *CAC*

A mid-Victorian
turquoise beadwork tea
cosy, 15in (38cm) wide.
£160-200   *C*

Cross Reference
Bags & Purses

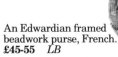

Beadwork trimming, 8in
(20cm) long.
£18-25   *PC*

An Edwardian framed
beadwork purse, French.
£45-55   *LB*

Lace

A pink silk crepe de chine boudoir cap, with ecru lace trim, c1910.
£30-40 *LB*
Crepe de chine is more expensive.

A Victorian cotton nightgown, with broderie anglaise trim.
£70-100 *LB*

A Victorian lady's boudoir cap with Valencia lace trim and satin ribbons.
£25-30 *LB*

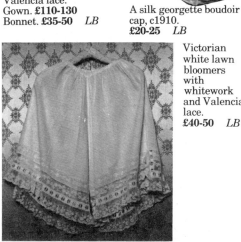

A Victorian lawn baby gown and bonnet, with hand tucked panels of Valencia lace.
Gown. **£110-130**
Bonnet. **£35-50** *LB*

A silk georgette boudoir cap, c1910.
£20-25 *LB*

Victorian white lawn bloomers with whitework and Valencia lace.
£40-50 *LB*

A pair of open-gusset bloomers with original price tag.
£15-25 *PC*

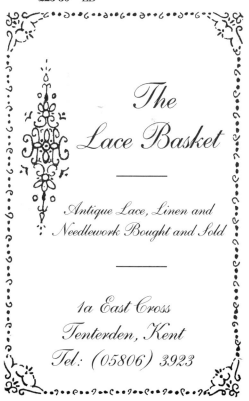

Lace Cushions

Lace cushions are made up mainly with antique lace but some modern textiles and pads are used.

A round cushion, 13in (33cm) diam.
£30-35 *CBA*

A Victorian embroidered lace edged neck pillow, with linen panel, 20in (50cm) long.
£35-45 *CBA*

An individually designed embroidered boudoir cushion with lace trimming, 22in (55cm) square.
£40-50 *CBA*

A square cushion with blue broderie anglaise trim, 20in (50cm) square.
£40-45 *CBA*

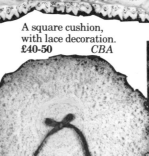

An oblong cushion, 15 by 12in (38 by 30.5cm).
£30-35 *CBA*

A square cushion, with lace decoration.
£40-50 *CBA*

An Edwardian boudoir cushion, with embroidered lace and thread work trim, 18in (45cm) square.
£30-40 *CBA*

A round cushion with pink bow, 12in (30cm) diam.
£30-35 *CBA*

An oblong cushion.
£30-35 *CBA*

Lace Making

A collection of Honiton
lace bobbins, one dated
1814, one carved with the
name Mary.
£12-30 each   *PC*

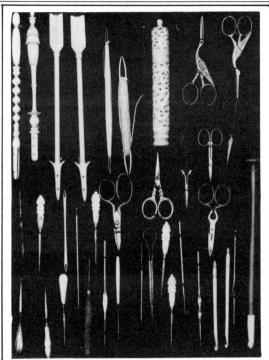

A collection of
needlework tools
including a Canton ivory
needle case with netting
needles, scissors and
spindles.
£180-200   *CSK*

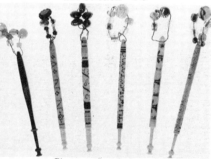

Six carved and stained
turned bone bobbins,
with inscriptions and
spangles, c1840.
£80-100   *P*

Two tatting and netting
shuttles, largest with
silver inlay, the smaller
one with mother-of-pearl,
4 and 3in (10 and 7.5cm)
wide.
£5-15   *PC*

A Georgian
weighted box
with drawer, used for
lace making.
£125-175   *PC*

Cross Reference
Sewing

Georgian thread winders
and box, in bone and
ivory.
£25-50   *PC*

Two wooden lace bobbins.
£6-18   *PC*

Lace curling tongs.
£25-35   *LB*

Pictorial

A silkwork picture, painted and embroidered in bright colours, late 18thC, 11½ by 14½in (29 by 36cm).
£100-120　*P*

An embroidered picture worked in coloured silks, early 18thC, 25in (63cm) wide, framed and glazed.
£700-800　*CSK*

A Regency petit point scene in original frame, 22in (55cm) wide.
£150-200　*OSc*

An embroidery fragment, depicting a sheep surrounded by stylised flowers, on red velvet, 18thC, 20in (50cm) wide.
£90-100　*LRG*

A silk picture worked in moss and satin stitch, mounted in frame, inscribed on back, late 18thC, 9½in (24cm) high overall.
£150-200　*Bon*

A silk and sequinned picture, c1900, 32½in (81cm) wide.
£100-180　*OSc*

A Japanese wallhanging, worked in applied floss silk and cord, with brocade border and printed cotton lining, 19thC, 98in (250cm) long.
£200-300　*P*

An embroidered picture worked in coloured wools with two peacocks eating fruit, 15in (38cm) wide, framed and glazed.
£140-160 *CSK*

An embroidered wool picture, in the style of Mary Linwood, c1800, 23in (58cm) square, framed and glazed.
£450-550 *CSK*

A woolwork picture, 12 by 8in (30 by 20cm).
£10-20 *CAC*

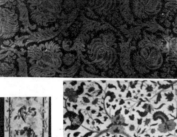

A length of Italian brocade, in crimson and yellow silk, mid-17thC, 83in (212cm) long.
£100-150 *P*

An embroidered picture worked in coloured silk, details in painted silk, c1800, 10in (25cm) wide, glazed and framed.
£240-270 *CSK*

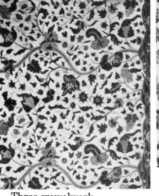

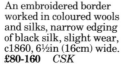

An oval silkwork picture, with rural scene, late 18thC, 11in (28cm) wide.
£180-200 *P*

Three crewelwork wallhangings, repaired, largest 83in (211cm) long.
£200-300 *Bon*

A pair of crewelwork curtains, worked in wool on natural cotton ground, English, some wear, early 18thC, 70in (178cm) long.
£400-600 *CSK*

An embroidered border worked in coloured wools and silks, narrow edging of black silk, slight wear, c1860, 6½in (16cm) wide.
£80-160 *CSK*

A length of Spanish blue silk brocade, c1760, 70in (178cm) long.
£100-150 *CSK*

Samplers

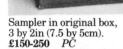

A needlework sampler by Elizabeth Cooper aged 10 years, 1842, 17½ by 13in (44 by 33cm), framed and glazed.
£350-450 *P*

Sampler in original box, 3 by 2in (7.5 by 5cm).
£150-250 *PC*

A German pattern book for sampler making.
£200-275 *PC*

A sampler dated 1860, 14in (35cm) wide.
£30-50 *OSc*

A sampler by Sarah Hockenhull, aged 11, early 19thC, 12½in (31.5cm) wide.
£200-400 *WIL*

A needlework sampler by Martha Bell, 1822, 19in (47cm) wide, framed and glazed.
£250-300 *P*

A needlework sampler on linen, by Sarah S. Bagshaw, dated March 28 1829, 14in (35cm) wide overall.
£250-350 *Bon*

A sampler by Anne Henshaw, 1714, 8in (20cm) wide, framed and glazed.
£800-900   *CSK*

A needlework sampler entitled Retirement and dated 1839.
£100-120   *OSc*

A needlework sampler by Jean Riddoch aged 18 years, April 1826, 11½in (29cm) wide, framed and glazed.
£350-400   *P*

A framed and glazed sampler, worked by Mary Stevens, 1797, 12½in (31cm) wide.
£150-200   *Bon*

DID YOU KNOW?

The earliest examples of samplers date back to the 16th Century. The word sampler derives from 'Exampler', a demonstration of needlework skills. This is why samplers were often produced by schoolchildren as a means of learning a variety of stitches.

An early Victorian needlework sampler by Martha Bitterson, signed and dated 1841, 16½ by 17½in (41 by 43cm), in glazed frame.
£450-500   *Bea*

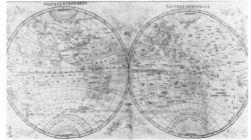

A map sampler by Mary Mellor, 1822, from Sandbach, Cheshire, 43in (108cm) wide, framed and glazed.
£600-700   *CSK*

Shawls

A Paisley wool shawl,
c1830, 65 by 126in (164
by 320cm).
£100-150   *P*

A Chinese silk
embroidered shawl.
£50-80   *LB*

A Norwich wool shawl,
early 19thC, 65in
(166cm) square.
£75-100   *P*

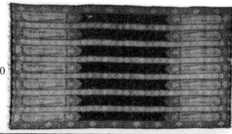

A Norwich Leno silk
gauze shawl, c1840, 69
by 135in (174 by 344cm).
£160-200   *P*

A Norwich black silk
shawl, woven in cotton,
c1840, 67in (170cm)
square.
£100-150   *P*

A printed Paisley shawl,
c1860, 63 by 129in (160
by 328cm).
£120-150   *P*

A black wool shawl,
possibly Paisley, c1850
71 by 135in (180 by
344cm).
£100-120   *P*

A Victorian English silk
hand embroidered shawl,
65in (165cm) square.
£100-120   *LB*

An ivory silk shawl,
printed in red, yellow
and green, probably

French, c1850, 67 by
130in (168 by 332cm).
£200-220   *P*

A silk shawl, probably
Norwich, c1870, 68in
(172cm) square.
£300-350 *P*

A French shawl, c1860,
64 by 127in (162 by
328cm).
£160-200 *P*

A Paisley 'moon' shawl,
c1840, 67in (170cm)
square.
£200-250 *P*

A reversible Paisley
shawl, c1870, 67in
(168cm) square.
£150-200 *P*

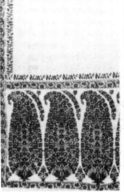

A Kashmir shawl in
cream wool and silk,
repaired, c1820, 120 by
53in (304 by 134cm).
£60-100 *CSK*

A French woven shawl,
mid-19thC, 138 by 63in
(352 by 160cm).
£100-150 *P*

A Chinese ivory silk
shawl, embroidered in
coloured silks, 19thC.
£150-200 *P*

A triangular shawl in
Brussels bobbin and
needlepoint appliqué,
mid-19thC.
£320-400 *P*

An Indonesian shawl of
cotton Itak, woven with a
design of animals and
grotesques, Sumba, 91 by
50in (232 by 128cm).
£160-200 *P*

A silk shawl, woven with
flowers, possibly
Norwich, c1840, 64 by
68in (162 by 172cm).
£700-750 *CSK*

Norwich turnover silk
shawls, c1840.
£50-70 each *P*

General Textiles

Handkerchiefs

A Victorian tapework handkerchief, 12in (30.5cm) square.
£15-25   *LB*

A lawn handkerchief, with Honiton lace surround, mid-19thC.
£120-150   *P*

This handkerchief was apparently offered to the Princess of Wales as a gift, which she declined in 1868.

A Victorian Irish lace handkerchief, 13in (35cm) square.
£25-35   *LB*

A Victorian Honiton lace handkerchief.
£15-25   *LB*

Lace bordered handkerchiefs.
£40-50 each   *P*

An ecru Maltese lace silk handkerchief, damaged.
£8-12   *LB*

Parasols

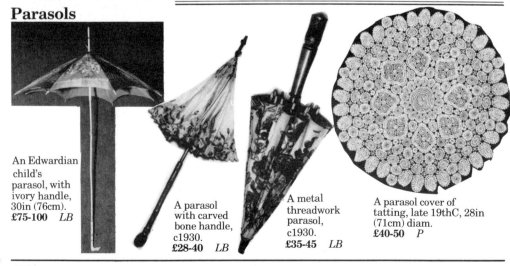

An Edwardian child's parasol, with ivory handle, 30in (76cm).
£75-100   *LB*

A parasol with carved bone handle, c1930.
£28-40   *LB*

A metal threadwork parasol, c1930.
£35-45   *LB*

A parasol cover of tatting, late 19thC, 28in (71cm) diam.
£40-50   *P*

Patchwork & Quilts

A pieced quilt, North
Star, c1890.
£200-250 *CNY*

A Victorian child's
collapsible parasol.
£45-65 *LB*

A material covered
parasol, c1930.
£25-35 *LB*

An appliqué quilt, c1870.
£600-650 *CNY*

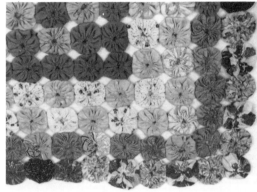

A Devonshire knots
patchwork, c1910, 58in
(147cm) square.
£60-80 *CAC*

Carpet cushions, made
from early 20thC kilims.
£25-30 each *OSc*

A needlework rug,
Kashmir, 91 by 127in
(231 by 322cm).
£450-500 *CSK*

A quilted patchwork
place setting.
£18-25 *CAC*

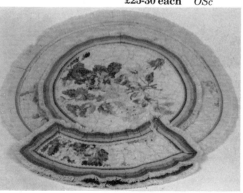

Tiles

Ivanhoe Series,
Wedgwood brown
transfer tiles, designed
by Thomas.
£35-60 *VF*

A Minton blue and white
tile, transfer printed
from a copper engraving
by William Wise, signed,
12in (30.5cm) square.
£40-100 *VF*

Months of the year by
Wedgwood, in blue.
£25-65 *VF*

DID YOU KNOW?
Medieval inlaid tiles were made for abbey and parish
churches until the Dissolution of the Monasteries
when the specialised knowledge was lost. Minton
spent a decade perfecting the technique
'rediscovered' in 1830 by Samuel Wright though,
ironically, there was a flourishing inlaid tile
industry just across the Channel in West Flanders.

Minton brown tiles,
Alfred burning the
cakes, an early English
series.
£20-45 *VF*

A pair of Minton,
Hollins, tiles, hand
coloured in brown/cream.
£18-30 *VF*

The Watteau series,
Minton, blue and white.
£25-40 *VF*

Majolica glaze moulded
tiles, by Flaxman Tile Co.
£25-40 *VF*

A Minton set of Tennyson
Idylls of the King,
designed by Moyr Smith.
£22-35   *VF*

A set of 12 biblical
scenes, Minton, Hollins.
£15-28   *VF*

A set of 10 lustre tiles,
designed by Lewis Day
for Maw & Co., c1880.
£25-65   *VF*

Majolica glaze tiles,
unmarked, unusual as in
3 colours.
£7-15   *VF*

Two of Rosebud series,
unmarked, possibly
William Godwin Tile Co.
£15-25   *VF*

Minton tiles, designed by
William Wise.
£25-55   *VF*

A set of 6 Minton,
Hollins, Venus & Adonis
series, by J. Moyr Smith.
£20-45   *VF*

FURTHER READING

Austwick, J. and B., *The Decorated Tile,* The Pitman House 1980.
Barnard, Julian, *Victorian Ceramic Tiles,* London 1972.
Berendson, Anne, *Tiles, A General History,* London 1967.
Garner, F. H. and Archer, M., *English Delftware,* London 1972.
Horne, J., *A Catalogue of English Delftware Tiles,* London 1980.
Jonge, C. H. de, *Dutch Tiles,* Pall Mall Press 1971.
Korf, D. *Dutch Tiles,* New York 1964.
Lane, Arthur, *Guide to the Collection of Tiles: Victoria and Albert Museum,* London 1960.
Ray, Anthony, *English Delftware Tiles,* Faber, London 1972.

TILES

Arts & Crafts design tiles, designed by Lewis F. Day for Pilkington, green and blue, pre-1900, 6 by 12 (15 by 30.5cm) and 6in (30.5cm) square.
£20-80 each *VF*

A galleon tile, c1930.
£2-15 *VF*

This was probably an art college student's test item.

DID YOU KNOW?____
Victorian tile catalogues can sometimes be found in antiquarian bookshops.

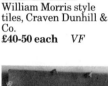

William Morris style tiles, Craven Dunhill & Co.
£40-50 each *VF*

Minton Elfin series, c1875.
£20-30 *VF*

A Barbotine tile.
£15-28 *VF*

Craven Dunhill & Co., Jolly Friar, light brown majolica glaze, 12 by 6in (30.5 by 15cm).
£25-35 *VF*

A.M.L. Ltd., majolica glazed Art Nouveau tiles.
£10-38 *VF*

Arts & Crafts design hand painted lustre tiles, Craven Dunhill & Co, red on a cream ground.
£10-30 *VF*

Bowls by moonlight, sporting pastimes, attributed to Malkin Edge & Co., c1895.
£22-35 *VF*

DID YOU KNOW?_____
The ridges and design on the reverse of tiles were to assist adhesion when fixing.

Water, Air, Fire, Earth
series.
£20-35 *VF*

A Maw & Co. lustre tile,
wood block printed and
hand filled.
£20-35 *VF*

A portrait tile of Rt. Hon.
David Lloyd George,
modelled by Geo.
Cartlidge after
photograph by Ernest H.
Mills.
£40-65 *VF*

Hand painted cottage
scene.
£7-25 *VF*

A four colour Art
Nouveau majolica glazed
tile.
£6-25 *VF*

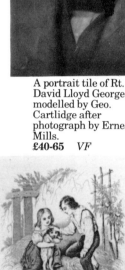

A Minton tile, with black
and white transfer.
£10-18 *VF*

A Minton tile from the
Rustic Figures series,
c1885.
£18-40 *VF*

A stencilled Barbotine
tile, unmarked.
£5-12 *VF*

Five colour Art Nouveau
tiles.
£3-18 *VF*

A Pilkington Willow
pattern design, c1905.
£12-18 *VF*

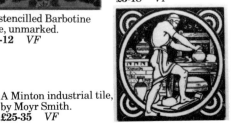

A Minton industrial tile,
by Moyr Smith.
£25-35 *VF*

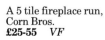

A 5 tile fireplace run,
Corn Bros.
£25-55 *VF*

TILES

A framed Art Nouveau tile.
£22-25 *PGA*

A tile with snowdrop pattern.
£7-10 *VB*

Josiah Wedgwood & Sons, Etruria tile.
£22-35 *VF*

Five William de Morgan lustre tiles, 6in (15cm) square.
£550-600 *CSK*

A blue and white tile.
£12-15 *COB*

A German Art Nouveau tile, 6½ by 10½in (16 by 28cm).
£280-300 *P*

Charlotte Rhead tiles.
£150-200 each *PGA*

Art Nouveau tube lined majolica glaze tiles.
£5-20 *VF*

A Gothic style hall chair with a tile set in the back.
£40-60 *VF*

A set of 4 tiles depicting country scenes, brown transfer, 6in (15cm) square.
£15-20 each *WRe*

A tile.
£8-10 *VB*

Six Mintons tiles, in black and white, four signed W. Wise, 20thC, 6in (15cm) square.
£110-120 *WIL*

An Art Nouveau pottery wall plaque, by Ernst Wahliss, impressed marks, 16in (41cm) diam.
£300-400 *P*

A set of 9 Victorian Mintons pottery tiles, scenes from Aesops Fables.
£250-300 *JW*

A tile, c1890.
£7-10 *VB*

A set of Minton tiles, blue and white with yellow border, 6in (15cm) square.
£150-180 *OSc*

A Victorian mahogany hanging shelf, with Wedgwood tiles inset, Midsummer Night's Dream.
£150-200 *VF*

A majolica glazed woman's head, green, no marks.
£15-25 *VF*

A set of 10 tiles.
£50-60 *VB*

Tins

A Huntley & Palmer's biscuit tin, c1903, 7in (18cm) wide.
£25-35   *BC*

A Cerebos Salt tin.
£10-15   *K*

A Sharp's Toffee bucket, 7lb size, c1930.
£50-60   *K*

C.W.S. Biscuits.
Poor Condition.
£10-15
Good Condition.
£30-50   *K*

A typical 1890s Christmas or gift biscuit tin.

A Cadbury's chocolate tin, 8in (20cm) wide.
£7-10   *AL*

Thorne's Newcream Toffee tin, 7lb size, double sided.
£30-40   *K*   *This would have been a retailer's tin from which the sweets were dispensed.*

A miniature or sample Clarnico tin, c1920.
£10-15   *K*

A Sharp's toffee tin, decorated with flamingoes.
£7-10   *VB*

R.M.S. Queen Mary, Benson's toffee tin, 10in (25.5cm) wide.
£15-20   *BC*

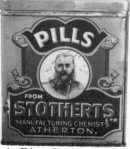

An Edwardian transfer printed string tin, Pills from Stotherts.
£35-45   *K*

Mazawatee Tea, 'Old Folks at Home'.
£15-30   *K*

Pioneer Brand, printed
in black on a mottled gold
ground, with paper label.
£10-20 *K*

A Japanese tin.
£5-8 *VB*

A W. & R. Jacob & Co.,
Coronation coach, c1936.
£180-200 *P*

A W. R. Jacob & Co.
houseboat, c1923.
£100-120 *P*

'Rattler' Navy Cut, early
20thC.
£35-50 *K*

A Huntley & Palmers
basket tin, c1905.
£50-60 *P*

A Mettoy O.K. Biscuits
delivery van tin, some
rust, 9½in (24cm) long.
£70-100 *P*

DID YOU KNOW?____
Missionaries kept their
Bibles in Huntley and
Palmer tins to protect
them from the ravages of
white ants.

Bryant & May and
Huntley & Palmers tins,
early 20thC.
£50-120 each *P*

An Art Deco design
transfer printed string
tin, Stotherts Pills, for a
shop counter.
£30-40 *K*

DID YOU KNOW?_____
Never wash transfer-printed tins, since they bloom
very badly. They may be wiped with a slightly damp
and very soft cloth but if in doubt leave alone.

An enamelled tin.
£10-12 *VB*

Royalty

'A Stitch in Time', 6½in (16.5cm) wide.
£6-10 *MB*

A Macfarlane Lang biscuit tin, the portrait by Marcus Adams, 9½in (24cm) wide.
£10-15 *BC*

An Oxo Coronation souvenir money box, 3in (7.5cm) high.
£5-8 *BC*

A Meltis Elizabeth II tin.
£3-5 *VB*

A Jubilee tin, 1935.
£12-15 *BC*

Commemorative tins.
£6-10 each *BC*

Not many of these tins were produced and are already in demand.

A Victory 'V' drawer tin.
£15-25 *BC*

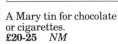

Cross Reference
Ceramics
Commemorative

A Mary tin for chocolate or cigarettes.
£20-25 *NM*

These tins were a gift by Queen Mary, wife of George V, to all the troops for Christmas 1914.

Cottage tins;
Top. Tuckers Toffee, c1950.
£5-10
Bottom. Macfarlane, Lang & Co., tin, doubles as a money box, 1938.
£75-95 *K*

Toiletries

18thC razors.
£35-45 each *CBA*

A powder compact, with watch, c1930, 4in (10cm) diam.
£200-250 *PAT*

Silver nail buffers.
£15-20 each *VB*

A silver shaving brush, London 1840.
£25-30 *VB*

A Rolls Razor, in original box with instructions.
£10-12 *WHA*

A pair of razors, signed Plum Bristol, with tortoiseshell guards and silver mounts, in leather case, early 19thC, 7in (18cm) wide.
£150-180 *CSK*

A Coty compact, designed by Lalique.
£18-25 *ZIG*

A Cutex manicure set, with Bakelite case, c1929, 6½in (16.5cm) wide.
£25-30 *PAT*

Tools

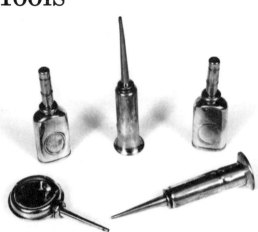

A copper oil can, 4½in (11.5cm) high.
£8-10   *AL*

Brass oil cans, 3½ to 5in (9 to 12.5cm) high.
£10-12 each   *AL*

| **Cross Reference** |
| Automobilia |

A scuppett, used for digging dykes, scooping grain etc.
£10-15   *OSc*

A glass cutter, A. Shaw & Son, London.
£5-10   *AL*

A plane, with brass fittings.
£30-35   *AL*

A brass mortice gauge, 7in (18cm) long.
£40-50   *SAD*

A Swedish brass blow lamp, 10½in (27cm) long.
£30-35   *SAD*

An eel cleaver, 19thC.
£30-40   *OSc*

A spokeshave.
£5-8   *VB*

A tape measure by John Rabone & Co., 3½in (9cm) diam.
£20-30   *AL*

A Stanley gauge, with
brass trim.
£8-12 *AL*

A boxwood folding rule,
by Rabone, 36in (91.5cm)
long.
£10-15 *AL*

A mahogany set square.
£10-15 *AL*

A solid brass plane.
£35-45 *AL*

A spirit level, with brass
trim, 8in (20.5cm) long.
£20-30 *SAD*

A spirit level, Parry &
Butt Ltd., Birmingham
9in (23cm) long.
£15-20 *AL*

A set square, with brass
fittings.
£8-12 *AL*

A grease box for cart
wheels, 3in (7.5cm) high.
£20-25 *AL*

A wood scorer, 10in
(25.5cm) long.
£7-10 *SAD*

A wooden spokeshave.
£8-12 *AL*

Various agricultural
tools.
£20-50 each *TM*

A brass spokeshave.
£20-30 *AL*

413

Machinery

A seed drill, J. L. Maltby, Ironmongers, Newark.
£30-40 *TM*

r. A Green's push mower.
£100-120 *TM*

l. A Ransomes lawn edge trimmer.
£20-30 *TM*

c. A Webb's push cylinder mower.
£5-10 *TM*

Hobbies fret saws.
£30-50 each *TM*

A single furrow horse drawn plough, Ruston Hornsby Ltd., XRPB No. 4.
£55-65 *TM*

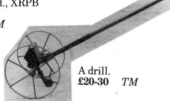

A drill.
£20-30 *TM*

l. An Atco cylinder motor mower.
£25-35 *TM*

r. A Ransomes cylinder motor mower.
£45-55 *TM*

A Victorian hand cart, with iron rimmed wheels, initialled C.W.D.
£120-150 *TM*

A barrow drill.
£30-40 *TM*

A wooden framed potato rocking riddle.
£30-50 *TM*

TOYS
Diecast
Aircraft

Dinky pre-war aeroplanes, in original boxes.
£350-450 *CSK*

Dinky pre-war 62h Hawker-Hurricanes.
£160-200 *P*

Dinky D.H. Comet, c1970, in original box.
£50-70 *Bon*

Dinky pre-war French set No. 60 Avions, very slightly chipped, c1937, in original box.
£5,500-6,000 *CSK*

Dinky pre-war 60r Empire Flying boat 'G-ADHM', in original box, with instructions.
£120-150 *CSK*

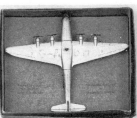

Cross Reference
Aeronautica

Dinky pre-war aircraft, 60g DH comet aeroplane, early type, 2 examples, 60e General Monospar, parts missing, and 60h Singapore Flying Boat.
£200-250 *P*

Dinky Avro 'York' air liner, c1950, original box.
£50-70 *Bon*

French Dinky Supertoys set No. 60, in original box.
£280-300 *CSK*

Automobiles

Dinky delivery vans and
racing car.
£100-350 each *CSK*

Dinky post-war
commercial vehicles.
£10-20 each *CSK*

Dinky 39 series,
American cars, in
original paintwork,
c1939.
£30-50 each *CSK*

Assorted Dinky post-war
cars.
£20-25 *CSK*

Dinky Supertoys, in
original boxes.
£100-150 each *CSK*

Corgi 482 Chevrolet Fire
Chief car.
£65-75 *MIN*

Corgi 303 Mercedes Benz
300SL Roadster.
£75-100 *MIN*

Corgi 221, Chevrolet
New York taxi.
£65-85 *MIN*

Corgi 154 Ferrari F1
Racer.
£45-55 *MIN*

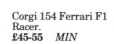

Corgi 271, Ghia 5000
Mangusta with De
Tomaso chassis.
£45-55 *MIN*

Dinky sports car
post-war, in original
box
£40-50 *CSK*

Corgi 241 Ghia L 6.4.
£75-85 *MIN*

Corgi 430 Bermuda Taxi.
£75-100 *MIN*

Corgi 258 The 'Saint's' Volvo, P.1800.
£75-100 *MIN*

Dinky tanker, c1950.
£50-70 *Bon*

Dinky tanker, c1950.
£80-100 *Bon*

Dinky post-war 100 series sports cars, in original boxes.
£40-50 each *CSK*

Dinky post-war 36 series cars, c1947.
£35-45 each *CSK*

Corgi 318, Lotus Elan S2.
£65-75 *MIN*

Matchbox cars, c1930, original boxes.
£10-15 each *Bon*

Corgi 305 Triumph TR3 sports car.
£85-95 *MIN*

Corgi cars, c1960, in original boxes.
£20-30 each *Bon*

Corgi 342 Lamborghini P400 with charging bull.
£45-55 *MIN*

Corgi 150S Vanwall racer.
£45-55 *MIN*

Dinky delivery van, c1950.
£200-250 *Bon*

Dinky commercial van, c1950, original box.
£50-70 *Bon*

417

Dinky Supertoys
commercial vehicles.
£10-20 each   *CSK*

Dinky Supertoys fire
engine, c1960, original
box.
£15-20   *Bon*

Dinky cars, c1960, in
original boxes.
£25-35 each   *CSK*

Corgi 319 Lotus Elan
Coupe.
£65-75   *MIN*

Corgi 263 Rambler
Marlin.
£45-55   *MIN*

A Dinky Supertoys 918
Guy Van, with box.
£150-170   *CSK*

Taylor & Barrett Fire
Engine and Escape, with
operatives, original box.
£120-140   *CSK*

Britains No. 1400
Bluebird, original box.
£150-170   *CSK*

French Dinky post-war
cars, in original boxes.
£40-50 each   *CSK*

Corgi 245 Buick Riviera.
£65-75   *MIN*

Dinky Supertoys 514
Guy Van, with box.
£150-200   *CSK*

Dinky, 917 Guy Van,
slight wear, with box.
£200-250   *CSK*

Two French Dinky toys,
post-war, with original
boxes.
£75-100 each   *CSK*

Spot-On model cars, in original boxes.
£50-60 each   *CSK*

Scamold clockwork die-cast Grand Prix racing cars, in original boxes.
£120-140 each   *CSK*

Corgi Chipperfields Circus models, some chipped.
£25-35 each   *CSK*

Dinky Supertoys, 514 Guy Van and 923 Big Bedford van, in original paintwork.
£150-200 each   *CSK*

Dinky Supertoys lorries and trucks, in original boxes.
£50-60 each   *CSK*

Lesney, Models of Yesteryear, 1st issue, trucks, in original boxes.
£50-70 each   *CSK*

Britains set No. 1656, Railton car, original box.
£100-140   *CSK*

A Dinky pre-war 2nd series 28m Wakefield's Castrol Oil van, damaged.
£650-700   *CSK*

Various diecast toys, pre-war, worn and damaged.
£10-15 each   *CSK*

Dinky pre-war 28/2d Oxo delivery van, worn.
£60-80   *CSK*

French Dinky post-war commercial vehicles, in original boxes.
£100-150 each   *CSK*

Spot-On cars.
£25-35 each   *CSK*

TOYS/DIECAST

Dinky Supertoys commercial vehicles, in original boxes.
£80-100 each *CSK*

Dinky pre-war 33 series, 33r Railway Mechanical Horse and Trailer van, damaged, c1935.
£50-60 *CSK*

Dinky pre-war 28 series van, some damage.
£100-120 *CSK*

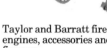

Tootsie Toys, with original paintwork.
£70-80 each *CSK*

Taylor and Barratt fire engines, accessories and firemen.
£300-350 *CSK*

Dinky pre-war 24h two-seater sports Tourer, slight fatigue.
£80-100 *P*

Lesney Moko, early large scale models.
£20-30 each *P*

A Shackleton toy, No. 1690 Foden and No. 1691 Dyson trailer, with clockwork mechanism in cab, c1960.
£220-250 *CSK*

Various Dinky pre-war toys.
£35-55 each *CSK*

Dinky pre-war toys, chipped, c1937.
£80-100 each *CSK*

Dinky post-war racing cars, in original boxes.
£25-30 each *CSK*

Tekno, trucks, boxed.
£20-30 each *P*

Lesney, Models of
Yesteryear, Gift Set
No. G.-7, in original box.
£200-250 *CSK*

Cast metal model cars,
battery operated and
wind-up models, c1950.
£50-60 each *CNY*

Three Spot-On 263
vintage Bentleys, 2 in
original boxes.
£70-100 *CSK*

A Dinky pre-war 28/2
series Kodak van, c1936.
£700-750 *CSK*

Matchbox toys, 2nd
issue, c1964.
£15-20 each *Bon*

Dinky pre-war vehicles,
c1935.
£60-80 each *CSK*

Tekno, Cementbil, 778
Benzinbil, 779
Sandtruck, 779 Sand
Truck, boxed.
£20-50 each *P*

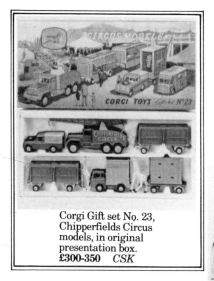

Corgi Gift set No. 23, Chipperfields Circus models, in original presentation box.
£300-350   *CSK*

Dinky pre-war set No. 42, Police Hut, Motor Cycle Patrol and Policemen, c1939, in original box.
£180-200   *CSK*

Spot-On cars, in original boxes.
£30-40 each   *CSK*

Dinky Supertoys, Guy van and lorries.
£50-100 each   *CSK*

Spot-On, 271 Express Dairy Van, in original box.
£20-30   *CSK*

Spot-On, set No. 260, The Royal Presentation set, with models, in original box.
£200-250   *CSK*

Spot-On Tonibell Ice Cream van, in original box.
£40-50   *CSK*

Other

Dinky pre-war set No. 50, Ships of the British Navy.
£170-200   *CSK*

Triang Minic, 1:2000 scale, waterline ships, in original boxes.
£30-50 each   *CSK*

Dinky pre-war set No. 17, passenger train.
£300-350   *CSK*

Military

Dinky 673 Scout car.
£55-65 *MIN*

Dinky 674 Austin Champ.
£55-65 *MIN*

French Dinky 820 Renault army ambulance.
£100-120 *MIN*

French Dinky 822 half-track M3.
£100-120 *MIN*

Dinky 677 Armoured Command car.
£100-120 *MIN*

French Dinky 814 AML Panhard armoured car.
£100-120 *MIN*

Britains Army Lorry, c1950.
£50-60 *Bon*

Britains set 1321, large armoured car, c1937.
£2,000-2,500 *P*

Britains searchlight, c1950.
£30-50 *Bon*

French Dinky 821 Mercedes Unimog army truck.
£100-120 *MIN*

Dinky 676 armoured personnel carrier.
£55-65 *MIN*

Dinky 641 Army 1-ton truck.
£35-45 *MIN*

Dinky 693 7.2 Howitzer.
£45-55 *MIN*

Dinky 688 Field artillery tractor.
£55-65 *MIN*

Dinky 670 Armoured car.
£55-65 *MIN*

423

Dinky military vehicles.
£35-45 each *CSK*

Cross Reference
Toy Soldiers

Dinky transporter and
tank, c1960.
Tank. **£15-20**
Truck. **£20-30** *Bon*

French Dinky 817 AMX
13 tonne tank.
£100-120 *MIN*

French clockwork army
boiler truck, c1950.
£100-120 *Bon*

Dinky 643 Army water
tanker.
£55-65 *MIN*

Britains Anti-Aircraft
gun, c1950.
£30-50 *Bon*

Britains set 1431 Army
co-operation autogiro,
with pilot in original box.
£280-300 *P*

Britains Army
Ambulance, with
stretcher patient,
original box, c1950.
£50-60 *Bon*

Lineol ambulance, with
clockwork mechanism,
c1936.
£550-600 *CSK*

Dinky 686 25-Pounder
Field Gun.
£35-45 *MIN*

Dinky 623 Army covered
lorry.
£65-75 *MIN*

Marx, armoured floating
tank transporter, boxed.
£45-55 *P*

French Dinky 815 E.B.R.
Panhard tank.
£85-95 *MIN*

French Dinky post-war
military vehicles, in
original boxes.
£20-30 each *CSK*

Model Railways

A Bassett-Lowke remodelled gauge 0 model of the LNER 4–6–2 and tender No. 4472, repainted in green livery, c1937.
£300-350 *CSK*

Three Bing gauge 1 MR four wheel coaches, some damage, c1912.
£120-150 *CSK*

A Hornby electric model of the LMS 4–6–2 locomotive and tender No. 6201 'Princess Elizabeth', c1938, slight damage.
£800-850 *CSK*

A rare Hornby gauge 0 clockwork No. 1 LNWR train set, some chipping, c1922.
£320-350 *CSK*

A rare early Hornby gauge 0 clockwork model of the LNWR 0–4–0 and tender 2663 'George The Fifth', some damage, c1924.
£100-150 *CSK*

A Hornby gauge 0 3-rail electric model of the LMS 4–4–2 locomotive and tender, slight chipping.
£700-800 *CSK*

A Hornby gauge 0 electric model of the SR 4–4–0 E420 locomotive and tender No. 900 'Eton', c1937.
£620-650 *CSK*

A rare and early Marklin gauge 1 clockwork model of the CLR 'Steeplecab' 0–4–0, some damage, c1901.
£2,200-2,500 *CSK*

Three very rare gauge 1 CLR passenger coaches, slight damage, c1903.
£6,000-6,500 *CSK*

A Bassett-Lowke gauge 0 clockwork BR goods set, c1960.
£300-350 *CSK*

A rare Bing live steam, spirit fired model of a German 4–6–2 Pacific Class locomotive and twin-bogie, c1927.
£2,000-2,500 *CSK*

A Bassett-Lowke gauge 0 electric model of the LMS 4–6–0 locomotive and tender No. 6100 'Royal Scott', in original LMS maroon livery.
£320-350 *CSK*

A Hornby gauge 0 electric model of the GWR 0–4–0 No. E120 special locomotive and tender No. 4700, slightly worn, c1935.
£420-450 *CSK*

A rare gauge 0 electric model of the SBB CFF 're 4/4' No. 427 diesel electric locomotive by H and A Gahler, Switzerland, c1947.
£650-700 *CSK*

A Hornby gauge 0 clockwork model of the LNER 4–4–0 No. 2 special locomotive and tender ND 234 'Yorkshire', in original paintwork.
£500-550 *CSK*

A Hornby gauge 0 model of the LMS 4–4–0 No. E220 special locomotive and tender No. 1185, slight damage, c1938.
£400-450 *CSK*

A rare Marklin gauge 0 model of the 0–4–0 electric locomotive RS 1020, c1927.
£350-400 *CSK*

Hornby gauge 0 rolling stock, 1924.
£300-350 *CSK*

A Japanese Gasoline car, in original box, 5½in (15cm) long, c1930.
£200-250 *CSK*

A detailed No. 1172 electric brass model of the New York Central Railway No. J-1e 4–6–4 'Hudson' locomotive and bogie tender, unpainted, in original box, c1965.
£520-550 *CSK*

A rare Marklin gauge 1 clockwork model of the GNR 4–4–2 'Atlantic' locomotive and tender No. 1427, c1907, some repairs.
£1,000-1,400 *CSK*

A Marklin gauge 1 live steam spirit fired model of a GNR 4–4–0 locomotive and 6 wheel tender, damaged and restored, c1909.
£600-700 *CSK*

A gauge 1 live steam spirit fired model of the MR 4–4–0 locomotive and tender No. 1000, by Bing for Bassett-Lowke, c1912.
£1,500-1,800 *CSK*

A gauge 00 3-rail electric Flying Scotsman train set, including coaches, locomotives and tender, by Trix Twin Railway for Bassett-Lowke, c1931.
£300-400 *CSK*

A gauge 1 electric model of the LNWR 4–4–0 locomotive, No. 513, Precursor, by Bing for Bassett-Lowke, c1911.
£1,000-1,500 *CSK*

A gauge 0 clockwork model of the CR 4–6–0 locomotive and bogie tender No. 50, by Marklin for Bassett-Lowke, repainted by D. Barrington Holt, c1918.
£450-500 *CSK*

Three gauge 1 LMS bogie coaches, original paintwork, slight damage.
£550-650 *CSK*

A Bassett-Lowke gauge 0 clockwork repainted model of the LMS 4–6–0 locomotive and tender No. 6102.
£250-350 *CSK*

A Bassett-Lowke gauge 0 live steam spirit fired model of GWR locomotive and tender, damaged, c1936.
£250-350 *CSK*

Three gauge 1 hand painted Pullman bogie coaches, slight damage, by Marklin, c1923.
£700-900 *CSK*

A Marklin gauge 1 clockwork model of the GER 0–6–0 locomotive, c1914.
£800-1,000 *CSK*

A Hornby gauge 0 van, damaged, c1928.
£100-150 *CSK*

A painted tinplate station made for the French market, by Marklin, early 1900s, 17in (43cm) long, with 0–4–0 locomotive and tender, 3 coaches, by Marklin, c1900.
£3,500-4,000   *P*

A 3½in gauge model of an 0–6–0 locomotive, 10 by 20in (25 by 50cm).
£800-1,000   *CSK*

A Marklin gauge 1 3-rail electric model of the NBR 4–4–2 locomotive and tender, damaged and worn, c1913.
£1,200-1,500   *CSK*

A Hornby 3-rail electric model of the SR 4–4–0 locomotive and tender, original paintwork, slight damage, c1933.
£650-750   *CSK*

Hornby gauge 0 rolling stock, in original boxes.
£500-600   *CSK*

Bassett-Lowke 3RE 460 LNER Flying Scotsman and 8-wheeled tender, mint condition.
£750-850   *P*

A Bing gauge 0 live steam spirit fired model of the LNWR locomotive, damaged, c1906.
£250-350   *CSK*

A 3½in gauge gas fired model of the SR 2–6–0 locomotive and tender, by W. Huggett, Ruislip, 46in (115cm).
£800-1,000   *CSK*

A Bassett-Lowke gauge 0 live steam spirit fired model of LNER 2–6–0 locomotive and tender, damaged.
£350-450   *CSK*

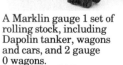

A Marklin gauge 1 set of rolling stock, including Dapolin tanker, wagons and cars, and 2 gauge 0 wagons.
£350-450   *CSK*

An electric model of the SR 2–6–0 'Mogul' locomotive and tender No. 897, c1927.
£800-850   *CSK*

A gauge 1 LMS dining car, by Carette for Bassett-Lowke, slight wear, c1924.
£130-160   *CSK*

Ten Bassett-Lowke
pre-WWI wagons,
7 boxed.
£600-800   *P*

A gauge 1 CIWL sleeping
car, by Bing, damaged,
c1902.
£500-600   *CSK*

A Hornby gauge 0 3-rail
electric model of the
Metropolitan Railway
E120 special type, Bo-Bo
locomotive, lacks lamps.
£300-400   *CSK*

A Bing gauge 0
clockwork train set, with
a LMS 0–6–0 locomotive
and tender, and
3 Pullman coaches,
c1925.
£800-1,000   *CSK*

A rake of three Darsted
gauge 0 CIWL Bogie
coaches, in original
boxes, c1965.
£800-850   *CSK*

A gauge 0 3-rail electric
20v model of the LMS
4–6–2 locomotive and
tender, some wear, in
fitted box.
£650-750   *CSK*

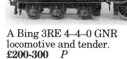

A Bing 3RE 4–4–0 GNR
locomotive and tender.
£200-300   *P*

A 4in gauge LMS model
tank engine, heavy goods
type, steam driven, on
oak stand.
£1,200-1,500   *WW*

Eight Hornby Dublo
3-rail electric model
locomotives, with
original paintwork, some
rusting, all in blue boxes.
£400-500   *CSK*

A 5in gauge model of the
LSWR Adams 4–4–0
locomotive and tender,
by D. W. Horsfall, c1970,
58½in (147cm).
£4,000-5,000 *CSK*

A 5in gauge model of the
GWR 45XX class 2–6–2
locomotive and tender,
by R. Seymour, 40in
(101cm).
£2,000-2,500 *CSK*

A Hornby pre-war gauge
0 clockwork No. 2 tank
goods set, with LNER
4–4–4 locomotive, and a
quantity of rolling stock,
in original box.
£300-400 *CSK*

A Dinky Express
Passenger train set,
c1955, 12in (30cm) long.
£25-30 *Bon*

Hornby pre-war gauge 0
No. 0 vans, including a
Bing LNWR wagon.
£250-350 *CSK*

A Bing electric
locomotive, Continental
style, c1939.
£1,000-1,500 *Bon*

A Hornby signal arm,
signed, c1939.
£30-40 *Bon*

A Hornby Dublo train
set, c1950.
£30-50 *Bon*

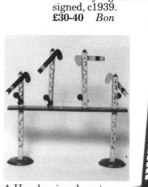

A Hornby signal gantry,
post war, in original box.
£40-50 *Bon*

A Bing gauge 1
clockwork model of the
MR 2–4–0 locomotive
and tender, c1910.
£250-350   *CSK*

A 7mm 2-rail electric
model of the LMS 4P5F
4–6–0 locomotive and
tender No. 4835, built by
F. Rider, 18in (45cm).
£400-600   *CSK*

Two early Hornby gauge
0 wagons, slight wear
and replacement wheels,
c1923.
£300-400   *CSK*

A Marklin electric metro
type train, The Flying
Hamburger, c1938.
£200-300   *Bon*

A French Hornby 3-rail
electric model of SNCF
TNC locomotive, with
accessories, damage,
c1960.
£250-350   *CSK*

A Hornby wine wagon,
c1937.
£40-50   *Bon*

A 5in gauge model of the
BR class 9 2–10–0
locomotive and tender,
Evening Star, built by
A. Dixon, 73in (183cm)
long.
£8,500-9,500   *CSK*
This model is new.

Hornby gauge 0 wagons.
From **£100-250 each**
CSK

A Hornby No. 1
passenger train set with
clockwork mechanism,
c1921, in original box.
£400-500   *Bon*

A Marklin Shell tanker,
c1937, no box.
£80-100   *Bon*

A Hornby gauge 0 3-rail electric model of the GWR 0–4–0 locomotive and tender, working headlamp, original paintwork, c1935.
£1,000-1,200 *CSK*

A Hornby gauge 0 clockwork LMS No. 1 passenger train set, including an 0–4–0 locomotive and tender, with 2 coaches and a quantity of track, original paintwork, c1925, with box.
£350-450 *CSK*

A Bassett-Lowke LNWR 4–4–2 tank engine No. 44, with clockwork mechanism and key, 12in (30cm) long.
£700-800 *McC*

A Hornby gauge 0 4–4–4 LMS clockwork tank engine, finished in black livery.
£100-200 *WIL*

Three gauge 0 bogie coaches, including a Bing coach, a Hornby passenger coach and a Pullman coach, all original paintwork and boxes, slight wear.
£300-400 *CSK*

A gauge 0 clockwork model of the MR 4–4–0 saddle tank locomotive, by Bing for Bassett-Lowke, c1923.
£300-400 *CSK*

A Kibri gauge 0 W. H. Smith & Son kiosk, with ten national newspapers, c1928, 3½in (8.5cm), in original box.
£200-300 *CSK*

A Hornby gauge 0 3-rail electric model of the LMS locomotive and tender, original paintwork, bulb lacking, c1938.
£500-600 *CSK*

Two Hornby gauge 0 No. 2 SR coaches, in original boxes.
£450-550 *CSK*

A gauge 0 live steam spirit fired model of the LMS 2–6–0 mogul locomotive and tender, by Bassett-Lowke, repainted.
£400-500 *CSK*

A Marklin covered wagon, c1937.
£80-100 *Bon*

A Bing gauge 0 3-rail electric model of the MR 4–4–0 locomotive and tender, original paintwork, replacements, c1920.
£200-300 *CSK*

A Bassett-Lowke gauge 0 3-rail electric model of the LMS 4–6–0 locomotive and tender, Royal Scot, some repainting, c1937.
£500-600 *CSK*

Cross Reference
Railways

A locomotive lettered B & O R R, c1907.
£1,000-1,500 *CNY*

A clockwork Mickey Mouse circus set, c1935.
£600-700 *CNY*

A Rainbow set of black cast iron locomotive, green tender, orange baggage car, and blue and red pullman cars, in original box with track, c1920.
£300-400 *CNY*

A Marklin gauge 1 3-rail electric model of a Continental 4–4–0 Compound locomotive and tender, damaged.
£200-300 *CSK*

A 5in gauge model of the GWR Director Class 4–4–0 locomotive and tender, 62in (156cm).
£3,000-3,500 *CSK*

Two Ives Union stations, with platform cover, c1928.
£900-1,200 *CNY*

President's Special Set of locomotive with 3 cars, c1926.
£500-700 *CNY*

A Bassett-Lowke gauge 0 3-rail electric model for the LMS Suburban Electric train driving unit No. 1652, a Bing lithographed goods yard and signal train, and a Hornby No. 1 level crossing.
£250-350 *CSK*

433

Model Soldiers

Courtenay No. 7, foot
figure of Sir Warin
Bassingborne, signed.
£300-400   *CSK*

Courtenay No. 15, foot
figure of Sir John Bloyon,
damaged.
£350-450   *CSK*

Courtenay No. 15c,
English archer, signed.
£200-300   *CSK*

Courtenay No. F1, Piers
de Cramand, signed XI.
£450-550   *CSK*

Courtenay No. Z2, foot
figure of Sir John of
Landas, signed.
£350-450   *CSK*

Courtenay No. H10,
mounted figure of Lord
de la Warr, signed,
damaged.
£1,000-1,200   *CSK*

Courtenay, No. 5/1, foot
figure of Sir
Bartholomew
Burghursh, signed.
£1,500-1,800   *CSK*

A Bing painted tinplate
cannon, c1910, 10in
(25cm).
£100-150   *CSK*

Britains set No. 39A,
Royal Horse Artillery,
Khaki Gun Team,
damage.
£400-500   *CSK*

Britains set No. 1330,
R.E. General Service
Limbered Wagon,
original box.
£300-400   *CSK*

Britains set No. 144A,
Royal Horse Artillery,
damaged.
£300-400   *CSK*

Britains set No. 213, The
Highland Light Infantry,
original box.
£650-750   *CSK*

Britains set No. 1291,
Band of the Royal
Marines, original box.
£300-400 *CSK*

Britains set No. 39A, The
Royal Horse Artillery
Khaki Gun Team.
£500-600 *CSK*

Franklin Mint Ltd.,
54mm scale hand
painted pewter figures,
52nd Light Infantry,
Oxfordshire Regiment,
95th Foot, Chasseur 6th
Regiment de Chasseurs a
cheval, in show case.
£100-150 *CSK*

Britains set No. 83,
Middlesex Imperial
Yeomanry, in original
damaged box.
£300-400 *CSK*

Britains set No. 460,
Colour Party of the Scots
Guards, in original box,
c1933.
£350-450 *CSK*

Courtenay Tournament
Knights, William, Earl
of Wiltshire, R.G. and Sir
James Audley,
damaged.
£300-400 *CSK*

Heyde, 90mm scale, 11th
Hussars, all damaged.
£200-300 *CSK*

Britains rare set No.
1904, Officers and Men of
the U.S. Army Air Corps,
original box, c1940.
£1,600-1,800 *P*

Britains set No. 8, 4th
Queens Own Hussars,
original box.
£120-150 *CSK*

Britains early set No. 46,
The 10th Duke of
Cambridge's Own
Bengal Lancers, in
original box, dated
1.11.1902.
£350-450 *CSK*

Britains set No. 1349,
North West Mounted
Police, slight damage,
c1933, in original box.
£50-100 *CSK*

435

A selection of Lineol
70mm scale figures, the
faces with paint, c1936.
£75-150 each *P*

Franklin Mint Ltd.,
54mm scale, hand
painted pewter figures,
The Fighting Men of the
British Empire, 1502- to
the present day, c1980, in
show case.
£150-200 *CSK*

Britains set, Pipers of the
Scots Guards, c1980, in
original box.
£100-150 *Bon*

Britains set No. 2101,
United States Marine
Corps Colour Guard,
some damage.
£60-100 *CSK*

Britains set, The Life
Guards, c1950, in
original box.
£100-150 *Bon*

Schneider, 40mm scale,
Austrian pontoon wagon
and wagon train,
Austrian Infantry,
original box.
£100-150 *CSK*

Britains lead soldiers,
British Infantry.
£50-100 *TAV*

Schneider, 40mm scale,
Austrian Hungarian
Hussars, c1910,
damaged, in original box.
£50-100 *CSK*

A set of 52mm scale British Fusiliers, German, some damage, c1900.
£150-200 *P*

Britains part set No. 1287, Military Band, c1934.
£130-180 *CSK*

Hausser-Elastolin, 7cm scale, British Army Ambulance.
£150-200 *CSK*

Britains set No. 1440, Royal Artillery, slight damage.
£1,500-2,500 *P*

Britains set No. 2010, Airborne Infantry.
£100-150 *CSK*

Britains assorted cavalry, including 4 Skinners Horse, 4 1st Bombay Lancers and 3 Red Army, Cavalry Parade Uniform, Officers.
£100-150 *CSK*

Britains set No. 2096, Drum and Pipe Band of the Irish Guards.
£150-200 *CSK*

Britains set No. 109, Royal Dublin Fusiliers, c1906.
£100-150 *CSK*

Kober, 40mm scale, Austrian Hungarian Band, c1910, original box. **£100-150** *CSK*

Britains set No. 1893, Royal Indian Army Service Corps, 23 figures.
£150-200 *CSK*

Britains post-war set
No. 39, King's Troop,
Royal Horse Artillery,
some damage.
£150-200 *CSK*

Britains set No. 1629,
Lord Strathcona's Horse
figures, c1938.
£1,800-2,000 *P*

Britains set of 5 Royal
Horse Guards, 1937.
£850-950 *P*

Britains set No. 1293,
Durban Light Infantry,
Armies of the World,
c1934.
£1,300-1,500 *P*

Britains set No. 146,
Royal Army Service
Corps wagon, damage, in
original box.
£80-100 *CSK*

Britains Queen Mary's
Dolls House toy soldiers,
comprising 20 miniature
figures, one sixth of the
normal size of a Britains
toy soldier, box in mint
condition.
£4,000-5,000 *P*

Britains set No. 1291,
Band of the Royal
Marines, 17 figures,
some re-touching.
£150-200 *CSK*

Britains converted Band
of the Royal Navy, 26
figures.
£150-180 *CSK*

Britains United States
cavalry, 3 figures, some
damage, c1940.
£650-750 *P*

Britains set No. 16, The
Buffs, East Kent
Regiment, 1st version,
c1894, original box.
£350-450 *P*

Britains set No. 13, 3rd
Hussars, damage, c1930,
original box.
£180-240 *P*

British Infantry 1815.
£90-100 *P*

Britains set No. 127, 7th
Dragoon Guards, c1930.
£300-400 *P*

First World War German
Infantry, 12 figures.
£200-300 *P*

Britains set of British
Infantry, slight damage,
c1940.
£1,500-1,700 *P*

American Hero Cowboy
and Indian set, by
Selchow & Righter Co,
with 6 Britains figures,
c1930, original box.
£200-300 *P*

Britains set No. 2112,
United States Marine
Corps, 14 figures, with
U.S. Army Band, 13
figures.
£100-150 *CSK*

Model Figures & Animals

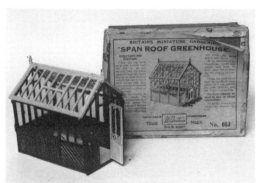

Britains Home Farm
series horse rake, c1950,
original box.
£50-60 *Bon*

<table>
<tr><td>Cross Reference
Toys
Tinplate</td></tr>
</table>

Britains Garden
Greenhouse in original
box.
£65-70 *Bon*

Britains Garden Shelter.
£65-70 *Bon*

DID YOU KNOW?

After the Second World War, there was a move away
from the popularity of toy soldiers. Many
manufacturers produced ranges of civilian figures,
zoos, farms and gardens being especially popular.

A straw-work Noah's
Ark, approx. 111
animals, Erzegebirge,
Germany, damage,
c1860, 13in (33cm) long.
£400-500 *CSK*

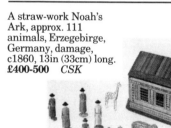

A painted wood Noah's
Ark, approx. 205
animals, Erzegebirge,
Germany, some damage,
c1870, 24in (61cm) long.
£1,000-1,200 *CSK*

A scratch built model of a
Tudor pub surrounded by
figures, c1920, 17in
(43cm) high.
£100-150 *LRG*

Britains Coronation
figures, original boxes.
£60-70   *Bon*

Britains farmyard pieces.
£2-5 each   *CAC*

Britains farmyard pieces.
£2-5 each   *CAC*

Britains Racing Colours,
set No. 1480, c1937,
original box.
£130-150   *CSK*

DID YOU KNOW?_____
Britains Home Farm series was so comprehensive
that it even included a village idiot. Numbered 587 in
the catalogue, it is now one of the most sought after
figures and an obvious target for fakers.

A set of painted lead
alligators forming a
band, bases stamped
M.S. 5/1216, Germany,
c1935.
£200-300   *CSK*

Britains Hunting
Display set No. 235, Full
Cry, slight damage,
c1939.
£300-350   *CSK*

Britains farm items.
£200-300   *CSK*

DID YOU KNOW?___
Miller's Collectables
Price Guide is designed
to build up, year by year,
into the most
comprehensive reference
system available.

Britains miniature
gardening set.
£300-400   *CSK*

A Noah's Ark toy, with wooden animals and figures, inscribed Irene's Ark, c1848, 17in (43cm) long.
£500-600 *CNY*

A wooden Noah's Ark by Erzegebirge, Germany, damage, c1860, 22in (55cm) long.
£900-1,000 *CSK*

A Victorian schoolroom toy, with figures and desks, probably German, c1870.
£450-550 *CNY*

Britains farm items.
£140-180 *CSK*

Britains assorted farm items, many chipped.
£400-500 *CSK*

The Equestrienne, a painted metal circus horse with lady rider, by Britains, c1910, 6½in (16cm) wide.
£250-350 *CSK*

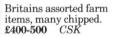

Britains Famous Football Teams, Derby County, damage, original box.
£250-350 *CSK*

A painted wood and composition rocking horse, German, late 19thC, 10½in (26cm) long.
£700-800 *CSK*

A wood and straw-work Noah's Ark with approx. 125 animals, 8 figures, slight damage, 23½in (59cm).
£800-1,000 *P*

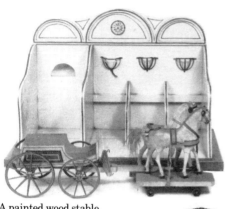

A painted wood stable block, German, c1907, 21½in (55cm) wide.
£1,100-1,400   *CSK*

A German child's wood and paper lithographed puppet stage in Palladian style building, with wood and papier mâché figures, late 19thC, 29in (73cm) wide.
£200-300   *P*

Marklin working models, German, c1936.
£170-200   *CSK*

A plastic robot, Dux-Astroman, No. 150, battery operated remote control, W. German, c1950, 12in (30.5cm), original box.
£200-300   *CSK*

A toy carousel, 19thC, 18in (45cm) diam.
£700-800   *AP*

Money Banks

Magic Bank, by J. & E. Stevens Co., c1876, 5in (13cm) high.
£350-450   *CSK*

American cast iron money bank, Hall's Lilliput bank.
£250-350   *P*

A cast iron mechanical bank, 'I Always Did 'Spise a Mule', probably by J. Harper & Co, c1910, 10½in (26cm) long.
£250-350   *CSK*

A painted cast iron mechanical money box, marked 'Patd Dec 23 1873' and 'Tammany Bank', 5½in (14.5cm).
£150-200   *OT*

Model Ships & Toys

A George Scott carved
and painted wood model
ferry boat, Wilson Line,
City of Chester, 24in
(61cm) long.
£200-300 *CNY*

Cross Reference
Shipping

Two G. Johnson painted
carton waterline model
boats.
£300-400 *CNY*

A painted wood waterline
dreadnought, probably
by Carette, c1904, 5in
(13cm) long, original box.
£300-400 *CSK*

A painted wood model of
the steamship President
Coolidge, 40in (100cm)
wide, on wood stand.
£1,000-1,500 *CNY*

A painted wood model of
the steamship Titanic by
George Scott, 52in
(130cm) long.
£600-800 *CNY*

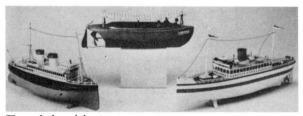

Three clockwork boats.
Left. **£400-500**   Centre. **£600-700**   Right. **£700-800** *CNY*

A fine wood and metal
electric powered model of
cruiser Kotick, RSMYC,
c1930, probably by Clyde
Model Dockyard,
restored, 33in (83cm) wide.
£600-700 *CSK*

A live steam pressure petrol fired model of the Thames river launch Donola, by Kingdom Yacht and Engineering Co. Teddington, modelled by L. G. Hewlett, 87in (222cm).
£1,300-1,500 *CSK*

A display model of the RNVR River Class Minesweeper, Carron, modelled by J. M. G. Brown, 39in (99cm) wide.
£700-900 *CSK*

A fine model of the clipper Cutty Sark, built by J. A. Evans, 2 by 3in (5 by 7.5cm).
£600-700 *CSK*

An Arnold four-funnel ocean liner, with clockwork mechanism, slight damage, c1920, 12in (30cm) long.
£300-400 *CSK*

A waterline model of Royal Navy frigate HMS Ajax, built by Capt. D. O. Head, 70in (177cm).
£1,700-2,000 *CSK*

| Cross Reference |
| Toys |
| Tinplate |

Bassett-Lowke No. 9 model with clockwork mechanism, c1935, 24½in (62cm) long, original wood case.
£400-500 *CSK*

Untersee-Boote, a painted metal model submarine, with clockwork mechanism, by Bing, damaged, repainted, c1910, 12in (30cm).
£250-350 *CSK*

A rare clockwork battleship, by Carette, restored, c1914, 19in (48cm) long.
£700-800 *CSK*

A waterline model of an estuary tug, with deck details, 15in (37cm) wide.
£300-400 *CSK*

Teddy Bears

Two Steiff pale plush teddy bears, with black button eyes and thread stitched nose, marked with Steiff button in left ear.
Smallest. **£300-400**
Largest. **£500-600**   *P*

A cinnamon plush covered teddy bear, probably Steiff, some wear, growler inoperative, c1908, 24in (61cm) high.
£1,500-1,800   *CSK*

A honey plush covered teddy bear, with Steiff button in ear, one pad moth-eaten, 13½in (34cm) high.
£450-550   *CSK*

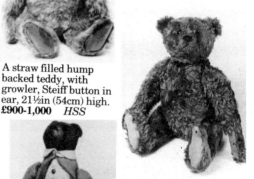

A straw filled hump backed teddy, with growler, Steiff button in ear, 21½in (54cm) high.
£900-1,000   *HSS*

A clockwork somersaulting teddy bear, by Bing of Nuremburg, button missing, 9in (22.5cm) high.
£550-650   *CSK*

A cinnamon plush covered teddy bear, probably Steiff, c1905, 21in (53cm) high.
£1,500-1,800   *CSK*

A golden plush covered standing clockwork bear, probably by Gebr. Bing, with button reading DRP DIV DRGM, c1933, 8in (20cm) high.
£400-500   *CSK*

A plush covered pull-along bear, with growl ring, Steiff button, c1920, 23in (58cm) long.
£400-500   *CSK*

A silver plush covered teddy bear, with Steiff button, 14in (35cm) high.
£550-650   *CSK*

A blond plush covered teddy bear with pronounced hump, Steiff button in ear, 30in (75cm) high.
£500-600 *CSK*

A plush covered polar bear, with Steiff button, c1913, 16in (40cm) long.
£400-500 *CSK*

A blond plush covered teddy bear, Steiff button missing, growler inoperative, 13in (33cm) high.
£300-400 *CSK*

A blond plush covered teddy bear, with growler, Steiff button in ear, 32in (80cm) high.
£700-800 *CSK*

A honey plus covered pull-along bear, probably Steiff, c1908, 6in (15cm) high.
£300-400 *CSK*

A family of Steiff teddy bears, in brown and beige plush, tallest 11in (29cm) high.
£450-550 *CSK*

A blond plush covered teddy bear with growler, with Steiff button in ear, replacement pads, 17in (43cm) high.
£450-550 *CSK*

A strawberry blond plush covered teddy bear, with plain Steiff button in ear, c1903, 12in (30cm) high.
£500-600 *CSK*

A selection of teddy bears.
£100-300 *CEd*

A set of miniature bisque teddy bears, The Three Bears, original crocheted clothes, ear chip, largest 2in (5cm) high.
£400-500 *CSK*

Steam Engines

A live steam, spirit fired model of a single funnel steam boat, by Radiguet, some damage, c1885, 20in (50cm) high.
£800-1,000   *CSK*

A Bing live steam spirit fired stationary steam set with brass boiler, with chimney and burner, c1900, 16 by 14in (40 by 35cm).
£1,600-1,800   *CSK*

A rare live steam, spirit fired stationary steam set, possibly American, original paintwork, late 19thC, 8½in (22cm) high.
£200-300   *CSK*

A model of a petrol engined lighting plant, 17 by 28in (44 by 71cm) overall.
£800-1,000   *CSK*

A Märklin live steam, spirit fired horizontal stationary steam engine No. 4160/7, German, c1920, 11in (29cm) deep, in original wooden box, with accessories.
£1,300-1,500   *CSK*

Hercules, a live steam spirit fired stationary steam set, by E. Plank, lacking burner, c1900, 15in (37cm) high.
£200-300   *CSK*

A Carette hot air engine, original paintwork, c1911, 15in (38cm) high.
£650-750   *CSK*

A live steam spirit fired vertical engine by Bing, No. 130/116, German, lacking chimney, scorched, c1912, 20½in (52cm) high.
£300-400   *CSK*

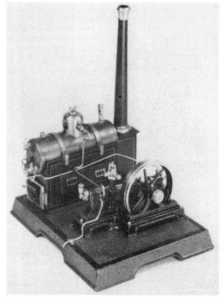

A model 4-pillar triple expansion vertical reversing marine engine, 8 by 12in (20 by 30cm).
£800-900   *CSK*

An unusual mechanical sculpture on a studded brass wooden display base, 14½ by 11in (37 by 28cm).
£100-150   *CSK*

A single oscillating cylinder vertical reversing over-crank stationary engine, 11½ by 7in (29 by 18cm).
£800-900   *CSK*

A model of a single cylinder horizontal mill engine, late 19thC, 37in (93cm) wide.
£550-650   *CSK*

A model of a vertical reversing single cylinder engine, late 19thC, 21½ by 13½in (54 by 34cm).
£450-550   *CSK*

A stationary steam plant, built by Radiguet, late 19thC, 17 by 10in (43 by 25cm), on cast iron base.
£700-900   *CSK*

A model of a Stuart 8-pillar triple expansion vertical reversing surface condensing marine engine, by N. W. Downes, Luton, 8 by 9in (20 by 23cm).
£900-1,000   *CSK*

A model of a twin cylinder vertical reversing marine engine, 11½ by 10½in (29 by 26cm).
£1,100-1,300   *CSK*

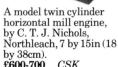

A model twin cylinder horizontal mill engine, by C. T. J. Nichols, Northleach, 7 by 15in (18 by 38cm).
£600-700   *CSK*

449

A model of a three pillar twin cylinder compound vertical condensing stationary engine, 13in (32cm).
£2,500-2,700 *CSK*

A spirit fired steam engine by Doll et Cie, lacking chimney, c1920, 12in (30cm) wide.
£100-150 *WIL*

A Bing live steam spirit fired portable engine, original paintwork, c1928, 10 by 8in (25 by 20cm).
£500-600 *CSK*

A Bing live steam spirit fired portable engine, restored, c1912, 8½ by 7½in (21 by 19cm).
£400-500 *CSK*

A small single cylinder engine, by C. Cole, c1940, 26in (65cm) long.
£250-350 *CSK*

Ironside, a restored and repainted live steam, spirit fired steam roller, by Wilesco, c1928, 11in (28cm) long.
£200-250 *CSK*

A Stevens Model Dockyard 3in gauge live steam spirit fired model of an early 2–2–0 locomotive, damaged, c1900.
£200-300 *CSK*

A model Stuart Swan twin cylinder marine engine, by R. Hutchings, 14½in (36cm) high.
£900-1,000 *CSK*

A brass and chromium plated scale model of a steam driven Silver Ghost Rolls Royce, boiler concealed underneath the seat, 22in (55cm) long.
£1,000-1,200 *HSS*

A Doll & Co. live steam spirit fired electric plant, with burner and chimney, German, worn, repaired, c1930.
£100-150 *CSK*

Tinplate

Aircraft

A printed and painted tri-engine plane, with clockwork mechanism, by Wells, restored, c1936, 21in (54cm) wide.
£450-550 *CSK*

Four printed and painted aeroplanes, c1950.
£200-300 *CSK*

A printed and painted high-wing monoplane, clockwork mechanism, German, c1920, 8½in (21cm) long.
£200-300 *CSK*

Automobiles

A Burnett lithographed tinplate bus, with clockwork mechanism, slight damage, c1920, 9in (22cm) long.
£1,100-1,400 *CSK*

A Fischer lithographed penny toy limousine, German, c1924, 5in (13cm) long.
£150-200 *CSK*

A rare Carette painted landaulette, with clockwork mechanism, slight wear, German, c1912, 11in (28cm) long.
£1,500-2,000 *CSK*

A lithographed and painted open tourer, with clockwork mechanism, by G. Levy, damage, c1924, 9½in (24cm) long.
£200-300 *CSK*

Two Burnett lithographed and painted tinplate vehicles, slight damage, c1920, 7in (18cm) long.
£650-850 each *CSK*

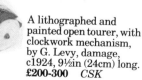

Two Orobr lithographed and painted tinplate vehicles, German, c1920, 8½in (21cm) long.
£200-400 each *CSK*

A Tipp lithographed and painted limousine, with clockwork mechanism, German, c1928, 9in (22cm) long.
£250-350 *CSK*

A C.I.J. clockwork
tinplate P2 model Alfa
Romeo, paintwork poor
condition.
£600-700 *CEd*

A Schuco Ingenico
Electric remote control
car, 5311/56, painted
tinplate and plastic, with
a Larreto 5330 trailer,
W. Germany, c1956, in
original box.
£200-300 *CSK*

Kiddycraft Traffic Set,
with clockwork vehicles
and Britains figures,
some damaged, c1938,
original box.
£1,000-1,200 *CSK*

A lithographed taxi, with
original paintwork, with
clockwork mechanism,
slight wear, by Fischer,
c1910, 8½in (21cm) long.
£1,500-1,800 *CSK*

A printed and painted
tinplate fire engine, with
clockwork mechanism,
by Distler, some rust,
c1936, 15½in (39cm)
long.
£300-500 *CSK*

A printed and painted
four-seater open tourer,
with clockwork
mechanism, by Distler,
No. 578, c1928, 12in
(31cm) long.
£2,000-2,400 *CSK*

Two Schuco Elektro-
Control vehicles,
W. Germany, c1960, in
original boxes.
£150-350 each *CSK*

A Rossignol printed and
painted tinplate
limousine, with
clockwork mechanism,
French, damaged, c1933,
14in (36cm) long.
£600-800 *CSK*

A Fischer lithograph
tinplate limousine, with
clockwork mechanism,
German, worn, c1925,
8in (20.5cm).
£170-200 *CSK*

A printed and painted
pick-up truck, with
clockwork mechanism,
by Lehmann, EPL
No. 570, c1912, 7in
(17cm) long.
£500-600 *CSK*

An early tinplate car,
'Tut Tut', EPL No. 490,
with clockwork
mechanism, some
damage, by Lehmann,
c1910, 7in (17cm) long.
£80-120 *CSK*

A Distler Electromatic
7500, a printed and
painted tinplate Porsche
W. German, c1950, 10in
(25.5cm).
£300-350 *CSK*

l. A Distler spring action
delivery van, c1920,
6½in (16.5cm).
£350-400
c. A Kellerman penny toy
covered wagon and pair,
5½in (14cm).
£90-120

r. Muller & Kadedar,
clockwork motorcycle
and sidecar, with rider
and passenger, 7in
(18cm) long.
£1,200-1,500 *P*

A Marx clockwork MD
War Department
streamlined ambulance,
boxed, 14in (36cm).
£300-350 *P*

A Marx Hi-Way
Express delivery lorry,
15½in (40cm).
£60-80 *P*

Carr's Biscuits London
Transport double decker
bus tin, in original
paintwork, c1948, 10in
(25.5cm) long.
£400-450 *CSK*

'Oho', EPL 545, a printed
and painted tinplate
motor car, with
clockwork mechanism,
by Lehmann, worn,
c1910, 3in (7.5cm).
£220-250 *CSK*

453

Hessmobile, a lithographed and painted tinplate two-seater car, with a hand-cranked, flywheel mechanism, by Hess, worn, c1908, 9in (23cm) long.
£200-250   *CSK*

A printed and tinplate limousine, with clockwork mechanism, by K. Bub, damaged, c1926, 11½in (29cm).
£700-750   *CSK*

A Tipp painted and lithographed tinplate motor coach, with clockwork mechanism, some rust, c1928, 10½in (26cm).
£120-140   *CSK*

Hessmobile, No. 1022, printed and painted tinplate landaulette, with flywheel mechanism, by Hess, c1924, 7½in (19cm).
£300-350   *CSK*

A printed and painted tinplate Carter Paterson delivery van, with clockwork mechanism, by Tipp, lacks driver and wheel loose, c1930, 10in (25cm) long.
£900-1,000   *CSK*

A hand painted limousine, with clockwork mechanism, by Carette, c1912, 10½in (27cm) long.
£1,000-1,200   *CSK*

Ito, EPL 679, a lithographed and painted tinplate limousine, with clockwork mechanism, by Lehmann, c1920, 7in (18cm) long.
£400-450   *CSK*

Swift, a printed and painted tinplate racing car, with clockwork mechanism, by Seidel, slight rust, c1928, 11in (28cm) long.
£170-200   *CSK*

A painted tinplate model of Major Gardner's record car, with friction drive mechanism, British, slight chipping, c1939, 10in (25.5cm) long.
£350-400   *CSK*

A 'De Dion' hand enamelled tinplate car, by Bing, c1904, 8in (20cm) long.
£2,500-3,000   *CSK*

A Distler printed and painted tinplate limousine, No. 525, with clockwork mechanism, German, c1927, 6½in (16.5cm).
£220-250   *CSK*

A Distler limousine
No. 579, with clockwork
mechanism, worn, c1928,
12in (30.5cm) long.
£280-300 *CSK*

Fischer lithographed
tinplate penny toys,
c1920.
£40-50 each *CSK*

A hand enamelled
four-seater open tourer,
No. 3358/21, by Carette,
slight damage, c1911,
8½in (21cm) long.
£3,000-3,500 *CSK*

Greppert and Kelch, a
spring action
lithographed tipper
lorry, 8½in (21cm) long.
£240-260 *P*

A Kingsbury Sunbeam
racer, clockwork, box
damaged.
£550-600 *LAY*

Motorcycles

Mac 700, a printed and
painted tinplate
motorbike and rider,
with clockwork
mechanism, by Arnold,
W. German, slight
damage, c1955, 7½in
(19cm).
£200-300 *CSK*

Mac 700, a printed and
painted tinplate
motorbike and rider,
with clockwork
mechanism, by Arnold,
W. Germany, damaged,
c1955, 7½in (19cm) long.
£140-160 *CSK*

A clockwork
lithographed and
painted tinplate toy, U.S.
Zone Germany, c1950.
£40-50 *CSK*

Echo, EPL No. 725, a
printed and painted
tinplate motor cyclist,
with clockwork
mechanism, by
Lehmann, c1910, 9in
(23cm) long.
£2,000-2,500 *CSK*

Wilhelm Krauss, a
spring action
lithographed AA Road
Services motorcyclist
and sidecar, 7in (18cm)
long.
£8,500-9,500 *P*

Figures & Animals

A tinplate pool player, printed and painted, with clockwork mechanism, stamped P.W., German, c1912, 7in (18cm) long.
£400-450   *CSK*

A mechanical hand painted tinplate clown band, with hand driven reed musical box, defective, by Gunthermann, c1910, 9½in (24cm) long.
£850-900   *CSK*

A Lehmann tinplate novelty monkey, Tom 385, finished in polychrome enamels, early 20thC.
£50-80   *WIL*

Our New Clergyman, a stained and carved wood, metal and tinplate model, probably by F. Martin, clockwork mechanism defective, c1890, 10½in (27cm) high.
£1,600-2,000   *CSK*

Cross Reference
Dolls

Miss Blondin, a printed and painted tinplate tightrope walker, by Lehmann, slight wear, c1888, 8½in (21.5cm).
£4,500-5,000   *CSK*

Busy Lizzie, a printed and painted tinplate parlour maid, with clockwork mechanism, German, c1924, 7in (18cm).
£300-350   *CSK*

A Lehmann 'Lo & Li' tinplate toy.
£1,200-1,500   *HP*

Dancing Sailor, EPL 535, a printed and painted tinplate sailor, with clockwork mechanism, defective, by Lehmann, c1912, 7½in (19cm) high.
£80-100   *CSK*

Flying Bird, painted tinplate bird, by Lehmann, damaged, c1900, 7in (18cm).
£80-120   *CSK*

A painted and lithographed tinplate clown, with clockwork mechanism, by Gunthermann, c1924, 9in (23cm) long.
£80-100   *CSK*

A singing bird in cage, with clockwork mechanism in base of cage, German, some chipping, c1920, 4in (10cm) high.
£350-400   *CSK*

Zulu, EPL 721, a painted and lithographed tinplate ostrich pulling a mail cart, with clockwork mechanism, by Lehmann, c1920, 7½in (19cm) long.
£600-650   *CSK*

A hand painted maid, with clockwork mechanism, probably by Gunthermann, slight wear, c1903, 8in (20.5cm).
£550-600   *CSK*

'Le Gai Violiniste', a painted tinplate musician, with clockwork mechanism, by F. Martin, damaged, c1907, 8in (20cm) high.
£70-100   *CSK*

A hand enamelled tinplate woman pushing a cart, probably by Gunthermann, some damage, c1903, 7½in (19cm) long.
£480-500   *CSK*

Fighting Cocks, No. 118, 2 printed and painted cockerels on a carriage, with clockwork mechanism, by Einfalt, c1935, 9½in (24cm).
£180-200   *CSK*

A painted and lithographed tinplate hansom cab, with clockwork mechanism, probably by Gunthermann, c1908, 8½in (22cm).
£1,200-1,500   *CSK*

Spaceships

A printed and painted tinplate rocket fighter, with clockwork mechanism, by Marx, American, c1950, in original box, 12in (30.5cm).
£200-300   *CSK*

'Soucoupe a Réaction', a printed tinplate flying saucer, with friction mechanism, by SFA Paris, c1950, original box, 7in (18cm).
£80-100   *CSK*

Sparkling Fighter Ship, by Marx, 12in (30cm).
£130-150   *P*

A clockwork rowing boat
with oarsman, by
Arnold, boxed.
£140-160 *P*

Cross Reference
Toys
Ships
Shipping

A Bing lithographed
tinplate ocean liner, No.
10/31/1, with clockwork
mechanism, German,
lacks mast with flag,
c1920, 7in (18cm) long.
£160-200 *CSK*

A painted tinplate river
paddle steamer, with
clockwork mechanism,
by Uebelacker,
Nuremburg, damaged,
c1902, 11in (28cm) long.
£500-550 *CSK*

A Third Series painted
tinplate clockwork ocean
liner, by Bing, slight
damage, c1925, 16in
(40.5cm) long.
£1,800-2,000 *CSK*

Clockwork tinplate boats.
£150-300 each *CNY*

A Bing hand painted
tinplate battleship, some
damage, c1912, 21in
(53cm) long.
£1,200-1,500 *CSK*

An Arnold four funnel
ocean liner, with
clockwork mechanism,
German, some parts
missing, c1920, 15½in
(39cm) long.
£300-350 *CSK*

A Bing motor boat, hand
painted with clockwork
mechanism, German,
slightly chipped, c1908,
9in (23cm).
£400-450 *CSK*

A painted tinplate gun
boat, with clockwork
mechanism, probably by
Bing, c1920, 16in
(40.5cm) long.
£250-300 *CSK*

Fleischmann No. 855 oil
tanker, a painted
tinplate model, with
clockwork mechanism,
some damage, c1936,
26in (66cm).
£550-600 *CSK*

Miscellaneous

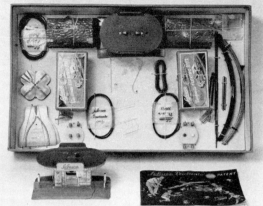

A lithographed tinplate garage, by Greppert & Kelch, c1924.
£350-400   *CSK*

Schuco-Varianto 3010 motorway, a tinplate and plastic remote control set, U.S. Zone W. Germany, c1955.
£120-150   *CSK*

A printed and painted tinplate robot, battery operated, by Horikawa, c1960, 15½in (39cm) high.
£270-300   *CSK*

Daiya battery operated Space Conqueror Man of Tomorrow, and a Japanese N.A.S.A. space station.
£360-400   *P*

The Climbing Miller, a printed and painted tinplate windmill, with pulley mechanism, by Chad Valley, c1924, 16½in (42cm) high, in original box.
£150-180   *CSK*

A German tinplate and clockwork tractor, and airship.
£50-200 each   *HSS*

A Bing painted and lithographed tinplate garage, c1925.
£300-350   *CSK*

A Marklin gauge 1 mainline station, hand enamelled, some pieces missing, c1903.
£700-800   *CSK*

Games

A jigsaw puzzle, by
Raphael Tuck & Sons.
£10-15   *FAL*

DID YOU KNOW?_____
The invention of jigsaw puzzles is credited to a
London cartographer John Spilsburg during the
1760s. The first recorded examples were maps,
cut-up and used as an aid to teach geography.

A printed paper on wood
picture block, German,
in original box with
illustrated lid, c1890.
£270-300   *CSK*

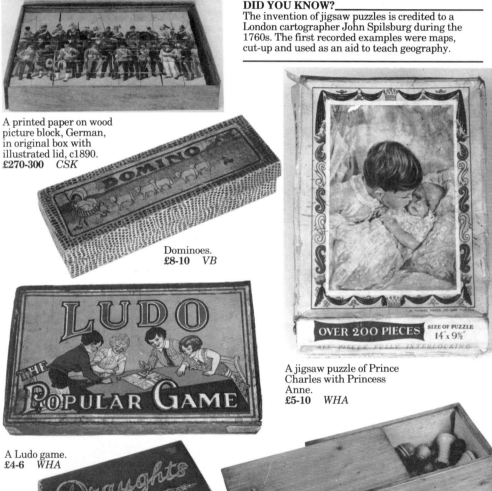

Dominoes.
£8-10   *VB*

A Ludo game.
£4-6   *WHA*

A jigsaw puzzle of Prince
Charles with Princess
Anne.
£5-10   *WHA*

Draughts.
£3-5   *VB*

A chess set.
£10-15   *VB*

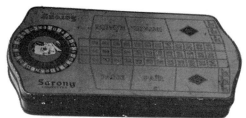

A cigarette tin depicting gambling game, 12½in (32cm) wide.
£25-30   *COB*

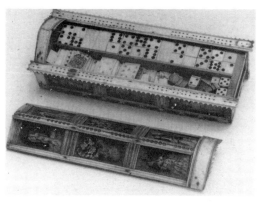

A 'Prisoner of War' carved bone games box, some damage, 10in (25.5cm).
£400-500   *Bea*

Card Playing

A News Round Game, 'Counties of England', late 19thC.
£55-65   *PC*

A pair of ivory hand markers of Whist.
£50-70   *AL*

A 'What's Trumps' Whist marker.
£10-15   *VB*

Cross Reference
Playing cards

Counters

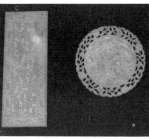

Mother-of-pearl markers.
£5-8 each   *VB*

A playing card shuffler.
£25-35   *WHA*

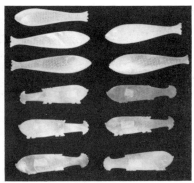

Victorian and Georgian mother-of-pearl counters.
£1-3 each   *VB*

General

Automobiles

A painted
wood and metal Daily
Mail van, by Lines Bros,
worn and rusted, c1928,
19½in (50cm) long.
£150-200   *CSK*

Tri-ang Minic Armoured
Assault Group, vehicles
with friction drive
mechanisms, in original
box, some damage, c1955.
£60-80   *CSK*

Two Schuco cars, U.S.
Zone German,
windscreen broken,
c1950.
£60-80 each   *CSK*

Two fairground
motorbikes, shaped wood
with polychrome painted
decoration, c1920, 44in
(111.5cm) long.
£100-150 each   *LRG*

A collection of penny and
carpet toys, mainly
German, varied
condition, c1920.
£15-20 each   *P*

Tri-ang Minic cars and
jeeps, in original boxes.
£10-15 each   *CSK*

Johillco motor cars and
lorries, c1930.
£50-60 each   *CSK*

Clockwork

A.G.L. 'Golden Arrow' land speed record car, British, axle broken, original box, c1933, 16½in (42cm).
£450-500 *CSK*

Sunbeam Silver Bullet, a printed and painted land speed record car, with clockwork mechanism, by Gunthermann, worn, c1933, 22in (56cm) long.
£200-250 *CSK*

A Tri-ang clockwork road roller, with box, c1950.
£30-40 *Bon*

A clockwork Art Deco style saloon, Mercedes 540K, known as the 'Autobahn-Kurier', by Tipp & Co., parts loose, c1935, 13½in (34cm).
£2,000-2,500 *P*

A printed and painted saloon, with clockwork mechanism, by Falk, c1933, 18in (45.5cm) long.
£700-750 *CSK*

Constructor Cars

A Meccano No. 1 Car Constructor Outfit, assembled as a sport coupe, c1935.
£300-350 *CSK*

A Meccano No. 2 Motor Car Outfit, c1933.
£500-550 *CSK*

A Meccano No. 2 Car Constructor Outfit, assembled as a racing car, c1935.
£500-550 *CSK*

A Meccano No. 2 Car Constructor Outfit, assembled as a sports two-seater, some replacements, c1936.
£450-500 *CSK*

A Meccano No. 2 Motor Car Outfit, assembled as a Grand Prix racing car, with clockwork mechanism, c1934.
£500-550 *CSK*

Disney

A group of bisque Disney figures, c1930.
£450-500 *CNY*

Cross Reference
Coca-Cola

A collection of Disney related books, 1933-40.
£500-550 *CNY*

A Disney Coca-Cola popcorn holder, c1960.
£8-10 *PC*

A Sutcliffe clockwork Nautilus submarine, from 20,000 Leagues Under The Sea, in original box, 9½in (24cm) long.
£80-120 *WIL*

Cross Reference
Ephemera

Mechanical

A bisque headed Jack-in-the-box, with musical movement, the box 4½in (11cm) high.
£300-350 *CSK*

A hand carved and stained wood clockwork toy of 2 animated dancers, The Juba Dancers, American, c1880, 9½in (24cm) high.
£270-300 *CSK*

A clockwork automaton figure of a bear drummer, probably Descamps, c1880, 27in (68.5cm) high.
£1,000-1,200 *CSK*

A Scottish terrier automaton, by Descamps, 11in (28cm) high.
£200-250 *CSK*

A French painted wood mechanical toy, hat lacking, c1860.
£300-350 *CSK*

Models

A ¼-scale flying model of the De Havilland DH2 Tiger Moth, Serial No. T-5854, 67in (170cm) wingspan.
£500-550   *CSK*

1933 SJ Dusenberg with Weymann Speedsters body, 1:15th scale, by Gerald Wingrove, 15in (38cm) long.
£3,200-3,500   *ONS*

Rocking Horses

An Edwardian painted wood dapple grey rocking horse, probably by Lines Bros, lacks stirrups and reins, c1924.
£200-250   *CSK*

A Ken Bright pine rocking horse, 1971.
£3,000-3,500   *C*

Stuffed Animals

A plush covered nodding Boston terrier, with pull growl, French, c1910.
£500-550   *CSK*

A plush covered Jemima Puddle Duck, one eye lacking and quacker inoperative, 14in (35.5cm).
£150-180   *CSK*

A Steiff velvet covered rabbit, c1905, 13in (33cm) high.
£170-200   *CSK*

A flock covered papier mâché pull-along rabbit, with inscription C. L. Braithwaite 1843, lacking wheels, 5in (12.5cm).
£100-120   *CSK*

Treen

Treen is a generic term for anything made of wood. The most popular woods used for drinking vessels and food containers were beech, chestnut and occasionally elm. Other woods used include: alder, apple, lime, pearwood, poplar, sycamore, walnut and yew. From the 18thC onwards a variety of imported timbers were used, for example boxwood, ebony, lignum vitae, mahogany, maple and teak.

A yew pin cushion,
c1840, 6in (15cm).
£160-200 *Cas*

A lignum vitae snuff pot,
c1850, 12in (30.5cm).
£450-500 *Cas*

A pair of coquilla nut
goblets, c1720, 3½in
(9cm) high.
£600-650 *Cas*

A pair of mahogany
coasters, c1820.
£350-400 *Cas*

A Scandinavian chip
carved tankard, 1860.
£450-500 *Cas*

A rosewood gallery glass,
1840.
£600-700 *Cas*

A Scandinavian chip
carved spice pot, c1850.
£250-300 *Cas*

A pair of walnut spill
vases, 1870.
£130-160 *Cas*

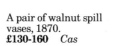

A walnut tobacco jar, 9in
(23cm).
£300-350 *Cas*

A turned wood goblet,
c1850, 12in (30.5cm)
high.
£180-200   *Cas*

A Victorian mahogany
pincushion.
£60-80   *PC*

A ring gauge, 19thC.
£30-40   *PC*

A Victorian globe on iron
stand.
£350-450   *PC*

A turned walnut hat pin
stand, c1850, 3½in (9cm)
high.
£135-155   *Cas*

A carved lignum vitae
salt, c1840.
£85-95   *Cas*

An oak spice container,
17thC.
£300-400   *PC*

A fruit knife stand, with
horn handled knives,
c1840, 9in (23cm) high.
£85-95   *Cas*

A fruitwood bobbin
stand, 18thC.
£300-400   *PC*

An oak goblet, 18thC,
10in (25.5cm) high.
£350-400   *Cas*

TREEN

An illustrated offertory box, 17thC.
£300-400 *PC*

A Victorian seal.
£20-30 *PC*

A sycamore mixing bowl, 17thC.
£100-120 *PC*

A coopered cider bottle, c1870.
£120-150 *Cas*

Cross Reference
Writing

An engine turned lignum vitae ink and quill stand, c1840, 2in (5cm) high.
£65-85 *Cas*

A Scandinavian peg tankard, 18thC.
£400-500 *PC*

An elm pestle and mortar, c1800.
£200-220 *Cas*

A tricorn bottle stand, late 18thC.
£80-100 *PC*

A fruitwood spice grinder, c1700.
£550-600 *Cas*

A boxwood medicine bottle case, c1870, 4½in (11.5cm) high.
£75-100 *Cas*

An elaborate mechanical
fire bellows, early 19thC.
£400-500 *PC*

A pair of fruitwood salts,
17thC.
£150-200 *PC*

A turned beech salt,
c1840, 6in (15cm).
£140-160 *Cas*

An elm dry store jar,
c1850, 15in (38cm) high.
£250-300 *Cas*

A magnum wine coaster
on wheels, c1860, 8½in
(21.5cm) diam.
£250-300 *Cas*

An oak hanging message
board, 17thC.
£300-400 *PC*

A fruitwood mortar,
c1800, 5½in (14cm) high.
£120-150 *Cas*

A feathered coopered
piggin, c1800, 7in (18cm)
high.
£150-180 *Cas*

A Scottish coopered pot
and cover, c1850, 5in
(12.5cm).
£140-160 *Cas*

A walnut extending
turned stand, late 18thC.
£250-300 *PC*

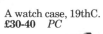

A watch case, 19thC.
£30-40 *PC*

A lignum vitae
bowl, c1800, 3½in (9cm)
diam.
£120-140 *Cas*

A chocolate whisk.
£40-50 *PC*

TREEN

An hour glass, c1800, 8in (20.5cm) high.
£420-450 *Cas*

A fruitwood artist's palette, by Robinson of Long Acre, c1870.
£150-200 *Cas*

An ash string barrel, c1870.
£200-250 *Cas*

A cheese scoop and sheath, 19thC.
£30-40 *PC*

A mahogany single bottle coaster, c1800.
£270-300 *Cas*

A tortoiseshell box with applied silver decoration.
£50-60 *PC*

A selection of fruitwood double measures, early 19thC.
£60-80 each *PC*

A mahogany gavel, c1840, 8½in (22cm).
£85-95 *Cas*

A fruitwood plumb line, 19thC.
£30-40 *PC*

A pair of mahogany candlesticks, c1820, 21½in (54cm) high.
£750-850 *Cas*

An expanding wool
winder.
£9-12 *VB*

A matchbox cover.
£3-5 *VB*

A pair of fruitwood
candlesticks, c1880, 10in
(25.5cm) high.
£140-160 *Cas*

A miniature chest, mock
ebony painted with
boxwood stringing, 6in
(15cm) high.
£25-30 *OSc*

A Scandinavian carved
birch wood goblet and
cover, signed and dated
1904.
£350-400 *Cas*

A Victorian fruitwood
wig powderer.
£40-50 *PC*

A pair of rosewood
'cannon barrel'
candlesticks, c1850,
8½in (21.5cm) high.
£150-200 *Cas*

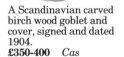

Beechwood glove
stretchers, 19thC.
£30-50 *PC*

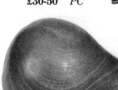

A lignum vitae paper
weight, 19thC, 5½in
(14cm).
£270-300 *PC*

Two toddy holders, 4in
(10cm) high.
£15-20 each *OSc*

A pair of rosewood vases,
c1880, 10½in (26.5cm)
high.
£170-200 *Cas*

471

TREEN

An 18thC looking glass.
£220-250 *PC*

A mahogany lacemaker's lamp stand, 19thC, 7in (18cm) high.
£65-75 *PC*

Cross Reference
Egg cups

A Victorian carved romantic figure, signed E.W., dated 1867, 23½in (60cm) high.
£750-850 *Cas*

Coquilla nut snuff boxes.
£400-500 each *PC*

A George III mahogany deportment board.
£80-100 *PC*

A carved wood tobacco jar, in the form of a drinking monk, lead lined, c1860.
£550-600 *Cas*

A late Victorian bucket.
£40-50 *PC*

Carved coquilla nutmeg graters.
£60-80 *PC*

A nutcracker, late 19thC.
£20-30 *PC*

An egg cruet, with horn top and feet, 8in (20.5cm) high.
£35-45 *AL*

472

An oak letter box, 13½in
(34cm) high.
£1,800-2,000 *C*

A Dutch oak foot warmer,
18thC, 11in (28cm) wide.
£350-450 *PC*

A pair of twisted walnut
candlesticks, c1840,
15½in (39cm) high.
£120-150 *Cas*

A pair of carved oak
candlesticks, c1850.
£120-150 *Cas*

A sycamore sugar caster,
18thC.
£150-200 *PC*

Wooden nut crackers.
£60-100 each *AL*

A pill board.
£400-500 *PC*

*These boards were used
by apothecaries for the
manufacture of tablets on
a small scale.*

Cross Reference
Candlesticks

A pair of olivewood
travelling candlesticks,
known as the Brighton
Bun, c1880.
£85-95 *Cas*

A pair of oak sifters, with
silver tops, late 18thC.
£200-250 *PC*

A nutmeg grater in the
form of an acorn.
£100-120 *AL*

473

TREEN

A mahogany cheese
board, 18thC, 8½in
(21cm) diam.
£160-200 *PC*

A mahogany cheese
coaster, on brass casters,
c1800.
£350-400 *PC*

An unusual faceted
candle box, 18thC.
£200-300 *PC*

A Victorian rosewood
money box, 6in (15cm)
wide.
£30-40 *MB*

A pair of Victorian
travelling fruitwood
candlestands and snuffer.
£60-80 *PC*

A rosewood glass topped
pill box, 19thC.
£30-40 *PC*

A lignum vitae egg cup.
£7-10 *VB*

A turned wood stand,
late 18thC.
£200-250 *PC*

A pine sock dryer.
£40-50 *PC*

A sycamore scoop, 18thC.
£30-40 *PC*

A decoy duck, late 19thC.
£100-120 *PC*

A very rare ale coaster,
17thC.
£800-1,000 *PC*

A Georgian mahogany
book carrying stand.
£600-800   *PC*

A double wig stand,
18thC.
£150-200   *PC*

An inlaid violin case,
with original interior,
early 19thC.
£250-300   *MB*

A dice shaker.
£6-10   *VB*

A butler's open carrying
candle box.
£200-250   *PC*

A fruitwood chalice,
19thC.
£80-100   *PC*

A bank sovereign and
half sovereign checker.
£500-600   *PC*

A lacquer work cabinet
brush, 27in (68.5cm).
£30-40   *OSc*

Heroin scales, 19thC.
£120-140   *PC*

A turned sycamore
chalice, 18thC.
£150-200   *PC*

Tunbridgeware

A Tunbridgeware banjo, c1860.
£400-500 *VB*

A Victorian inlaid rosewood box, 5in (13cm) wide.
£60-70 *MB*

A Victorian rosewood inlaid Tunbridgeware box.
£100-150 *MB*

A Tunbridgeware box decorated with ebony, 6½in (16cm) long.
£120-140 *MB*

A Tunbridgeware container.
£40-50 *PC*

DID YOU KNOW?

The earliest examples of Tunbridgeware date back to the end of the 17th century, consisting of small boxes covered with floral marquetry. Sometimes painted, these boxes were usually decorated using a variety of wood veneers; holly, plum, yew, cherrywood and sycamore. Diseased oak known as Emerald Rot provided the green wood.

Tunbridgeware beads.
£30-70 *VB*

Very early Tunbridgeware boxes.
£40-45 *VB*

A selection of boxes.
£20-50 each *VB*

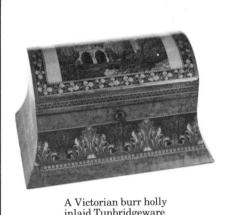

A Victorian burr holly inlaid Tunbridgeware casket, showing Bayham Abbey.
£550-650 *MB*

A pin tray and pill box.
£40-60 *VB*

Assorted picture frames.
£20-50 each *VB*

A collection of sewing
items.
£25-50 each *VB*

A box with bird's eye
maple pattern, c1830,
8in (20cm).
£80-90 *VB*

Two boxes.
Small. **£50-60**
Large. **£90-100** *VB*

Two cribbage boards.
£40-80 *VB*

Letter opener, brooches,
counter box.
£20-50 each *VB*

A box, 7in (17.5cm) wide.
£120-140 *VB*

477

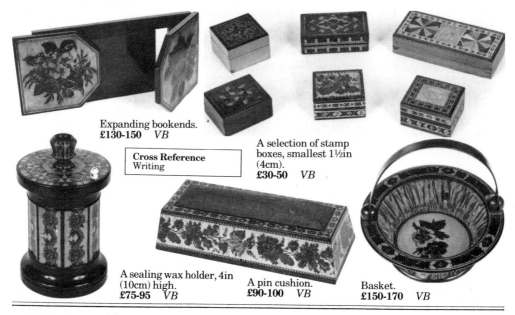

Expanding bookends.
£130-150 *VB*

Cross Reference
Writing

A selection of stamp
boxes, smallest 1½in
(4cm).
£30-50 *VB*

A sealing wax holder, 4in
(10cm) high.
£75-95 *VB*

A pin cushion.
£90-100 *VB*

Basket.
£150-170 *VB*

Mauchlineware

Mauchline (pronounced Mochlin), is a small Scottish town near Ayr, which gave its name to this very collectable range of decorative Scottish souvenir ware.

The industry was at its peak during the 1860s and continued until 1933 when the box works burnt down, effectively ending production.

A vast array of goods was produced, sent to all corners of the U.K. and the Commonwealth, providing a rich area for collectors today.

A collection of
Mauchlineware
miniature boxes and
container, 3in (7.5cm).
£10-20 each *AL*

A Mauchlineware watch
holder.
£35-45 *VB*

A collection of
Mauchlineware.
£500-600 *CSK*

Tartan Ware

Bridge scoreboards, 3 by
2in (7.5 by 5cm).
£50-70 *AL*

Autograph book, bible,
Mary Queen of Scots and
a prayer book.
£70-120 *EUR*

Cross Reference
Serviette rings

Tartan ware paper
knives.
£30-50 each *EUR*

A selection of pen knives.
£25-75 each *EUR*

Serviette rings.
£20-25 each
Pin cushions.
£35-55 each *EUR*

Propelling pencils.
£75-100 each *EUR*

A box with motto, 4in
(10cm) wide.
£100-150 *EUR*

Needlecase.
£120-140

Pen knife.
£35-45

Nib case.
£65-75 *EUR*

TARTANWARE

Various containers for sewing items.
£50-75 *EUR*

Needle holders.
£50-75 *EUR*

Two boxes.
£55-65 each *EUR*

Lady of the Lake, bound in tartan.
£120-140 *EUR*

A money box, 2½in (6cm) high.
£70-80 *EUR*

A dice shaker.
£30-40 *EUR*

A watch holder box.
£65-75 *EUR*

A large and a small box, 1½ and 2½in (4 and 6cm) high.
£50-80 *EUR*

A pin cushion box, 2in (5cm) high.
£75-100 *EUR*

A pin cushion box.
£100-120 *EUR*

A brooch.
£40-60 *EUR*

An egg cup and egg.
£45-55 *EUR*

Walking Sticks

Walking sticks or canes evolved from the staves used by travellers to protect themselves in the Middle Ages. These sticks were used for defence and were not usually decorated. More ornate sticks became fashionable in Europe in the late 15thC, and spread to England during the reigns of Henry VII and Henry VIII. The carrying of canes increased in popularity and became an important fashion accessory. Since the First World War and the decline in the formality of menswear the popularity of walking sticks has decreased.

Dual Purpose Sticks

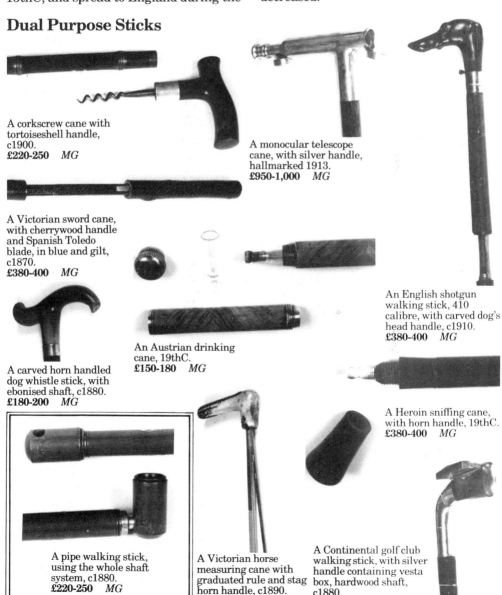

A corkscrew cane with tortoiseshell handle, c1900.
£220-250 *MG*

A monocular telescope cane, with silver handle, hallmarked 1913.
£950-1,000 *MG*

A Victorian sword cane, with cherrywood handle and Spanish Toledo blade, in blue and gilt, c1870.
£380-400 *MG*

An Austrian drinking cane, 19thC.
£150-180 *MG*

An English shotgun walking stick, 410 calibre, with carved dog's head handle, c1910.
£380-400 *MG*

A carved horn handled dog whistle stick, with ebonised shaft, c1880.
£180-200 *MG*

A Heroin sniffing cane, with horn handle, 19thC.
£380-400 *MG*

A pipe walking stick, using the whole shaft system, c1880.
£220-250 *MG*

A Victorian horse measuring cane with graduated rule and stag horn handle, c1890.
£170-200 *MG*

A Continental golf club walking stick, with silver handle containing vesta box, hardwood shaft, c1880.
£400-450 *MG*

Ivory Handled

A German carved ivory stag being attacked by a wolf handle, on a malacca shaft, c1860.
£650-700 *MG*

An ivory and silver pique inlaid handled stick, with malacca shaft,
£460-500 *MG*

An ivory horse head handled stick, with silver collar and ebony shaft, c1890.
£400-500 *MG*

A Japanese ivory handled stick, inlaid with shibayama, silver collar and ebonised shaft, signed, late 19thC.
£520-550 *MG*

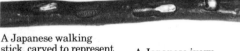

A Japanese walking stick, carved to represent natural wood, inset with 2 climbing snakes and an ivory skull, c1880.
£370-400 *MG*

A Japanese ivory handled stick with ebony shaft, c1890.
£480-500 *MG*

A carved ivory parrot handled stick, on an ebonised shaft, c1870.
£270-300 *MG*

A marine ivory head of a Maori warrior, with sulphur glass eyes, hardwood shaft, late 19thC.
£550-600 *MG*

A Victorian carved ivory dog's head stick, with silver collar, presentation inscription and dated 1883.
£275-300 *MG*

Gold Handled

An American presentation gold plated handle cane, with ebony shaft, dated 1884.
£400-450 *MG*

A French cane with gold handle, deeply chased, Paris hallmark, c1840.
£1,200-1,500 *MG*

Ladies Canes

A hardwood ball handled cane, inlaid with silver, with twisted ebonised shaft, c1870.
£125-150 *MG*

A crystal ball handled ladies cane, with gilt collar, on partridge wood shaft, c1880.
£120-150 *MG*

A cloisonné and silver cane, with ebonised shaft, c1900.
£190-220 *MG*

Whale Bone

A narwhal walking stick, with natural twist, wooden handle, c1840.
£950-1,000 *MG*

A whale bone walking stick, carved with barley twist, c1840.
£850-1,000 *MG*

A Victorian silver hare's head handled cane, London hallmark, 1884.
£600-650 *MG*

A Victorian malacca cane, engraved with owner's name, c1870.
£125-150 *MG*

Silver Topped

Miscellaneous

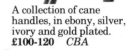

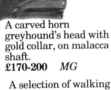

A silver plated spurred boot, on partridge wood shaft, c1840.
£120-150 *MG*

A pewter dog's head handled cane, with ebonised shaft, engraved with owner's name, c1870.
£120-150 *MG*

A collection of cane handles, in ebony, silver, ivory and gold plated.
£100-120 *CBA*

An Art Nouveau silver handled gentleman's cane, with rosewood shaft, French hallmark, c1880.
£220-250 *MG*

A carved horn greyhound's head with gold collar, on malacca shaft.
£170-200 *MG*

A silver topped malacca cane, English, late 19thC.
£60-80 *MG*

A selection of walking sticks.
£8-25 each *AL*

Carved Wooden Sticks

A carved wooden goose head walking stick, with glass eyes, c1870.
£150-170 *MG*

A carved wood hand holding a ball, c1870.
£160-200 *MG*

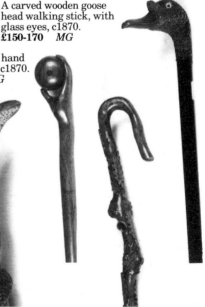

A heavy hardwood country walking stick, carved with natural pattern, c1840.
£160-200 *MG*

A German WWI walking stick, with monkey's head handle.
£110-140 *MG*

A carved and painted duck's head handle, on carved hardwood shaft, c1920.
£90-120 *MG*

A Victorian carved wood dog's head with leather collar, on stepped malacca shaft, c1860.
£125-150 *MG*

A malacca cane with carved and painted cobra twisted around entire length, c1850.
£300-350 *MG*

A country walking stick, carved with animal heads and acorns, mid-19thC.
£180-200 *MG*

Watches

A Swiss nickel keyless lever watch, signed for J.C. Vickery, 13.5cm diam, in leather and silver mounted case.
£350-400 *P*

A gold pair cased verge watch, signed Wm. Plumley, Ludgate Hill, 5215, with signed and numbered cap, the inner case marked London 1769, 5cm diam.
£950-1,000 *P*

A Swiss silver Masonic watch, 5.8cm high.
£750-850 *P*

A gold verge watch, 18thC, 4.2cm diam.
£700-750 *P*

A Swiss gold and enamel cylinder watch, the gilt bar movement signed Grohe Geneve, with enamel dial, the cuvette signed and numbered 6186, 3.6cm diam.
£200-300 *P*

A gilt metal hunter cased verge watch, for the Turkish market, the movement with pierced cock numbered 6157, the enamel dial signed Ralph Gout, London, 4.9cm diam, with gilt metal chatelaine.
£260-300 *P*

A Swiss silver and banded agate chatelaine watch, the cylinder movement with black dial, 7in (17.5cm) long.
£250-300 *P*

A French gold and enamel form watch, decorated in enamel, damaged, early 19thC, with gold chain.
£600-700 *P*

A silver pair cased verge pocket watch, the engraved cock signed Geo. Hewitt, Marlboro, 18thC, 5cm diam.
£250-300 *CSK*

An 18ct gold hunter cased keyless lever watch, signed F. Duffner, London 1922, Class A Kew Certificate, the case marked London 1921, 5.4cm diam.
£800-900 *P*

A silver pair cased repousse verge pocket watch, signed Jno. Wilders.
£300-350 *CSK*

An Astro-Navigator's watch set, signed J. W. Benson, London, 5.1cm diam each, in pig skin case.
£330-350 *CSK*

A gilt repoussé verge pocket watch, with chatelaine, signed Al. Foisseau, London, 18thC, 5cm diam.
£500-600 *CSK*

An 18ct gold minute repeating full calendar and moonphase chronograph pocket watch, in plain hunter case, 5.5cm diam.
£2,000-3,000 *CSK*

An 18ct gold hunter pocket watch, signed Willm. Best, 16B Wimpole Street, Cavendish Square, London, 4.6cm diam.
£400-450 *CSK*

A silver pair cased Freemason's verge pocket watch, signed Thos. Lees, Bury, enamel dial cracked, 5.4cm diam.
£150-200 *CSK*

A stainless steel open-faced 24 hour deck watch, signed Longines Watch Company, 21 jewels, adjusted to temperature and 5 positions, numbered 6018973, 5.3cm diam.
£400-450 *CSK*

A Continental verge calendar movement.
£250-300 *CSK*

An 18ct gold open-faced pocket watch, signed James Whitelaw, Edinburgh, 5cm diam.
£400-450 *CSK*

A silver pair cased verge pocket watch, signed Marc Grangier, London, late 17thC, 5cm diam.
£900-1,000 *CSK*

A Continental silver pair cased pocket watch, signed Cabrier, London.
£500-600 *CSK*

Wristwatches

A gentleman's steel wristwatch, by Pierce, 3.2cm diam.
£160-200 *P*

An American gold gentleman's wristwatch, by Bulova, 3.8cm long.
£260-300 *P*

A gold Longines chronograph wristwatch, with presentation case, with inscription, c1928, 3.3cm diam.
£1,600-1,800 *CSK*

A White metal buckle clasp containing a watch, inscribed Tavannes and Hermes.
£250-350 *CSK*

A gentleman's steel and gilt metal wristwatch, by Baume & Mercier, 3.3cm diam.
£400-450 *P*

A Swiss two colour gold gentleman's wristwatch, by Supra, 2.7cm diam.
£180-200 *P*

An 18ct gold Cartier wristwatch, numbered 780911134, with cabochon winder.
£1,400-1,600 *CSK*

A stainless steel Jaeger-le Coultre Memovax alarm wristwatch, 3.4cm diam.
£200-250 *CSK*

A Swiss gold gentleman's wristwatch, the movement stamped D.R.P., signed Tiffany & Co., 4cm long.
£650-750 *P*

A Swiss gold gentleman's wristwatch, by Vacheron and Constantin, 2.8cm diam.
£1,600-1,800 *P*

A Swiss gold gentleman's wristwatch, by Movado, 3.6cm diam.
£300-350 *P*

A Swiss gold ladies wristwatch, by Rolex, 2.7cm diam.
£280-300 *P*

DID YOU KNOW?
Miller's Collectables Price Guide is designed to build up, year by year, into the most comprehensive reference system available.

A Swiss gold Rolex
Prince wristwatch,
4.2cm long.
£2,000-2,500 *P*

An 18ct gold wristwatch,
the movement signed
Russells Limited, and
numbered 263656, the
case marked London
1926, 3.3cm diam.
£280-300 *P*

An 18ct gold gentleman's
wristwatch, by J. W.
Benson, London, the
movement signed and
numbered F4331, the
case marked London
1916, 3.4cm diam.
£420-480 *P*

A steel and enamel ladies
digital wristwatch,
3.4cm.
£50-60 *P*

A Swiss two colour gold
Rolex Prince wristwatch,
the signed movement
numbered 8103, 4.3cm
long, with original
presentation case, with
rating certificate dated
26th June, 1930.
£2,500-3,000 *P*

A steel oyster perpetual
bubble back gentleman's
wristwatch, by Rolex,
marked Serpico Y Laino,
on steel bracelet.
£400-450 *P*

A Swiss gold gentleman's
wristwatch, by Longines,
the signed movement
numbered 5154538, the
signed dial marked for
Alex Scott, Glasgow,
3.1cm long.
£340-380 *P*

A stainless steel Zenith
El Primero automatic
chronograph wristwatch.
£350-400 *CSK*

A stainless steel
Breitling chronograph
wristwatch, the signed
movement jewelled to
the centre with 17 jewels.
£200-250 *CSK*

A Swiss gold gentleman's
wristwatch, by Patek
Philippe, numbered
923149, 3.4cm diam.
£1,400-1,600 *P*

A stainless steel Rolex
wristwatch, 'Railway'
model, numbered 018118
1862, the signed
movement further
inscribed Extra Prima
Observatory, with 17
jewels and numbered
79974.
£1,100-1,300 *CSK*

A Swiss gold ladies
wristwatch, by Cartier,
2.4cm diam, with box.
£460-500 *P*

A gold wristwatch, signed Longines Galli, Zurich.
£350-400 *CSK*

A Dunhill wristwatch.
£250-300 *CSK*

An 18ct gold automatic wristwatch, signed Baume and Mercier, Geneve.
£800-900 *CSK*

A gentleman's wristwatch, in heavy yellow metal case, inscribed Audemars Piguet and Co., Geneve, Super, numbered 45731, 3.4cm diam.
£400-450 *CSK*

An 19ct gold chronograph wristwatch, signed Universal, Geneve, 3.3cm diam.
£600-650 *CSK*

A stainless steel calendar and moon phase wristwatch, inscribed Universal Geneve, 3.4cm diam.
£275-300 *CSK*

A stainless steel Breitling Navitimer, 4cm diam.
£300-350 *CSK*

A stainless steel Rolex Oyster Perpetual Turn-o-Graph wristwatch, 3.4cm diam.
£200-250 *CSK*

A World War II German pilot's wristwatch, signed Laco, numbered 13652, 5.5cm diam.
£400-450 *CSK*

A silver cased watch.
£400-450 *CSK*

An 18ct gold wristwatch, signed Van Cleef & Arpels, the movement signed Piaget, 3.3cm.
£550-650 *CSK*

An automatic Masonic wristwatch.
£400-450 *CSK*

A Swiss gold gentleman's wristwatch, by Rolex, enamel dial damaged, 3.6cm diam.
£250-300 *P*

Watchstands

19thC watchstand.
£75-125   *P*

An Anglo-Indian ivory
watchstand, 19thC, 11in
(28cm) high.
£150-200   *P*

An Indian ebony watch
and inkstand, 8in
(20.5cm) high.
£110-120   *P*

A rosewood watchstand
and miniature sewing
box, with thimble stand
and pin cushion, 19thC,
7in (18cm) high.
£220-250   *P*

Whistles

North Eastern Railway
wooden guard's whistles.
£12-15 each   *ONS*

Ivory watchstand ,
19thC.
£140-180   *P*

A selection of whistles,
including 'The ACME'.
£3-6 each   *AL*

Brass whistles.
£5-8 each   *AL*

A Metropolitan Police
whistle, No. 020082.
£5-8   *AL*

Cross Reference
Walking Sticks
Railways
Police

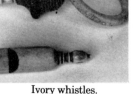

Ivory whistles.
Top. **£30-35**
Bottom. **£20-25**   *AL*

Writing Accessories

Pens

A 1940s fountain pen.
£130-150 *JAS*

A Parker Vacuumatic
pen, c1940.
£110-150 *JAS*

A Conway Stewart pen
and pencil set, in original
box.
£12-15 *ZIG*

A Parker fountain pen,
c1935.
£140-160 *JAS*

A Swan pen, c1931.
£110-120 *JAS*

A Conway Stewart
fountain pen, c1938.
£75-85 *JAS*

A Parker Lucky Curve
vest pen, c1924.
£140-160 *JAS*

A Croxley pen, c1940.
£65-85 *JAS*

A collection of mother-of-
pearl, ivory, bone, silver,
ebony and quill pens and
pen holders.
£5-10 *Bon*

A Parker Duofold Special
Lucky Curve pen, c1927.
£230-250 *JAS*

A Conway Stewart
Dinkie vest pen, c1924.
£65-75 *JAS*

A Conway Stewart
Dinkie, c1935.
£65-85 *JAS*

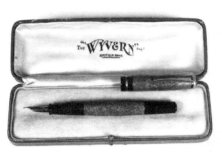

A Wyvern pigskin
covered fountain pen, as
used by the Royal Family
during the 1940s.
£110-120   *JAS*

*Wyvern also used lizard
and crocodile on their
pens.*

A Parker pen with 12ct
rolled gold cap, c1948.
£140-160   *JAS*

An Irish bog oak pen.
£40-50   *JAS*

A rolled gold Parker 61,
c1956, with original box.
£165-185   *JAS*

Dip pens.
£30-40 each   *JAS*

A fountain pen with 18ct
rolled gold case, c1933.
£150-200   *JAS*

A Waterman pen, c1936.
£65-85   *JAS*

Pencils

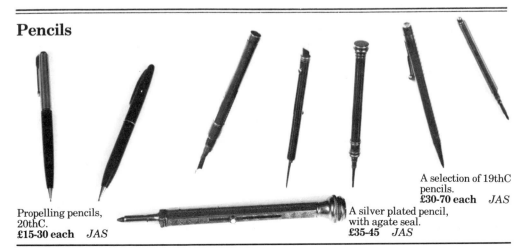

A selection of 19thC
pencils.
£30-70 each   *JAS*

Propelling pencils,
20thC.
£15-30 each   *JAS*

A silver plated pencil,
with agate seal.
£35-45   *JAS*

Pen Holders

A Cricketers brass pen tray.
£25-35 *JAS*

An Art Deco green glass pen holder.
£15-20 *CBA*

A plated pen rack.
£35-45 *JAS*

A lacquer pen tray.
£20-30 *JAS*

A papier mâché pen rack.
£55-65 *JAS*

A lacquer pen tray, c1873, 10in (25.5cm) long.
£50-60 *JAS*

A Victorian cast iron pen rack.
£30-40 *JAS*

A Victorian brass pen rack.
£45-55 *JAS*

A chrome pen holder, c1935.
£45-55 *DEC*

A desk set, c1931.
£130-150 *JAS*

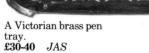

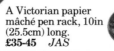

A Victorian brass pen tray.
£30-40 *JAS*

A Victorian papier mâché pen rack, 10in (25.5cm) long.
£35-45 *JAS*

Inkwells

An Austrian bear inkwell, c1870.
£60-80 *JAS*

A Victorian silver plated inkstand, 3in (7.5cm) square.
£75-85 *JAS*

A Florentine inkwell, marked, 5½in (14cm) high.
£75-85 *CBA*

An Italian inkwell, 19thC, 8in (20cm) high.
£150-180 *CBA*

A hobnail ink pot, 4in (10cm) high.
£175-200 *JAS*

A Royal Crown Derby blue and white inkwell, c1890, 2½in (6cm) high.
£40-50 *CBA*

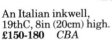

An early Victorian glass ink pot, with brass lid.
£55-65 *JAS*

A pair of Georgian inkwells, with seals inside caps.
£55-65 *JAS*

A German inkwell with copper lid, 19thC.
£85-95 *JAS*

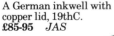

A Victorian Sheffield plate inkwell from a travelling case.
£65-75 *JAS*

An ink bottle, damaged, c1880, 2½in (6cm) high.
£25-35 *JAS*

A late Victorian silver inkwell, London 1902.
£85-95 *JAS*

Letter Holders

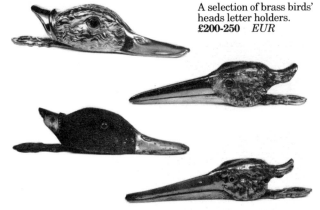

A selection of brass birds' heads letter holders.
£200-250   *EUR*

A paper holder with initials TA.
£7-10   *VB*

Cross Reference
Treen

Paper Knives

Paper knives.
£3-7   *VB*

Top. A Sheffield silver paper knife, c1928.
£40-50
Centre. An ivory and silver paper knife, Birmingham c1903.
£65-75
Bottom. A silver paper knife, Birmingham 1891.
£50-60   *JAS*

A Victorian Tartan ware paper knife.
£30-40   *JAS*

Paper Knives, top Mauchline ware.
£10-12
Centre: rosewood.
£5-8
Bottom: crested.
£4-6   *VB*

Book marks and letter openers.
£4-20 each   *VB*

A Victorian ivory paper knife and a silver and tortoiseshell paper knife.
£30-70 each   *JAS*

Blotters

A plated blotter.
£35-45 *JAS*

An Art Deco chrome
blotter, 5½in (14cm).
£20-30 *DEC*

A Victorian
brass blotter,
c1890.
£50-60 *JAS*

A silver blotter,
Birmingham c1911.
£140-160 *JAS*

Seals

A six scene brass cube
seal.
£14-16 *VB*

A blue agate seal set,
with silver trim.
£90-120 *JAS*

Bakelite and wooden
seals.
£4-8 each *VB*

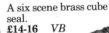

A mahogany pencil/ruler
with seal, 12½in (32cm).
£20-30 *AL*

A 19thC seal.
£20-30 *PC*

Brass seals.
£8-10 *VB*

A selection of agate,
mother-of-pearl, bone
and bloodstone seals.
£2-12 *VB*

A rotating bloodstone
and agate seal.
£18-20 *VB*

A seal in the form of a
cupid balanced on a hoop,
the base with the name
Alice, early 20thC.
£120-150 *WIL*

General

A Persian pencil box,
early 19thC.
£90-120 *JAS*

A silver nib brush,
Birmingham 1913.
£40-50 *JAS*

A letter rack, paper knife
and letter holder.
£6-16 *AL*

A Victorian 1887 Jubilee
book mark.
£20-30 *MB*

A brass bound oak pen
box, with swivel lid, 11in
(28cm) wide.
£175-200 *MB*

A Victorian brass shop
bell.
£55-65 *JAS*

A Victorian embosser.
£25-30 *MB*

A pen knife in the shape
of a shoe.
£5-10 *VB*

Gold leaf holders.
£16-18 *VB*

Brass handled scissors,
early 19thC.
£60-80 *JAS*

Ladies gilded steel
straight edges, one
inscribed Helena
Steelchiors 1824, 11in
(28cm) long.
£90-120 *CSK*

Cross Reference
Boxes

An Art Deco desk set,
c1930, 9in (23cm).
£75-100 *CBA*

A Victorian coromandel
and brass desk blotter,
11½ by 8in (29 by 20cm).
£60-80 *MB*

DIRECTORY OF SPECIALISTS

This directory is in no way complete. If you wish to be included in next year's directory or if you have a change of address or telephone number, please could you inform us by December 31st 1989. Entries will be repeated in subsequent editions unless we are requested otherwise. Finally we would advise readers to make contact by telephone before a visit, therefore avoiding a wasted journey, which nowadays is both time consuming and expensive.

AUCTIONEERS SPECIALISING IN COLLECTABLES

London

Bonhams at Chelsea,
65/69 Lots Road, London, SW10
Tel: 01-351 7111

Christie's South Kensington
Ltd, 85 Old Brompton Road,
London, SW7
Tel: 01-581 7611

Onslow Auctioneers,
Metro Store, Townmead Road,
London, SW6
Tel: 01-793 0240

Phillips,
10 Salem Road, London, W2
Tel: 01-229 9090

Avon

Taviner's Auction Rooms,
Prewett Street, Redcliffe, Bristol
Tel: (0272) 265996

Dorset

Garnet Langton Auctions,
Burlington Arcade,
Bournemouth
Tel: (0202) 22352

Gloucestershire

Specialised Postcard Auctions,
25 Gloucester Street,
Cirencester
Tel: (0285) 659057

Norfolk

Glennies,
Wensum Hall, Wensum Street,
Norwich
Tel: (0603) 633558

James,
33 Timberhill, Norwich
Tel: (0603) 624817/625369

Nottingham

Neales,
192 Mansfield Road,
Nottingham
Tel: (0602) 624141

East Sussex

Wallis & Wallis,
West Street Auction Galleries,
Lewes
Tel: (0273) 473137

DEALERS SPECIALISING IN COLLECTABLES

AERONAUTICA

London

Alfie's Antique Market,
13-25 Church Street, London,
NW8
Tel: 01-723 6066

Hampshire

Cobwebs,
78 Northam Road, Southampton
Tel: (0703) 227458

AUTOMOBILIA

London

Grays Antique Market,
AAA Stand 121, 58 Davies
Street, London, W1
Tel: 01-629 7034

Sarah Baddiel,
S.12 Grays Mews, London, W1
Tel: 01-408 1239/01-452 7243

Brian R. Verrall & Co,
20 Tooting Bec Road, London,
SW17
Tel: 01-672 1144

Kent

Falstaff Antiques Motor
Museum,
63-67 High Street, Rolvenden,
Nr Cranbrook
Tel: (0580) 241234

Hampshire

Cobwebs,
78 Northam Road, Southampton
Tel: (0703) 227458

Lincs.

The Complete Automobilist
Dept 1, The Old Rectory,
Greatford, Nr Stamford
Tel: (077 836) 312

S. Yorkshire

Bardwell Antiques,
919 Abbeydale Road, Sheffield
Tel: (0742) 584669

BAROMETERS

London

Patrick Capon,
350 Upper Street, Islington,
London, N1
Tel: 01-354 0487/01-467 5722

Avon

Barometer Shop,
3 Lower Park Row, Bristol
Tel: (0272) 272565

Cheshire

Derek Rayment Antiques,
Orchard House, Barton Road,
Barton, Nr Malpas
Tel: (0829) 270429

Essex

It's About Time,
863 London Road,
Westcliff-on-Sea
Tel: (0702) 72574

Hereford & Worcs

Barometer Shop,
New Street, Leominster
Tel: (0568) 3652

Somerset

Bernard G. House
(Mitre Antiques),
Market Place, Wells
Tel: (0749) 72607

BOTTLES

London

Rob Gee,
Flea Market, Camden Passage,
London, N1
Tel: 01-226 6627

Georgian Village – 1st Floor,
Islington Green, London, N1
Tel: 01-226 1571/5393

Isle of Wight

Kollectarama,
Old Railway Station,
Horringford, Arreton
Tel: (0983) 865306

BOXES

London

Barham Antiques,
83 Portobello Road, London,
W11
Tel: 01-727 3845

Berks

Boxes From Derek McIntosh,
10 Wickham Road, Stockcross,
Newbury
Tel: (0488) 38295

Mostly Boxes,
92 & 52B High Street, Eton,
Windsor
Tel: (0753) 858470

Yorkshire

Danby Antiques,
65 Heworth Road, York
Tel: (0904) 415280

BUCKLES

London

Moderne,
Stand 5, Georgian Village,
Camden Passage, N1

Monica Jaertelius, The Mall,
Camden Passage, N1
Tel: 01-546 2807

Ziggurat,
Stand J.22, Grays Mews,
1-7 Davies Mews, W1
Tel: 01-630 7943

Avon

Jessie's Button Box,
Great Western Antique Centre,
Bartlett Street, Bath
Tel: (0272) 299065

BUTTONS

London

The Button Queen,
19 Marylebone Lane, W1
Tel: 01-935 1505

Avon

Jessie's Button Box,
Great Western Antique Centre,
Bartlett Street, Bath
Tel: (0272) 299065

BUTTON HOOKS

London

David Hogg,
S.141 Grays Antique Market,
58 Davies Street, W1
Tel: 01-493 0208

Noelle Antiques,
S.26 Chelsea Antiques Market,
253 Kings Road, SW3
Tel: 01-352 5581

Kent
The Variety Box,
16 Chapel Place, Tunbridge
Wells
Tel: (0892) 31868/21589

N. Wales
Paul Gibbs,
25 Castle Street, Conwy
Tel: (0492) 593429

CAMERAS
London
Jessops,
65 Great Russell Street, WC1
Tel: 01-831 3640

Vintage Cameras Ltd,
254 & 256 Kirkdale, Sydenham,
SE26
Tel: 01-778 5416/5841

Herts
P. Coombs,
87 Gills Hill Lane, Radlett
Tel: (0923) 856949

CARD CASES
London
Eureka Antiques,
105 Portobello Road, W11
(Saturdays)

Grays Antique Market,
58 Davies Street, W1
Tel: 01-629 7034

Avon
Carr Linford,
10-11 Walcot Buildings, London
Road, Bath
Tel: (0225) 317516

Cheshire
Eureka Antiques,
18 Northenden Road, Sale
Tel: (061 962) 5629

Shropshire
F. C. Manser & Son Ltd,
53 Wyle Cop, Shrewsbury
Tel: (0743) 51120

CERAMICS
ART DECO
London
Beverley,
30 Church Street, Marylebone,
NW8
Tel: 01-262 1576

Monty & Anita,
Stand V14-V15 Antiquarius,
135-141 Kings Road, SW3
Tel: 01-351 5382

Jane & Bjarne Olsen
(Maling Ware),
Alfie's Antique Market, T103 &
T104, 13-25 Church Street, NW8
Tel: 01-706 2969/01-870 7905

A.J. Partners (Shelley),
M12 Antiquarius,
135-141 Kings Road, SW3
Tel: 01-376 3772

Past & Present,
York Arcade, Unit 5, Camden
Passage, N1
Tel: 01-833 2640

Patrician Antiques,
1st Floor Georgian Village,
Camden Passage, N1
Tel: 01-359 4560/01-435 3159

Van Den Bosch,
1st Floor Georgian Village,
Camden Passage, N1
Tel: 01-359 4560/01-398 5410

Essex
A. Waine,
Tweedale, Rye Mill Lane,
Feering, Colchester

Lancs
A.S. Antiques,
26 Broad Street, Pendleton,
Salford
Tel: 061-737 5938

Shropshire
Expressions,
17 Princess Street, Shrewsbury
Tel: (0743) 51731

Wales
Paul Gibbs Antiques,
25 Castle Street, Conwy
Tel: (0492) 593429

Warks
Castle Antiques,
1 Mill Street, Warwick
Tel: (0926) 498068

E. Yorks
Tim Barnett,
Carlton Gallery, 60A Middle
Street, Driffield
Tel: (0482) 443954

W. Yorks
Muir Hewitt,
Halifax Antiques Centre,
Queens Road/Gibbet Street,
Halifax
Tel: (0442) 66657/366657

DOULTON
London
Britannia,
Stand 101, Grays Antique
Market, 58 Davies Street, W1
Tel: 01-629 6772

The Collector,
Alfie's Antique Market,
13-25 Church Street, NW8
Tel: 01-883 0024/01-706 4586

Doug Pinchin,
Dixons Antique Centre,
471 Upper Richmond Road
West, East Sheen, SW14
Tel: 01-878 6788/01-948 1029

Leicester
Janice Williamson,
9 Coverdale Road, Meadows
Wiston, Leicester
Tel: (0533) 812926

COMMEMORATIVE
London
Britannia,
Stand 101, Grays Antique
Market, 58 Davies Street, W1
Tel: 01-629 6772

British Commemoratives,
1st Floor, Georgian Village,
Camden Passage, N1
Tel: 01-359 4560

East Sussex
Leonard Russell,
21 Kings Avenue, Mount
Pleasant, Newhaven
Tel: (0273) 515153

GOSS & CRESTED
CHINA
London
British Commemoratives,
1st Floor, Georgian Village,
Camden Passage, N1
Tel: 01-359 4560

Hants
Goss & Crested China Ltd,
62 Murray Road, Horndean
Tel: (0705) 597440

Kent
The Variety Box,
16 Chapel Place, Tunbridge
Wells
Tel: (0892) 31868/21589

E. Yorks
The Crested China Company,
Station House, Driffield
Tel: (0377) 47042

STAFFORDSHIRE
London
Gerald Clark Antiques,
1 High Street, Mill Hill Village,
NW7
Tel: 01-906 0342

Jacqueline Oosthuizen,
1st Floor, Georgian Village,
Camden Passage, N1
Tel: 01-226 5393/01-359 4560
and
Chelsea Antique Market,
Unit 30, 253 Kings Road, SW3
Tel: 01-352 6071/5581

Jonathan Horne,
66B & C Kensington Church
Street, W8
Tel: 01-221 5658

Kent
Dunsdale Lodge Antiques,
Westerham
Tel: (0959) 62160

Suffolk
Crafers Antiques,
The Hill, Wickham Market
Tel: (0728) 747347

W. Midlands
Ray & Diane Ginns,
39 Norman Road, Northfield,
Birmingham
Tel: 021-476 8319

Wiltshire
Bratton Antiques,
Market Place, Westbury
Tel: (0373) 823021

TORQUAY
POTTERY
London
Jacqueline Oosthuizen,
1st Floor, Georgian Village,
Camden Passage, N1
Tel: 01-226 5393/01-359 4560
and
Chelsea Antique Market,
Unit 30, 253 Kings Road, SW3
Tel: 01-352 6071/5581

POT LIDS
London
Rob Gee,
Flea Market, Camden Passage,
N1
Tel: 01-226 6627

E. Sussex
Ron Beech,
150 Portland Road, Hove
Tel: (0273) 724477

SPONGEWARE
London
Robert Young Antiques,
68 Battersea Bridge Road, SW11
Tel: 01-228 7847

Avon
Robert Pugh,
13 Walcot Buildings, London
Road, Bath
Tel: (0554) 772613

Kent
Angela Page Antiques,
Tunbridge Wells
Tel: (0892) 22217

CORKSCREWS
London
David,
141 Grays Antique Market,
Davies Street, W1
Tel: 01-493 0208

Beds
Christopher Sykes Antiques,
The Old Parsonage, Woburn
Tel: (0525) 290259

Cumbria
Bacchus Antiques,
Longlands at Cartmel
Tel: (044 854) 475

E. Sussex

Chateaubriand Antiques Centre,
High Street, Burwash
Tel: (0435) 882535

DOLLS

London

Antique Dolls,
Stand L14 Grays Mews,
1-7 Davies Mews, W1
Tel: 01-370 2043

Pat Walker,
Georgian Village, Camden Passage, N1
Tel: 01-359 4560/01-435 3159

Yesterday Child,
24 The Mall, Camden Passage, N1
Tel: 01-354 1601/(0908) 583403

Cheshire

Dollectable,
53 Lower Bridge Street, Chester
Tel: (0244) 44888/679195

Glos

Lillian Middleton's Antique Dolls Shop,
Days Stable, Sheep Street, Stow-on-the-Wold
Tel: (0451) 31542

Hants

Toys Through Time,
Fareham
Tel: (0329) 288678

Kent

Hadlow Antiques,
No. 1 The Pantiles, Tunbridge Wells
Tel: (0892) 29858

Surrey

Victoriana Dolls,
Reigate
Tel: (0737) 249525

E. Sussex

Dolls Hospital,
17 George Street, Hastings
Tel: (0424) 444117/422758

DOLLS HOUSE FURNITURE

Essex

Blackwells of Hawkwell,
733 London Road,
Westcliff-on-Sea
Tel: (0702) 72248

COCKTAIL/ DRINKING

London

Beverley,
30 Church Street, Marylebone, NW8
Tel: 01-262 1576

EPHEMERA

CIGARETTE CARDS

London

Murray Cards (International) Ltd,
51 Watford Way, Hendon Central, NW4
Tel: 01-202 5688

Avon

Winstone Stamp Company,
S.82 Great Western Antiques Centre, Bartlett Street, Bath
Tel: (0225) 310388

Middlesex

Albert's Cigarette Card Specialists,
113 London Road, Twickenham
Tel: 01-891 3067

Somerset

The London Cigarette Card Co Ltd,
Sutton Road, Somerton
Tel: (0458) 73452

Suffolk

W. L. Hoad,
9 St Peter's Road, Kirkley, Lowestoft
Tel: (0502) 587758

COMICS

London

Forbidden Planet,
71 New Oxford Street, W1
Tel: 01-379 6042

Gosh Comics,
39 Great Russell Street, WC1
Tel: 01-636 1011

Heroes,
21 Canonbury Lane, Islington, N1
Tel: 01-359 8329

Somerset

Yesterday's Paper,
40 South View, Holcombe Rogus, Wellington
Tel: (0823) 672774

GREETINGS CARDS

London

Images (Peter Stockham),
16 Cecil Court, Charing Cross Road, WC2
Tel: 01-836 8661

Pleasures of Past Times,
11 Cecil Court, Charing Cross Road, WC2
Tel: 01-836 1142

MATCHBOXES

Kent

Kollectomania,
4 Catherine Street, Rochester
Tel: (0634) 45099

POSTCARDS

London

Memories,
18 Bell Lane, Hendon, NW4
Tel: 01-203 1772/01-202 9080

Cheshire

Avalon,
1 City Walls, Northgate Street, Chester
Tel: (0244) 318406

Essex

R.F. Postcards,
17 Hilary Crescent, Rayleigh
Tel: (0268) 743222

Kent

Mike Sturge,
39 Union Street, Maidstone
Tel: (0622) 54702

Norfolk

Bluebird Arts,
1 Mount Street, Cromer
Tel: (0263) 512384/78487

E. Sussex

John & Mary Bartholomew,
The Mint Arcade, 71 The Mint, Rye
Tel: (0797) 225952

W. Sussex

Bygones, Collectors Shop,
123 South Street, Lancing
Tel: (0903) 750051/763470

BEER MATS

W. Midlands

Roger Summers,
92 Nursery Road, Edgbaston, Birmingham

PLAYING CARDS

London

Intercol (Yasha Beresiner),
1A Camden Walk, Islington Green, N1
Tel: 01-354 2599

SCRIPOPHILY

Essex

G.K.R. Bonds Ltd.,
PO Box 1, Kelvedon
Tel: (0376) 71138

FANS

Kent

The Variety Box,
16 Chapel Place, Tunbridge Wells
Tel: (0892) 31868/21589

Shropshire

F. C. Manser & Son Ltd,
53-54 Wyle Cop, Shrewsbury
Tel: (0743) 51120

FISHING

Shropshire

Vintage Fishing Tackle Shop and Angling Art Gallery,
103 Longden Coleham, Shrewsbury
Tel: (0743) 69373

Scotland

Jamie Maxtone Graham,
Lyne Haugh, Lyne Station, Peebles
Tel: (072 14) 304

Jess Miller,
PO Box 1, Birnam, Dunkeld, Perthshire
Tel: (03502) 522

GOLFING

London

Sarah Baddiel,
The Book Gallery, B.12 Grays Mews, 1-7 Davies Mews, W1
Tel: 01-408 1239/01-452 7243

King & Country,
Unit 46, Alfie's Antique Market, 13-25 Church Street, NW8
Tel: 01-724 3439

GLASS – EARLY 18thC/19thC

London

Christine Bridge,
78 Castelnau, SW13
Tel: 01-741 5501

Pryce & Brise,
79 Moore Park Road, Fulham, SW6
Tel: 01-736 1864

Mark J. West – Cobb Antiques,
39B High Street, Wimbledon Village, SW19
Tel: 01-946 2811/01-540 7982

Avon

Somervale Antiques,
6 Radstock Road, Midsomer Norton, Bath
Tel: (0761) 412686

Kent

Variety Box,
16 Chapel Place, Tunbridge Wells
Tel: (0892) 31868/21589

Warwickshire

Sharon Ball,
Stratford-on-Avon Antique Centre, Ely Street, Stratford-on-Avon
Tel: (0789) 204180

GLASS – 20thC

London

Frank Andrews – Monart and Vasart,
Unit 21, 290 Westbourne Grove, W11
Tel: 01-881 0658

Beverley – Cloud Glass,
30 Church Street, NW8
Tel: 01-262 1576

The Scottish Connection,
Alfie's Antique Market,
13-25 Church Street, NW8
Tel: 01-723 6066

Stephen Watson – Powell,
Alfie's Antique Market,
13-25 Church Street, NW8
Tel: 01-723 0678

HAIRDRESSING/ HAT PINS
London
Ursula,
P16, 15 & 14 Antiquarius,
135 Kings Road, SW3
Tel: 01-352 2203
Kent
The Lace Basket,
1A East Cross, Tenterden
Tel: (05806) 3923

Variety Box,
16 Chapel Place, Tunbridge
Wells
Tel: (0892) 31868/21589

INKWELLS
London
Jasmin Cameron,
Green & Stone, 259 Kings Road,
SW3
Tel: 01-352 0837/6521

David,
141 Grays Antique Market,
Davies Street, W1
Tel: 01-493 0208

Patrician,
1st Floor, Georgian Village,
Camden Passage, N1
Tel: 01-359 4560/01-435 3159
Berkshire
Mostly Boxes,
92 & 52B High Street, Eton,
Windsor
Tel: (0753) 858470
Kent
Ann Lingard,
Ropewalk Antiques, Rye
Tel: (0797) 223486

JEWELLERY

VICTORIAN/ EDWARDIAN
Glos
Lynn Greenwold,
Digbeth Street,
Stow-on-the-Wold
Tel: (0451) 30398
Kent
Old Saddlers Antiques,
Church Road, Goudhurst,
Cranbrook
Tel: (0580) 211458

Norfolk
Peter Howkins,
39, 40 and 135 King Street,
Great Yarmouth
Tel: (0493) 844639

ART DECO
London
Pierre De Fresne 'Beaux Bijoux',
Q 9/10 Antiquarius, 135 Kings
Road, SW3
Tel: 01-352 8882

Ziggurat,
J22 Grays Mews, 1-7 Davies
Mews, W1
Tel: 01-630 7943

KITCHENALIA
London
David,
141 Grays Antique Market,
Davies Street, W1
Tel: 01-493 0208
Kent
Penny Lampard,
28 High Street, Headcorn
Tel: (0622) 890682

Up Country,
Old Corn Stores, 68 St John's
Road, Tunbridge Wells
Tel: (0892) 23341
Lancs
Kitchenalia
(Prop. Susan Cook),
89 Berry Lane, Longridge
Tel: (077 478) 5411
Surrey
Wych House Antiques,
Wych Hill, Woking
Tel: (04862) 64636
E. Sussex
Ann Lingard,
Rope Walk Antiques, Rye
Tel: (0797) 223486

LUGGAGE
London
Stanhope Bowery,
Grays Antique Market, Davies
Street, W1
Tel: 01-629 6194

MILITARIA
MEDALS
Hants
Charles Antiques,
101 The Hundred, Romsey
Tel: (0794) 512885
E. Sussex
Wallis & Wallis,
West Street Auction Galleries,
Lewes
Tel: (0273) 480208

ARMS & ARMOUR
London
Michael German,
38B Kensington Church Street,
W8
Tel: 01-937 2771

E. Sussex
George Weiner,
2 Market Street, The Lanes,
Brighton
Tel: (0273) 729948

W. Yorks
Andrew Spencer Bottomley,
The Coach House,
Thongsbridge, Holmfirth
Tel: (0484) 685234

ARMS & MILITARIA
Surrey
West Street Antiques,
63 West Street, Dorking
Tel: (0306) 883487
E. Sussex
Wallis & Wallis,
West Street Auction Galleries,
Lewes
Tel: (0273) 480208

METALWARE
London
Christopher Bangs,
SW11
Tel: 01-223 5676

Jack Casimir Ltd,
The Brass Shop, 23 Pembridge
Road, W11
Tel: 01-727 8643
Avon
Nick Marchant,
13 Orwell Drive, Keynsham,
Bristol
Tel: (0272) 865182
Beds
Christopher Sykes,
The Old Parsonage, Woburn
Tel: (0525) 290259
Kent
Old Saddlers Antiques,
Church Road, Goudhurst,
Cranbrook
Tel: (0580) 211458
Oxfordshire
Key Antiques,
11 Horse Fair, Chipping Norton
Tel: (0608) 3777
ORIENTAL
London
Ormonde Gallery,
156 Portobello Road, W11
Tel: 01-229 9800/(042482) 226
Dorset
Lionel Geneen Ltd,
781 Christchurch Road,
Boscombe, Bournemouth
Tel: (0202) 422961
E. Sussex
Chateaubriand Antique Centre,
High Street, Burwash
Tel: (0435) 882535

PERFUME BOTTLES
London
Patrician Antiques,
1st Floor, Georgian Village,
Camden Passage, N1
Tel: 01-359 4560/01-435 3159

Trio (Theresa Clayton),
Grays Mews, 1-7 Davies Mews,
W1
Tel: 01-629 1184

Ziggurat,
J22, Grays Mews, 1-7 Davies
Mews, W1
Tel: 01-630 7943
Shropshire
F. C. Manser & Son Ltd,
53-54 Wyle Cop, Shrewsbury
Tel: (0743) 51129

POLICE MEMORABILIA
London
David,
141 Grays Antique Market,
Davies Street, W1
Tel: 01-493 0208
Dorset
Mervyn A. Mitton,
161 The Albany, Manor Road,
Bournemouth
Tel: (0202) 293767

RADIOS
London
The Originals,
Stand 37, Alfie's Antique
Market, 13-25 Church Street,
NW8
Tel: 01-724 3439
Hereford & Worcs
Radiocraft,
56 Main Street, Sedgeberrow,
Nr Evesham
Tel: (0386) 881988

SCIENTIFIC & MEDICAL INSTRUMENTS
London
David Weston Ltd,
44 Duke Street, St James's, SW1
Tel: 01-839 1051/2/3
Beds
Christopher Sykes,
The Old Parsonage, Woburn
Tel: (0525) 290259
Surrey
David Burn,
116 Chestnut Grove, New
Malden
Tel: 01-944 7356

SEWING

London
The Thimble Society of London,
The Bees, S134 Grays Antique
Market, 58 Davies Street, W1
Tel: 01-493 0560

Kent
The Variety Box,
16 Chapel Place, Tunbridge
Wells
Tel: (0892) 31868/21589

Suffolk
Crafers Antiques,
The Hill, Wickham Market
Tel: (0728) 747347

SHIPPING

Hants
Cobwebs,
78 Northam Road, Southampton
Tel: (0703) 227458

SILVER

London
Donohoe,
L25/7 M10/12 Grays Mews,
1-7 Davies Mews, W1
Tel: 01-629 5633/01-455 5507

Goldsmith & Perris,
Stand 327, Alfie's Antique
Market, 13-25 Church Street,
NW8
Tel: 01-724 7051

The London Silver Vaults,
Chancery House, 53-65
Chancery Lane, WC2
Tel: 01-242 3844

Kent
The Variety Box,
16 Chapel Place, Tunbridge
Wells
Tel: (0892) 31868/21589

Oxfordshire
Thames Gallery,
Thameside, Henley-on-Thames
Tel: (0491) 572449

Shropshire
F. C. Manser & Son Ltd,
53-54 Wyle Cop, Shrewsbury
Tel: (0743) 51120

TARTANWARE

London
Eureka Antiques,
Geoffrey Vanns Arcade,
105 Portobello Road, W11
(Saturdays)

Grays Antique Market,
58 Davies Street, W1
Tel: 01-629 7034

Cheshire
Eureka Antiques,
18 Northenden Road, Sale
Tel: 061-962 5629

TEXTILES
SAMPLERS

London
Sophia Blanchard,
Alfie's Antique Market, Church
Street, NW8
Tel: 01-723 5731

Matthew Adams Antiques,
69 Portobello Road, W11
Tel: 01-579 5560

QUILTS, PATCHWORK, COSTUME

London
The Antique Textile Company,
100 Portland Road, Holland
Park, W11
Tel: 01-221 7730

The Gallery of Antique Costume
& Textiles,
2 Church Street, Marylebone,
NW8
Tel: 01-723 9981

LINEN & LACE

London
Antiquarius,
135-141 Kings Road, SW3
Tel: 01-351 5353

Audrey Field,
Alfie's Antique Market,
13-25 Church Street, NW8
Tel: 01-723 6066

Kent
Antiques & Interiors,
22 Ashford Road, Tenterden
Tel: (05806) 5462

The Lace Basket,
1A East Cross, Tenterden
Tel: (05806) 3923

E. Sussex
Chateaubriand Antique Centre,
High Street, Burwash
Tel: (0435) 882535

TILES

E. Sussex
Ann Lingard,
Rope Walk Antiques, Rye
Tel: (0797) 223486

The Old Mint House,
Pevensey
Tel: (0323) 762337

Wales
Paul Gibbs Antiques,
25 Castle Street, Conwy
Tel: (0492) 593429

Victorian Fireplaces
(Simon Priestley),
Ground Floor, Cardiff Antique
Centre, 69/71 St Mary Street,
Cardiff
Tel: (0222) 30970/226049

TINS & METAL SIGNS

London
Keith, Old Advertising,
Unit 14, 155A Northcote Road,
Battersea, SW11
Tel: 01-228 0741/6850

Avon
Michael & Jo Saffell,
3 Walcot Buildings, London
Road, Bath
Tel: (0225) 315857

TOYS
MECHANICAL

London
Stuart Cropper,
Grays Mews, 1-7 Davies Mews,
W1
Tel: 01-629 7034

TEDDY BEARS

London
Pam Hebbs,
5 The Annexe, Camden
Passage, Islington, N1

DIECAST MODELS

London
Colin Baddiel,
Grays Mews, 1-7 Davies Mews,
W1
Tel: 01-408 1239/01-452 7243

Mint & Boxed,
110 High Street, Edgware,
Middx
Tel: 01-952 2002

Bucks
Cars Only,
4 Granville Square, Willen
Local Centre, Willen, Milton
Keynes
Tel: (0908) 690024

Norfolk
Trains & Olde Tyme Toys,
Aylsham Road, Norwich
Tel: (0603) 413585

Shropshire
Stretton Models,
12 Beaumont Road, Church
Stretton
Tel: (0694) 723737

W. Midlands
Moseley Railwayana Museum,
Birmingham
Tel: 021-449 9707

Wiltshire
David Wells,
Salisbury Antique & Collectors
Market, 37 Catherine Street,
Salisbury
Tel: (0425) 476899

Yorks
Andrew Clark,
42 Pollard Lane, Bradford
Tel: (0274) 636042

John & Simon Haley,
89 Northgate, Halifax
Tel: (0422) 822148

Wales
Corgi Toys Ltd,
Kingsway, Swansea Industrial
Estate, Swansea
Tel: (0792) 586223

GAMES

London
Donay,
35 Camden Passage, N1
Tel: 01-359 1880

TREEN

London
Simon Castle,
38B Kensington Church Street,
W8
Tel: 01-892 2840

Wynyards Antiques,
5 Ladbroke Road, W11
Tel: 01-221 7936

Bucks
A. & E. Foster,
Little Heysham, Forge Road,
Naphill
Tel: (024 024) 2024

TUNBRIDGEWARE

Berks
Mostly Boxes,
52B High Street, Eton
Tel: (0753) 858470

Kent
Strawsons Antiques,
33, 39 & 41 The Pantiles,
Tunbridge Wells
Tel: (0892) 30607

The Variety Box,
16 Chapel Place, Tunbridge
Wells
Tel: (0892) 31868/21589

E. Sussex
Barclay Antiques,
7 Village Mews, Little Common,
Bexhill-on-Sea
Tel: (0797) 222734

WALKING STICKS

London
Cekay Antiques,
Grays Antique Market,
58 Davies Street, W1
Tel: 01-629 5130

Michael German,
38B Kensington Church Street,
W8
Tel: 01-937 2771

WATCHES

London
City Clocks,
Lambs Passage, Chiswell
Street, EC1
Tel: 01-628 6749

Pieces of Time, Grays Mews,
1-7 Davies Street, W1
Tel: 01-629 2422

Philip Whyte,
32 Bury Street, St James's, SW1
Tel: 01-321 0353

DIRECTORY OF MARKETS & CENTRES

This directory is in no way complete. If you wish to be included in next year's directory or if you have a change of address or telephone number, please could you inform us by December 31st 1989. Entries will be repeated in subsequent editions unless we are requested otherwise.

London

Alfies Antique Market,
13-25 Church Street, NW8
Tel: 01-723 6066
Tues-Sat 10-6pm

Angel Arcade,
116-118 Islington High Street,
Camden Passage, N1
Open Wed & Sat

Antiquarius Antique Market,
135/141 Kings Road, Chelsea, SW3
Tel: 01-351 5353
Open Mon-Sat 10-6pm

Bermondsey Antiques Market,
corner of Long Lane and
Bermondsey Street, London, SE1
Friday 5am-2pm

Bermondsey Antique Warehouse,
173 Bermondsey Street, SE1
Tel: 01-407 2040/4250
Open 9.30-6.30pm, Thurs 9.30-8pm,
Fri 7-5.30pm. Closed Sat and Sun

Bond Street Antiques Centre,
124 New Bond Street, W1
Tel: 01-351 5353
Open Mon-Fri 10-5.45pm,
Sat 10-4pm

Camden Antiques Market,
Corner of Camden High Street,
and Buck Street, Camden Town,
NW1
Thurs 7-4pm

Camden Passage Antique Centre,
357 Upper St Pierrepont Arcade,
Islington, N1
Tel: 01-359 0190
Stalls open Wed 8-3pm (Thurs
Books 9-4pm), Sat 9-5pm

Chelsea Antiques Market,
245-253 Kings Road, SW3
Tel: 01-352 5689/9695/1424
Open 10-6pm

Chenil Galleries,
181-183 Kings Road, SW3
Tel: 01-351 5353
Mon-Sat 10-6pm

Corner Portobello Antiques Supermarket,
282, 284, 288, 290 Westbourne
Grove, W11
Tel: 01-727 2027
Open Fri 12-4pm, Sat 7-6pm

Covent Garden Antiques Market,
Jubilee Market, Covent Garden
Piazza, WC2
Tel: 01-240 7405
Mon only 6-4pm

Cutler Street Antiques Market,
Goulston Street, near Aldgate
End, E1
Sun 7-2pm

Crystal Palace Collectors Market,
Jasper Road, Westow Hill, Crystal
Palace, SE19
Tel: 01-761 3737
Open Wed, Thurs 9-4pm, Fri,
Sat 9-5pm, Sun 10-3pm

Dixons Antique Centre,
471 Upper Richmond Road West,
East Sheen, SW14
Tel: 01-878 6788
Open 10-5.30pm, Sun 1.30-5.30pm.
Closed Wed

Franklin's Camberwell Antiques Market,
161 Camberwell Road, SE5
Tel: 01-703 8089
Open 10-6pm, Sun 1-6pm.
Closed Mon

Georgian Village Antiques Market,
100 Wood Street, Walthamstow,
E17
Tel: 01-520 2443/989 4914
Open 10-5pm. Closed Thurs

Georgian Village,
Islington Green, N1
Tel: 01-226 1571
Open Wed 10-4pm, Sat 7-5pm

Good Fairy Open Market,
100 Portobello Road, W11
Tel: 01-351 5950
Open Sat 6-5pm

Grays Antique Market,
58 Davies Street, W1
Tel: 01-629 7034
Open 10-6pm. Closed Sat

Grays Mews,
1-7 Davies Street, W1
Tel: 01-629 7034
Open 10-6pm. Closed Sat

Grays Portobello,
138 Portobello Road, W11
Tel: 01-221 3069
Open Sat 7-4pm

Greenwich Antiques Market,
Stockwell Street by "The Letting
Office", Greenwich, SE10
Open Sat & Sun 9-4pm

Greenwich Antiques Market,
Greenwich Market, College
Approach (near Cutty Sark), SE10
Tel: 01-240 7405
Open Sat & Sun 10-4pm

Hampstead Antique Emporium,
12 Heath Street, Hampstead, NW3
Tel: 01-794 3297
Open 10-6pm. Closed Mon

L'aiglon Antique Centre,
220 Westbourne Grove, W11
Tel: 01-221 1121
Open 10-6pm

The London Silver Vaults,
Chancery House,
53-65 Chancery Lane, WC2
Tel: 01-242 3844
Open 9-5.30pm. Closed Sat pm

The Mall Antiques Arcade,
Camden Passage, Islington, N1
Tues, Thurs, Fri 10-5pm,
Wed 7.30-5pm, Sat 9-6pm

Northcote Road Antiques Market,
155A Northcote Road, Battersea,
SW11
Tel: 01-228 6850
Open Mon-Sat 10-6pm,
Sun 12-5pm

Pierrepont Arcade,
Camden Passage, N1
Tel: 01-359 0190
Open Wed & Sat

Portobello Road Market,
London, W11
Open Sat 5.30-5pm

Red Lion Market,
165/169 Portobello Road, W11
Open Sat 5.30-5pm
Tel: 01-221 7638/229 4010

Roger's Antique Gallery,
65 Portobello Road, W11
Tel: 01-351 5353
Open Sat 7-5pm

Rochefort Antique Gallery,
32/34 The Green, Winchmore Hill,
London, N21
Tel: 01-886 4779/01-363 0910
Open 10-1pm, 2.30-6pm

Streatham Traders & Shippers Market,
United Reform Church Hall,
Streatham High Street, SW16
Tel: 01-764 3602
Open Tues 8-3pm

World Famous Portobello Market,
177 Portobello Road and
1-3 Elgin Crescent, W11
Tel: 01-221 7638/229 4010
Open Sat 5-6pm

York Arcade,
80 Islington High Street, N1
Tel: 01-837 8768
Open Wed Sat 8-5pm, Tues,
Thurs, Fri 11-3pm

Greater London

Antiques Arcade,
22 Richmond Hill, Richmond,
Surrey
Tel: 01-940 2035
Open Tues, Thurs, Fri 10.30-5.30,
Sun 2-5.30pm

Beckenham Antique Market,
Old Council Hall, Bromley Road,

Beckenham, Kent
Tel: 01-684 5891
Open Wed 9.30-2pm

Bromley Antique Market,
United Reformed Church Halls,
Widmore Road, Bromley, Kent
Open Thurs 7.30-3pm

Emperor Antiques Centre,
1 Vicarage Road, Bexley
Tel: (0322) 524990
Open 9-12 & 1-6pm

Surbiton Antique Centre,
55 Brighton Road, Surbiton
Tel: 01-390 8721
Open 10-5.30pm. Closed Wed
Open Sun 11-1pm

St Elphege's Church Hall,
Stafford Road, Wallington, Surrey
Tel: 01-642 7378/01-642 4722
Open Wed 8.30-2.30

Avon

Bartlett Street Antiques Centre,
7-10 Bartlett Street, Bath
Tel: (0225) 66689/330267/310457
Open 9.30-5. Wed 8-5pm

Bath Antique Market,
Guinea Lane, Paragon, Bath
Tel: (0225) 337638/22510
Open Wed 6.30-2.30pm

Bath Saturday Antiques Market,
Walcot Street, Bath
Tel: (0225) 60909
Open Sat 7-5pm

Great Western Antique Centre,
Bartlett Street, Bath
Open Wed 7.30-4pm

Great Western Antique Centre,
Bartlett Street, Bath
Tel: (0225) 24243/28731/20686/
310388
Open 9.30-5pm Mon-Sat

Bristol Antique Market,
St Nicholas Markets,
The Exchange, Corn Street
Tel: (0272) 260021
Open Thurs & Fri 9-4pm

Clifton Antiques Market,
26/28 The Mall, Clifton, Bristol
Tel: (0272) 741627
Open 10-6pm. Closed Mon

Beds

Antiques Finder,
59 North Street, Leighton Buzzard
Tel: (0525) 382954
Open 10-5pm. Closed Thurs

The Woburn Abbey Antiques Centre,
Woburn
Tel: (0525) 290350
Open every day 11-5pm Nov to
Easter. 10-6pm Easter to Oct

Berks

Hungerford Arcade,
High Street, Hungerford
Tel: (0488) 83701
Open 9.30-5.30pm, Sun 10-6pm

Reading Emporium,
1A Merchant Place (off Friar
Street), Reading
Tel: (0734) 590290
Open 9-5pm

Twyford Antiques Centre,
1 High Street, Twyford
Tel: (0734) 342161
Open 9.30-12.30pm & 1.30-5.30pm
Open Sun. Closed Wed

Bucks

Old Amersham Antique Centre,
20-22 Whieldon Street,
Old Amersham
Tel: (0494) 431282
Open 10-6pm

Regency Antiques,
Great Missenden Arcade, 76 High
Street, Great Missenden
Tel: (024 06) 2330
Open 10-5pm. Closed Thurs

Marlow Antique Centre,
5 Spittal Street, Marlow
Tel: (06284) 76837
Open 9.30-5.30pm, Sun 10.30-5pm

Olney Antiques Centre,
Rose Court, Olney
Tel: (0234) 712172
Open 10-5.30pm, Sun 12-5.30pm

Bell Street Antiques Centre,
20/22 Bell Street, Princes
Risborough
Tel: (084 44) 3034
Open 9.30-5.30pm, Sun 11-5pm

Tingewick Antiques Centre,
Main Street, Tingewick
Tel: (028 04) 7922
Open 10.30-5 inc. Sun

Cambs

Collectors Market,
Dales Brewery, Gwydir Street
(off Mill Road), Cambridge
Open 9.30-5pm

Silhouette Antique Centre,
Chequers Street, Fenstanton
Tel: (0480) 66746/63269
Open 10-5pm Fri-Sun

Willingham Antiques & Collectors
Market,
25-29 Green Street, Willingham

Cheshire

Chester Antique Hypermarket,
41 Lower Bridge Street, Chester
Tel: (0244) 314991
Open 10-5pm

City Road Antique Centre,
32 City Road, Chester
Tel: (0244) 41818
Open 9.30-5.30pm

E.R. Antiques Centre,
122 Wellington Street
(off Wellington Road), Stockport
Tel: (061 429) 6646
Open 12-5.30pm

Guildhall Fair,
Watergate Street, Chester
Open Thurs 10-4pm

Saracens Head Inn,
Warburton
Tel: (0253) 725788
Open Wed 2-10pm

Stancie Cutler Antique &
Collectors Fairs,
Nantwich Civic Hall, Nantwich
Tel: (0270) 666802
Open 1st Thurs each month
12-9pm, Bank Hols & New Years
Day. 2nd Sat of each month
Collectors Market 9-4pm, 10-6pm

Nantwich Antique Centre,
The Old Police Station, Welsh Row,
Nantwich
Tel: (0270) 624035
Open 10-5.30pm. Closed Wed

Cornwall

Waterfront Antique Complex,
1st Floor, 4 Quay Street, Falmouth
Tel: (0326) 311491
Open 10-5pm

New Generation Antique Market,
61/62 Chapel Street, Penzance
Tel: (0736) 63267
Open 10-5pm

Truro Antique Centre,
108 Kenwyn Street, Truro
Tel: (0872) 78400
Open 9.30-5pm

Cumbria

Carlisle Antique & Craft Centre,
Cecil Hall, Cecil Street, Carlisle
Tel: (0228) 21970
Open 9-5.30pm

Cockermouth Antiques Market,
Courthouse, Main Street,
Cockermouth
Tel: (0900) 824346
Open 10-5pm

Devon

Dartmoor Antiques Centre,
Off West Street, Ashburton
Tel: (0364) 52182
Open Wed 9-4pm

The Antique Centre on the Quay,
The Quay, Exeter
Tel: (0392) 214180
Open 10-5pm

The Antique Centre,
Abingdon House, 136 High Street,
Honiton
Tel: (0404) 2108
Open 10-5pm

Newton Abbot Antiques Centre,
55 East Street, Newton Abbot
Tel: (0626) 54074
Open Tues 9-3pm

Barbican Antiques Market,
82-84 Vauxhall Street, Barbican,
Plymouth
Tel: (0752) 266927
Open 9.30-5pm

Dorset

Painted Lady Antique Centre,
5 West Allington, Bridport

Tel: (0308) 25885
Open 9.30-5pm

Antique Market,
Town Hall/Corn Exchange,
Dorchester
Tel: (0963) 62478
Open one Wed each month

Colliton Antique & Craft Centre,
Colliton Street, North Square,
Dorchester
Tel: (0305) 69398/62444
Open daily

Antique Market,
Digby Hall, Sherborne
Tel: (0258) 840224
Open one Thurs each month

Sherborne Antique Arcade,
Mattar Arcade, 17 Newlands,
Sherborne
Tel: (0935) 813464
Open 9-5pm

Barnes House Antiques Centre,
West Row, Wimborne Minster
Tel: (0202) 886275
Open 10-5pm

Durham

The Imperial Antiques Arcade,
Grange Road, Darlington
Tel: (0325) 481685
Open 10-4pm. Closed Wed

Essex

Battlesbridge Antiques Centre,
Battlesbridge
Tel: (0268) 734005/763500/763344

Sheredays Antiques Centre,
Billericay
Tel: (0277) 624356
Open 10-4.30pm. Closed Thurs

East Hill Antiques Centre,
29 East Hill, Colchester
Tel: (0206) 868623
Open 9.30-5pm, Thurs 9.30-1pm

Trinity Antiques Centre,
7 Trinity Street, Colchester
Tel: (0206) 577775
Open 9.30-5pm

Epping Saturday Market,
rear of 64-66 High Street, Epping
Tel: (0378) 73023/4
Open every Sat am

Great Baddow Antique & Craft
Centre,
The Bringy, Church Street,
Great Baddow
Tel: (0245) 76159
Open 10-5pm, Sun 12-5pm

Kelvedon Antiques Centre,
139 High Street, Kelvedon
Tel: (0376) 70896
Open 10-5pm

Maldon Antiques & Collectors
Market,
United Reformed Church Hall,
Market Hill, Maldon
Tel: (078 75) 2826
Open first Sat every month

Orsett Hall Antiques Fair,
Orsett Hall, Prince Charles
Avenue, Orsett

Tel: (0702) 714649
Open 2nd Sun each month except
6th March, 1st May, 18th Sept

Gloucestershire

Cirencester Antique Market,
Market Place, Cirencester
Tel: 01-240 0428
Antique Forum Ltd
Open Fri

Gloucester Antiques Centre,
Severn Road, Gloucester
Tel: (0452) 29716
Open Mon-Fri 9.30-5pm,
Sat 9.30-4.30pm, Sun 1-5pm

Antique Centre,
London House, High Street,
Moreton-in-Marsh
Tel: (0608) 51084
Open 9.30-5.30pm

Painswick Antique Centre,
New Street, Painswick
Tel: (0452) 812431
Open 10-5pm, Sun 2-5pm

Cotswold Antique Centre,
The Square, Stow-on-the-Wold
Tel: (0451) 31585
Open 10-5.30pm

Tewkesbury Antiques Centre,
78 Church Street, Tewkesbury
Tel: (0684) 294091
Open 9.30-5pm

Hampshire

Folly Antiques Centre,
College Street, Petersfield
Tel: (0730) 64816
Open 9.30-5pm, Thurs 9.30-1pm

The House of Antiques,
4 College Street, Petersfield
Tel: (0730) 62172
Open 9.30-5pm. Closed Thurs pm

St George's Antiques Centre,
10A St George Street, Winchester
Tel: (0962) 56317
Open 10-4.30pm

Hereford & Worcester

Leominster Antiques Market,
14 Broad Street, Leominster
Tel: (0568) 2189
Open 10-5pm, Sat 10-4pm

The Great Malvern Antiques
Arcade,
Salisbury House, 6 Abbey Road,
Malvern
Tel: (06845) 5490
Open 9.30-5pm

Hertfordshire

St Albans Antique Market,
Town Hall, Chequer Street,
St Albans
Tel: (0727) 50427
Open Mon 9.30-4pm

By George! Antiques Centre,
23 George Street, St Albans
Tel: (0727) 53032
Open 10-5pm

The Herts & Essex Antique Centre,
The Maltings, Station Road,
Sawbridgeworth
Tel: (0279) 722044

Humberside

New Pocklington Antiques Centre,
26 George Street, Pocklington
near York
Tel: (0759) 303032
Open Mon-Sat 10-5pm

Kent

Canterbury Antique Centre,
Ivy Lane, Canterbury
Tel: (0227) 60378
Open 9-5.30pm

Canterbury Weekly Antique
Market,
Sidney Cooper Centre, St Peters
Street, Canterbury
Open Sat 8-4pm

Hoodeners Antiques & Collectors
Market,
Red Cross Centre, Lower Chantry
Lane, Canterbury
Tel: (022 770) 437
Open first Sat monthly 9-4.30pm

Malthouse Arcade,
High Street, Hythe
Tel: (0303) 60103
Open Fri & Sat 10-6pm

Hythe Antique Centre,
5 High Street, Hythe
Tel: (0303) 69643
Open 10-5.30pm

Rochester Antiques & Flea
Market,
Corporation Street, Rochester
Tel: 01-240 0428
(Antique Forum Ltd)
Open Sat 9-2pm

Sandgate Antiques Centre,
61-63 High Street, Sandgate
Tel: (0303) 48987
Open 10-6pm, Sun 11-6pm

The Antiques Centre,
120 London Road, Sevenoaks
Tel: (0732) 452104
Open 9-1pm, 2-5.30pm

Tudor Cottage Antiques Centre,
22-23 Shipbourne Road, Tonbridge
Tel: (0732) 351719
Open 10-5.30pm

Tunbridge Wells Antique Centre,
Union Square, The Pantiles,
Tunbridge Wells
Tel: (0892) 33708
Open 9.30-5pm

Castle Antiques Centre,
1 London Road, Westerham
Tel: (0959) 62492
Open 10-5pm

Lancashire

Last Drop Antique & Collectors
Club,
Last Drop Hotel, Bromley Cross,
Bolton
Open Sun 11-4pm

Bygone Times Antique,
Eccleston (6 mins from J 27, M6)
Open 7 days-a-week 8-6pm

Eccles Antique Centre,
325/7 Liverpool Road, Patricroft
Bridge, Eccles

Tel: 061-789 4467
Open 12-6pm

Manchester Antique
Hypermarket,
Levenshulme Town Hall,
965 Stockport Road, Levenshulme,
Manchester
Tel: 061-224 2410
Open 10-5pm

Royal Exchange Shopping Centre,
Antiques Gallery, St Ann's
Square, Manchester
Tel: 021-834 3731/834 1427
Open 9.30-5.30pm

North Western Antique Centre,
New Preston Mill (Horrockses
Yard), New Hall Lane, Preston
Tel: (0772) 794498
Open 8.30-5.30pm, Sat, Sun by app.

Walter Aspinall Antiques,
Pendle Antique Centre, Union
Mill, Watt Street, Sabden near
Blackburn
Tel: (0282) 76311
Open Mon-Thurs 9-8pm,
Fri-Sat 9-5pm, Sun 11-4pm

Leicestershire

The Antiques Complex,
St Nicholas Place, Leicester
Tel: (0533) 533343
Open 9.30-5.30pm

Oxford Street Antiques Centre Ltd,
16-26 Oxford Street, Leicester
Tel: (0533) 553006

Carillon Antiques,
64 Leicester Road, Loughborough
Tel: (0509) 237169
Open 10-5pm. Closed Wed

Lincolnshire

Boston Antiques Centre,
12 West Street, Boston
Tel: (0205) 61510
Open 9-5.30pm

Hemswell Antique Centre,
Caenby Corner Estate, Hemswell
Cliff near Gainsborough
Tel: (042 773) 389, (0652) 61616
Open 10-5pm 7 days-a-week

The Lincolnshire Antiques Centre,
Bridge Street, Horncastle
Tel: (06582) 7794
Open 9-5pm

Talisman Antiques,
51 North Street, Horncastle
Tel: (065 82) 6893
Open 10.30-5pm. Closed Mon

Eastgage Antique Centre,
Black Horse Chambers,
6 Eastgate, Lincoln
Tel: (0522) 44404
Open 9.30-5pm

Norfolk

Coltishall Antiques Centre,
High Street, Coltishall
Tel: (0603) 738306/737631
Open 10-5pm

Norfolk House Antiques Centre,
Norfolk House Yard
(off St Nicholas Street), Diss

Tel: (0379) 51433
Open 9.30-5pm

Fakenham Antique Centre,
Old Congregational Chapel,
14 Norwich Road, Fakenham
Tel: (0328) 2941
Open 10-5pm, Thurs 9-5pm

The Old Granary Antique &
Collectors Centre,
King Staithe Lane,
(off Queens Street), King's Lynn
Tel: (0553) 775509
Open 10-5pm

Cloisters Antiques Fair,
St Andrew's & Blackfriars Hall,
St Andrew's Plain, Norwich
Tel: (0603) 628477
Open Wed 9.30-3.30pm

Norwich Antiques & Collectors
Centre,
Quayside, Fye Bridge, Norwich
Tel: (0603) 612582
Open 10-5pm

Angel Antique Centre,
Pansthorn Farmhouse, Redgrave
Road, South Lopham, near Diss
Tel: (037 988) 317
Open 9.30-6pm inc Sun

Swaffham Antiques Centre,
Cranglegate, Market Place,
Swaffham
Tel: (0760) 21277/21052
Open 10-1pm, 2-5pm

Wymondham Antique Centre,
No 1 Town Green, Wymondham
Tel: (0953) 604817
Open 10-5pm

Northamptonshire

The Village Antique Market,
62 High Street, Weedon
Tel: (0327) 42015
Open 9.30-5.30pm,
Sun 10.30-5.30pm

Antiques & Bric-a-Brac Market,
Market Square, Town Centre,
Wellingborough
Tel: (0905) 611321
Open Tues 9-4pm

Northumberland

Colmans of Hexham,
15 St Mary's Chare, Hexham
Tel: (0434) 603812/605522

Nottinghamshire

Castle Gate Antiques Centre,
55 Castle Gate, Newark
Tel: (0636) 700076
Open 9-5.30pm

Newark Antiques Centre,
Lombard Street, Newark-on-Trent,
Tel: (0636) 605504
Open 9.30-5pm

Newark Antique Warehouse,
Kelham Road, Newark
Tel: (0636) 74869
Open 9-5.30pm

Nottingham Antique Centre,
British Rail Goods Yard, London
Road, Nottingham
Tel: (0602) 54504/55548
Open 9-5pm. Closed Sat

Top Hat Antiques Centre,
66-72 Derby Road, Nottingham
Tel: (0602) 419143
Open 9.30-5pm

Oxfordshire

Burford Antiques Centre
(at the roundabout), Cheltenham
Road, Burford
Tel: (099 382) 2552/3227
Open 10-5.30pm

Cotswold Gateway Antique
Centre,
Cheltenham Road, Burford
Roundabout, Burford
Tel: (099 382) 3678/2450/2618
Open 10-5.30pm, Sun pm-5.30pm

Chipping Norton Antique Centre,
Ivy House, Middle Row, Chipping
Norton
Tel: (0608) 44212
Open 10-5pm inc Sun

Deddington Antique Centre,
Laurel House, Bull Ring, Market
Square, Deddington
Tel: (0869) 38968
Open 10-5pm

Oxford Antiques Centre,
The Jam Factory, 27 Park End,
Oxford
Tel: (0865) 739071
Open 10-5pm. Closed Mon

Antique & Collectors Market,
Town Hall, Thame
Tel: (0844) 28205
Open 8.30-3.30pm. Second Tues
each month

The Lamb Arcade,
High Street, Wallingford
Tel: (0491) 35048/35166
Open 10-5pm, Sat 9.30-5pm,
Wed 10-4pm

Wallingford Antiques Gallery,
4 Castle Street, Wallingford
Tel: (0491) 33048
Open 10-5.30pm, Sun 2-5.30pm

Span Antiques,
6 Market Place, Woodstock
Tel: (0993) 811332
Open 10-1pm, 2-5pm. Closed Wed

Shropshire

Stretton Antiques Market,
36 Sandford Avenue, Church
Stretton
Tel: (0694) 723718

Ironbridge Antique Centre,
Dale End, Ironbridge
Tel: (095 245) 3784
Open 10-5pm, Sun 2-5pm

Pepper Lane Antique Centre,
Pepper Lane, Ludlow
Tel: (0584) 6494
Open 9-5.30pm

St Leonards Antiques,
Corve Street, Ludlow
Tel: (0584) 5573
Open 9-5pm

Shrewsbury Antique Centre,
15 Princess House, The Square,
Shrewsbury
Tel: (0743) 247704
Open 9.30-5.30pm

Shrewsbury Antique Market,
Frankwell Quay Warehouse,
Shrewsbury
Tel: (0743) 50916
Open 10-5.30pm, Sun 12-5pm

Somerset
Guildhall Antique Market,
The Guildhall, Chard
Open Thurs 8-4pm
Crewkerne Antique Centre,
42 East Street, Crewkerne
Tel: (0460) 76755
Open 9.30-5.30pm
Dulverton Antique Centre,
Lower Town Hall, Dulverton
Tel: (0398) 23522
County Antiques Centre,
21/23 West Street, Ilminster
Tel: (0460) 54151
Open 10-5pm
Silver Street Antique Centre,
23 Silver Street, Taunton
Tel: (0823) 271604
Open Mon 8-3.30pm
Taunton Antique Centre,
27/29 Silver Street, Taunton
Tel: (0823) 289327
Open Mon 9-4pm
Wells Antique Centre,
6A Mill Street/High Street, Wells
Tel: (0749) 74820
Open 10-4pm

Staffordshire
Rugeley Antique Centre,
161/3 Main Road, Brereton near
Rugeley
Tel: (08894) 77166
Open 10-5.30pm
The Antique Centre,
128 High Street, Kinver
Tel: (0384) 877441
Open 10-5.30pm
Antique Market,
The Stones, Newcastle-under-
Lyme
Tel: (088 97) 527
Open Tues 7-2pm
Barclay House Antiques,
14-16 Howard Place, Shelton,
Stoke-on-Trent
Tel: (0782) 274747/657674
Open 9.30-6pm
Tutbury Mill Antiques,
6 Lower High Street, Tutbury near
Burton-on-Trent
Tel: (0283) 815999
Open 7 days 9-6pm

Suffolk
Waveney Antiques Centre,
Peddars Lane, Beccles
Tel: (0502) 716147
Open 10-5.30pm
St Edmund's Antique Centre,
30 St John's Street, Bury St
Edmunds
Tel: (0284) 64469
Open 9.30-5.30pm
Gil Adams Antique Centre,
The Forresters Hall, High Street,

Debenham
Tel: (0728) 860777
Open 9.30-5.30pm
Long Melford Antiques Centre,
The Chapel Maltings, Long
Melford
Tel: (0787) 79287
Open 10-5.30pm
Old Town Hall Antiques Centre,
High Street, Needham Market
Tel: (0449) 720773
Open 10-5pm
The Barn,
Risby, Bury St Edmunds
Tel: (0284) 811126

Surrey
Surrey Antiques Centre,
10 Windsor Street, Chertsey
Tel: (0932) 563313
Open 10-5pm
The Antiques Arcade,
77 Bridge Road, East Molesey
Tel: 01-979 7954
Open 10-5pm
Hampton Court Revival Antique
Centre,
52 Bridge Road, Hampton Court
Tel: 01-979 3552
Closed Wed
Englefield Green Antiques Centre,
1 St Judes Road, Englefield Green
near Egham
Tel: (0784) 71293
Open 9.30-5.30pm, Sun 1.30-5pm
Victoria & Edward Antiques
Centre,
61 West Street, Dorking
Tel: (0306) 889645
Open 9.30-5.30pm
Bourne Mill Antiques,
Guildford Road, Farnham
Tel: (0252) 716663
Open 9.30-5.30pm
Farnham Antiques Centre,
27 South Street, Farnham
Tel: (0252) 724475
Open 9.30-5pm
Maltings Monthly Market,
Bridge Square, Farnham
Tel: (0252) 726234
First Sat monthly
The Antiques Centre,
22 Haydon Place corner of Martyr
Road, Guildford
Tel: (0483) 67817
Open 10-5pm. Closed Mon, Wed
Wood's Wharf Antiques Bazaar,
56 High Street, Haslemere
Tel: (0428) 2125
The Old Smithy Antique Centre,
7 High Street, Merstham
Tel: (073 74) 2306
Open 10-5pm
Reigate Antiques Arcade,
57 High Street, Reigate
Tel: (0737) 222654
Open 10-5.30pm
Fern Cottage Antique Centre,
28/30 High Street, Thames Ditton,
Tel: 01-398 2281

Sussex East

Bexhill Antiques Centre,
Quakers Mill, Old Town, Bexhill
Tel: (0424) 210182/221940
Open 6 days, 10-5.30pm

Brighton Antiques Gallery,
41 Meeting House Lane, Brighton
Tel: (0273) 26693/21059
Open 10-5.30pm

Jubilee Antique Cellars &
Collector's Market,
44-47 Gardner Street, Brighton
Tel: (0273) 600574
Open 9-5pm

Kollect-O-Mania,
25 Trafalgar Street, Brighton
Tel: (0273) 694229
Open 10-5pm

Prinnys Antique Gallery,
3 Meeting House Lane, Brighton
Tel: (0273) 204557
Open 10-5pm

Chateaubriand Antiques Centre,
High Street, Burwash
Tel: (0435) 882535
Open 10-5pm, Sun 12-5pm

Eastbourne Antique Market,
80 Seaside, Eastbourne
Tel: (0323) 20128
Open 10-5.30pm

Antique Market,
Leaf Hall, Seaside, Eastbourne
Tel: (0323) 27530
Open Tues, Sat 9-5pm

Hastings Antique Centre,
59-61 Norman Road,
St Leonards-on-Sea
Tel: (0424) 428561/221940
Open 10-5.30pm

Cliffe Antiques Centre,
47 Cliffe High Street, Lewes
Tel: (0273) 473266
Open 9.30-5pm

Lewes Antique Centre,
20 Cliffe High Street, Lewes
Tel: (0273) 476148
Open 10-5pm

Newhaven Flea Market,
28 South Way, Newhaven
Tel: (0273) 517207/516065
Open every day

Polegate Antiques Centre,
97 Station Road, Polegate
Tel: (032 12) 5277
Open 9-5pm. Closed Sat

Mint Arcade,
71 The Mint, Rye
Tel: (0797) 225952
Open 10-5pm every day

Seaford's "Barn Collectors"
Market & Studio Book Shop,
The Barn, Church Lane, Seaford
Tel: (0323) 890010
Open Tues, Thurs & Sat 10-4.30pm

Sussex West

Antiques & Collectors Market,
Old Orchard Building, Old House,
Adversane near Billingshurst

Arundel Antiques Market,
5 River Road, Arundel
Tel: (0903) 882012
Open Sat 9-5pm

Treasure House Antiques &
Collectors Market, rear of 31 High
Street, near Crown Yard Car Park,
Arundel
Tel: (0903) 883101
Open Sat 9.5pm

Almshouses Arcade,
19 The Hornet, Chichester
Open 9.30-4.30pm

Eagle House Antiques Market,
Market Square, Midhurst
Tel: (073 081) 2718
Open daily

Midhurst Antiques Market,
Knockhundred Row, Midhurst
Tel: (073 081) 4231
Open 9.30-5.30pm

Mostyns Antique Centre,
64 Brighton Road, Lancing
Tel: (0903) 752961

Petworth Antique Market,
East Street, Petworth
Tel: (0798) 42073
Open 10-5.30pm

Tyne & Wear

Vine Lane Antique Market,
17 Vine Lane, Newcastle-upon-
Tyne
Tel: 091-261 2963/232 9832
Open 10-5.30pm

Warwickshire

The Antiques Centre,
High Street, Bidford-on-Avon
Tel: (0789) 773680
Open 10-5pm, Sun 2-5.30pm.
Closed Mon

Dunchurch Antique Centre,
16/16A Daventry Road,
Dunchurch near Rugby
Tel: (0788) 817147
Open 7 days 10-5pm

Spa Antiques Market,
4 Windsor Street, Leamington Spa
Tel: (0926) 22927
Open 9.30-5.30pm

Antiques Etc,
22 Railway Terrace, Rugby
Open 10-5pm. Closed Tues & Wed

The Antique Arcade,
Sheep Street, Stratford-upon-Avon
Tel: (0789) 297249
Open 10.30-5.30pm

Stratford Antique Centre,
Ely Street, Statford-upon-Avon
Tel: (0789) 204180
Open 10-5.30 every day

Smith Street Antiques Centre,
7 Smith Street, Warwick
Tel: (0926) 497864
Open 10-5.30pm

Vintage Antique Market,
36 Market Place, Warwick
Tel: (0926) 491527
Open 10-5.30pm

Warwick Antique Centre,
20-22 High Street, Warwick
Tel: (0926) 495704
Open 6 days-a-week

West Midlands

Birmingham Antique Centre,
141 Bromsgrove Street,
Birmingham
Tel: 021-692 1414/622 2145
Open every Thurs from 9am

The City of Birmingham Antique
Market,
St Martins Market, Edgbaston
Street, Birmingham
Tel: 021-267 4636
Open Mon 7-2pm

Stancie Cutler Antique &
Collectors Fair,
Town Hall, Sutton Coldfield
Tel: (0270) 666802
Open 2nd Wed monthly 11-8pm

Wiltshire

London House Antique Centre,
High Street, Marlborough
Tel: (0672) 52331
Open Mon-Sat 9.30-5.30pm

The Marlborough Parade
Antiques Centre,
The Parade, Marlborough
Tel: (0672) 55331
Open 10-5pm

Antique Market,
37 Catherine Street, Salisbury
Tel: (0722) 26033
Open 9-5.30pm

The Avon Bridge Antiques &
Collectors Market,
United Reformed Church Hall,
Fisherton Street, Salisbury
Open Tues 9-4pm

Mr Micawber's Attic,
73 Fisherton Street, Salisbury
Tel: (0722) 337822
Open 9.30-5pm. Closed Wed

Yorkshire North

The Ginnel,
Harrogate Antique Centre
(off Parliament Street), Harrogate
Tel: (0423) 508857
Open 9.30-5.30pm

Grove Collectors Centre,
Grove Road, Harrogate
Tel: (0423) 61680
Open 10-5pm

Montpelier Mews Antique Market,
Montpelier Street, Harrogate
Tel: (0423) 530484
Open 9.30-5.30pm

West Park Antiques Pavilion,
20 West Park, Harrogate
Tel: (0423) 61758
Open 10-5pm. Closed Mon

Micklegate Antiques Market,
73 Micklegate, York
Tel: (0904) 644438
Open Wed & Sat 10-5.30pm

York Antique Centre,
2 Lendal, York
Tel: (0904) 641582/641445

Yorkshire South

Treasure House Antiques Centre,
4-10 Swan Street, Bawtry near
Doncaster
Tel: (0302) 710621
Open 10-5pm inc Sun

Yorkshire West

Halifax Antiques Centre,
Queens Road/Gibbet Street,
Halifax
Tel: (0422) 366657

Scotland

Bath Street Antique Galleries,
203 Bath Street, Glasgow
Open 10-5pm, Sat 10-1pm

Corner House Antiques,
217 St Vincent Street, Glasgow
Tel: 041-248 2560
Open 10-5pm

The Victorian Village,
53 & 57 West Regent Street,
Glasgow
Tel: 041-332 0808
Open 10-5pm

Wales

Pembroke Antique Centre,
The Hall, Hamilton Terrace,
Pembroke
Tel: (0646) 687017
Open 10-6pm

Cardiff Antique Centre,
69-71 St Mary Street, Cardiff
Tel: (0222) 30970

Jacobs Antique Centre,
West Canal Wharf, Cardiff
Tel: (0222) 390939
Open Thurs & Sat 9.30-5pm

Offa's Dyke Antiques Centre,
4 High Street, Knighton, Powys
Tel: (0547) 528634/528940
Open Mon-Sat 10-1pm, 2-5pm,
Wed 10-1pm

Swansea Antique Centre,
21 Oxford Street, Swansea
Tel: (0792) 466854

Channel Islands

Union Street Antique Market,
8 Union Street, St Helier, Jersey
Tel: (0534) 73805/22475
Open 9-6pm

INDEX

INDEX

papier mâché 130, 272, 492
paperweights 46-7, 309
polar expeditions 298
patriotic and political 303
naval 301
humorous 302
presentation discs 319
posters 321-3
rolling pins 195, 222
Rolling Stones, The 317
Michael Jackson 320

INDEX